1

A Chinese
Economic Revolution

State and Society in East Asia Series
Elizabeth J. Perry, Series Editor

A Chinese Economic Revolution

Rural Entrepreneurship in the Twentieth Century

Linda Grove

ROWMAN & LITTLEFIELD PUBLISHERS, INC.
Lanham • *Boulder* • *New York* • *Toronto* • *Plymouth, UK*

ROWMAN & LITTLEFIELD PUBLISHERS, INC.

Published in the United States of America
by Rowman & Littlefield Publishers, Inc.
A wholly owned subsidiary of The Rowman & Littlefield Publishing Group, Inc.
4501 Forbes Boulevard, Suite 200, Lanham, Maryland 20706
www.rowmanlittlefield.com

Estover Road
Plymouth PL6 7PY
United Kingdom

British Library Cataloguing in Publication Information Available

Library of Congress Cataloging-in-Publication Data
Grove, Linda, 1944-
  A Chinese economic revolution : rural entrepreneurship in the twentieth century /
Linda Grove.
      p. cm. — (State and society in East Asia)
  Includes bibliographical references and index.
  ISBN-13: 978-0-7425-5354-5 (cloth : alk. paper)
  ISBN-10: 0-7425-5354-X (cloth : alk. paper)
  1. China—Economic conditions—20th century. 2. Rural industries—China. 3.
Rural development—China. I. Title. II. Series.
  HC427.G76 2006
  338'.040951091734—dc22

                                                                    2006008484

Printed in the United States of America

♾™ The paper used in this publication meets the minimum requirements of
American National Standard for Information Sciences—Permanence of Paper
for Printed Library Materials, ANSI/NISO Z39.48-1992.

For Hidemi and Kei

Contents

Acknowledgments

I have worked on this book for twenty years and have accumulated debts to many individuals and institutions that supported the various stages of research. It is a great pleasure to acknowledge the assistance I have received. The first of those debts is to several generations of Gaoyang entrepreneurs who shared their experiences with me. Members of the prewar generation patiently answered my questions, while contemporary entrepreneurs took time out of their busy work schedules to explain technical and managerial practices, talk about the histories of their firms, and answer survey questions. Government and CCP officials in Gaoyang County supported every stage of this work, facilitating research visits and sharing their insights on their hometown. Other assistance came from managers and cadre of the state textile firms, the Gaoyang County Township and Village Enterprise Bureau, the editorial office for the County Gazetteer, officials of many townships and villages, and the county Foreign Affairs Office.

When I first began work on this project during the 1979–1980 academic year, economic reform policies had just been launched. I was one of the first cohort of scholars sponsored by the Committee on Scholarly Communications with the People's Republic of China. At that time protocols for social science research in rural China were just being developed. Every visit outside of Tianjin required an internal travel passport, and travel to areas that were not open to foreigners—which included most of the towns and counties in north China—was difficult to arrange. Colleagues at the Economic Research Institute of Nankai University worked unceasingly to get the permissions and make the arrangements for rural research. I owe a great debt of thanks to the late Prof. Ding Shixun, whose efforts made the first trip possible; to the late Prof. Liu Foding, who provided assistance for several later trips; and to Prof. Wang Yuru and Ms. Long Jingzhao of the Institute, who provided invaluable assistance during the research visits. In later years the late Prof. Wang Yongxiang of the Nankai history department, a native of Gaoyang, provided important assistance. Prof. Zhang Limin, head of the History Research Institute of the Tianjin Academy of Sciences, helped to arrange a number of the later visits, and he and his colleagues also provided assistance in searching materials in Tianjin archives. I have spent many happy hours in conversation about north China economic history with Prof. Zhang and his colleagues at the Tianjin Academy of Social Sciences, as well as with colleagues at Nankai's Institute of Economic Research and the Nankai history department. Qiao Weixiong and his colleagues at the Tianjin People's Political Consultative Conference arranged interviews with Tianjin businessmen involved in the pre-1949 textile industry. Prof. Chen Meijian of Hebei University generously shared interview data and research notes on the Gaoyang textile industry and assisted with the 1995 survey. Mr. Lin Lipan and Prof. Yang Suoting shared knowledge of the contemporary textile industries, and Prof. Yu Heping of the Chinese Academy of Social Sciences suggested analytical approaches and helped me obtain copies of rare journal articles.

The intellectual framework of this book has been strongly influenced by work with Japanese colleagues. In the early 1980s Prof. Kusamitsu Toshio introduced me to a group of Japanese scholars working on textile history, and over the years I have learned much from them and from scholars working on textile history issues in Japan, England, and India, especially Abe Takeshi, Tanimoto Masayuki, Saito Osamu, Douglas Farnie, David Jeremy, and T. K. Roy. My understanding of the textile trade in the East Asian context was greatly furthered by a joint project on commercial networks in Asia organized with Sugiyama Shinya. Sugihara Kaoru shared his knowledge of the global context of Asian trade and provided a number of opportunities for presentation of early drafts of arguments in this book. Kiyokawa Yukihiko introduced me to Japanese work on technology transfer, and Ohno Akihiko invited me to join a project on women's labor in Asia that led to rethinking the gender implications of this study. While I was working on this study of Gaoyang, I was also a member of a joint Sino-Japanese research team that was resurveying north China villages that had been included in the famous 1940s Mantetsu surveys of village customary law. That project provided rich opportunities for discussion of north China village life in the twentieth century. My thanks to the members of that research group: in Japan, Mitani Takashi, Hamaguchi Nobuko, Kasahara Tokushi, Nakao Katsumi, Oda Noriko, and Uchiyama Masao; and in China, Wei Hongyun, Zhang Hongxiang, Zhang Limin, and Zuo Zhiyuan, and their then research students Jiang Pei, Li Enmin, Qi Jianmin, and Zhang Si. The history of Gaoyang industry is closely linked to the economic development of Tianjin, and I have learned much from working with the Tianjin urban history research group, including

Hamaguchi Nobuko, Kawashima Shin, Kishi Toshihiko, Watanabe Tōru, and Yoshizawa Seiichiro, and from our joint projects with the Tianjin Academy of Social Sciences' Tianjin urban history group.

My thanks to colleagues who have read and commented on the manuscript at different stages. First to Joseph Esherick, Philip Huang, and Elizabeth Perry, colleagues in a joint rural research project in the 1980s, who read and commented on the early draft of the manuscript. R. Bin Wong, David Wank, and Kate Nakai have commented on numerous drafts of the manuscript, which has been greatly improved by their perceptive questions and comments.

During the years I was working on this book my mother-in-law, Kondo Aiko, and my sister-in-law, Masaki Midori, took loving care of my son so that I could do research work in China. There is no way to fully express my appreciation to them and to my husband, Kondo Hidemi, and our son Kei for their continuing support.

The work on this project was supported by a grant from the Committee on Scholarly Communications with the People's Republic of China and by a sabbatical grant from Sophia University.

List of Illustrations

TABLES

I

The Chinese "economic miracle" has captured the imagination of the world community in the early twenty-first century. We have watched one of Asia's largest and poorest countries break out of poverty into sustained economic growth. Rural industry has played a central role in contemporary Chinese growth. In the last two decades rural industry has provided jobs for several hundred million peasants. Income from industrial jobs has raised rural incomes, contributing to the creation of a vast domestic market that has helped to sustain high economic growth rates. At the same time, rural industry has made important contributions to China's export drive, producing low-cost consumer goods that have flooded world markets.

While much has been written about Chinese rural industry, most of the literature takes the economic reform policies initiated in 1978 as the starting point, and few scholars have asked questions about the links between traditional Chinese business practices and contemporary growth.[1] *A Chinese Economic Revolution* takes a different approach, locating contemporary Chinese rural industry in a century-long development trajectory and exploring links between managerial practices in present-day rural firms and traditional Chinese business practices. We will examine those links through the history of the Gaoyang weaving district, from its rise in the first decade of the twentieth century to the present.

During the early decades of the twentieth century, the Gaoyang industrial district, located on the North China Plain south of Beijing, was one of China's most successful new rural weaving centers. Our narrative will show how a local entrepreneurial community recognized the opportunities presented by a state-sponsored technology transfer program, and how regional leaders built on and transformed traditional Chinese business practices to create

1

innovative firms and marketing networks able to sustain continued growth. In the process, local entrepreneurs provided employment for thousands of rural weaving households that came to invest in the new technology and to share in the prosperity that the industrial district created.

The book will trace the history of the Gaoyang industry during three discontinuous phases of growth. The first phase began in the early twentieth century and ended in 1937, when the outbreak of the war with Japan cut access to raw materials and markets. The second phase of growth began at the end of the war, in the summer of 1945, and continued until the new socialist state decided in 1953–1954 to socialize commerce and industry. This decision put the textile industries under a state monopoly and brought an end to private firms, as well as rural weaving. The third phase of growth began after the launching of the economic reforms in 1978 and continues to the present day. The Gaoyang industrial district today is one of China's leading producers of cotton towels, wool blankets, knitting yarn, and other textile products.

The development of a new style of rural textile production in Gaoyang was closely linked to changes in the global economy. The forces that would eventually transform China's handicraft textile industry grew out of changes in the industrial centers of England, halfway around the world. Beginning in the late eighteenth century, the introduction of mechanized spinning and weaving had transformed the English cotton industry. By the mid-nineteenth century rapid industrial growth had led to the saturation of English markets and pushed manufacturers to seek new customers overseas, particularly in Asia.[2] At first, British manufacturers exported cotton piece goods, but the piece goods were soon followed by exports of machine-spun cotton yarn. While the former cut into the market for locally produced cotton cloth, the latter was used as a raw material for manufacture. In response to these developments, by the 1870s Chinese officials were drafting plans for the mechanization of the domestic cotton industry, and by the 1890s and early 1900s government officials and private investors had begun initiatives to reorganize the cotton industry. That reorganization took two forms: establishment of mechanized spinning and weaving mills, and the development of new-style rural weaving districts that used machine-spun yarn.

Gaoyang and several other weaving districts, including Baodi and Weixian in North China and Nantong in central China, created a new style of industrial production described by one Chinese scholar as having the "head and tail outside," that is both the supplies of raw materials and the markets were outside the local community.[3] Much like the export-processing zones set up in many contemporary developing countries, the new-style weaving districts mobilized the abundant labor resources of rural China to process imported raw materials. Unlike the modern export-processing zones, the new weaving districts of early twentieth-century China produced goods for the domestic market, goods designed to serve as substitutes for a flood of imports that threatened to engulf the Chinese economy.

Several generations of Gaoyang entrepreneurs took part in the effort to build a thriving industrial district. Tracing the footsteps of the first generation, we will begin by exploring the world of traditional Chinese business practices, a world in which businessmen got their start as young apprentices who were the first to rise in the morning and the last to go to bed at night. Those who wanted to succeed in business had to learn the trade from the bottom up, mastering a language, a technology, accounting, and business and market practices that were specific to the trade they entered. Many dreamed of saving enough money to start businesses of their own. As the Gaoyang industrial district developed during its three phases of growth, successive generations of young men—and in the third phase of growth also young women—were able to realize the Gaoyang dream of "being one's own boss." Through the Gaoyang story we will encounter the entrepreneurial spirit that permeates the local economic system and has resulted in the birth of thousands of small factories and firms. We will come to know some of the entrepreneurs and their firms and the challenges they have faced in different periods and under different political regimes. By the end of the story, we should be closer to understanding the mechanisms that have fueled small-scale industry and helped to transform the Chinese economy.

Gaoyang is located in central Hebei Province, 35 kilometers east of the former provincial capital at Baoding, 130 kilometers southeast of Beijing, and 150 kilometers from Tianjin, the major port city in North China. When I first visited in May 1980, the town, which was small and dusty, was home to a population of about fifteen thousand. The only hints of what had once been a booming commercial center were some stone-faced buildings that had previously served as the headquarters of wealthy merchant firms and the three-story building that had been the headquarters of the chamber of commerce. With its periodic markets and small shops that served a rural population of close to two hundred thousand, Gaoyang looked like many other North Chinese country towns. One of the few things distinguishing it were the state-owned textile factories that employed the town's small working class. A short walk beyond the factories on the southern edge of town brought one into the seemingly timeless world of North China village life. During the winter months the horizon of the nearly flat plains seemed to stretch into infinity. The sun-dried-brick houses and their surrounding walls, the same color as the barren fields, blended into the flat horizon, and the only interruptions in the vast panorama of land and scattered villages were the dark trunks and branches of trees whose leaves, in summer, would shade the village lanes.

The central government had launched the economic reforms policies in late 1978, but during that first visit I saw little evidence of change. Peasants still worked in collective teams on their communal land, and each village was allowed to run only one small village enterprise. Most village-run work-shops produced coarse textiles, particularly a rough cotton cloth used for baling goods in the town's state factories. In some of the small village factories young male weavers wove on the same kind of iron gear looms that had brought prosperity to rural weavers seven decades earlier. In 1980 Gaoyang was still recovering from the Cultural Revolution factional disputes that had torn the communal fabric of almost every village in the region, and rural residents lived with the aftereffects of economic policies that had forced local communities to grow grain—leaving the rural population with enough to eat, but little to spend on other forms of consumption.

The lack of funds for investment in infrastructure could be seen every-where. Only the main roads that linked Gaoyang to Baoding and Tianjin were paved. In the dry season this made little difference, but when the summer rains came, the unpaved dirt roads that linked villages to the main roads became rivers of thick viscous mud that brought all traffic to a stop.

A decade and a half later, Gaoyang presented a very different face to the outside world. The rapid growth of the textile industry had created resources for both private and public investment, transforming town and countryside. The town was once again the center of a dynamic business-centered culture that drew workers and traders from all over the country. Expansion of the textile industry had touched off a building boom. Paved highways had re-placed dirt roads, and a circular bypass road had been constructed around the center of the town. Factories and businesses lined the bypass, along with impressive multistory buildings of banks and government offices. Almost all of the older buildings in the center of town had been torn down and re-placed by new multistory shops and trading firms. At night food and drink stands lined the town's main streets. Karaoke sets with large-screen monitors were set up for entertainment, and bars and restaurants did a lively business. Almost all of Gaoyang's new factories and trading firms were private enter-prises, and almost all of the capital invested in industry came from local sources.

INDUSTRIAL DISTRICTS AND THE GAOYANG MODEL OF GROWTH

While this book is about the successful development of one industrial dis-trict, it has wider implications for understanding the dynamics of small-scale enterprises in China and the alternative route to modern economic growth that they represent. Taking the Gaoyang experience as one model of rural in-dustrial growth I will explore two different dimensions of that experience: the activities of individual entrepreneurs and firms on the one hand, and the structure of industrial organization on the other. In considering the activities of individual entrepreneurs and firms I will stress the characteristic features

Figure Intro.1.   Contemporary Gaoyang. Overview of Gaoyang in 2005. (Photo provided by the Gaoyang County government office.)

of small-firm organization in twentieth-century China and their relation to past business practices. How did entrepreneurs create new organizations on the basis of traditional business practices? What forms of finance did they use in the absence of a modern banking system? How did entrepreneurs find markets for their goods and determine market demand? How did they organize their firms and recruit employees, and what happened when capital holdings increased? Finally, was rural industry successful primarily because it had a lower wage bill?

Turning to the structural features of the local political economy within which small-scale firms have flourished, this book will examine Gaoyang as an industrial district. The term "industrial district" describes an industrial structure in which a large number of small firms in the same line of business are concentrated in a limited geographical area. This form of industrial organization gives rise to a distinctive business culture, characterized by a complex mixture of competition and cooperation between independent firms that share values and knowledge, and to a distinctive pattern of relations of cooperation between managers and workers.[4] Physically the Gaoyang industrial district includes the town of Gaoyang, which is the administrative center of the county, several smaller market towns, and several hundred villages spread across five counties. In the prewar period the town of Gaoyang was surrounded by high walls; most of the wholesale firms that controlled the textile trade were located within the town walls. Dyeing and finishing factories were located in areas just outside the town walls and in nearby villages. Weavers worked on looms set up in their own compounds in the more than one hundred villages that were part of the industrial district. (See map 1.1 in chapter 1.)

Focusing on Gaoyang as an industrial district, I will ask what kind of social relations prevailed in this industrial district. How did firms relate to each other, and how did managers relate to their workers? What kinds of organizations and institutions were created to serve collective interests? How did changes in the political regime affect rural industrial practices? The resulting findings counter the common assumption that rural industry is backward and that "modern" forms of mass production will inevitably replace it. *A Chinese Economic Revolution* argues that rural industrialization represents an alternative to urban-centered mass production. Chinese rural industry has played an important role in the industrial revolution of the long twentieth century, and is likely to continue to follow its own development trajectory.

Charles Sabel and Jonathan Zeitlin touched off academic discussion of the industrial district in an article that argued for such districts as an "alternative to mass production."[5] This article appeared at almost the same time as Sabel and Michael Piore's book *The Second Industrial Divide*, which argued that our contemporary economy is moving toward new forms of industrial organization incorporating more flexible forms of production.[6] In the years since the publication of those seminal works, there has been a growing literature on the problems of flexible production and accumulation and their implications for both history and contemporary society.[7]

In the same years that economic historians and sociologists examining industrial districts were starting to challenge the narratives that had focused on mass production as the primary path to modern economic growth, business historians began to look again at the role of small firms in that process. Just as the dominant narrative in economic history stressed the rise of large-scale modern industry, the major approach in business history focused on the rise of the modern integrated business firm. Alfred Chandler, the leading scholar of modern business history, argued that the benefits to be derived from economies of scale would eventually lead to the dominance of large-scale firms in most lines of manufacturing.

Both the economic historians' models of modern industrial growth and the business historians' models of the rise of the large, integrated firm were based on the study of patterns of development in the initial cohort of industrializing nations. When scholars turned to examine similar issues in late-developing countries, they incorporated ideas derived from dual-economy theories into their conceptual frameworks. Theories of economic dualism assume that late-developing states will import (or "transfer") advanced technology from already industrialized economies. Development based on imported technology produces a sharp division between a modernizing sector, characterized by technologically sophisticated facilities, higher rates of productivity, and higher wage rates, and the so-called traditional sector marked by backward technology, lower productivity, and lower wage rates. Dual-economy models usually assume that growth will displace the backward, small-scale, and rural industrial sectors, replacing them with mass production units.[8] Although these models were derived from the experiences of market-based economic systems, planners in socialist China shared many of the same suppositions about the scale and scope of industry. They, too, believed that mass production was the most efficient way to meet economic goals, and after 1950 they strove to funnel investments into large-scale state-owned enterprises.[9]

The questions raised in recent years with regard to the inevitable triumph of the large integrated firm and mass production have implications for not only the study of historical economic systems, but also policy decisions in contemporary developing economies. Those who have challenged the dominant narratives in economic and business history note that not all products or all markets are necessarily suited to the mass production of standard goods: the market has niches for a wide range of products, including limited-circulation and one-of-a-kind, as well as standardized items. There is also a wide range of market conditions, some well suited to standardized production and others requiring frequent shifts in style. While large firms are most efficient at producing standard products and serving predictable markets, small firms using flexible means of production better serve these other markets.[10]

The industrial district as a form of organization is a crucial part of the story of small-scale industrial development in China. Later parts of this book will explore the economic and institutional factors that influenced the choice of this industrial structure during the three phases of growth. Here I simply set the stage for this exploration by briefly considering theories about how industrial districts function.

Many of our ideas about industrial districts come from the work of one of the early twentieth century's greatest economists, Alfred Marshall. Marshall, who is best known for his contributions to the marginal revolution, was among the first to focus attention on the industrial district as a distinctive form of industrial organization.[11] Marshall stressed the role of the industrial district in creating external economies, that is, economies external to the individual firm. Such external economies make it possible, he held, for the small firms in an industrial district to benefit from something like the economies of scale that are often seen as the key to the success of mass production. In the industrial district, economies of scale function not within single firms, but within the industrial district as a whole. Successful development of small-scale industry, Marshall argued, requires a critical mass of producers concentrated in one region. In industrial districts, individual small firms can share communal resources, which no single firm can afford. In such districts, according to Marshall, "The mysteries of the trade become no mysteries, but are as it were in the air, and children learn many of them unconsciously. Good work is rightly appreciated, inventions and improvements in machinery, in processes and the general organization of the business have their merits promptly discussed: if one man starts a new idea, it is taken up by others and combined with suggestions of their own; and thus it becomes the source of further new ideas."[12] In industrial districts small firms share a common market. Although the output of any single firm might be quite small, the total regional output volume is large, making industrial districts major manufacturing centers.

Contemporary economists with an interest in economic agglomeration have tested Marshall's theories, looking at the relation between transportation costs and industrial concentration and the relation between labor markets and concentration.[13] Most of the studies use data on industry in already developed countries, and most focus on industrial clustering as part of the study of urban economies.[14] Gaoyang represents a different style of industrial clustering, a form that also was common in Japan during most of the twentieth century. In this form of clustering, industry is located in rural villages or small towns and draws on a rural labor force that has not completely severed ties to agriculture. New-style industrial districts first appeared in the late nineteenth and early twentieth centuries and most made use of technologies and inputs that were newly available as a result of the growth of foreign trade.

We need to distinguish these new-style industrial districts like Gaoyang from earlier forms of regional specialization. Regional specialization in industrial production has, of course, long been part of the economy in almost all parts of the world. China also had its traditional industrial districts, regions famed for production of iron goods, ceramics, silk, and many other specialized products. In those earlier handicraft industries, regional specialization was the result of comparative advantage, with industries concentrating in regions with ready access to raw materials, or in regions where the climate was particularly appropriate for the production of raw materials that fed into such industries.

The comparative advantage of new industrial districts like Gaoyang derived from institutional factors rather than from what might be seen as "natural" locational or resource advantages. Central among these was a complex network of business relationships. Since the raw materials used in processing were readily available to all comers, in the initial stages of development, any of dozens of rural regions had the potential to become new weaving centers. However, once Gaoyang entrepreneurs established close ties with yarn wholesalers and native banks in Tianjin and with customers in markets throughout the country, it became more difficult for newcomers to compete.

Gaoyang merchants provided a large and reliable market for yarn importers, and the special advantages in terms of credit and trust that were one of the benefits of membership in the Gaoyang merchant clique made it easier for individual firms to operate. In investigating the Gaoyang comparative advantage, we thus need to explore not only the macroeconomic environment, but also the actions of individuals and groups of businessmen whose strategic choices influenced the development of their own firms and shaped many of the features of the industrial district.

While the general patterns that I will identify in the Gaoyang case are not peculiar to Chinese modern industrial development, the particular forms that they have taken have been strongly influenced by the larger economic and institutional environment, as well as by traditional Chinese business practices and the specific strategic choices made by Gaoyang businessmen. In some countries, Italy and India being two prominent examples, government policies have deliberately protected small-scale industries.[15] In Japan, institutional links between large and small firms in the forms of networks and subcontracting have preserved an important role for small-scale industries. By contrast, the three regimes (imperial, republican, and socialist) that have governed China over the last century have offered little in the way of formal protection for small-scale industries. Small-scale industry's survival has been strongly linked to its ability to mobilize independent capital resources in an economic system that has been generally characterized as capital short.

RECOVERING ENTREPRENEURIAL VOICES

To explore in depth the development of small-scale enterprise in Gaoyang over the past century requires recovering the voices and experiences of several generations of rural entrepreneurs and workers. This has not been an easy task. One of the great challenges of studying Chinese business history, particularly the history of small industrial firms, is the general lack of firm records. The absence of such materials in contemporary archives does not mean that firms did not keep written records. Chinese businessmen were almost always literate and numerate. All of the larger Gaoyang firms had teams of accountants and clerks who kept the books and received daily written reports from sales branches all over the country. In spite of what must have been a huge body of written documentation at the firm level, today almost no records survive.[16] In the absence of firm-level records, others sources have to be used to try to re-create the world of small-scale business enterprises.

Prewar Survey Data. The starting point for this study was a well-known economic survey undertaken in the 1930s by researchers from the Nankai Institute of Economics.[17] The Nankai Institute was interested in teaching

Chinese economic history to its students, but found that there were few materials on the Chinese economy. To fill this gap it undertook a series of studies on industry in Tianjin and nearby rural areas. Wu Zhi, a 1928 graduate of
Nankai University who later joined the institute research staff and was responsible for devising many of the early Nankai price indexes, was assigned
the task of undertaking a survey of the largest and most important of the
North China rural weaving districts, Gaoyang.

Wu Zhi recruited a team of three assistants and developed a plan for a projected six-month survey of Gaoyang industry. The research team settled in
Gaoyang in February 1933 and established close working relationships with
some of the leading entrepreneurs. Since the Nankai Institute had already
gained a reputation for its statistical compilations and analysis, one of the
main tasks of the young research team was gathering as much statistical data
as possible.[18]

Wu Zhi's report on the Gaoyang survey, published in 1936 as *Xiangcun
zhibu gongye de yige yanjiu* (A study of the rural weaving industry), focused
on the role of the merchant entrepreneurs who coordinated the Gaoyang
system. In the report Wu used modern accounting methods to estimate production costs, business overhead, and profit ratios. In addition he provided
an outline history of the development of Gaoyang industry, undertook a
sample survey of several hundred weaving households in an attempt to understand the role of weaving in the family economy, and investigated the
production and marketing systems.

Wu Zhi's study set a high standard for its day, and it has been read by economic historians ever since.[19] As a source for the kind of questions that I was
interested in exploring, it also had problems, however. Although Wu provided an outline of the historical development of the Gaoyang industrial system, his statistical data all came from his own surveys; thus while it provided
a detailed snapshot of the weaving industry in the early 1930s, data on earlier development trends was quite sketchy. A second major problem was the
absence of data on individual firms. To gain the cooperation of business
leaders, Wu had assured those who cooperated with him that no one would
be able to identify individual firms and entrepreneurs. While the study provides an invaluable description of Gaoyang industry in the early 1930s, the
reader does not get a sense of who the entrepreneurs were, or how they had
come to build their successful firms.

I was thus faced with two tasks: first, to find records on Gaoyang industry
that would expand the time frame of coverage, and, second, to recover the
histories of individual firms. Over the years I have discovered a number of
accounts, mostly in Japanese, that provide data to sketch in long-term development trends. Gaoyang industry was one of the major customers for
Japanese yarn exporters in the early part of the twentieth century. Japanese
consular services and trade organizations conducted periodic surveys of in-

dustry, intended as guides for Japanese exporters. The earliest of the Japanese reports was written in 1911 and the last, a Japanese survey of the effects of the war on Gaoyang industry, was undertaken in 1942. Although it is impossible to reconstruct consistent time series data, the reports do provide a series of anchors that confirm the periodization in Wu Zhi's survey.

Oral History Interviews. The work of reconstructing the histories of individual firms began during a research visit to China in 1979–1980. For that year my research home was the Nankai Institute for Economic Research in Tianjin, the descendant of the prewar organization that had done the original survey on Gaoyang. In the spring of 1980, I made a first trip to Gaoyang, where I interviewed people who had been involved in the prewar textile industry, visited factories that had descended from prewar firms, and toured villages that had once been heavily involved in weaving. It was during that first visit that I began to explore the human dimensions of the Gaoyang story, to learn about the early entrepreneurs from people who had worked in their firms as apprentices, accountants, and branch office managers. Old weavers discussed their lives and recalled what the situation had been in the 1930s. I also read work-committee reports from the early 1950s that described the struggle between state and private firms in the course of collectivization. The visit also brought home the importance of understanding technological issues. Factory managers spent hours describing the technical sides of their operations and carefully demonstrated the different kinds of equipment that had been used and how the equipment had changed over the years.

Archival Sources. The Gaoyang Chamber of Commerce, the organization that represented the interests of textile entrepreneurs, was founded in 1906. Qing government regulations subordinated county-level chambers of commerce to the chambers of commerce of a province or major urban center. The Gaoyang Chamber of Commerce was subordinate to the Tianjin Chamber of Commerce. The archives of the Tianjin Chamber of Commerce have been preserved in their entirety, with more than ten thousand files covering the years from the chamber's founding in 1903 to the early 1950s. Records of the Gaoyang Chamber of Commerce, including reports, petitions, and other correspondence are included in the Tianjin chamber archives.[20]

Studying the Contemporary Textile Industry. I became interested in the contemporary textile industry after receiving a letter from Nankai friends in 1984 that reported the revival of household weaving in Gaoyang. Following the year I spent in China in 1979–1980, I had written a draft of a monograph that ended with the story of how household weaving came to an end in the early 1950s as a result of the socialization of commerce and industry. The report from Gaoyang that rural industry was starting up again raised a new set of interpretive problems, and before revising the draft I wanted to visit again and see for myself what forms the new rural industry took. I spent ten days in Gaoyang in the summer of 1988 and discovered that not only was rural industry booming, managerial forms resonated strongly with practices common in the rural textile industry in the prewar period. Thus began an extended reconsideration of the situation in Gaoyang that included visits in 1988, 1990, 1991, 1995, and 1996.

These research visits produced several kinds of data that have been used in the second part of this book. Each visit included briefings by county government officials, lengthy discussions with the cadres responsible for rural industry, and extensive and repeated interviews with factory owners, raw-materials dealers, finished-goods traders, workshop owners, and workers. To get a better understanding of where Gaoyang industry fits in the Chinese industrial structure, I consulted textile experts at various institutions in Tianjin who have generously shared their knowledge of both technological and economic questions. As my study extended in time, discussions with contemporary entrepreneurs suggested ways of rethinking prewar Gaoyang industry.

Survey Materials. The visits, interviews, and informal conversations produced general statistical data and gave me a sense of the overall operation of the contemporary Gaoyang system. It also led to a series of hypotheses about the similarities and differences between the experience of rural industry in the past and in the contemporary period that I have tried to verify through surveys of selected firms.

I have used two surveys I conducted in Gaoyang as major sources for the chapters on the third phase of growth. The first of these surveys, completed in the spring of 1992, looked at women workers in state and private industry. The survey targeted 160 workers, 80 chosen from women workers at two privately owned wool spinning mills, and 80 from women workers at one of the state firms in the county that produced hand-printed fabrics for the export market. Researchers from Nankai University helped in designing and administering the survey, which was supplemented by extensive qualitative interviewing with managers and workers in the three factories.

The second survey, conducted in May 1995, gathered data on a random sample of thirty-four larger private firms. County government officials cooperated by encouraging private entrepreneurs to participate in the survey, which Chinese research assistants or I individually administered to the manager of each of the selected factories.

The surveys have provided the hard data for reconstruction of the development patterns of firms in the 1980s and 1990s. Much of the knowledge I have gained about how firms grew, the careers of the leading entrepreneurs, and the broader cultural context in which they operate, came from more informal forms of investigation. As I got to know more people in Gaoyang, casual meetings began to supplement structured interviews, and I learned much in the course of conversations over meals and drinks, lessons in local gambling customs, and excursions to local tourist sites. It was then that entrepreneurs and officials relaxed and talked about daily life, gossiping about colleagues and friends, their struggles with other enterprises, taxes and how to avoid them, and an almost endless list of other topics of interest. Obviously not all of my informants were speaking the literal truth, but such occasions provided opportunities to see how local officials and entrepreneurs viewed their own community and the rapid changes that were taking place in the 1980s and 1990s.

This book is thus based on a wide range of sources, all of which have contributed to the total picture of the Gaoyang industrial district over almost a century of development. The book stresses the interconnection between traditional business practices in China and the first phase of growth, and emphasizes the part played by Gaoyang's own business traditions in the dynamic patterns of development during the second and third phases of growth. I should note, however, that in arguing for close links between earlier rural industrial practices and contemporary industrial growth, I am pointing to connections that I see rather than to ones identified by contemporary local officials or entrepreneurs. Most Gaoyang entrepreneurs today operate in a business culture that takes as a given, as the natural way of organizing and operating a business, the organizational forms that I have problematized. Entrepreneurs have organized their firms in a certain manner because they believe that this is the best solution to the specific problems that they face. Few, if any, know that they are using forms similar to those that their fathers and grandfathers might have used many decades earlier. While most local entrepreneurs have some vague notion of the Gaoyang tradition in the textile industry, with the exception of those elders who were active in the prewar period, they have little interest or knowledge of the history of earlier practices. Gaoyang entrepreneurs have not consciously chosen to organize their businesses in "traditional" ways. That nevertheless the practices they use replicate many of the earlier forms in itself suggests much about the survival of a commercial and industrial tradition deeply embedded in Chinese economic practice.

NOTES

1. William Byrd and Lin Qingsong, *China's Rural Industry: Structure, Development and Reform* (Oxford: Oxford University Press, for the World Bank, 1990); John Wong, Rong Ma, and Mu Yang, *China's Rural Entrepreneurs: Ten Case Studies* (Singapore: Times Academic Press, 1995); Susan Young, *Private Business and Economic Reform in China* (Armonk, NY: Sharpe, 1995; Jean Oi, *Rural China Takes Off: Institutional Foundations of Economic Reform* (Berkeley: University of California Press, 1999).

2. See my essay "Rural Manufacture in China's Cotton Industry, 1890–1990," in *The Fibre That Changed the World: The Cotton Industry in International Perspective,*

1600–1990s, ed. Douglas A. Farnie and David J. Jeremy (Oxford: Oxford University Press, 2004), 431–59.

3. Editorial Committee for Zhongguo Nongcun Shichang Moshi Yanjiu, *Zhongguo nongcun shichang moshi yanjiu* (Beijing: Xinhua Shudian, 1993).

4. Sebastiano Brusco, "Small Firms and the Provision of Real Services," in *Industrial Districts and Local Economic Regeneration,* ed. Frank Pyke and Werner Sengenberger (Geneva: International Institute for Labour Studies, 1992), 177–96.

5. Charles Sabel and Jonathan Zeitlin, "Historical Alternatives to Mass Production: Politics, Markets and Technology in Nineteenth-Century Industrialization," *Past and Present* 108 (August 1985), 133–76.

6. Michael J. Piore and Charles Sabel, *The Second Industrial Divide* (New York: Basic Books, 1984). See also Charles Sabel and Jonathan Zeitlin, *World of Possibilities: Flexibility and Mass Production in Western Industrialization* (Cambridge: Cambridge University Press, 1997); and Michael Storper and Robert Salais, *Worlds of Production: The Action Framework of the Economy* (Cambridge: Harvard University Press, 1997).

7. David Harvey, *The Condition of Postmodernity* (Oxford: Basil Blackwell, 1989). The essays included in Sabel and Zeitlin's *World of Possibilities* exemplify the range of such work by those working on European economic development.

8. Suzanne Berger and Michael Piore, *Dualism and Discontinuity in Industrial Societies* (Cambridge: Cambridge University Press, 1980); Sabel and Zeitlin, *World of Possibilities*.

9. The Chinese textile industry offers a good example of the struggles between state planners pushing for larger-scale production, and local interests pulling in the opposite direction. For a fuller explanation of this argument, see my essay, "Rural Manufacture in China's Cotton Industry, 1890–1990."

10. Philip Scranton, "Diversity in Diversity: Flexible Production and American Industrialization, 1880–1930," *Business History Review* 65 (Spring 1991), 27–90; and Robert Salais and Michael Storper, "The Four 'Worlds' of Contemporary Industry," *Cambridge Journal of Economics* 15 (1992), 169–93.

11. Alfred Marshall, *Principles of Economics*, eighth ed. (London: Macmillan, 1920), chapter 10. Mark Blaug, *Economic Theory in Retrospect*, fourth ed. (Cambridge: Cambridge University Press, 1985), 382–83. See also the rich Japanese literature on *sanchi*, or producing districts. Konosuke Odaka and Minoru Sawai, *Small Firms, Large Concerns: The Development of Small Business in Comparative Perspective* (Oxford: Oxford University Press, 1999).

12. Marshall, *Principles of Economics*, 271.

13. For an overview of recent economic work on the industrial district, see Bjorn T. Asheim, "Industrial Districts: The Contributions of Marshall and Beyond," in *The Oxford Handbook of Economic Geography*, ed. Gordon L. Clark, Maryann P. Feldman, and Meric S. Gertler (Oxford: Oxford University Press, 2000), 413–31.

14. Masahisa Fujita, Paul Krugman, and Anthony J. Venables, *The Spatial Economy: Cities, Regions and International Trade* (Cambridge, MA: MIT Press, 2000).

15. On Italy, see Berger and Piore, *Dualism and Discontinuity in Industrial Societies*; on India, see the World Bank study edited by Ian M. D. Little, Dipak Mazumdar, and John M. Page, Jr., eds., *Small Manufacturing Enterprises: A Comparative Study of India and Other Economies* (New York: Oxford University Press, 1987).

16. Most of the records seem to have been destroyed during the anti-Japanese war and the civil war that followed.

17. Bao Juemin, "Jiefang qiande Nankai Daxue Jingji Yanjiusuo" *Tianjin Wenshi Ziliao Xuanyi* 19 (March 1982).

18. Wu Zhi in an interview on June 9, 1980, in Beijing.

19. Tōa Kenkyūjo produced a translation in 1942.

20. Tianjin Dang'an Guan, Tianjin Shehuikexueyuan Lishi Yanjiusuo, and Tianjin-shi Gongshangye Lianhehui, *Tianjin Shanghui dang'an huibian,* 10 volumes (Tianjin: Tianjin Renmin Chubanshe, published between 1989 and 1998).

1

Creating an Industrial District

Three factors played significant roles in initiating the growth of the modern Gaoyang weaving industry. Two of those factors are the familiar actors in narratives of industrial development: the state and private entrepreneurs. The state appears in the industrial promotion policies implemented in the metropolitan province of Zhili[1] under the governorship of Yuan Shikai, and the private entrepreneurs in the activities of a group of small-town businessmen who seized the opportunities offered by the industrial promotion program. The third factor that contributed to industrial growth was a Japanese export promotion program that supplied raw materials on easy credit terms. It was the coincidence and interaction of the three factors that led to the explosive growth of rural industry in the years between 1908 and 1910 which, in turn, made Gaoyang a model that other communities strove to emulate.

YUAN SHIKAI'S INDUSTRIAL PROMOTION POLICIES

When Yuan Shikai was appointed governor-general of Zhili and commissioner of the northern ports in 1901, the North China region was facing a major economic crisis. The immediate cause of the crisis was the Boxer Rebellion, which had swept across North China from 1898 to 1900, and the foreign intervention that had followed in its wake. The deeper economic problems facing Zhili Province in the early twentieth century, however, were the result of growing population pressure on the land. That problem had been severely aggravated by the decline of the rural textile industry which provided cash income to rural farm families. The central part of Zhili Province was part of the great North China Plain, a flat loess region that stretched from the

Taihang Mountains to the sea. The area was dry, alternately plagued by droughts and floods, and home to a rural population of roughly twenty million in the early twentieth century. Cotton grew well in the soil of the plains region, and since the early eighteenth century rural housewives had produced cotton fabrics for home use and for sale in the frontier regions of the northeast and northwest. By the late nineteenth century income from cotton textile production was an important supplement to rural household budgets.[2]

The decline of the rural textile industry was one of the consequences of the economic, social, and political changes that had been initiated by the opening of Tianjin as a treaty port in 1861.[3] While the native textile industries in central and southern China had faced foreign competition after the opening of the first treaty ports in the 1840s, the crisis in the north became obvious in the 1890s when foreign imports began to make significant inroads into North China markets.

The industrial promotion policies implemented in Zhili in the last decade of the Qing were designed to deal with two aspects of this crisis: rural industries would produce goods for the domestic market that could effectively compete with foreign imports and absorb surplus rural labor, providing employment and raising rural standards of living. In the language of modern development economics, the goals were import substitution and labor absorption.

In the years after the opening of Tianjin as a treaty port, foreign goods had made significant inroads into the North China market for daily-use items. Yuan's advisers decided to promote industries to produce domestic substitutes for those foreign imports. Zhou Xuexi, one of Yuan's chief advisers, was put in charge of the new organization established to promote native industry, the Zhili Industrial Institute (Zhili Gongyiju).[4] Zhou described the situation at that time as follows: "Total foreign import and export trade is more than 90,000,000 taels, but exports are only one fifth of this. The imports are all manufactured goods while exports are all unprocessed materials. The only finished goods we export are straw hats and braid. Failure to develop our native industry means that all the profits of the trade are going to foreigners."[5] Tianjin foreign trade figures showed an annual import of approximately 7,000,000 bolts of cloth with a value of 20,000,000 taels.[6]

Yuan's program to promote the rural weaving industry was modeled on the recent successful import substitution programs in Japan.[7] Zhou Xuexi visited Japan, toured the textile districts, and came back determined to establish schools and demonstration factories using Japanese technology. For the weaving industry the crucial new technology was the iron gear loom, an improved handloom that, except for its power source, worked much like a power loom. The loom produced cloth that was similar to foreign imports produced on power looms. In 1904 the Industrial Institute demonstration factory was in operation with more than six hundred student-apprentices drawn from counties all over the province. The institute, with its subdivisions teaching weaving, dyeing and finishing, introduced modern textile techniques to students who were expected to return to their home counties and promote the new technology.

Zhou Xuexi chose as his chief foreign adviser Fujii Tsunehisa, a leader of industrial promotion in Japan. Fujii was a graduate of the Higher Industrial School, a Meiji predecessor of the engineering faculty of Tokyo Imperial University. Fujii had served as director of the Osaka Commodity Exhibition Center, one of the most successful regional industrial promotion organizations in Japan. Established in 1890, the center had played an active role in developing and promoting new products and technologies and providing information and technical guidance to local entrepreneurs.[8] Although Fujii received the high salary of 400 taels a month, he brought to Yuan's new enterprises years of experience in industrial promotion activities, and we can see his hand in the policies that developed in the following years.[9] Under Fujii's guidance industrial exhibitions were organized in 1906 and 1907 attracting more than fifty thousand visitors.[10]

Gentry and local officials all across the province were urged to play an active role in setting up factories to use the new technology: "Development can be extended from the township to the county, and from one county to the whole province. People who hear of it will be caught up in the spirit of the development and will exert all their efforts for salvation. No one will have to abandon the land and this will benefit the country. There will be no wandering poor. Not only will there be no poor, but the wealthy will have a way of protecting their wealth." Teams were sent out from Tianjin to visit each county to organize local support for industrial activities. Advertisements were posted announcing the visits and public lectures were scheduled for market days.[11]

Local response to the industrial promotion initiatives was strong and many counties started their own weaving factories; between 1904 and 1910 weaving factories were set up in ninety counties throughout the province.[12] The factories set up in Zhili were part of what Japanese observers visiting the Nanyang Exhibition in Nanjing in 1910 called a "boom in textile manufacture" that was sweeping China.[13]

Yuan's industrial promotion program in Zhili was one of the most comprehensive technology transfer experiments of the late Qing. Technology transfer has long been recognized as one of the most important economic development strategies open to late-developing countries. The technology transfer strategy is based on the import and adaptation of machinery and techniques from developed countries. Implementation of technology transfer policies is considerably more complex than may appear at first glance, involving more than simply the importation of equipment. Machinery is created for and adapted to specific patterns of social organization, and when it is implanted in a different social and economic environment, adaptation and innovation is necessary before the technology can be "domesticated" and its application made economically profitable. In many cases the adaptation of new technology requires structural changes in patterns of work organization and creates new forms of industrial and commercial organization.

In the context of the late Qing reform efforts, it is important to note that the role of the state, although crucial in industrial promotion policies, was also limited. Successful application of the new technology in commercially profitable local industries depended on the efforts of individuals in local communities. As we will see in the case of weaving, although the new technology was available to rural communities all over Zhili, it proved to be commercially profitable in only a small number of regions.

The new weaving technology did require changes in the social organization of work. The iron gear loom required a much larger investment, and those costs could only be justified if the loom was in constant use. This led to a shift from part-time handicraft weaving as a supplement to agriculture, to full-time weaving with agriculture in a subsidiary role. Accompanying this professionalization of weaving was a shift in the organization of household labor. Handloom cotton weaving had traditionally been women's work. In the new family workshops men became the weavers, with women and children assigned to reeling and other preparatory tasks.[14]

The higher productivity of the iron gear loom also necessitated major changes in commercial organization. The higher output per unit of labor time, together with the intensification of labor, increased the demand for supplies of yarn. The loom was used almost exclusively with machine spun yarns. Yarn supplies came from the few domestic modern spinning mills or from foreign sources. This created a new role for merchant entrepreneurs as intermediaries and their control over supplies of raw materials and markets led to the development of a putting-out system.[15]

One further organizational change was the concentration of production in a small number of specialized industrial districts. Before the introduction of this new technology, rural households in many counties had produced cloth for the market. The professionalization of weaving together with the changes in commercial organization led to a geographical concentration of production in industrial districts that successfully developed supply and marketing services. Merchants in the new industrial districts were among the first to recognize the opportunities presented by the new technology and to build the network of credit relationships with wholesale suppliers in the treaty ports that sustained the growth of the industry. Such industrial districts became centers for sophisticated processing and finishing factories, thus adding to the initial advantages created by the early establishment of a credit nexus.

TECHNOLOGICAL BEGINNINGS—THE IRON GEAR LOOM

While the social and institutional programs for promoting industrial development were an important element of the late Qing reform programs in Zhili, the fortunate selection of a new technology ideally suited to Chinese conditions was crucial to the rapid response to the promotion programs.[16] The older handloom weaving centers that had flourished since the Ming dynasty had all used simple wooden looms to produce a narrow plain-weave fabric.[17] The most efficient of the plain-weave looms produced approximately ten meters of fabric a day. The experts sent by Yuan Shikai to Japan in 1903 brought back reports on an iron gear loom used in small-scale factories.[18] The iron gear loom had been invented in Japan around 1887 and in the space of five to ten years had replaced the old-style Japanese handloom in many weaving districts. The iron gear loom used a wooden frame to support iron gears that were propelled by foot treadles, which were moved up

Figure 1.1.   Iron Gear Loom. Young weaver working on a modified iron gear loom in a village collective factory in 1980. (Photo by the author.)

and down by the weaver. The gears controlled the passing of the shuttle, the movement of the bar to beat the weft into a tight weave, and the beams for unwinding the warp and for winding on the finished fabric. The weaver's main tasks were providing the foot power to move the loom, keeping a watch for broken warp threads, and replacing used shuttles with full ones. This machine was much faster than older looms, allowing for 120 picks a minute versus a maximum of about 60 with the use of a wooden loom with a flying shuttle. Since almost all actions of the loom were mechanized, it produced a much smoother weave, required less skill to operate, and could produce approximately three times more cloth per working day.[19]

In making the choice for what modern scholars working in the field of development economics call an intermediate or appropriate technology, that is a technology that is less advanced than the state of the art technology that is available at the time,[20] Yuan Shikai's experts considered questions of cost efficiency and adaptability to existing Chinese conditions. Following their visits to a small weaving factory in Wakayama, they calculated the production costs, the wages that were earned by the weavers, and the profits to the owners, and then reported, "Although the steam machines of Europe and America are extraordinarily clever, they can not best these [looms]."[21]

While the iron gear loom had a relatively short period of popularity in Japan, coming into widespread use in the late 1890s and being replaced almost completely by power looms by the 1920s, it was to have a much longer life in China.[22] First introduced in 1903, it remained in use in weaving centers like Gaoyang until the early 1960s. The popularity of this loom was based on a number of factors, including its greater efficiency in comparison with traditional handlooms and the ease of operation, which meant that even untrained weavers could quickly master its operation and produce acceptable fabrics. At least as important was its low cost when compared with power looms. The average cost of an iron gear loom in Gaoyang was 30 to 40 yuan. While this was a large sum for a poor rural family, merchants who wanted to promote the weaving industry quickly began to sell the looms to potential weavers on credit. The returns on weaving were sufficient to cover repayment of loans within a year's time.[23]

The spread of the use of the iron gear loom also had important implications for the development of the Chinese machine-making industry.[24] While all of the power looms in Chinese factories in the prewar period were imported, the mechanisms of the iron gear loom were quickly copied by small metalworking factories in Tianjin's Santiaoshi district and the manufacture of iron gear looms and loom parts became an important part of the Tianjin metalworking industry. Two Japanese trading firms contracted with Santiaoshi factories to produce loom parts as well as whole looms, selling the finished products under Japanese brand-names.[25] Gaoyang weavers were the main customers for the new looms and one of the Gaoyang wholesale merchants,

Yang Musen, encouraged Santiaoshi production by providing capital to the Guo Tian Xiang workshop.[26] Account books of another firm show a great expansion in business between 1908 and 1910, with the manufacture of more than 1,500 looms in 1910. By the mid-1930s there were some 27,000 iron gear looms in use in the Gaoyang weaving district, most of which had been manufactured in Tianjin.

GAOYANG MERCHANTS AND THE NEW WEAVING INDUSTRY

The rural industrial movement promoted by Yuan Shikai met with an immediate response in Gaoyang. In Gaoyang, as in many other Zhili counties, weaving had for a long time been an important supplement to agriculture and the challenge from imported cloth had cut sharply into local income. While there are no contemporary statistics on production in the 1890s, one later estimate suggests that Gaoyang weavers had annually sold about 350,000 bolts of native cloth.[27] By 1905, production of cloth for the market had dropped to only 100,000 bolts.[28] That reduction by almost two-thirds created a sense of crisis among local merchants and pushed them to take action. In 1906 a group of merchants led by Zhang Xinghan, Han Weiqing, Yang Musen, and Li Bingxi organized the Gaoyang Chamber of Commerce. At the time the county town of Gaoyang had a population of only five thousand, and all of the men involved in the new organization were owners or managers of small commercial firms.

The merchants were determined to revive the cotton weaving industry. In 1908 Han Weiqing visited the Tianjin experimental factory and toured other North China areas that were starting local industry. Following this survey he borrowed several iron gear looms from the Industrial Institute, imported machine-spun yarn, and loaned the machines and raw materials to local weavers.[29] Members of the chamber of commerce also set up two experimental factories. Yang Musen, who would later become the single most successful Gaoyang entrepreneur, invested 10,000 yuan in a demonstration factory in his home village of Nanbianwu, just across the county border in Anxin. Two other merchants, Li Mengkuai and Shi Chunhe, jointly invested 10,000 yuan in another factory in Dazhuang village in neighboring Qingyuan County.[30] The weaving industry made a very rapid take-off from these modest beginnings. By 1909 there were 10,000 looms in the region and by 1910 15,000; Gaoyang weavers produced 950,000 bolts of cloth in 1909 and 1,480,000 bolts in 1910. Not all of the looms in this period were iron gear looms. A Japanese team of investigators estimated that in 1910 some 20 percent of the looms were iron gear looms; most of the rest were wooden looms with flying shuttles. Either loom could produce the foreign-style wide cloths that made up the main part of Gaoyang production, although the iron gear loom produced double the amount of cloth per unit of weaving time. By the middle of the next decade almost all of the weavers had switched to the iron gear loom and some had added jacquard devices to weave patterned fabrics. By 1910 there were more than ten yarn and cloth dealers in Gaoyang County and commercial houses were developing new trading networks.[31]

RECRUITING THE WEAVERS

To realize their goals, the merchants needed to convince peasants to invest in looms and learn the new technology. From the peasant weaver's point of view, economic incentives were major motivators.[32] Agrarian crisis had created a large population of rural underemployed who were ready to try any new endeavor that promised a steady supplement to agriculture income.

Gaoyang agriculture in the early twentieth century provides a classic illustration of what Philip Huang has described as involution in the North China peasant economy.[33] By the early twentieth century, the steadily rising rural population had expanded beyond the capacity of the land to support it. Although the land was poor and natural disasters frequent, the central Hebei plains were densely populated with households struggling to make a living on the unpromising land. In the Gaoyang area agricultural production depended on the weather. Rain was concentrated in two months during the peak of the growing season and too much or too little could bring swift disaster to a population living very close to the survival level. Flood and drought were frequent visitors to the region.[34]

In addition to the problems peasants faced with poor soil quality and natural disasters, land was generally scarce, as well as unequally distributed. Fully 80 percent of all households in the area lacked sufficient land to live by agriculture alone.[35] A survey of the weaving district in 1933 showed an average household of 5.52 persons with a farm of 14.95 *mu* of land. A more detailed study of 382 weaving households distributed over the five-county weaving area provides a clearer picture of land distribution and the overwhelming number of rural households below the subsistence level if income came from agriculture alone. This survey showed an average weaving household with 6.64 members and average landholdings of 17.88 *mu*. For a family of this size to survive by agriculture alone, a minimum of 32 *mu* would be required. Fully 64 percent of the households had less than 16 *mu*, or half of that required.[36]

The overall shortage of land and the alkaline nature of the soil were more direct causes of rural poverty in the Gaoyang region than was concentration of land in the hands of large landlords. In approximately 90 percent of the villages land was relatively equally distributed; in only 10 percent of the villages were there landlords with significant holdings.[37]

Most of the poorer peasants lived in small, three- or four-room sun-dried mud-brick houses which accommodated family members and provided shelter in the winter season for pigs, chickens, and whatever other animals a family possessed. Compilers of the local gazetteer noted that a foul odor pervaded most farm residences as a result of the crowded living conditions.[38] The vast majority of the peasant families survived on a repetitive diet of gruel, noodles, and steamed breads made from the millet and corn they raised. As one moved up the economic ladder from the very poorest to middle peasant status, total consumption levels of grains rose but there was only slight improvement in the variety of foods; middle peasant families, on average, consumed one-third to one-half more grain than their poor peasant neighbors and were also able to supplement their diet with some vegetables and sugar. Meat, fish, and breads made from the finer wheat flours were treats known only to the more fortunate peasant families for their annual New Year's feasts.[39]

By the early twentieth century many families found it impossible to maintain even these low consumption levels by farming alone and turned to alternative activities to supplement farm income. This situation, common across most of the North China plains, gave rise to several kinds of by-employment: long-term and short-term farm labor, seasonal migration to cities and the newly opened region of the northeast, and widespread handicraft industry. Each of these forms of supplementary employment brought hard-pressed households cash income that could be exchanged for grains and other necessities.

The weaving industry drew on this vast reservoir of rural underemployed and provided cash income to thousands of farm families. By the 1920s, 80 to 90 percent of Gaoyang area rural households were involved in the weaving industry and derived most of their income from weaving with farming continuing as a subsidiary enterprise. The rapid expansion of the weaving industry reversed the trend toward emigration common throughout central Hebei. By the 1920s Gaoyang had become the destination for immigrants from nearby counties; men flocked to the area seeking employment.[40]

IMPORT SUBSTITUTION

Early Gaoyang success was built on the production of piece goods made in imitation of foreign imports but sold at prices below those of imported goods. Major products included light-, medium-, and heavy-weight sheetings, T-cloth, drills, and old-style native cloth.[41] Some of the cloth was shipped unbleached while other lines were dyed and finished before sale. In general the unbleached cloth competed in the market with Japanese imports while dyed and finished goods competed with English imports.

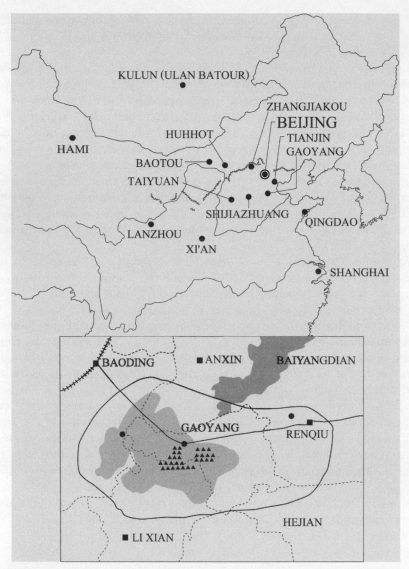

Map 1.1. The Gaoyang Industrial District. On the inset map, the solid line indicates the limits of the Gaoyang weaving district, the shaded area indicates the area where weaving was most common, and dots indicate the areas of jacquard weaving.

Gaoyang's success in producing import substitutes can be seen in Tianjin custom statistics. As a Japanese survey of 1911 noted, imports to Tianjin of British sheetings stood at 110,000 bolts in 1906 and 1907, but dropped by 50 percent in 1908, and stagnated at the 50,000-bolt level for the years down to 1911. The Japanese reporters attributed the British loss of market to the rise of Gaoyang cloth. Hardest hit of the British imports were their lowest priced items. In the market for coarse sheetings, Gaoyang cloth was 20 percent cheaper than English goods. Gaoyang's competitive position was further strengthened by the introduction of German and Italian chemical dyes, which were already being used by dyeing factories in 1910. In the case of competition between Japanese imported unbleached cloth and similar Gaoyang fabrics, the price differential was considerably less, falling in the range of 10 percent. Gaoyang products were making much deeper inroads into the Japanese market for T-cloth, a fabric that had originally been imported from India and was quite similar to shirting. The Japanese had seen the import volume in Tianjin drop from 136,240 bolts in 1906 to only 20,000 bolts in 1910.[42]

THE JAPANESE EXPORT CAMPAIGN AND THE GAOYANG COTTON INDUSTRY

From the beginning Gaoyang trade was enmeshed in a complicated and multistranded relationship with the global economy. The iron gear loom came from Japan and Chinese weavers were first trained to use it by Japanese teachers.[43] Further, while Gaoyang cloth was designed to substitute for imported goods, almost all of the yarn used in weaving was imported. In 1910 Japanese manufacturers had 70 percent of the Gaoyang market, and Japanese-supplied credit played an important role in the rapid development of the weaving industry. The rise of Gaoyang industry coincided with a major Japanese export campaign that included an export cartel. To better understand the links that motivated the Japanese to offer easy credit to Chinese merchants, we need to turn briefly to an examination of the structure and growth of the Japanese cotton industry in the late nineteenth century.

The Japanese market, like that of China, had been flooded by imported cotton goods after the opening of the first treaty ports in that country. As in China, the trade imbalances had stimulated domestic entrepreneurs to establish modern cotton-spinning and weaving mills. The first cotton-spinning mill was set up in Kagoshima in 1866. While the pace of development in the early years was quite slow, it increased dramatically during the 1890s, with total spindle capacity passing the million mark in 1898.[44] The boom in mill founding after the 1894–1895 Sino-Japanese War led to overcapacity that became very obvious in the depression of 1897–1898. The government intervened to prevent bankruptcies and industry leaders, all members of the Japan Cotton Spinner's Association, established a cartel to promote exports. Members of the association were assigned export quotas that were to be filled even if this meant selling at a loss. China was targeted as the most important market. With assistance from the government and loans from the Yokohama Species Bank, the export trade in cotton yarn picked up. By 1897, 25 percent of the total cotton yarn output of Japanese factories was being exported, with 94 percent going to China.[45] By the turn of the century, more than 40 percent of Japan's total cotton yarn output was going into the export market, primarily to China.

In Tianjin, one of the major Japanese trading companies, Mitsui Bussan, established a branch office and began selling Japanese cotton yarn directly to yarn firms in the city on credit.[46] The credit extended to Tianjin yarn wholesalers allowed them to sell on credit to their customers, including the Gaoyang entrepreneurs.[47] This made it possible for the Gaoyang entrepreneurs to develop their system of production with relatively limited investment capital.

CYCLES OF GROWTH IN THE WEAVING INDUSTRY

The Gaoyang weaving industry, which had dramatically expanded following the introduction of the iron gear loom, went into a major slump in the fall of 1910 and was showing no signs of recovery in 1911 when a Japanese survey team visited the area. The immediate cause of the decline in 1910 was a credit panic that was touched off by the collapse of several Shanghai native banks.[48] The native banks had been forced into bankruptcy as a result of loans for speculation on the international rubber market. When the speculative bubble in rubber shares burst, loans were called in. The practice of nested borrowing among native banks touched off a chain reaction, with ramifications in ever-widening circles. In the case of the 1910 panic, not only native banks, but most of the major foreign banks in Shanghai were involved, since many had extended unsecured "chop loans" to Chinese native banks. Losses on loans extended for rubber speculation bankrupted seven native banks; the foreign banks in turn called in their outstanding chop loans to native banks, widening the circle of native bank failures. As the panic spread, native banks in other cities were touched by the wave of the panic.

Gaoyang was drawn into the spreading panic since her yarn and cloth merchants bought yarn on credit from yarn wholesalers in Tianjin who offered generous credit terms. Those yarn wholesalers were in turn backed up by two sources of credit: credit offered by the foreign trading firms that imported yarn, and credit from Tianjin native banks. Gaoyang merchants in turn relied on those same Tianjin native banks to provide short-term loans to pay bills due to yarn wholesalers before payments on the sale of finished goods had come back into the firms' accounts. The panic initiated by instability in the Shanghai financial markets led Tianjin native banks to tighten credit. Since Gaoyang dealers operated with limited capital backing, they did not have sufficient capital to sustain the trade at previous levels. The immediate result was contraction in cloth production: Gaoyang yarn and cloth merchants pulled back their agents from regional marketing centers, and output fell to only 15 percent of the level of the previous year.[49]

The financial crisis of late 1910–1911 would prove to be a temporary setback. Although it is not clear when the recovery from the slump began, certainly by 1914 the industry had entered another boom period that was to last until 1920. This first boom period followed by a deep crisis established a pattern that was to be repeated several times. In the years before the beginning of the anti-Japanese war in 1937, Gaoyang industry was to see a series of boom periods, usually lasting four to five years, each followed by a crisis. While the direct cause touching off each crisis varied, the underlying problem of structural vulnerability to tightened credit was always present. Gaoyang firms, like many other small-scale firms in other parts of Asia, both in the past and in the present, operated with relatively limited capital. Since firms were heavily dependent on credit, credit contractions in the economy were quickly reflected in contractions in business turnover. Loosening of credit, on the other hand, could lead to rapid recovery.

While this pattern of credit tightening and loosening seemed to move in a cyclical pattern, other forces were also at work that provided for long-term change. Each crisis provided a stimulus to innovation, and each recovery period saw the introduction of innovations in technology, product, or marketing strategies that led to the expansion of production. The strategy of flexible specialization grew out of this pattern of crisis and response, shifting Gaoyang industry to a diversified product line with much greater value added.

While there are no precise figures on output during this boom period from 1914 to 1920, one Chinese observer estimated that in 1914 the Gaoyang merchant community earned 3,000,000 yuan in profits; the largest of the yarn and cloth wholesale firms owned by Yang Musen pulled in profits of approximately 130,000 yuan that year on a capital investment of about 20,000 yuan. The industry was doing so well that local merchants were talking about raising capital to set up their own spinning mill to supply yarn to weavers.[50] Signs of recovery could be seen everywhere. Perhaps the strongest indicators were the increase in the number of yarn and cloth wholesale merchants in the town and the expansion of the marketing region. Between 1912 and 1920, at least eighteen new wholesale firms opened business in Gaoyang.[51]

NEW STRATEGIES FOR SURVIVAL

The most important business innovation during the decade of the teens was the mastering of a system of direct marketing. In the early teens, Gaoyang firms began to set up direct sales agencies in important regional marketing centers. The direct sales agencies, which seem to have been a Gaoyang innovation, served two functions: first, they pushed the sale of cloth to regional wholesale merchants, and second, they gathered information on market demand so that new products could be designed to meet specific local needs and tastes.

The recovery that started in 1912 or 1913 and lasted through the First World War period was greatly aided by the withdrawal of European fabrics from the Chinese market. All across China, this same period saw the expansion of native industries that were temporarily freed from some of the pressure of foreign competition. British textile imports declined sharply and Gaoyang goods were able to move into markets that merchants had previously found it difficult to enter.

There were technical innovations, too, which improved Gaoyang cloth. The most important technical improvements were changes in the dyeing and finishing process. In the earliest period, some small dyeing workshops in Gaoyang had already started to shift from traditional vegetable dyes to modern chemical dyes. The learning process was accelerated when a German technician was hired to teach local dye masters how to use the chemical dyes more effectively.[52]

While unbleached shirtings and sheetings were still the mainstay of the Gaoyang trade, weavers were beginning to experiment with new fabrics. In the latter days of the Qing dynasty almost all Gaoyang cloth had been produced using low count yarns with the largest market share going to sixteen- and twenty-count yarns.[53] In the early teens, weavers began to move into the slightly higher-count yarns, particularly with greater use of twenty- and thirty-two–count yarns, which produced a slightly finer fabric. In 1915–1916, Japanese manufacturers introduced a new "gassed yarn" which had been singed in the production process to remove any stray fibers. Such yarn, introduced to improve the Japanese competitive position at a time when low-count yarns from Chinese domestic mills were starting to compete in the market, was used to produce a cloth called "patriotic cloth" (*aiguo bu*) which was primarily used to make the long Chinese traditional formal garment, the *changpao*.

Other new product innovations introduced in this period included stripes and checks, which were produced with yarn that was dyed before weaving; finer fabrics, including various kinds of gauzes woven with high-count yarns; and finally, in the very late teens, the introduction of various kinds of small-pattern weaves, which could be woven when a dobby device was used with the standard iron gear loom. All of these innovations contributed to the expansion of markets, but many of them also required higher levels of technical skill.[54] Several of these innovations, particularly the addition of a jacquard frame which was used for weaving patterned fabrics, were to be developed much more extensively in the 1920s and to become the mainstays of later Gaoyang cloth production.

This period also saw the development of a putting-out system in which weaving households worked for yarn and cloth merchants under an informal contract system. When weaving first began in 1908, most weavers bought yarn from a wholesale dealer and sold finished goods to wholesalers. By 1910, merchants had developed a system of informal contract; under this system, weavers exchanged finished cloth for yarn plus a payment that represented the piece wage for the finished goods. This putting-out system allowed cash-short weaving households to continue weaving from one market period to the next with no interruption. I refer to this system as an informal contract system since there were never any written contracts involved and since either the weaver or the merchant could sever the relationship at any time.

The wartime boom period came to an end in 1921, and for the next four years there was a general stagnation in the industry. While the recession was certainly not as dramatic as that of 1911, it led to some major restructuring. One of the chief causes of the recession was the return of foreign competition after the end of the First World War. During the war few European firms engaged in trade with China, but once the war ended they returned to the China market and the "golden age" for China's native industry came to an end. In the textile industry, one of the chief manifestations of the decline was instability in the price of yarn. Increased competition began to drive prices down. New spinning mills were established in Tianjin and Qingdao in the 1920s and already existing facilities in Shanghai were expanding. With foreign competitors reentering the market, the price of cotton yarn began to fall.[55] Yarn and cloth wholesalers found themselves caught in a situation where the profit rate per production unit began to fall as increased competition forced a faster fall in the price of finished goods than in raw materials prices.

The mainstay of the Gaoyang product line, cheap unbleached shirtings and sheetings, were hardest hit by the slump. Competition came from foreign imports that had reentered the market, as well as from new domestic producers. One of Gaoyang's strongest rivals was the new weaving center established in Wei County, Shandong. The weaving district in Wei County had been set up following the Gaoyang model, and some Gaoyang entrepreneurs had also made investments in the new Shandong weaving center. Wei County, which was located on the rail line from Qingdao to Jinan, had more convenient transportation links than Gaoyang, and as a result shipping charges were considerably lower.[56] The challenge from Wei County and other districts that strove to imitate Gaoyang's success first came in the market for unbleached cotton cloth, since that was the product that required the least skill. Just as Gaoyang had gotten its start in the production of cheap, plain cotton weaves, new industrial districts that wished to copy its success began their efforts in the same way, choosing the product lines that required the least in terms of technical skill and capital investment.

The response of the Gaoyang manufacturers to this challenge was to shift to the production of higher-value-added fabrics that required greater weaving skill and more investment in dyeing and finishing. While the Gaoyang choice may seem to be the only logical response to the situation, the choice was far from inevitable. Until the 1920s, the Baodi weaving district, located almost directly north of Tianjin, had followed a strategy very similar to that of Gaoyang, and had met with similar success. However, during the 1920s slump, Baodi manufacturers continued to produce cheap, unbleached cotton fabrics. By the late 1920s they were losing their competitive position and weaving in Baodi went into a permanent decline. In 1928, output volume for Gaoyang and Baodi was roughly equivalent at approximately 3,000,000 bolts of cloth each, but the total value of Gaoyang output stood at 30,600,000 yuan, while for Baodi total value was only 7,525,000 yuan.[57] The difference in value was the result of Gaoyang's production of higher-value-added items like yarn-dyed stripes and checks, and patterned fabrics.

TECHNOLOGICAL INNOVATION AND RECOVERY

The introduction of yarn-dyed striped and checked fabrics was the first of a series of product innovations which steadily moved Gaoyang producers into a new style of production that made the most effective use of their flexible production system and direct marketing networks. (See table 1.1.) Rather than trying to compete with new rivals in the lowest segments of the market, a competition that would almost inevitably be won primarily on the basis of lowest production costs, Gaoyang manufacturers chose to compete in the middle and upper segments of the market where a more diversified line of medium- and high-quality fabrics appealed to customers. This shift in strategy was made possible by the application of technologies that allowed for the production of new types of fabrics and was greatly assisted by the sales agency system, which also served to gather information on regional market demand. The two most important innovations were the introduction of the jacquard loom for the weaving of patterned fabrics and the use of rayon yarn to produce imitation silk fabrics.

The jacquard loom, which had been invented in France in 1800, was first brought to Gaoyang in 1914 by Su Bingheng who later was one of the found-

Table 1.1. Product Diversification

Period	White goods	Colored goods	Rayon	Rayon blends
1906–1915	Sheetings	Dyed sheetings		
1915–1917		Patriotic cloth		
		Gassed yarn cloth		
		Gassed yarn checks		
		Pongees		
1917–1919		Small-figured cloth		
		Striped cloth		
		Checked cloth		
		Bedding covers		
1919–1921				Gauze
1922–1925			Minghua	
			Poplin	
			Damask	
1926–1930		Serge	Spring crepe	
			Imitation Italian crepe	
1931–1933			Crepe georgette	
			Printed covers	

Source: Wu Zhi, *Xiangcun zhibuye de yige yanjiu,* chapter 5, part 2.

ing partners of a very successful family-run firm, Tong He (discussed in chapter two). Su Bingheng had mastered weaving on a jacquard loom as a student apprentice at the Zhili Industrial Institute in Tianjin. When he returned to Gaoyang at the end of his apprenticeship, he brought home a jacquard loom that he used to produce patterned cotton weaves. The market demand for such fabrics was quite limited, and the jacquard loom did not come into widespread use until Gaoyang manufacturers began to promote the use of rayon. Rayon fiber had been introduced in the late teens but at first could only be used to produce mixed weaves that used cotton yarn for the warp and rayon yarn for the weft. All-rayon fabrics became a possibility in 1926, when a Tianjin workshop discovered a way to process rayon yarn that increased its tensile strength. This made the synthetic fiber usable as both warp and weft. The Tianjin inventor tried to protect his monopoly on the sizing of rayon yarn, but several Gaoyang workers got jobs in his factory, mastered the technique which was technically quite simple, and returned to Gaoyang with the trade secret.

The production of all-rayon fabrics initiated a major boom period in Gaoyang trade. Rayon, the first synthetic fiber to hit the world market, was called synthetic silk in Chinese; it looked like silk, could be dyed a range of very attractive colors, and yet sold for prices considerably below the price of silk. Within the space of several years, Gaoyang output had risen to 600,000 bolts of rayon fabric a year. These light-weight fabrics were particularly welcomed in the southern part of the country, and Gaoyang firms sent agents to Sichuan, Hunan, and Hubei for the first time, and also shipped goods to southeast Asia.[58] For the weavers the new rayon fabrics brought high profits. The most attractive weaves were those in patterned designs woven on jacquard looms; this required higher investment from the weaver, but the profits per bolt of fabric were also higher. At the peak of the boom period, profits stood at four to six yuan per bolt, depending on the quality of the work and the difficulty of the design.

Production of rayon fabrics encouraged the growth of new subsidiary industries. Most important were the dyeing and finishing industries. Dyeing and finishing workshops were set up in the areas outside Gaoyang town and in nearby villages. Several of the larger yarn and cloth wholesale firms set up mechanized dyeing and finishing factories. This shift of investment from exclusively trade to involvement in production marked an important transitional stage in the development of Gaoyang capital. (See chapter two.) In addition to the dyeing and finishing factories and workshops, other small firms were set up to create the new designs and punch the cards for use on the jacquard looms.

THE 1930–1933 CRISIS IN GAOYANG WEAVING

The Gaoyang weaving industry, which had experienced boom conditions from 1926 to 1930, went into a severe slump beginning in 1930. By 1932 more than half of the looms were not operating. The slump of the early 1930s can be traced to a number of causes, including the effects of the Japanese invasion of the northeast, the general world depression, and the accumulated effects of a decade of civil war. As prices for agricultural goods fell, farm income was reduced and many families ceased cash cropping and returned to subsistence production of grains. The natural result was a general decline in disposable income and reduced demand for manufactured goods. This generalized rural depression lowered the demand for textiles since a consuming household could reasonably postpone purchase of cloth for at least a few years by patching and re-patching older garments.

The general secular decline in demand was made worse by the complete loss of a major regional market as the result of the Japanese invasion of the northeast. Since 1919 Gaoyang merchants had devoted much effort to cultivating Manchurian markets and had established outlet stores in the cities of Harbin, Shenyang, Liaoyang, Fengtian, Jilin, and Changchun. Since the population of the northeast was growing rapidly and there was little indigenous production of textiles, these markets were regarded as the most promising for Gaoyang's future.[59]After the Japanese seized the northeast in 1931 and set up their puppet-state of Manchukuo, the government declared that all trade with China was to be treated as foreign trade, subject to tariffs. In order to encourage Japanese trade and investment in the Manchurian economy, tariffs on cotton textiles were set at 50 percent of declared value. These high tariffs removed the price advantage that Gaoyang textiles had had in the markets of the northeast; not only the product of Gaoyang looms, but also that of all other Chinese producers was effectively shut out of the Manchurian market.[60]

Exclusion from the Manchurian markets made the anti-Japanese issue of direct concern to Gaoyang merchants, and in the last months of 1931 the chamber of commerce joined in the national wave of patriotic feeling and pledged its support for a boycott of Japanese goods. This left many Gaoyang merchants with large stocks of Japanese yarn for which there were no immediate markets. The price of Japanese thirty-two–count yarn, the most commonly used at that time, dropped precipitously in the early months of 1932 as small dealers and weavers shifted to the use of yarn from Chinese spinning mills.[61] While the price of Japanese yarn plummeted, the price of Chinese yarn dropped only slightly. When stocks of Chinese yarn were exhausted merchants were reluctant to invest in new stocks of the higher-priced yarn, and by the third month of the new year Chinese yarn had disappeared from the Gaoyang market.[62]

With the falling price of yarn, merchants were caught in the same trap that they had found themselves in during the slump of the early 1920s. Merchants were caught in a price squeeze when the price of finished goods fell faster than the price of raw materials. The lack of local credit and banking institutions left merchants with no source of commercial loans to tide them over the slump, and many of the smaller operators were forced out of business.[63]

RECOVERY AND NEW BOOM, 1934–1937

Wu Zhi's well-known survey of the weaving industry was undertaken in 1933, when the industry was at the deepest point of this major depression. Much later scholarship has assumed that the crash of the early 1930s represented the end of Gaoyang weaving. However, when I interviewed former merchants and weavers, most of them had only dim memories of the troubles of the early 1930s, but very vivid recollections of the boom that followed and lasted to the beginning of the war with Japan in the summer of 1937. They remember those years immediately preceding the war as the most prosperous in Gaoyang's history, when weavers were working nonstop to meet demand.

The prewar revival of Gaoyang industry was part of a general secular improvement of the whole Chinese economy at that time, with the recovery intensified by factors particular to the textile industry.[64] A combination of technological innovation and marketing changes allowed Gaoyang merchants to regain their competitive position despite the loss of the important markets in the northeast. In the years after 1934, cotton shirtings and sheetings played a reduced role in Gaoyang production; such goods had made up 55 percent of trade in 1932, but by 1934 had shrunk to only 20 percent of the total output.[65] Beginning in 1933–1934, the chief products were various kinds of rayon and rayon blends, and colored cotton goods, including printed fabrics, stripes, and checks, and cotton worsteds, cotton blankets, sheets, and tablecloths. As the product line suggests, Gaoyang manufacturers were serving markets for specialized goods.

There is little question that the revival of Gaoyang weaving in the immediate prewar period was strongly affected in very complex ways by the advance of Japanese imperialism. From the beginning, Gaoyang interests had been closely intertwined with those of Japan. The iron gear loom had come from Japan, Japanese manufacturers supplied raw materials, and, later, the Japanese invasion of the northeast effectively shut Gaoyang merchants out of those markets, which contributed to the major slump of the early 1930s. Japanese connections were also important in the mid-1930s recovery.

For the Japanese producers of rayon fiber, Gaoyang had constituted an important market in the 1920s and 1930s. The Japanese rayon industry had shifted to an export-oriented growth strategy in the 1920s. While manufacturers at first focused on the export of finished piece goods, the export of rayon fiber became increasingly important after the mid-1920s. As Japan moved aggressively into the world market for rayon fiber and goods, her trading partners responded by raising tariffs to protect their native industries. Chinese tariffs under the unequal treaties had been set at 5 percent of value on all imported goods. Tariff autonomy was one of the chief goals of the Nationalist government and following negotiations with the foreign powers in the late 1920s, the Chinese government began to raise tariffs to increase government revenue and also to protect native industries. Tariffs were first raised in 1928, and again in 1930. In 1930 the tariff on rayon piece goods and rayon yarn were both set at the same high rate of 45 percent, and subsequently, imports of rayon piece goods dropped dramatically. Rayon yarn, however, was a major raw material for weavers not only in the Gaoyang area but also in the Yangzi delta region, where former silk weavers had switched from silk to rayon and rayon blends.[66]

While the higher tariffs did not bring an end to the import of rayon fiber, they did significantly cut into profits. However, since rayon's selling point was its low price in comparison with silk, it was not possible to compensate for the full increase by raising the price of finished goods. When cheaper rayon yarn came onto the market in 1934 as a result of smuggling through the East Hebei zone, Gaoyang producers benefited directly.

The East Hebei Special Zone was a triangular-shaped area along the coast of the Gulf of Bohai north of Tianjin. It was set up in 1933 following the Tangku Truce, which ended a Japanese military incursion into the area south of the Great Wall. The Tangku Truce established a demilitarized zone that was administered by a Chinese police force; a pro-Japanese Chinese military officer headed the government set up in the zone, and the zone was effectively under Japanese control. Regular Chinese military forces were withdrawn following the truce agreement and officials of the Maritime Customs were also forced to withdraw. This sets up the conditions that led in 1934–1935 to an active smuggling trade, in which rayon fiber was one of the most important items. Rayon was exported from Japan to ports in the Japanese puppet-state of Manchukuo and then shipped on small boats to various ports on the coast of eastern Hebei; the goods were then trucked to Tianjin. Smuggled rayon sold for 83.84 yuan per hundred pounds versus a Tianjin price for legally imported goods of 98 yuan.[67]

As smuggling increased, Japanese importers in Tianjin strongly protested since they too were losing business. In 1934 the East Hebei zone government established a new tariff system for what it called "special trade." The new tariffs were only applicable to goods of Japanese manufacture and the tariff on rayon yarn was less than one-seventh of that set by the Nanjing government. Throughout the immediate prewar period Gaoyang merchants continued to benefit from the lower-priced rayon yarn that came in through East Hebei.[68]

Despite the fact that Gaoyang was largely dependent on Japanese imports for the raw materials used in both rayon and cotton weaving, Gaoyang fabrics got a huge boost in the mid-1930s from the national campaign to boycott Japanese goods. While Gaoyang had periodically played on its "national product" character, there is no question that, particularly in this period, demand increased as a result of the anti-Japanese boycotts. Merchants stressed the "native" origin of their goods and among the new products put on the market was a cotton worsted which was sold as "anti-Japanese worsted" (*kang-ri ni*).[69] Han Xianghui, who was the head of the Tianjin branch office of the large Gaoyang yarn and cloth dealer Da Heng, recalled that his company had been unable to meet the increased demand for cloth and in 1936 and 1937 had started to purchase shirtings and sheetings in Tianjin; the fabrics were dyed either in Tianjin or in Gaoyang, and after attachment of a Gaoyang trademark were marketed in the interior. At that time roughly equivalent qualities of Gaoyang and Japanese imported cloth brought in very different profits; on a bolt of Japanese cloth, the profit would be 0.4–0.5 yuan, while the equivalent Gaoyang cloth would bring in a profit of 1.0 yuan. Han attributed the difference to the higher demand for Gaoyang cloth as a result of the boycott movement.[70]

Gaoyang industry was operating at full capacity and struggling to keep up with market demand in the summer of 1937 when the war began. The

Japanese invasion cut Gaoyang off from its sources of raw materials and from the markets in the interior. Most of the entrepreneurs and managers of yarn and cloth dealers and the operators of finishing and dyeing factories fled, and the industry collapsed within the space of a few months. During the long war years there were several attempts by the Japanese to revive the weaving industry, but they met with very little success. In the next four chapters we will look at various aspects of Gaoyang industry during the prewar period, looking at the firms that led the textile industry and the social changes that rural industrialization brought to the community.

NOTES

1. The name Zhili referred to the province that was directly under the national administration. The province's name was changed to Hebei in 1928. Current borders of Hebei Province are slightly different from those of Qing Zhili.

2. A survey of rural textile industries was undertaken at the direction of the Zhili Gongyiju in 1905. Tianjinshi Dang'an Guan, Tianjin Shehui Kexueyuan Lishi Yanjiusuo, and Tianjinshi Gongshangye Lianhehui, eds., *Tianjin Shanghui dang'an huibian,* part 1, vol. 1, 970–72.

3. Treaty ports were cities opened to foreign residence and commerce as a result of treaties signed with foreign powers. The first five were opened after the Opium War, others through successive treaties. Tianjin was opened by treaty agreement in 1861, following the second Opium War.

4. Zhu Chunfu, "Zhou Xuexi yu Beiyang Shiye," *Tianjin Wenshi Ziliao Xuanyi* 1 (December 1978), 1–28; Zhu Chunfu, "Beiyang junfa dui Tianjin jindai gongye de touzi," *Tianjin wenshi ziliao xuanyi* 4 (October 1979, 146–62; Xu Jingxing, "Tianjin jindai gongye de zaoqi gaikuang," *Tianjin wenshi ziliao xuanyi* 1 (December 1978), 124–61.

5. Zhou Errun, *Zhili gongyizhi chubian, zhangbailei,* 1:1a (Tianjin: Zhili Gongyiju Printing Office, 1907).

6. *Zhili gongyizhi chubian, zhangbailei,* xia, 3:a–b.

7. Sun Xuemei, *Qingmo Minchu Zhongguoren de Riben guan—yi Zhilisheng wei zhongxin* (Tianjin: Tianjin Renmin Chubanshe, 2001).

8. Osaka Furitsu Shōhin Chinretsusho Soritsu Sanjunen Kinen Kyōsankai, *Kaiko Sanjunen* (Osaka, 1920). See Imazu Kenji, "Kōgyōka ni hatashita kangyō seisaku no yakuwari: Nōshōmushō shōkōgyō gishi ni meggute," in *Nihon no kōgyōka to gijutsu hatten,* ed. Kiyokawa Yukihiko and Minami Ryoshin (Tokyo: Tōyō Keizai Shimposha, 1987), 237–59.

9. See Minamisato Tomoki, "Chūgoku seifu koyō no Nihonjin," in *Kindai Ni-Chū kankei shiryō,* vol. 2 (Tokyo: Ryūkei Shosha, 1976), for salaries of Japanese employees of Chinese organizations in the late Qing.

10. *Zhili gongyizhi chubian, zhangbailei, shang,* 26a–27b.

11. *Zhili gongyizhi chubian, baogaolei, juan xia,* 4a–7a; *conglulei, juan shang,* 3a–b.

12. Peng Ziyi, ed., *Zhongguo jindai shougongye shi ziliao*, vol. 2 (Beijing: Sanlian, 1962), 528–32.

13. Nan'yō Kangyōkai Nihon Shuppin Kyōkai, ed. *Nan'yō Hakurankai kakusho shuppin chōsasho* (Tokyo, 1912), 1373.

14. See my article, "Mechanization and Women's Work in Early Twentieth Century China," in Yanagita Setsuko-sensei Koki Kinen Ronshū Henshō Iinkai, *Yanagita Setsuko-sensei koki kinen Chūgoku no dentō shakai to kazoku* (Tokyo: Kyūko Shoin, 1993), 95–120.

15. Under the putting-out system, merchants supplied raw materials to producers who worked in their own homes. The merchants collected the finished goods, paying the producers a "wage" for their work. Use of the iron gear loom in Japan led to similar changes in commercial organization and development of putting out.

16. Kiyokawa Yukihiko, "Gijutsu kakusa to dōnyu gijutsu no teichaku katei: Sen'yi sangyō no keiken o chūshin ni," in *Kindai Nihon no Keizai Hatten*, ed. Ogawa Kazushi and Minami Ryoshin (Tokyo: Tōyō Keizai Shinposha, 1975).

17. Chen Weiwei, ed., *Zhongguo fangzhi kexue jishu shi—gudai buben* (Beijing: Kexue Chubanshe, 1984).

18. *Zhili gongyizhi chubian, baogaolei xia*, 16a–17a. For a report on the iron gear loom in Tianjin, see "Tenshin chihō ni okeru shokufuki" in *Tenshin Nihonjin Shōgyō Kaigisho Hannenhō*, (1916), 61–66.

19. Ishii Tadashi, "Toyota Saekichi to shoki gijutsu no hatten." *Hatsumei* 76 (January-June 1979), 40.

20. Nicolas Jequier, ed. *Appropriate Technology—Problems and Promises* (Paris: Development Centre of the Organisation for Economic Co-Operation and Development, 1976); Austin Robinson, ed., *Appropriate Technologies for Third World Development* (London: Macmillan, 1979); Arghiri Emmanuel, *Appropriate or Underdeveloped Technology?* (Chichester: Wiley, 1982).

21. Zhou Errun, *Zhili gongyizhi chubian, baogaolei, xia*, 16b.

22. Kiyokawa Yukihiko, "Nihon orimonogyō ni okeru rikishokukika no shinten o meggute," *Keizai Kenkyū* 35:2 (April 1984).

23. Interviews with old weavers in Gaoyang in May 1980.

24. Kiyokawa Yukihiko, "Chūgoku sen'i kikai kogyō no hatten to zaikabō no igi," *Keizai Kenkyū* 34, no. 1 (January 1983), 22–39. Shanghai machine workshops began to make Tianjin-style iron gear looms in the early 1920s.

25. Sasaki Chōjiro and his wife were teachers in the Industrial Institute and later set up a company dealing in looms. See *Dai Nippon Bōseki Rengōkai Geppō* (April 25, 1915).

26. Nankai University History Department, ed., *Tianjinshi Santiaoshi zaoqi gongye ziliao diaocha* (mimeograph, 1958), 7–14; Gail Hershatter, *The Workers of Tianjin, 1900–1949* (Stanford: Stanford University Press, 1987).

27. Li Feng, "Wushinianlai shangye ziben zai Hebei xiangcun mianzhi shougongye zhong zhi fazhan jincheng," *Zhongguo Nongcun* 1, no. 3 (December 1934), 61–76.

28. Tianjinshi Dang'an Guan, Tianjin Shehuikexueyuan Lishi Yanjiusuo, and Tianjinshi Gongshangye Lianhehui, eds., *Tianjin Shanghui dang'an huibian*, vol. 1, 970–72.

29. *Tsūshō Ihō* (August 5, 1911).

30. Tianjinshi Dang'an Guan, Tianjin Shehuikexueyuan Lishi Yanjiusuo, and Tianjinshi Gongshangye Lianhehui, eds., *Tianjin Shanghui dang'an huibian*, vol. 1, 219–21.

31. *Tsūshō Ihō* (August 5, 1911).

32. Wu Zhi reported that in the late Qing, weavers could earn about 200 strings of cash a year from sale of cloth. At the same time, the income from working as a year-long hired laborer would have been about 20 strings of cash plus room and board (Wu Zhi, "Gaoyang zhi tubu gongye," in *Zhongguo jingji yanjiu*, ed. Fang Xianting [Changsha: Shangwu Yinshuguan, 1938], 2). During the late Qing and the early republic, many types of money circulated in China. "Strings of cash" refers to copper coins. Traditionally these were minted in one unit forms, and one thousand of the coins, strung together, were equal to one ounce of silver. Beginning in 1900 the government began to mint new-style copper cash, with face values of one, five, and ten copper units; these could be exchanged for minted silver coins, which were minted in one dollar units.

33. Philip C. Huang, *The Peasant Economy and Social Change in North China* (Stanford: Stanford University Press, 1985).

34. Shuili Shuidian Kexue Yanjiuyuan Shuilishi Yanjiushi, ed., *Qingdai Haihe Luanhe honglao dang'an shiliao* (Beijing: Zhonghua Shuju, 1981).

35. Ramon Myers, *The Chinese Peasant Economy* (Cambridge: Harvard University Press, 1970). Statistical data compiled by Lossing Buck (quoted in Meyers, 137) shows a 20 to 30 percent decline in the size of farms between 1870 and 1930. In calculating the amount of land in *mu* necessary to support a household by farming alone, I have used as a minimum level of five *mu* per person. (A Chinese *mu* is equivalent to roughly one sixth of an acre.) Jin Zheng has used the same 5 *mu* measurement in a study of Ding County, which is near Gaoyang in central Hebei province. See his "Shixi ersanshi niandai Ding Xian nongmin gengdi zhi buzu," *Hebei Daxue Xuebao* 2 (1991), 79–85.

36. Wu Zhi, *Xiangcun zhibu gongye de yige yanjiu* (Shanghai: Shangwu Yinshuguan, 1936), 108–9.

37. *Jizhong Daobao* (February 19, 1947).

38. *Gaoyang xianzhi* (1932), 147.

39. *Gaoyang xianzhi*, 146; Zhongyang Nongyebu Jihuaci, *Liangnian laide Zhongguo nongcun jingji diaocha huibian* (Shanghai: Zhonghua Shuju, 1952), 96–100.

40. Liang Xihui, "Gongshang fazhan yu renkou zhi guanxi," *Da Gong Bao* (March 31, 1937).

41. Both shirtings and sheetings were plain-weave cloths. Sheeting was made with relatively coarse yarn, twenty count or less, while shirting was made with yarn of twenty to twenty-six. (The count of yarn indicates whether the yarn is fine or coarse; the higher the count, the finer the yarn.) T-cloth was also a plain weave, made in imitation of Indian cotton cloth, and usually produced with sixteen- to twenty-four–count yarn. Drills were a variation on plain weave. In a plain weave, the warp and weft crossed one on one, while in a drill the warp went over one and then under two weft yarns. This produced a diagonal effect. What is called "native cloth" was woven with low-count, homespun yarns on wooden looms that produced a narrow-width cloth. Descriptions, drawings, and fabric samples can be found in Watanabe Kisaku, *Menshipu no kiso chishiki,* Osaka: Kyokutō Shoji Kabushiki Kaisha, 1950.

42. All figures are from the *Tsūhō Ihō* report of August 5, 1911. See also Kikuchi Takaharu, "Keizai kyōkō to Shingai Kakumei e no keisha," in *Chūgoku kindai no shakai kōzō*, ed. Kyōiku Daigaku Bungakubu Tōyōshi Kenkyūkai (Tokyo: Kyōiku Shoseki, 1960), 73–110.

43. This project was initiated during a period Douglas Reynolds has called "the golden decade" in Sino-Japanese relations. See his essay, "A Golden Decade Forgotten: Japan-China Relations, 1898–1907," *Transactions of the Asiatic Society of Japan*, fourth series, vol. 2, 1987; and Douglas Reynolds, *China, 1898–1912: The Xinzheng Revolution and Japan* (Cambridge: Harvard University Press, 1993).

44. In 1890, total spindle capacity in Japan was 277,000; by 1899 the total was close to 1,200,000 and by 1910 over 2,000,000. W. A. Graham Clark, *Cotton Goods in Japan and Their Competition on the Manchurian Market* (Washington: Government Printing Office, 1914), 40.

45. Takamura Naosuke, *Kindai Nihon mengyō to Chūgoku* (Tokyo: Tokyo Daigaku Shuppankai, 1982), 50–51; also, Christopher Howe, *The Origins of Japanese Trade Supremacy: Development and Technology in Asia from 1540 to the Pacific War* (London: Hurst, 1996).

46. The Mitsui Bunkō in Tokyo has credit ratings of Tianjin merchants for 1900.

47. In the early years the standard credit terms required payment three to four months after delivery of goods.

48. Kikuchi Takaharu, "Keizai kyōkō to Shingai Kakumei e no keisha." See also William Rowe, *Hankow* (Stanford: Stanford University Press, 1984).

49. *Tsūshō Ihō* (August 5, 1911).

50. *Zhili Shiye Zazhi* 4, no. 2 (February 1, 1915), 15.

51. Wu Zhi, *Xiangcun zhibu gongye de yige yanjiu*, 40.

52. *Zhili Shiye Zazhi* 4, no. 2 (February 1, 1915), 15.

53. The coarseness or fineness of yarn is measured by count—the higher the count, the finer the yarn. Watanabe Kisaku, *Menshipu no kiso chishiki* (Tokyo: Konan Shoin, 1950), 36.

54. Wu Zhi, *Xiangcun zhibu gongye de yige yanjiu*, 221–22.

55. For example, the price of a *bao* of sixteen-count yarn on the Tianjin market fell from 268.40 yuan in 1919, to 240.92 in 1920, to 210.28 in 1921, and to 204.19 in 1922. Wu Zhi, "Cong yiban gongchan zhidu de yanjin guancha Gaoyang zhibu gongye," *Zhengzhi Jingji Xuebao* (October 1934), 68.

56. Hokushi Keizai Chōsasho, ed., *I-Ken dofugyō chōsa hōkokusho* (Mantetsu Chōsabu, 1942).

57. Fang Xianting and Bi Xianghui, "You Baodi shouzhi gongye guancha gongye zhidu zhi yanbian," *Zhengzhi Jingji Xuebao* 4, no. 2 (January 1936), 261–329. Abe Takeshi has analysed similar differences in strategy in Japan. See his *Nihon ni okeru sanchi men'orimonogyō no tenkai* (Tokyo: Tokyo Daigaku Shuppankai, 1989).

58. "Tianjin Li Li Gongchang diaocha," in *Pingjian gongye diaocha*, ed. Beijing Shili Gaoji Zhiye Xuexiao (1937), 113–16.

59. Peng Ziyi, ed. *Zhongguo jindai shougongye shi ziliao*, vol. 3, 1045–47; Wu Zhi, *Xiangcun zhibu gongye de yige yanjiu*, 259–89.

60. *Gongshang Banyuekan* 5, no. 3 (February 1, 1933), 2–5, and 5, no. 12 (June 15, 1933), 126. In 1929, 13.51 percent of Chinese textiles had been marketed in the northeast; the loss of these markets was a major problem for the Chinese textile industry.

Fang Xianting, "Zhongguo mianfang zhiye zhi weiji," *Jingji Zhoukan* 8, *Da Gong Bao* (April 19, 1933). There is a discussion of the same changes on "native cloth" from the Nantong-Shanghai area in Xu Xinwu, *Jiangnan tubu shi* (Shanghai: Shanghai Shehui Kexue Chubanshe, 1992), 295–97.

61. Wu Zhi, "Gaoyang zhi tubu gongye," 688.

62. "Miansha mianbu pifashang de lishi qingkuang," Manuscript held by the Tianjin Zhengxie, June 1980.

63. In 1929 approximately 80,000 *bao* of cotton yarn had been imported but in 1932 it was down to 25,000. Rayon weaving also suffered heavy losses as the total import of rayon fiber fell from 20,000 crates in 1929 to 4,000 in 1932.

64. Ramon Myers, "The World Depression and the Chinese Economy 1930–36," in *The Economies of Africa and Asia in the Inter-War Depression,* ed. Ian Brown (London: Routledge, 1989), 253–78; Wang Yuru, "Economic Development in China between the Two World Wars (1920–1936)," in *The Chinese Economy in the Early Twentieth Century: Recent Chinese Studies,* ed. Timothy Wright (New York: St Martin's Press, 1992), 58–77.

65. Wu Zhi, *Xiangcun zhibu gongye de yige yanjiu*, 11–12. Gaoyangxian Renmin Zhengfu Caizheng Jingji Bangongshi, "Gaoyang xian 1954 nian shougongye diaocha gongzuo zongjie," mimeograph, 1954.

66. Kubo Tōru, "Nanking seifu no kanzei seisaku to sono rekishiteki igi," *Tochi seido shigaku,* 86 (January 1980), 38–55.

67. Nakamura Takafusa, "Nihon no Kahoku keizai kosaku," in *Kindai Nihon to Higashi Ajia,* ed. Kindai Nihon Kenkyūkai (Tokyo: Yamakawa Shupan, 1980), 173.

68. Given the nature of the trade, it is impossible to find official statistics on the level of Gaoyang consumption of rayon yarn for this period. One Japanese report on the East Hebei special trade estimated that 300,000 pounds of rayon fiber were entering Gaoyang every month. *Mantetsu Chōsa Geppō* 3, no. 2 (1936), 194.

69. Gaoyangxian Renmin Zhengfu Caizheng Jingji Bangongshi "Gaoyang Xian 1954 nian shougongye diaocha gongzuo zongjie," mimeograph, 1954.

70. Interview, May 28, 1960.

2

Gaoyang Entrepreneurs

Yuan Shikai's technology transfer initiatives created the possibility for rural industrial growth. Entrepreneurial vision led a group of small-town merchants to take advantage of the opportunity to create one of China's most famous rural industrial districts. The first generation of entrepreneurs founded firms that brought together new technology with a new form of organization, creating the industrial district. That first generation of firms also provided the models for later generations of investors and managers who founded new firms. Although those who followed were not innovators in the Schumpeterian tradition of entrepreneurship, they were key organizers of resources who risked capital in starting new firms.[1] The success of the pioneers gave rise to an entrepreneurial culture that nurtured thousands of small firms over the three phases of growth. Gaoyang people talk of the local entrepreneurial spirit as one in which everyone dreams of becoming the boss of his own firm, and the records show that thousands of individuals have risked capital to found independent workshops and firms.

It has become fashionable in recent years to treat Chinese entrepreneurial cultures as the product of Confucian cultural influences that are assumed to be common to all of Chinese society. Turning Max Weber's famous analysis on its head, some scholars have argued that Chinese culture is not a block to the development of capitalism, but rather a great facilitator of its development. Exactly what elements of Confucian culture have this effect is not always clear, but the appearance of a new version of dynamic capitalism in Chinese cultural areas has seemed to be sufficient proof of the links.

I do not believe that entrepreneurial traditions are common to whole cultural regions, and the links to macro-level religious and cultural traditions seem at best indirect. Some communities in North China have firmly embedded entrepreneurial traditions while other communities, separated by only short distances and presumably sharing in what could be called a "common culture," show no signs at all of the same entrepreneurial spirit.[2] It is my contention that the Gaoyang entrepreneurial spirit—and that of other local systems with similar entrepreneurial traditions—are not the product of some combination of vaguely defined cultural attributes, but rather the result of the historical development of local commercial and industrial systems. Pioneering individuals, who do fit Schumpeter's understanding of entrepreneurs, explored the possibilities for technological and business innovations within the economic and market contexts of their day; later entrepreneurs, inspired by the success of the pioneers, built on the models they provided.

This chapter examines the activities of the pioneering generation of Gaoyang entrepreneurs, using the histories of several firms to illustrate the patterns of development and the interaction of technological, marketing, and organizational innovation during the first phase of growth. As industry developed, the commercial and manufacturing system that supported its growth developed into an increasingly complicated system. On the eve of the war with Japan, Gaoyang County was home to 533 factories and commercial firms, including over 350 that were classified as medium scale or above. This number included more than 100 yarn and cloth wholesaling firms, 17 mechanized dyeing and finishing factories, more than 50 fabric printing and dyeing factories, and hundreds of smaller trading firms and workshops.[3]

Gaoyang's most successful firms can be divided into two large groups. The first group includes firms that began as yarn and cloth wholesalers and the second group includes firms that grew out of workshop-based weaving or dyeing operations. Together these two groups of firms represented the major forms of capital investment in the weaving industry. Contemporary observers would have regarded the major yarn and cloth wholesale firms as the most important players in Gaoyang industry. Not only did they boast the largest capital investment, their firms also had much longer histories. The leaders of the major trade organization, the Gaoyang Chamber of Commerce, usually were selected from the owners and managers of the largest of the wholesale firms. Firms in the second group, which got their start as weaving or dyeing operations, were relative newcomers. The oldest of these firms had been founded in 1917, and fewer of their proprietors or managers were leaders of the chamber of commerce. However, the latter group closely resembles the small-scale industrial firms that led the second phase of growth and those that have played a key role since the beginning of the economic reforms in the 1980s.

By 1937 the largest firms in the two categories had come to share certain similarities: most of the large wholesaling firms had added on mechanized dyeing and finishing factories, and many of the dyeing and weaving firms had their own sales networks. In spite of the surface similarities, the patterns of development and sources of success of the two categories of firms were different. In the discussion that follows, we will first look at the yarn and cloth wholesaling firms and then at the firms that grew out of workshop production.

YARN AND CLOTH WHOLESALING FIRMS

The yarn and cloth wholesalers engaged in several aspects of the textile trade. They imported yarn and sold it to independent weavers or put it out to contracted weavers. They also collected finished fabric from weavers, arranged for dyeing and finishing, and managed shipping and sales to markets in the interior. In addition to its main office in Gaoyang, a wholesale firm would have a number of branch offices (*waizhuang*). The Tianjin branch purchased raw materials and controlled finance through the treaty port's native banks. Other branches located in major markets in the interior sold finished goods to regional wholesale merchants and collected information and orders for future sales.

Entrance into and exit from the yarn and cloth wholesale business were quite common. Wu Zhi identified sixty yarn and cloth wholesale firms operating in Gaoyang in 1933. That number represented conditions during the prewar period's biggest depression. The industrial census of 1935, at the beginning of the prewar period's last great boom, reported a total of more than one hundred yarn and cloth wholesale firms. Earlier surveys, beginning with a Japanese survey in 1911, list names of prominent wholesaling firms. A comparison of the various lists shows that only a few of the largest firms were active from the beginning. Other firms that played a prominent role early on disappeared and new firms rose to take their place. Since there was little fixed capital investment in most yarn and cloth wholesalers, movement in and out of the wholesaling business was relatively easy.

The most important capital in the wholesaling trade was human capital, held in the forms of accumulated knowledge of the production process, products and markets, and the personal networks of connections that proprietors and managers controlled. This kind of human capital could be, and often was, rearranged. Some business partnerships survived for several decades, others broke up after only a few years. Since the proprietors and hired managerial personnel who possessed the requisite knowledge and connections were in high demand, there was a great deal of mobility from firm to firm. The largest firms, which had gotten into the trade early and were still in business in the 1930s, developed a dominating role in the local market and collective organizations. On the fringes of those large firms were scores of smaller firms that strove to emulate the success of the leaders.

Capital Generation among the Wholesaling Firms

Economic historians have generally assumed that China's early industrialization efforts failed and that structural problems in the traditional economy were among the chief causes of the failure. China lacked the necessary institutions to support modern industry; most importantly, it lacked a modern banking system. Albert Feuerwerker, expressed this commonly held view in a convincing way:

> The overall prospects for modern manufacturing industry in late-Ch'ing [Qing] China were limited. The institutions—a modern banking system in particular— for channelling non-treaty port savings into industry did not exist. . . . But it was not an absolute shortage of capital which constrained China's early industrial development. As of 1912, manufacturing firms registered with the Ministry of Agriculture and Commerce reported a total capitalization of Ch.$54,804,000. In the same year, traditional banks (ch'ien chuang, 'money shops') and pawnshops registered with the ministry were capitalized at a total of Ch.$164,854,000. The resources of the economy, limited as they were, remained sterilized in traditional vessels which only fundamental political change could shatter.[4]

Feuerwerker was not alone in this view. Victor Lippit and Carl Riskin made independent estimates of the potential surplus in the Chinese economy before 1937. Each concluded that one of the major causal factors in China's slow development was the inability of the government or of private sector institutions to mobilize the surplus that did exist in the Chinese economy.[5] Studies of many of the early private and joint public-private enterprises point to lack of capital as a prime factor in business failures. Many of the early modern enterprises experienced difficulty in recruiting shareholders and some were forced to start production while under-subscribed.[6] Modern banking institutions were just beginning to form, and most of the banks were unwilling to provide funds for industrial ventures.[7] It is therefore with some surprise that we discover a poor, relatively backward area like Gaoyang supplying adequate funds to give birth to such an extensive rural industrial district. Let us then turn to the question of capital accumulation and examine the sources of the funds invested in the rural textile industry.

Capital in the wholesale trade came from two major sources: locally generated capital and capital from outside the region that entered the Gaoyang market after industry started to develop. Wholesale firms drew their capital from two major sources: commercial capital, which was derived from the investment of profits made in other forms of trade, and managerial capital, which refers to capital accumulated by employees of textile firms that they later invested in independent enterprises.

Commercial capital, that is capital created out of the profits of commercial enterprises, was the most important source of investment capital in the weaving industry. Almost all of the early entrepreneurs drew their funds from commercial sources, primarily from trade in foreign goods and capital accumulated in the grain trade. Before the rise of the weaving industry Gaoyang was a small town with a population of less than 5,000 residents. In those days the largest merchants in town were the proprietors of eight firms that dealt in grain and handled money exchange. As the weaving industry began to prosper almost all the operators of the grain dealerships/native banks switched their capital into yarn and cloth wholesaling. The process of accumulation and reinvestment can best be illustrated by turning to the histories of individual firms. Let us begin with the largest and most successful of the Gaoyang firms, Fu Feng.

Yang Musen and the Fu Feng Enterprises

Yang Musen (1864–1939) founded the Fu Feng firm in Gaoyang in 1902 with an investment of 3000 strings of cash.[8] Yang Musen was the eldest son of Yang Shicong who came from the village of Nanbianwu, just across the

Figure 2.1. Yang Musen. Yang Musen, proprietor of Gaoyang's largest firm, Fu Feng. This photo appeared in the *Quanguo Shanghui Lianhehui Huibao*. In the photo, Yang is wearing several of the medals he was awarded by Yuan Shikai's government for distinguished charitable service.

county border in Anxin County. Yang Shicong had gotten his start at the age of nineteen as a village peddler of cloth, thread, and other foreign goods. The elder Yang purchased goods on credit from Qing Feng Yi, a Baoding foreign goods specialty firm. He transported his merchandise on carrying poles making tours of nearby towns and villages. As his small business prospered, he purchased a cart and was able to transport a wider variety of goods to his village customers. Yang and his partner Wang Laoxi developed a reputation for honesty in all of their business dealings, and when Qing Feng Yi needed a new business manager the two were hired for the position. The Yang family's first contact with Gaoyang came in 1881. In that year Qing Feng Yi decided to open a Gaoyang branch. Yang Shicong put up 5,000 strings of cash and had his eldest son Yang Musen appointed as manager of the branch store.

The Gaoyang branch of Qing Feng Yi prospered and the younger Yang gradually put away savings out of his salary and commissions. In 1902 he used 3,000 strings of cash to start a firm of his own, Fu Feng, which was also involved in the foreign goods trade. The main items in the foreign goods trade in North China in this period were imported fabrics and yarns, and so it was an easy step from trade in imported goods to trade in piece goods of domestic manufacture.

By 1906–1907 the yarn and cloth trade had become the main core of Fu Feng business, but the firm continued to deal in other miscellaneous goods until 1912.[9] Yang Musen was both owner and manager of the firm in the early years. Former employees of Fu Feng remember Yang as a man of few words, but one who had deep knowledge of the textile trade and who was an excellent judge of men. A self-made man who had grown rich through his business activities, he also came to play a leading role in the Gaoyang Chamber of Commerce.

By the early teens Fu Feng had claimed the position as the leading yarn and cloth wholesaler in Gaoyang, a position it maintained to the beginning of the war with Japan in 1937. An estimate by a former accountant for the firm suggests that the total commercial holdings of the Yang family stood at roughly 2,000,000 yuan on the eve of the war.[10]

The Managerial Capitalists of Hui Chang

The years during the First World War have often been described as the golden age of Chinese capitalism, a period when Chinese native capital, temporarily freed from competition with European interests, flourished. Gaoyang also saw a boom during those years, and Fu Feng, as the leading wholesale firm, made very high profits. At the end-of-the-year accounting in 1918, seven senior employees of Fu Feng demanded a higher percentage of the profits as their fair share of the firm's improved business. The seven argued that the high profits Fu Feng had earned were directly the result of their efforts. When Yang refused to accept their demand, the seven resigned from Fu Feng and joined together in a business partnership to establish Hui Chang.

Hui Chang thus got its start in 1919 as a partnership of the seven, each of whom put up 3,000 yuan. Chang Yihua, a Gaoyang native who had entered Fu Feng as an apprentice, served as manager, and another former Fu Feng employee became vice-manager. (This vice-manager did not invest capital in the firm, but was given a reduced share in the profits for his working contribution [*rengu*] to the partnership.) Hui Chang got its start in the midst of a boom in Gaoyang manufacture and very quickly prospered. By 1923, just four years after the founding of the firm, the original capital of 21,000 yuan had increased to more than 200,000 yuan. Hui Chang purchased thirty *mu* of land fronting on East Main Street and built an impressive stone and brick head office. By the eve of the war in 1937, Hui Chang was the second largest firm in Gaoyang with capital holdings of close to 1,000,000 yuan.

Hui Chang is representative of a very common form of capital accumulation in Gaoyang: managerial capital. Many wholesale firms used a system of managerial bonuses (*hongli*) as part of their wage system. These bonuses were paid out of a fixed percentage of the profits that was divided among senior employees of a firm. In most firms using such incentive payments, bonuses were paid to the higher-ranking employees as well as the chief manager, with the size of the bonus depending on an employee's rank in the firm. During the boom periods the most prosperous firms were making annual profits of 100 percent or more on invested capital. Even the 1 to 5 percent share of such profits that was standard payment for a high-ranking employee might provide the employee with sufficient capital after a few years to allow an individual to set up his own small wholesale business.

Managerial capital was a chief source of capital particularly among the smaller yarn and cloth wholesalers. Since the managers who had accumulated funds through bonuses also had the necessary skills, knowledge, and contacts, it was quite common for an individual or a group of individuals who had formerly been employees of a larger firm to break off and set up an independent firm using their own savings as capital.

Non-Native Investors

Chinese merchants were often sojourners, taking up residence for long periods of time in cities and towns far from their native place. In many markets sojourners monopolized the major lines of trade, far outnumbering native merchants. For example, Tianjin trade had long been dominated by natives of Huizhou who played a leading role in the salt trade. After Tianjin was opened to foreign trade, new merchant cliques from Canton and Ningbo had become major players in banking and commerce. On the regional level, there were smaller merchant cliques that played important roles in regional commerce. The first boom in Gaoyang industrial growth in the late Qing drew the notice of such outside investors, and by the second decade of the twentieth century capital from nearby regions began to flow into Gaoyang.

Among the sixty yarn and cloth wholesalers in Wu Zhi's survey, there were two major cliques of non-native merchants. One clique included merchants from the Nangong-Jizhou area of southern Hebei. Those in the other clique came from Shulu county in central-southern Hebei. When sojourner merchants established firms in Gaoyang, they usually sent managers and senior employees from their home base. In the firms owned by non-native capitalists, 10 percent or less of the employees were Gaoyang natives, with the majority of employees natives of the same place as the investor.

The native places of most of the outside investors had well-developed commercial traditions. Both Jizhou-Nangong and Shulu were relatively poor subsistence agricultural regions and their local gazetteers note that the lack of local investment opportunities had led many natives to invest in trade. In the case of Jizhou, natives had immigrated to Beijing in the mid-Qing and set up businesses in such trades as hardware, money exchange, used books, cloth, and carpets. After Tianjin was opened as a treaty port, Jizhou entrepreneurs moved to Tianjin where they established a number of native banks; by the early 1930s they were regarded as a regional banking clique (*bang*) alongside the more famous Guangdong, Ningbo, and Shanxi cliques.[11]

Organization of Wholesale Firms

Wholesale firms came in many sizes: the largest firms, like Fu Feng and Hui Chang, had more than two hundred employees, while the smallest firms might include only the proprietor or manager and several assistants. The wholesale firms were about evenly split between firms like Fu Feng that were owned by a single individual or family and those like Hui Chang that were owned by a business partnership.[12] In both types of firms, ownership and management were usually separated. This was true even in the case of Fu Feng, whose founder, Yang Musen, had exercised a crucial entrepreneurial role in the early years. When the firm was reorganized after the 1918 exit of the seven senior employees, Yang turned day-to-day management of the firm over to a hired manager. Wu Zhi had found when he surveyed the sixty firms in 1933 that only seven of the sixty firms were managed by their owners; the remaining fifty-three all used hired managers.

Gaoyang wholesale firms share many similarities with what Philip Scranton has identified as "proprietary capitalism" in medium- and small-scale Philadelphia textile firms. The Philadelphia firms, like those in Gaoyang, were engaged in production of specialty goods for a diversified market. The strategies of closely linking production and marketing and of using technologies adapted to flexible strategies of production were also similar. But in the Philadelphia case, ownership and management of the firm were, at least in the first generation, almost always in the hands of the proprietor who founded the firm and directed its early growth.[13]

To understand why Gaoyang wholesaling firms usually separated ownership and management we need to consider several factors. Many of the investors who entered the trade in later years lacked the trade-specific knowledge necessary to manage a wholesaling firm, and it was thus natural that such individuals and partnerships would hire professionals who did have that knowledge. In the cases of the pioneering entrepreneurial generation, however, the explanation seems to be related to patterns of firm expansion. As firms prospered they often invested in branches and related firms, and owner-proprietors usually stepped back from day-to-day management of individual units of their group of firms and turned over operational activities to hired managers.

Professional managers were almost always chosen from a pool of individuals who had gained knowledge of the textile business through apprenticeship and employment in textile firms.[14] An apprenticeship, which lasted for three years, provided the first stage of formal training. During an apprenticeship, the trainee was expected to master knowledge specific to the trade as well as such general skills as accounting and protocols for dealing with customers. Young candidates for apprenticeship needed an introduction from someone who knew the manager in order to enter the firm. Before beginning a commercial apprenticeship it was assumed that a young man would already have acquired basic literacy and numeracy, and would be able to write with an acceptable hand. Most Gaoyang wholesaling firms employed at least one or two apprentices, with the larger firms employing up to ten or more. On completion of the apprenticeship a young employee might continue to work for the firm that had trained him or might move on to employment in another firm.[15]

Within the firm the manager usually had complete control over day-to-day operations of the business. Most managers worked on a contract with the investor. In hiring a professional manager the investor had two basic options with regard to salary. About half of the Gaoyang firms employed managers on a fixed salary that might be supplemented by a bonus if the firm did unusually well. In most cases, the salary paid to the manager was in the range of 100 to 200 yuan a year, with the highest paid manager making 350 yuan a year.[16] In addition to the cash wage, the firm supplied housing and food and an expense account to cover the costs of business entertaining. The other option was a system in which the manager was given a share (*rengu*) in the company based on his contribution of knowledge and skill. Rather than receiving a fixed salary, the manager received a percentage of the profits—5 to

8 percent if his contribution was exclusively labor, and up to 10 percent if he had invested capital as well as labor in the firm. The final amount of his salary would not be determined until the end of the accounting year. Prior to that time the manager and senior employees who were slated to receive bonuses could borrow interest-free funds from the firm against anticipated income.

Most managers worked on three-year, renegotiable contracts. At least in theory, though increasingly less so in practice, the firm was created for only three years, with the investor entrusting a certain amount of capital to the manager to run the business during the contracted period. In the early years, when most firms operated out of rented headquarters and held most of their investment in circulating capital, it was easier to disband a partnership at the end of three years. In later years, when the more prosperous firms had built impressive buildings to house their offices and had invested funds in pioneering marketing systems and developing brand-names, the dissolution of partnerships among the major firms became less common.

Most managers were obligated to provide a general accounting every year, and a comprehensive accounting at the end of the three-year contract. In most cases the investor would meet with the manager once a year, most commonly on the sixth day of the Lunar New Year when reports on the company's general situation were presented and account books reviewed. At that time, the investor could make recommendations on the direction of the firm and on personnel matters. Since the accounting measures involved were very complicated and included the keeping of a large number of account books that recorded different aspects of the business transactions, the manager and the accountants were the only ones who had a comprehensive understanding of exactly how well the firm was doing.[17] It was not uncommon for a manager to manipulate the annual financial report in order to achieve his desired goals. For example, if a manager wanted to retain more of the profits in order to expand the business and thought the investor might not agree with his decision, he might underreport profits.

Within the firm, the manager supervised a staff of anywhere from ten to one hundred employees in the Gaoyang main headquarters. The larger firms were subdivided into sections, with submanagers taking responsibility for specific areas of the business. These subdivisions included an accounting office, which had a team of accountants to keep track of the amounts of yarn put out to contract weavers, record the volume of finished goods, record orders from sales branches, and keep records of prices, wages, and goods in stock. A second subdivision included the senior staff responsible for purchase and collection of finished goods from weavers. Since some of the weavers worked on contract to the firm and some were working on their own account, methods of collection varied. In either case, employees in this division were among the most skilled in the firm. Goods were collected from weavers on only two or three days out of every ten-day market cycle.[18] On purchasing days hundreds of weavers came with their finished goods, and employees had to make quick decisions as to the quality of the work and appropriate payment. A third subdivision of the firm was responsible for organizing the warehouses and keeping track of stock, both yarn and finished goods. These employees were also responsible for sending goods out to dyeing and finishing factories, and preparing orders for shipment to sales branches throughout the country.

Since the traditional Chinese firm was not only a work place but also a substitute home for its employees, who usually lived on the premises, every firm also had several cooks who prepared meals for the whole staff. Most other housekeeping chores for the firm were handled by the apprentices; apprentices worked for the longest hours, with the lowest-ranking jobs going to the newest recruits.

Each firm also employed large numbers of people in its sales branches outside of Gaoyang. For example, Fu Feng had more than one hundred employees working in its sales branches. Fu Feng's largest branches were in Xi'an (fourteen employees), and Zhangjiakou, Taiyuan, and Yuci (Shanxi) (ten each). Smaller sales branches often had only two or three employees. The most important of the branches, particularly the one located in Tianjin, which was responsible for acquisition of raw materials and for the handling of financial accounts that were cleared through Tianjin native banks, was headed by a vice-manager. Vice-managers, like managers, were usually employed on three-year contracts and often received a share of the profits. When all of the employees were added together, both those working in Gaoyang and those working in the sales branches, the total staff of a large wholesale firm might number over two hundred.

Patterns of Growth in Wholesale Firms

Most of the early firms were organized as general trading companies, and only shifted to concentrate exclusively on the yarn and cloth trade in the early teens, when Gaoyang's position as an industrial district seemed assured. The earliest firms engaged in relatively simply exchange activities: buying yarn from Tianjin wholesalers, transporting and selling the yarn to weavers, buying cloth, and selling the cloth to wholesale merchants who came to trade in the Gaoyang market. While there was an internal logic that linked the various activities, most of the steps in the process were independent exchanges mediated through the market. It was not long before the pioneering firms began to elaborate their organizations, taking on new tasks and more complex forms of organization. The growth patterns in the wholesale firms followed two trajectories: the first included strategies that led to vertical integration and the second involved spinning off independent firms that often duplicated operations of the parent firm. Let us first examine the move toward vertical integration of the wholesale firms.

There were three chief steps in the process of vertical integration. Historically the first step involved the move into distribution, specifically the setting up of sales agencies to directly market goods to regional wholesale merchants. Establishing sales agencies required more capital, an increased staff, and a more elaborate system of internal communication within the firm. It added to the firm's efficiency, not only by more aggressive marketing, but also by allowing for a greatly intensified flow of information on regional market demand that could be incorporated into production plans.

The second step involved development of a putting-out system that brought formerly independent weavers under the wholesaler's control. Contract weavers worked to the firm's orders, using raw materials the firm provided but working on their own machines in their own family workshops. The use of contract weaving gave the firm reliable sources of supply during boom periods when short supply drove up purchasing prices. It also allowed the firm to adjust production to the demand for specific types and designs of fabrics. The system of contract weaving developed in the mid-teens in response to the move out of the market for cheap, plain-weave fabrics and into more upscale and specialty markets. For the wholesale firm, contract weaving required a much larger investment in capital, since the firm had to supply raw materials to weavers rather than leaving it to weaving households to purchase on their own account.

How much did it cost for a wholesale merchant to maintain a contract weaver? In the early 1930s, Li Feng estimated that a wholesaler made an investment of approximately 560 yuan per contracted loom. This investment included the costs of the raw materials currently on the loom, those in the preparatory process, and the accumulated but not yet sold finished cloth. His estimates assumed that a firm had to count on a cycle of at least three months from the import of yarn to the return through final sale.[19] The majority of Gaoyang wholesalers were small firms with less than one hundred weaving households under contract, but the largest operators, like Fu Feng, had one thousand looms under contract.[20]

Putting-out in Gaoyang was related to the move from plain-weave fabrics to yarn-dyed goods and patterned fabrics. It represented the first stage of backward integration from trade into production. However, when a wholesale firm contracted with weavers, its investment was still in what can be broadly termed circulating capital—raw materials, goods in process, and finished goods. It was not long after the introduction of contract weaving that some of the larger wholesale firms took a more radical step and invested in processing factories for dyeing and calendering. This represented the first major investment in fixed capital assets that could not be used for other purposes. The earliest investments were in factories using handicraft techniques, but by the mid-1920s the dyeing and finishing factories began to in-troduce mechanized equipment.

With this final step we have the fully mature wholesale firm with its con-trol over the supply of raw materials, weaving, dyeing, finishing, and final distribution. To get a clearer picture of how this integrated system devel-oped, let us look at the later development of Fu Feng.

Fu Feng: Patterns of Growth

Fu Feng was founded in 1902 and established its first sales branches in 1912, opening an office in Tianjin to manage yarn purchases and sales of-fices in Beijing, Nangong, and Xingji. The sales branches did so well that the firm opened additional sales branches in 1915 in Zhangjiakou, Kulun (con-temporary Ulan Batour, Mongolia), Baotou, Taigu, and Luoyang. As we can see, while the first set of sales offices were all located in the North China re-gional market, by the mid-teens Fu Feng was moving into frontier markets in the northwest and Mongolia. At this point the staff of Fu Feng had grown to include approximately fifty employees and capital had increased to about 200,000 yuan. The firm was doing so well that Yang Musen decided to invest some of his profits in the construction of a new and enlarged headquarters in Gaoyang.

In 1917 Fu Feng set up a branch firm, the Fu Feng Dyeing and Calender-ing Factory, as a wholly owned subsidiary. It employed twenty workers and was supervised by a manager and vice-manager. In the beginning the factory processed goods produced by the parent firm's contract weavers. In the 1920s both calendering and dyeing were mechanized. In the early 1930s the factory grew steadily; capacity increased from 50,000 bolts of fabric a year in 1932 to 80,000 in 1934. On the eve of the war, annual capacity stood at 100,000 bolts of fabric and the factory employed a workforce of two hundred men.[21]

At the end of 1918, the dispute between Yang Musen and his senior em-ployees led to their exit from the firm and the reorganization of Fu Feng. Yang took for himself the title of general manager (*zongjingli*), appointed his third brother, Yang Baosen, as his assistant, and turned day-to-day manage-ment of the Fu Feng operations over to a hired manager Ding Yunge. In later years Ding played a major role in the management of Fu Feng and in the Gaoyang Chamber of Commerce.

The Fu Feng firm and its directly owned factory continued to grow throughout the 1920s and into the 1930s. In the late 1920s new sales branches were opened in Shanghai, Hankou, Xi'an, Lanzhou, Pingliang, and Chengdu. The move to the south coincided with the popularity of rayon and patterned-fabric weaving. Thus, on the eve of the war, Fu Feng had grown to employ two hundred men in its Gaoyang headquarters and its nationwide distribution system, and an additional two hundred workers in its dyeing and processing factory.

The story of Fu Feng, however, does not end with this completion of the process of vertical integration into both production and distribution. Beginning in 1925 Yang Musen began to invest some of his profits in a series of related firms, or *lianhao*.[22] The first of the related firms was the Da Heng yarn and cloth wholesale firm established in 1925. An independent manager was appointed to oversee the activities of Da Heng. Da Heng then replicated the vertical integration process that had characterized the growth of Fu Feng, adding on sales agencies for distribution, taking on contract weavers, and in 1935 setting up its own processing plant, the Da Heng Factory, a mechanized dyeing and calendering factory with sixty employees. By the mid-1930s Da Heng was one of the major players in Gaoyang, boasting a staff of twenty in its headquarters and an additional eighty working in its sales agencies throughout the country.

In 1931 Yang Musen supplied 10,000 yuan capital to his eldest son, Yang Mingchen, to set up the Yuan Feng yarn and cloth wholesale firm. In 1933 the eldest son of Yang Baosen (Yang Musen's younger brother and chief assistant), founded the Jiu Feng yarn and cloth wholesale firm in the family's native village of Nanbianwu. Jiu Feng, in addition to dealing in yarn and cloth, also owned a weaving factory with thirty jacquard looms. Jiu Feng set up branch sales agencies in Baoding, Gaoyang, Shijiazhuang, and Hankou.

Finally in 1933, Yang Musen's two younger sons were provided with 240,000 yuan to set up the Da Feng wholesale firm. The two brothers hired a professional manager, Wu Kuanlun, to run the business for them. Wu tried unsuccessfully to gain control over the cotton-yarn market in Gaoyang. That failure, and another unsuccessful effort to set up a native bank in Gaoyang, led to the termination of Wu's contract and his replacement by a new manager, a former branch manager from Fu Feng. With a new and more stable management in place, Da Feng developed rapidly as a yarn and cloth wholesaler. By 1936 its staff had grown to sixty-four, and profits that year had risen to 200,000 yuan.

In addition to these investments in the textile trade, Yang Musen also provided investment funds to members of his family to set up the Fu Rong Import-Export Company in Tianjin, which operated between 1928 and 1930. This firm, owned by Yang's second son, was set up with an investment of 300,000 yuan. The firm, with its headquarters in the French Concession, had a reputation as a modern enterprise, hiring only college graduates for its office staff and setting up offices in New York, Osaka, and Singapore. Its main lines of business were the import of cotton and rayon yarn and foreign piece goods, and the export of native products. Fu Rong was the exclusive agent for certain products of the Soviet Union, and as a result of that trade got involved in a dispute with the powerful warlord Zhang Xueliang in 1929. Since

Fu Rong was not very profitable, the firm was closed in 1930 and the capital invested to establish the Fu Feng native bank in Tianjin in 1931.

The final member of the Fu Feng group of related firms was the Yuan Feng Flour Mill, established in 1934 as a subsidiary of the Yuan Feng wholesale firm. The mill's proprietor was Yang Jianming, eldest grandson of Yang Musen, who had 30,000 in capital provided by his father, the owner of the Yuan Feng wholesale firm.

This brief recounting of the development of related firms in the Yang family enterprise group will lead most readers to assume that the pattern of development must be closely related to the logic of family division within the Yang family. As we will see, the explanation is not so simple. Before discussing the family and business logics involved, we should note that this pattern of horizontal expansion—which involved the setting up of firms that were in competition with each other—was not peculiar to the Yang family group. Hui Chang, which had been founded as a business partnership of former senior employees of Fu Feng, followed a similar pattern of development. Hui Chang set up two related wholesale firms: Hui Kang and He Da Tong. Hui Kang was established in 1932 with 40,000 yuan in capital from Hui Chang. By the eve of the war it had grown to be a medium-sized wholesale firm with thirty employees and six sales agencies. He Da Tong was of similar size and operation. While the related firms set up by Yang Musen and his family were often in direct competition with the mother firm, in the case of Hui Chang the related firms set up their sales offices in cities where Hui Chang was not operating, and there seems to have been more coordination between the firms than in the case of the Yang family enterprises.

The pattern that we can see with Fu Feng and Hui Chang was repeated by all of Gaoyang's larger commercial firms. Once a firm reached a certain size, rather than continuing to expand the operations of the main firm, investors tended to pull out some of their capital and invest it in related firms. No single logic seems to explain the practice. To take the Yang family enterprise group as an illustration, some of the related firms were set up to give younger members of the family an opportunity to run their own independent businesses. However, the timing of the establishment of new firms does not necessarily match stages in the process of family division. (See figure 2.2.)

Let us look first at the cases that do seem to be related to the process of family division. Yang Shicong, Yang Musen's father, died in 1929. Yang Musen, as eldest son, took responsibility for managing the family's inheritance. After setting aside funds for charitable activities, including construction of a hospital and of wells to provide water in times of drought, he divided some of the inheritance among the younger generation. It was shortly after this that his eldest son (Yang Mingchen) set up Yuan Feng, his third and fourth sons set up Da Feng, and his nephew set up Jiu Feng. Many of these firms were founded in 1933, at a time when Gaoyang was still in a major

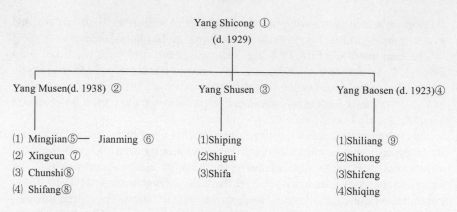

①Yang Shicong: Manager of Qing Feng Yi, Baoding wholesaler

②Yang Musen: Founder of Fu Feng

③Yang Shusen: Managed family land in Nanbianwu, Anxin County

④Yang Baosen: Chief manager of Fu Feng 1918 to death in 1923

⑤Yang Mingjian: Founder of Yuan Feng wholesaler in 1933

⑥Yang Jianming: Founder of Yuan Feng flour mill

⑦Yang Xingcun: Founder of Fu Rong Trading Company (Tianjin) 1928

⑧Yang Chunshi, Yang Shifang: Co-founders of Da Feng Wholesaler 1933

⑨Yang Shiliang: Founder of Jiu Feng wholesaler 1933

Figure 2.2.   Yang Family Genealogy and Firms

slump, not the time that would normally have been chosen for the founding of new firms. The fact that several of these firms were established in the same year by different branches of the family suggests that in these cases inheritance after the death of Yang Shicong was the impetus for the division of capital.

Not all of the Yang family enterprise spin-off firms, however, can be explained by the logic of family division. For example, the first major related firm, Da Heng, was set up in 1925 when there had been no change in the family composition, and investment in the new firm was made in Yang Musen's own name. Gaoyang business was unusually good in 1924, and Fu Feng is reported to have made profits of 300,000 yuan. In 1924–1925, not only Fu Feng but a number of wholesale firms set up related firms. For the Yang family, 1928 was another boom year and investment funds were taken out of the profits to found the Fu Rong Import-Export Company; the founding of this new firm was also separate from the process of family division.

Normally when we see an investor dividing his funds among a number of investment opportunities we assume that the strategy is designed to reduce risks. The risk avoidance logic does not fully explain the pattern of investment in Gaoyang. Although it was not unknown for a wholesale firm to go into bankruptcy when others were doing well, most of the business failures occurred during periods of general secular decline. If investors wanted to diversify to hedge against losses, they would not have put their funds into firms that were engaged in almost identical operations.

Two other factors seem to have greater explanatory value. First are calculations as to the optimal size of a firm. Chinese-style commercial management required that the chief manager keep a very careful eye on all stages of the business operation. Branch managers were expected to report to the head office everyday by mail or telegraph and to send weekly summary reports of their activities and of market conditions in their region. Employees in the home office were strictly supervised and managers kept a sharp eye on the books. The management style in most commercial firms depended more on the personality and skills of the general manager, less on elaboration of formal written rules. While some large Chinese firms had written regulations, few Gaoyang firms had such written codes. In a management style that depended on the daily supervision of senior managers and direct communication of instructions, the optimal size of the firm was considerably smaller than it would be for a more bureaucratized style of organization. Few wholesale firms were ready to cross the line dividing traditional commercial practice from more modern business management. Hui Chang came closer than other firms to making the transition: at Hui Chang apprentices were recruited through a competitive examination rather than through personal introductions, managers ran formal study sessions for apprentices during the evening hours, and employees all wore a standard uniform rather than the traditional long gown (*changpao*) of the merchant class. However, most of the managers and many of the investors in wholesale firms had themselves been trained through apprenticeships in commercial firms. While the firms they ran were innovative in many other ways, in terms of internal management most still held to time-honored methods of operation, and these traditional practices placed limits on the size of the firm.

The second explanation that has been given for this practice is related to financial customs used by Chinese native banks. Negishi Tadashi, one of prewar Japan's leading experts on Chinese business, argued that related firms could more easily acquire credit. When a Chinese native bank extended credit to a firm, the size of the credit line was only indirectly related to the capital of the firm applying for the loan. Loans were given on the basis of trust, and trust involved an estimation of the total reserves of a capitalist and the firms in which he held investments. If firm A of a group of related firms asked for credit, the bank would estimate how much credit to extend only after taking into account all of the holdings of related firms in the group. If a second firm in the group went to the same native bank for a loan, the process would be repeated. Thus an investor who wished to have access to as much

credit as possible was able to acquire more credit if his investments were in
a series of firms, rather than if all of the investment was in a single firm.[23]
Since credit was a crucial key to the success of wholesale firms, this consideration also may have played a role in entrepreneurial decisions to split off
part of the capital to set up competing firms in the same line of business.

Financing the Wholesale Firm

Gaoyang wholesalers had relatively limited capital holdings, but were able
to operate a system that did an annual business turnover in peak periods of
more than 4,000,000 bolts of cloth with a value of over 35,000,000 yuan. The
key to success was the ability to acquire and effectively use credit from a
number of different sources.[24] Table 2.1 shows the average assets and liabilities of the sixty wholesale firms in Wu Zhi's study.[25]

The data point to two ways in which firms obtained credit: the first way
supplied credit for the purchase of raw materials, and the second way, which
involved the use of funds deposited with the wholesale firm for a fixed period of time, provided credit for general operations. Credit for the purchase
of raw materials was almost always extended by organizations outside of the
Gaoyang community, while deposits placed with a firm came primarily from
sources within the Gaoyang community. Let us look first at the outside
sources of credit, and then at those within the community.

**Table 2.1.   Average Assets and Liabilities of Sixty Yarn
and Cloth Wholesalers, March 1933**

Category	Value (yuan)	Percentage
Assets		
Cash and savings	13,578	26.9
Sales on credit	7,298	14.4
Goods in stock	19,783	39.1
Raw materials in stock	7,309	14.5
Land and buildings	1,843	3.6
Equipment	720	.4
Total	50,531	99.9
Liabilities		
Credit purchases	20,042	39.7
Loans for fixed terms	17,284	34.2
Invested capital	8,918	17.6
Unpaid interest and savings	4,287	8.5
Total	50,531	100

Source: Wu Zhi, *Xiangcun zhibu gongye de yige yanjiu* (Shanghai: Shangwu Yinshuguan, 1936), 53.

Gaoyang was one of the major markets for Tianjin yarn wholesalers, who were the first intermediaries in a chain that linked foreign import firms with their rural yarn consumers. Foreign importing firms sold yarn to Tianjin yarn wholesalers on credit, and the wholesalers sold the yarn to wholesale merchants from Gaoyang and other industrial districts.[26] The sources and terms of credit varied from period to period, fluctuating with secular shifts in the Chinese economy. Before 1921, Gaoyang merchants relied on credit offered by Tianjin middlemen. After 1921, the development of Chinese domestic spinning mills increased the supply of cotton yarn and drove down the price. As the profits for Tianjin middlemen fell and they became less willing to do business on credit, sources of credit for purchasing raw materials became more diversified. Some firms turned to short-term loans from native banks while others continued to cultivate relations with wholesale merchants willing to extend credit. A former Tianjin branch manager for Da Heng, Han Xianghui, recalled that his firm purchased yarn through wholesale dealers rather than directly from factory producers because the wholesalers were more likely to extend credit. Han recalled that when he wanted to purchase yarn he would agree with the wholesaler on volume and price, and the wholesale agent would ship the goods to Gaoyang. Formal purchase contracts were rarely necessary since relationships of trust had been established between the large Gaoyang firms and their Tianjin trading partners. Both parties used traditional Chinese bookkeeping methods and each party simply recorded the transaction in his running account books, one as a debit and the other as a credit. Normally the account would be settled about a month after the purchase of the yarn.[27]

Although accounts were normally settled in about a month, the customary system for settling accounts divided the financial year into three periods, with settlement required only at the end of each trimester. Book credit provided by Tianjin wholesalers bore no interest. Only if a Tianjin dealer found himself short of cash and had to call for payment of outstanding debts would the Gaoyang branch manager be forced to take out a loan from a native bank to pay off his debts.

Just as we can plot the progress of the yarn as it passed out of the treaty ports and into the production process, we can also follow the progress of credit. So far we have concentrated on the second stage of that process, that is, the transfer of credit from the Tianjin wholesaler to his Gaoyang trading partner. In most cases the Tianjin wholesaler had himself purchased goods on credit, possibly from the manufacturers or their agents, including domestic spinning mills and foreign importing firms, or from native banks.

If we turn our attention away from the treaty port origins of the credit and try to follow its journey as it activates the production process, we can see that the credit was parceled out by the Gaoyang wholesalers in ways that allowed them to expand production. Yarn bought on credit in Tianjin was sold or put out directly to weavers, or sold, usually on credit, to smaller wholesale firms and weaving and dyeing workshops. As the credit moved further away from its origins, the time limit for repayment shortened. Gaoyang merchants usually had at least several months to repay their debts to Tianjin wholesalers, but would usually allow less time to their debtors. Credit reached the furthest from its starting point when it entered the marketing network and was offered by marketing agents to their customers, cloth wholesalers and retailers in regional markets. At that point, terms for payment rarely extended beyond thirty days.

At each stage of the production and exchange process credit was transferred from one partner to the next, transfers being accomplished through accounting methods that usually recorded credits and debits in the account books of the trading partners. While it was assumed that debts would be paid off on a regular schedule, due dates on credit were flexible. Within the Gaoyang market, credit was transferred back and forth between larger and smaller wholesalers and dyeing and weaving shops and the intervention of cash or of formal financial institutions such as native banks was quite rare. Promissory notes (*batiao*) were traded in lieu of currency. When a firm was faced with a sudden demand for cash, the firm had to check its own account books and then send an employee, known as a runner (*paojie*), to collect on the promissory notes it held. Since any firm could pay its debts with promissory notes that it held on third parties, it was frequently necessary to trace the whole system of credits and debits back to its origins. Such clearing of debts might require several days of running the streets and would ultimately involve a majority of the firms. There was no regular system for clearing of promissory notes, but normally there would be only three or four major adjustments a year in response to cash demands of one of the major firms.

The system of local promissory notes was linked to a complex system of trading in which the original debits accrued in the purchase of raw materials were repaid with profits from the sale of finished goods. The sales branches transferred their returns via local native banks to native banks in Tianjin and the Tianjin branch manager used the remittances to repay debts. Promissory notes could be used as credit guarantees for yarn purchases in Tianjin, although the largest wholesale firms rarely were asked for such guarantees. When promissory notes were used as credit guarantees, they were traded in Tianjin at a 3 percent discount.[28]

What happened when a wholesale firm found that it had overextended and could not meet the demand for payment of debts? While it was difficult for a wholesaler to refuse payment to a Tianjin creditor, within the local market there was little a creditor could do. When the manager of a firm lacked funds to meet obligations, he would first ask the investor in his firm to supply additional capital. If the investor refused, the manager would follow local custom and invite his local creditors to a meal, explain the reasons for the firm's difficulties, and announce that the firm was going out of business. As a result of this practice, bankruptcy was known as "eating a hot pot" (*chi huoguo*) after the meal served to the creditors. Although Gaoyang firms were not legally incorporated, the investors were only held responsible to the extent of their invested capital. It was not uncommon for the manager and employees of a bankrupt firm to seek financial backing from other investors and establish a new firm.[29]

Depositing Funds with Commercial Firms

The second major means of obtaining credit was acceptance of funds deposited with the firm. Friends of the owners or managers could deposit funds with a firm. They would agree on the rate of interest (which was usually higher than the interest rates of other financial institutions)[30] and deposit the funds for a fixed period of time, also agreed on at the time of the original negotiations. The manager could use the deposited funds in the same way that invested capital was used. However, unlike those who had invested in the firm, depositors of funds had no claim on the profits.[31]

The most common sources of such deposits were wealthy people in the community and high-ranking employees of the firm. Higher-ranking employees of the firm usually received bonuses at the end of every financial year. Depositing the funds with the firm at a fixed interest rate was an easy way to assure a steady return to income.

One may ask why such funds were not simply added to the paid-up capital. To answer the question, we must begin with an explanation of how partnerships divided profits. Traditional Chinese business partnerships balanced the interests of the investors and higher-ranking employees of the firm with a carefully calculated arrangement of claims on profits. Any change in that calculation would destroy the balance among partners and between the investors and employees. The practice of depositing funds at fixed interest rates allowed the firm access to increased capital while maintaining the balance between those who had claims on the profits of the firm. In many Gaoyang firms, fixed-term deposits were an important source of capital, one that tended to increase in boom periods.[32]

The successful manager of a wholesale firm was adept at manipulating these various sources of credit to sustain the growth of his firm. The careful nurturing of a network of personal connections smoothed access to credit and allowed the manager to expand his firm's business. Establishing a reputation as an honest and reliable businessman was essential to that process.

The business practices described above, which were commonly used by businessmen in the first part of the twentieth century, were in no way unique to Gaoyang firms. Yarn and cloth wholesalers were simply adapting conventional Chinese business practices to new uses. In the process of that adaptation, the Gaoyang entrepreneurs created the fully integrated whole-sale firm, with control over production through contract weaving, investment in industrial production in the form of mechanized dyeing and weaving, and involvement in distribution as seen in the system of sales branches. In creating the wholesale firm, managers had drawn on the large repertoire of traditional Chinese commercial practices, changing and adapting more generalized practices to meet the specific needs of the yarn and cloth whole-sale trade. The other major group of Gaoyang investors, the proprietors of workshops and small-scale factories, used other strategies. Let us turn to consider organizational forms in small-scale manufacturing enterprises.

FROM WORKSHOP TO SMALL-SCALE FACTORY PRODUCTION

The second set of major players in the industrial district was firms that developed out of small workshops. By the late 1930s there were dozens of small factories that had developed out of home workshops. For most of these firms, mastery of new technologies was a crucial factor in their success. In this section I will look at three such firms as illustrating the dynamics of this kind of development. Although each of the three firms' experiences was slightly different, they shared a common commitment to the application of modern technology to production.

While the yarn and cloth wholesale firms drew most of their higher-ranking personnel from men who had been trained through commercial apprenticeships and continued to use relatively traditional organizational forms, the firms that got their start as workshops were most commonly founded by graduates of technical training schools. These firms highly valued technical knowledge. As the firms matured, many of them became involved in contract weaving and some established distribution networks. At a quick glance they resemble the wholesaling firms. However, the ethos of such firms was different from that of the large wholesale firm with its base in traditional commercial culture. The commitment of the workshop-based firms to technological innovation also led to very different fates during the war years. While the fortunes of most of the major wholesaling firms declined in the early war years, many of the workshop-based firms survived into the 1950s.

The Su Family and Tong He

Su Zhaoquan (1860–1924), father of the brothers who started Tong He, was a rural intellectual who had earned the lowest-level examination degree under the Qing dynasty.[33] The family had long been struggling at the bottom rungs of entry into the local elite. A great-grandfather had been a petty official and a grandfather had been a small-town merchant. Su Zhaoquan earned the *xiucai* degree, the first step on the examination ladder, and then spent the rest of his life as a respected local schoolteacher. Throughout his life he continued to cultivate his family's small farm. Passionately concerned about the fate of his country, Su Zhaoquan believed that industrialization was the salvation of China and encouraged his sons to pursue education for practical occupations.

Su Bingheng, the eldest son, born in 1890, received his early education in Gaoyang and Baoding and then went as an apprentice-student to the Industrial Institute established by Yuan Shikai. At the Industrial Institute he entered the weaving division where he mastered the art of pattern weaving, learning to use both the traditional Chinese draw loom and the iron gear loom with a jacquard device. After graduation Bingheng worked for a weaving workshop in Tianjin for a short period of time. In 1914 he purchased an iron gear loom with a jacquard device and returned to Gaoyang where he wove at home. He was the first person in the Gaoyang area to use a jacquard loom for patterned weaving, and it was not long before neighbors came to study with him. Bingheng invested the profits from weaving in the purchase of more looms with jacquard devices. By 1918, the family workshop had seven looms and Bingheng hired ten employees to work with him.

Success in pattern weaving depended on weaving skills, but also on the attractiveness of the designs woven into the fabrics. The second son of the Su family, Bingjie (born in 1897), entered the weaving and dyeing division of the Tianjin Higher Industrial School, graduating with a degree in textile design in 1918.[34] Bingjie returned home to work with his older brother in the family workshop. By 1919 their workshop was producing more than one thousand bolts of patterned fabric a year. At that point, the brothers decided to expand their home workshop into a factory. Since both Bingjie and Bingheng were trained in technical matters, they called back their third brother to join them as manager of the firm.

Bingzhang (born in 1901) was not yet twenty at the time he took over as manager of the Tong He factory. While his two elder brothers had gotten technical educations, Bingzhang had received training in business management. After graduating from the commercial school, sponsored by the Gaoyang Chamber of Commerce, he began an apprenticeship with the Yu Feng Tai wholesaling firm. In the years of formal study and apprenticeship he had acquired knowledge of the commercial side of the textile industry. Bingzhang, like his two older brothers, had been influenced by his father's dream of national salvation through industrialization. The new factory founded by the Su brothers was named Tong He,[35] a name selected by Su Zhaoquan to signify owners and workers cooperating together.

The Tong He factory was started with an investment of 8,000 yuan; the factory had forty jacquard looms and simple dyeing and finishing machinery and employed a staff of sixty workers. The Su brothers were fortunate in the timing of their new venture. The factory had just been completed when rayon yarn appeared in the market and they began to specialize in patterned rayon fabrics. The new synthetic fabrics were very popular and Tong He prospered. Profits were reinvested in the firm.[36] By 1934 the firm had outgrown its original factory buildings, and land was purchased to set up a second factory complex alongside the original one. New jacquard looms were purchased, bringing the total to eighty. At this point the brothers decided to experiment with powered looms. They bought an electric power generator and purchased seven of the latest-model Toyota power looms. They also bought a truck for shipment of goods. By 1937, the firm had fixed assets worth 250,000 yuan and circulating capital of 100,000 yuan, and employed four hundred people in the factory and business offices.

While contemporaries regarded Tong He as the most progressive of the Gaoyang firms, it was also a mixed operation. As the company developed its processing plant for fabric dyeing and finishing, the capacity of that division exceeded the output of the weaving sheds. By the early 1930s Tong He had started to take on contract weavers, most of whom lived in the village of Beishawo where the factory was located. Tong He also established a distribution system, setting up sales branches in Xuchang, Nanyang, Hankou, Xuzhou, Wei County, Xi'an, and Luoyang. Since the factory was located in a village a few kilometers from town, Tong He also had a business office in town with a telephone link to the village factory.

As manager of the firm, Su Bingzhang established a reputation as a very enlightened entrepreneur who was interested in new ideas and who was willing to back those ideas with money. Tong He was interested in acquiring employees with advanced technical skills and offered high salaries to entice such individuals to work for the firm. Su Bingzhang kept in close contact with the chamber of commerce–sponsored technical school, always on the lookout for promising teachers and graduates. He hired one instructor from the school on a part-time basis and got him to write a guide for workers. On another occasion he persuaded Tian Jiepei, a Gaoyang native and graduate of the Tianjin Higher Technical School who had gone on to graduate from a Japanese technical school, to sign on as an adviser to Tong He.

Tong He's organization was more modern than that of many of its rivals and the firm strove to stay at the front lines of technological innovation. The Su brothers were among the first in Gaoyang to experiment with power looms, and in 1934, when a new type of chemical dyes came on the market, they were among the first to invite German technicians to act as advisers while they mastered their use. There were also innovations on the managerial side. In 1934 Su Bingzhang was invited by Li Shizeng to tour the Yangzi region and visit a number of industrial projects sponsored by Li and his associates. Following that trip, Su Bingzhang and Li Futian, a teacher at the technical school who had accompanied him, wrote a small pamphlet describing the trip and laying out their proposals for reforms in Gaoyang industry.[37]

Some of the lessons of that trip were applied to Tong He's own internal management practices. After returning to Gaoyang, Su Bingzhang switched from a system of fixed wages to an incentive-wage package based on piece wages and bonuses. He also began to deduct 5 percent from the wages of each employee to put into a year-end bonus fund. Other changes were designed to improve the working atmosphere. A cafeteria was set up to provide better meals and a gardener was hired to raise fresh vegetables. Working hours at Tong He were already shorter than at other Gaoyang factories. When Tong He was first established, workers were expected to work twelve to thirteen hours a day, but by the mid-1930s most workers were on the job for nine hours a day and free time in the evenings was often given over to company-organized recreational activities, including sports teams. While the welfare package for workers seems small by contemporary standards, in Gaoyang in the 1930s, Tong He workers had a better deal than those at any other firm in the area.

Tong He had gotten its start as the first Gaoyang factory to produce patterned fabrics and was well placed to take advantage of the boom in the market for patterned rayon fabrics in the 1920s and 1930s. However, the firm's first-mover advantage in patterned weaving only lasted for a short time. Su Bingheng had been generous in sharing knowledge of jacquard weaving with others in the community and it was not long before the number of jacquard loom weavers increased dramatically. Tong He maintained its lead in the industry by introducing new fabric patterns designed by Bingjie and by constantly remaining alert to new technologies in weaving, dyeing, and finishing of fabrics.

Li Enbo and the En Ji Dyeing and Fabric Printing Firm

The En Ji Dyeing and Fabric Printing Firm was founded by Li Enbo who, like Su Bingjie, studied at the Tianjin Higher Industrial School, graduating from the dyeing department in 1918. Li came from a poor rural family and was only able to go to school after an uncle recognized his talent and offered to help. After finishing elementary school he entered the Tianjin Higher Industrial School. After graduation he worked in Tianjin for several years and then returned to Gaoyang in 1923. His uncle put up 3,000 strings of cash, and with this capital backing Li started a small dyeing workshop, Tian Zhen Sheng. Li's factory got a major boost in the early 1920s since his was the only one in Gaoyang that could dye rayon fabrics. He earned 20,000 yuan during the first year, and reinvested all of the profit. By 1927, Li's total capital holdings had reached 34,000 yuan and he decided to further expand production. He bought mechanized equipment for dyeing and calendering fabrics, added on more dyeing vats, and increased his workforce from ten to forty. Results were seen almost immediately; by the end of 1928 his capital had increased to 100,000 yuan. Ever eager to enlarge his operations, in 1930 Li bought one hundred *mu* of land on the eastern edge of town and set up a new factory with the latest mechanized equipment. In honor of the new venture, he renamed the firm En Ji. By the eve of the war, En Ji was one of the four largest dyeing and calendering factories in Gaoyang.

In the first years En Ji had worked on contract to wholesale firms, dyeing and calendering fabrics to order. However, in 1934 En Ji set up a network of contract weavers, reaching a maximum of 150 looms under contract. Li Enbo also experimented with a sales network, opening two sales agencies in 1935, one in Xi'an and the other in Beijing. The Xi'an branch was not very successful and closed within the year, but the Beijing outlet proved very profitable and continued in operation to the beginning of the war.

The key to En Ji's success was the application of new technology and the exploitation of first-mover advantage. Li Enbo had a deep knowledge of chemical dyeing technology. He regularly undertook research on new processes and was willing to take risks in using new technologies. He was able to parlay his skills into a temporary monopoly over business in dyeing rayon fabrics. When he first began to dye rayon fabrics, his workshop charged 2 yuan per bolt. As others began to copy his dyeing techniques, the fees fell, reaching a price of 0.70 yuan per bolt. At that point, Li Enbo sought new technology. Li visited a higher-school classmate in Shanghai, where he discovered the fashion for printed rayon fabrics. After spending several months in Shanghai studying the process, he returned to Gaoyang where En Ji became the first firm to print rayon fabrics. Again the technological jump on rivals led to windfall profits. The funds were reinvested in improved equipment for En Ji factory.

Li Enbo was willing to take risks with regard to technology, but proved to be a hard taskmaster for his workers. The workday at En Ji normally began at four in the morning, and laborers often worked until seven or eight in the evening. There were no welfare benefits for the workers of En Ji, although the success of the firm did guarantee reasonably safe jobs. While Li Enbo, coming from a very different family background from the Su brothers of Tong He, shared little of their progressive management style, En Ji, like Tong He, prided itself on using the highest quality German dyestuffs and up-to-date technology to produce high-quality goods that could compete with any of the Tianjin weaving and dyeing factories.

The Li Family and He Ji

The He Ji Dyeing Factory started out as a commercial firm, but like Tong He and En Ji, its success rested on the mastering of new technologies. The firm was established in 1919 as a partnership between two brothers, Li Shu-liang (1883–1954) and Li Zhongliang, and two of their friends, Yang Aiqing and Sun Yueqi. The Li brothers who played a major role in starting the firm began as wholesale merchants of dyestuffs. In 1913 the German representative of a major German dyestuffs wholesaling firm visited Gaoyang to promote the use of German chemical dyes. The Li brothers agreed to serve as the exclusive local agent for the German import-export firm. Li Zhongliang also set up a small dyeing workshop in the town using German dyes.[38]

In 1915 supplies of German dyes were cut off due to the deepening of the war in Europe, and the value of the stocks the Li brothers had on hand rose dramatically. Since China did not yet have a chemical dyestuffs industry of its own, all supplies came from overseas; when it became obvious that the war would drag on, buyers rushed to stockpile dyes. During the space of only a few months stocks originally worth only 3,000 to 4,000 yuan rose in value to over 200,000 yuan. These unexpected one-time profits formed the capital base for the He Ji Dyeing Factory. In 1919 the firm bought land on the southern edge of the town and set up a factory. In 1923 the He Ji partners decided to mechanize, the first Gaoyang factory to do so, and purchased dyeing and calendering equipment from Germany; German technicians came to the factory to set up the equipment. By 1937 He Ji employed two hundred workers and was one of the most prosperous dyeing factories in Gaoyang.

He Ji, like Li Enbo's En Ji and the Su family's Tong He, had started out as an enterprise centered on production—in this case dyeing and calendering—but then expanded its activities to include contract weaving. On the eve of the war He Ji had approximately three hundred looms under contract and was engaged in dyeing and finishing work on contract to other wholesale firms as well as dyeing and finishing fabric on its own account.

In 1926 one of the partners in He Ji, Li Shuliang, invested some of his profits in the He Ji Soda Company, which began to manufacture alkali products for the dyeing industry. At the time there were more than one hundred dyeing workshops in the Gaoyang area, all of which used alkali products. Before this, all of the factories were supplied by the Yung Lee Soda Company, a firm that had been established by the finance ministry of the Beijing government in 1915 and which had been given special tax benefits and a monopoly on sales within a one hundred *li* radius of its factory.[39] The He Ji Soda Company was set up with a listed capital of 10,000 yuan in 1926. The following year its capital was expanded to 33,000 yuan, and further expansion in 1934 led to a listed capital investment of 200,000 yuan. Li Shuliang was the general manager of He Ji Soda Company and his partners included Wang Caichen from Shuchang County, Hao Deqin from Renqiu, and Chang Muru, Dong Xinxiang, Deng Shengsan, and Feng Deming from Gaoyang.[40] Li's new firm set up a soda factory in Hangu, near the salt fields on the coast. It was

not long before He Ji's Red Elephant brand products began to challenge the
Yung Lee monopoly, and Yung Lee took He Ji to court, contending that they
had received exclusive rights to sell alkali products in the Tianjin area. The
case came to the attention of the national government in Nanjing. Li
Shizeng, the Nationalist party elder, came from the same lineage as the Li
brothers of He Ji and with his assistance He Ji won its legal battles. After losing the court battle, Yung Lee decided on a price war, lowering the price of
their products from 9 yuan a barrel to 5.6 yuan. Li Shuliang again sought the
assistance of Li Shizeng, who stepped in to persuade the Industrial Bank to
back the firm, giving them enough support to survive the price war and
continue in business.[41]

Although none of the partners in the He Ji firms were themselves graduates of technical schools, the firms made major efforts to hire employees with
advanced technical training. All of the division chiefs of the He Ji Dyeing Factory had graduated from technical schools. Efforts were made to invite German technicians to the factory to supervise the introduction of new dyes and
dyeing processes. Thus, although the investors in He Ji had started in the
trade in cloth and dyestuffs, the pattern of development of this firm places it
in the same category as Tong He and En Ji, firms whose growth was built on
the use of new technologies.

Often when we think about the development of China's modern industries, we assume that urban industry must have been more technologically
advanced than rural industry. Such a notion follows naturally from the theories of dualistic economic development that have shaped the study of the
economic history of late-developing countries. The history of the Gaoyang
weaving and dyeing firms poses serious challenges to such formulations.
While not all of the weaving, dyeing, calendering, and fabric printing firms
were as progressive as those discussed above, Gaoyang had the reputation
in the 1920s and 1930s as Tianjin's major competitor. By the mid-1920s Tianjin was home to a number of large spinning mills. Dyeing and weaving, however, were still dominated by small firms.[42] Pattern-weaving firms in Tianjin
complained of the advantages held by Gaoyang firms like Tong He: not only
were the costs of production lower, but the Gaoyang firms were not bur-
dened by factory taxes that were paid by all Tianjin firms, however small
they might be.[43]

Gaoyang dyeing firms not only had the advantage of lower production
costs, they also enjoyed a technological advantage. It was rare for small Tianjin firms to employ technicians with the kinds of skills that were common to
Gaoyang dyeing firms. It was that technological advantage that added to the
overall reputation of Gaoyang cloth in the 1930s. As Gaoyang production
moved increasingly into the upper ends of the market for specialty goods,
dyeing, calendering, and finishing techniques came to play a more significant role, and it was firms like Tong He, En Ji, He Ji, and their numerous

smaller rivals and imitators that made significant contributions to the industry's development.

GAOYANG FIRMS AND THE STUDY
OF CHINESE BUSINESS HISTORY

Much of the debate on traditional Chinese business practice has focused on the family firm and whether that form of organization blocked economic development.[44] In the Gaoyang case, there is little question that entrepreneurial firms played a crucial role in initiating regional economic development. Were the Gaoyang firms radically different from the traditional family firms that have often been seen as incapable of making the transition to modern capitalism? Or have existing theories on the small family firm in China misunderstood their potential for development?

Those who argue for the limitations of the family firm look to the work of Alfred Chandler on Western business history. In a series of books comparing American and European business firms and practices, Chandler argues that the family-controlled firm was, in the long run, less likely to continue to grow. For Chandler, the secret of the successful firm was found in the full exploitation of the cost advantages of the economies of scale and scope. The key to exploitation of those advantages lay in a three-pronged investment in production facilities, marketing and distribution networks, and development of professional managerial capabilities.[45] Early writing on Chinese business history in English followed Chandler's model, noting the weakness of the traditional Chinese business firm.

Two major factors have been cited as the chief deficiencies in the traditional Chinese firm. First is what is called "the successor problem." The strong-willed founders were reluctant to relinquish power to successor generations. Even when the founder was willing to transfer power to his successors, the family firm limited potential candidates for high-level managerial positions. By a third or fourth generation, company growth was blocked, and internal disputes over succession to managerial positions led to segmentation and eventually to disintegration of the company. The second major factor blocking expansion of family enterprises was said to be conservative financial policy. Family firms were reluctant to go to outside sources for financing and were not willing to sacrifice short-term profits for long-term firm expansion.

Wong Siu-lan has described a four-stage cycle that he believes characterized the development of the Chinese family firm. On the basis of extensive research on family-run firms in Hong Kong, he argues that the first and second stages of firm development were characterized by dynamic growth, with stagnation and potential disintegration setting in only after the firm matured and leadership passed to a second or third generation of the family. Linking the cycle to development of the family itself, Wong argues against the prevailing theory that links failure of family firms to the complex claims on authority and property presented by the extended Chinese family. Rather, Wong asserts, the success of a firm made development of the extended family possible by providing assets that could best be managed collectively. However, he too sees the potential for the family firm to run into difficulties in a second or third generation. As the number of younger members of the family increased, competition for positions in the firm and disputes over equitable division of profits take their toll, and those in power are gradually compelled to assume caretaker rather than innovator roles. When that happens, further expansion of the firm is blocked.

If we were to apply Wong's four-stage cycle to the Gaoyang firms, we would find that their patterns of development fit his model very nicely. For example, Wong's model assumes rapid capital accumulation and reinvestment during the second stage of growth, a pattern that is quite common in Gaoyang firms. The Yang family's Fu Feng enterprise group seems to resemble very closely the patterns one would expect in the third stage of development, that is, segmentation of the firm with different members of the larger family taking responsibility for different segments of the group of firms. However, since the coming of the war with Japan cut off the natural process of development of the Gaoyang firms, it is impossible to know how the firms that were still vigorous and expanding in 1937 would have developed.

One major problem in the application of theories of the family firm to Gaoyang enterprises is the prominent position of business partnerships in which the partners share no family connections. On the basis of his work on Hong Kong firms, Wong argues that business partnerships were inevitably unstable. He believes that in most cases one of the partners would come to hold a dominant role in the partnership and eventually convert the partnership into something resembling a family firm. Partnerships were quite common among Gaoyang firms, accounting for approximately half of the total number of wholesale firms. The best known of those business partnerships, Hui Chang, grew to be one of the biggest players in the Gaoyang market while maintaining the partnership form. While business partnerships were technically created for only three years, there is no evidence to suggest that Gaoyang partnerships were more likely to fail than family-owned firms. And, as we will see in later chapters, during the second and third phases of growth, business partnerships were the leading form of management in the Gaoyang industrial district. It is also important to recall that important managerial decisions were usually in the hands of professional personnel, not in the hands of family members or partners. As a result, the Gaoyang firms experienced fewer problems with succession than the Hong Kong family-owned firms that were the subjects of study for Wong Siu-lan and many others who have written about Chinese managerial practices.

Theories of the family firm help to explain some of the characteristics of Gaoyang firms, but not all. Business historians most commonly look at individual firms or groups of firms, less commonly at the development of regional economic systems. This is primarily because classic business history has taken the large industrial firm as its subject. While some historians of China have looked at large business firms in China in the prewar period,[46] many of the contemporary theoretical discussions of business history issues have been inspired by the successful development of Chinese capitalism in Hong Kong and Taiwan and among overseas Chinese in Southeast Asia. In both the Hong Kong and Taiwan cases, small and medium-sized firms, often family owned, have played a leading role. This phenomenon has led scholars interested in such problems to look beyond the individual firm to the larger business environment that has shaped patterns of growth.

Gary Hamilton has argued that the institutional environment has been of crucial importance to the development of Chinese-style capitalism. In an essay tracing the development of Chinese business institutions, Hamilton argues that the Chinese business environment was characterized by a complex market economy and a relatively weak state that was little concerned with developing a framework of legal institutions to govern the economy. As a result, the institutional framework that eventually emerged was created and guaranteed through self-regulating organizations among the interested parties themselves. Out of this came the merchant guilds and native place associations that came to play important roles in Chinese commerce. Hamilton refers to the business strategies that developed within this environmental context as "regional collegiality," which was to become the basis for the networks of personal relations that continue to characterize Chinese business practice to the present day.[47] The practice of regional collegiality and the use of network strategies to link the interests and obligations of numerous small and medium-sized firms created a distinct business environment.

Prewar Gaoyang firms, much like the highly competitive small firms of contemporary Taiwan, are important illustrations of the role that small, often family-based, firms can play in promoting regional economic growth. This is not to deny that many Gaoyang firms were unstable. The contract nature of business partnerships, a business culture that legitimized easy entrance and exit, and a style of doing business in which credit was relatively easily acquired created a highly competitive local market. Within that competitive market, individual firms prospered and declined. Some, like Fu Feng, Hui Chang, and Tong He, developed into fully mature firms involved in a wide range of activities. Other firms found niches specializing in one segment of the production, processing, marketing, or distribution process. Some partnerships were of long duration while others survived for only a few years.

The rise and decline of individual firms did not alter the long-term growth trajectory of the industrial district. While some firms might have chosen to exit, others entered to take their place. The number of active firms fluctuated, increasing during boom periods, contracting during recessions, but the overall industrial structure showed little change after reaching maturity in the mid-1920s.

NOTES

1. See Tony Fu-Lai Yu, *Entrepreneurship and Economic Development in Hong Kong* (London: Routledge, 1997).

2. I have worked with Japanese and Chinese colleagues on a project re-surveying villages studied in the 1940s by the research bureau of the South Manchurian Railroad. In the five villages we surveyed, successful entrepreneurship was rare. Mitani Takashi, ed., *Chūgoku noson henkaku to kazoku, sonraku, kokka—Kahoku noson chōsa no kiroku,* vol. 2 (Tokyo: Kyūko Shoin, 2000).

3. After Wu Zhi completed his study of Gaoyang, Nankai sociologist Chen Xujing and his students studied the ways in which development of rural industry had affected the local community. One of Chen's students, Liang Xihui, published the results, "Gongshang fazhan yu renkou zhi guanxi," in the *Jingji Zhoukan* of *Da Gong Bao* on March 31, 1937.

4. Albert Feuerwerker, "Economic Trends in the Late Ch'ing Empire, 1870–1911" in *The Cambridge History of China,* vol. 11, ed. John K. Fairbank and Kwang-ching Liu (Cambridge: Cambridge University Press, 1980), 39–40.

5. Victor Lippit, "The Development of Underdevelopment in China," *Modern China* 4, no. 3 (1978), 251–328; Carl Riskin, "Surplus and Stagnation in Modern China," in *China's Modern Economy in Historical Perspective,* ed. Dwight H. Perkins (Stanford: Stanford University Press, 1975), 49–84.

6. Suzuki Tomoo, *Yōmu undō no kenkyū* (Tokyo: Kyūko Shoin, 1992).

7. High returns from pawnbroking made it difficult to find funds for industry.

8. The data on histories of firms comes from oral history interviews with relatives of entrepreneurs and former employees. I have compared the interview data with contemporary written reports and archival materials when possible. Estimates of profits are only rough indications. Prof. Chen Meijian of Hebei University also shared her interview notes with me. See her study, *Gaoyang zhibuye jianshi, Hebei Wenshi Ziliao,* vol. 19, 1987.

9. This was true of the Gaoyang headquarters, but some of the branches in frontier regions continued barter trade. For details on the barter trade, see my article "International Trade and the Creation of Domestic Marketing Networks in North China, 1860–1930," in *Commercial Networks in Modern Asia,* ed. S. Sugiyama and Linda Grove (Richmond, Surrey: Curzon, 2001), 96–115.

10. Most of the details on the Yang family come from interviews. Estimates of profits during different periods can also be found in several sources, including Wu Zhi, *Xiangcun zhibu gongye de yige yanjiu* (Shanghai: Shangwu Yinshuguan, 1936). Information on the Yang family native bank can be found in Minami Mantetsu Chōsabu, *Tenshin no ginkō* (1942), 222 and 275.

11. See Minami Mantetsu Chōsabu, *Tenshin no ginkō*, for details on the Jizhou banking clique.

12. Wu Zhi found that of the sixty wholesale firms, twenty-five were partnerships. Wu Zhi, *Xiangcun zhibu gongye de yige yanjiu*, 43–43.

13. Philip Scranton, *Proprietary Capitalism: The Textile Manufacture at Philadelphia, 1800–1885* (Philadelphia: Temple University Press, 1983).

14. All of the merchants I interviewed reported that their training had been in the same line of work in which they had made their career.

15. Wu Zhi, 46. Former apprentices recall the years of apprenticeship as ones of hard work; they were expected to be the first to rise and the last to go to bed. Most managers expected their apprentices to be busy all the time, assisting the regular employees of the firm and spending any spare moments practicing the abacus and calligraphy. There were no formal classes and the young recruits were expected to learn by watching and remembering what their seniors did.

16. These figures come from Wu Zhi's 1932 survey of sixty wholesale firms, *Xiangcun zhibu gongye de yige yanjiu*.

17. Zhongguo Kexueyuan Jingji Yanjiusuo, et al., *Beijing Reifuxiang* (Beijing: Sanlian Shudian, 1959), 53, describes eighteen different account books.

18. The lunar calendar organized time into ten-day cycles or weeks, with three ten-day cycles per month. Marketing schedules moved on the ten-day cycle, with markets being specified as occurring on x and x days out of a ten-day cycle. A market that ran on a 3-7 schedule would meet on the third, seventh, thirteenth, seventeenth, twenty-third, and twenty-seventh days of the month.

19. Li Feng, "Wushinianlai shangye ziben zai Hebei xiangcun mianzhi shougongye zhong zhi fazhan jincheng," *Zhongguo Nongcun* 1, no. 3 (December 1934), 61–76.

20. Wu Zhi, *Xiangcun zhibu gongye de yige yanjiu,* 79, chart 25. Former Fu Feng employees reported that the firm had five hundred contract weavers during the 1932–1933 slump and close to one thousand by 1935.

21. *Ji-Cha Diaocha Tongji Zongkan* 1, no 6, 49–60.

22. There does not seem to be a standard translation for this term.

23. Negishi Tadashi, *Shōji ni kan suru kankō chōsa hōkokusho—"Hegu" no kenkyū* (Tokyo: Tōa Kenkyūsho, 1943). See particularly 512–16.

24. Wu Chengming, "Zhongguo minzu ziben de tedian," *Jingji Yanjiu*, no. 6 (1956), 111–37.

25. The table shows the amount of capital invested in wholesale operations at the time of founding.

26. Ding Shixun, "Tianjin miansha pifa shanghe shilue," *Nankai Xuebao*, no. 4/5 (1981): 47–54.

27. See Nishikawa Kiichi, *Menkōgyō to menshi menpu* (Shanghai: Nihondō Shobō, 1924), 366–85, on the cotton-yarn trade in Tianjin.

28. Fong, *Rural Industries in China.* Industry Series of the Nankai Institute of Economics (Tianjin: Nankai Institute of Economics, 1933), 44–45.

29. This local practice with regard to bankruptcy was not in accordance with Republican law, nor with traditional commercial practice that held investors responsible for the debts to the extent of their ability to pay.

30. The lack of formal financial institutions may have encouraged this practice. In the mid-1930s a bank branch was established in Gaoyang.

31. The depositors were using the firm as an alternative to a bank. From another perspective, the funds can be seen as a private loan to the firm.

32. Negishi, *Shōji ni kan suru kankō chōsa hōkokusho.*

33. Data on Tong He comes from my interviews and those of Prof. Chen Meijian with Su Bingqi (1909–1997), the youngest of the Su brothers. While his three older brothers ran Tong He, Su Bingqi continued his studies. He became one of China's most prominent archaeologists and was the only one of the brothers still alive in the 1980s. Su Bai, ed., *Su Bingqi Xiansheng jinianji* (Beijing: Kexue Chubanshe, 2000).

34. The Higher Technical School had been founded in 1902. It went through many name changes and continues as a university-level technical training institution to the present day. Alumni records from 1947 list more than thirty Gaoyang natives among students and graduates. *Hebei shengli gongxueyuan xiaoyoulu,* 1947.

35. The character "He" was written with an irregular Chinese character composed of the element for "person" on the top, and the *gong* of "worker" on the bottom.

36. Su Bingqi insisted that his family was very different from the Yang family. The Yangs, he said, behaved like landlords after they became rich, but his brothers continued to live a very simple life, eating coarse grains along with their workers and pouring the profits into expansion of the firm.

37. Su Bingzhang and Li Futian, *Jiangnan shiye canguan ji.* This small volume (73 pages) was privately published in 1936.

38. There is some difficulty in identifying this German firm. All informants used the Chinese name for I. B. Farben, but that conglomerate was only founded after the First World War. *Dai Nippon Bōseki Rengōkai Geppō* mentions the use of dyes from the Farvenfabriken friedr Bayer & Co. Elberbeld. *Geppō,* April 25, 1915, 7.

39. Mantetsu Tenshin Jimusho Chōaka, *Shina in okeru san, sōda oyobi chisso kōgyō*(1936), 3.

40. Feng was listed as manager of a Gaoyang wholesale firm.

41. Details on He Ji Soda Company can be found in Mantetsu Tenshin Jimusho Chōsaka, *Shina in okeru san, sōda oyobi chisso kōgyō* (1936), 54–56.

42. On Tianjin pattern weaving, see *Tianjin Gongshang Ye,* vol. 1 (Tianjin Tebieshi Shehuiju 1930), 63–83.

43. *Tianjin Gongshang Ye,* vol. 1 (Tianjin Tebieshi Shehuiju, 1930), 63.

44. Wellington K. K. Chan, "The Organization Structure of the Traditional Chinese Firm and Its Modern Reform," *Business History Review* 46 (Summer 1982), 218–35; Siu-lan Wong, "The Chinese Family Firm: A Model," *The British Journal of Sociology* 36, no. 1 (1985), 58–72; Susan Greenhalgh, "Families and Networks in Taiwan's Economic Development," in *Contending Approaches to the Political Economy of Taiwan,* ed. Edwin A. Winckler and Susan Greenhalgh (Armonk, NY: Sharpe, 1988); Gary Hamilton and Kao Cheng-Shu, "The Institutional Foundations of Chinese Business: The Family Firm in Taiwan," *Comparative Social Research* 12 (1990), 135–51; and Gary Hamilton, ed., *Business Networks and Economic Development in East and Southeast Asia* (Hong Kong: Centre of Asian Studies, University of Hong Kong, 1991).

45. Alfred C. Chandler, Jr., *Scale and Scope: The Dynamics of Industrial Capitalism* (Cambridge: Harvard University Press, 1990).

46. Sherman Cochran, *Big Business in China: Sino-Foreign Rivalry in the Cigarette Industry, 1890–1930* (Cambridge: Harvard University Press, 1980).

47. Gary Hamilton, *Business Networks and Economic Development in East and Southeast Asia*, 48–65. See also Hamilton and Nicole Woolsey Biggart, "Market, Culture and Authority: A Comparative Analysis of Management and Organization in the Far East," *American Journal of Sociology* 94 (1988): S52–S93.

3

Rural Weavers

The entrepreneurial firms in the town coordinated the production of a vast army of peasant weavers who worked in their homes or in village workshops to produce several million bolts of cotton and rayon fabric every year. The weavers' activities were supported by other small production units, including dyeing workshops that bleached and dyed the yarn used in producing striped and checked fabrics, sizing workshops that processed rayon yarn, craftsmen who punched the pattern cards for the jacquard looms, metalworking shops that produced loom parts, and carpenters who produced the wooden loom frames. The activities of these thousands of small production units were coordinated through a variety of arrangements, including putting-out, subcontracting, fee-based processing, and market-mediated exchange.

One of the features of the Gaoyang system—and one of the keys to its success—was the division of the burden of investment among many small producers. Weavers invested in looms, dyers in vats and dyes, and jacquard card operators in machines for punching cards. The capital requirements for each individual unit were quite small, making it possible for thousands of relatively poor rural actors to find niches in the system.

This chapter will consider four major questions related to rural weaving. How was production organized? How did weaving change the family economy? What were the social implications of this new style of organization? How did rural industry survive in the face of fierce competition from modern domestic and foreign industry?

ORGANIZATION OF PRODUCTION

Many of our ideas about rural weaving have been shaped by the idealized image of the independent English handloom weaver working in his cottage surrounded by the members of his family and weaving at a pace that was interrupted by Sundays and holidays of the weaver's own choosing. While we can find similar cottage weavers in Gaoyang—families in which the father wove and the rest of the work of preparation was done by the women and children of the household—there was a range of other styles of organization, which included the use of hired labor, the organization of small weaving factories, and the establishment of larger weaving factories and cooperatives. The various forms of weaving organization can be roughly divided into four major categories: individual weaving households, family-run workshops, small weaving factories, and cooperatives.

In 1933, there were thirty thousand iron gear looms in the weaving district spread across a five-county area in more than one hundred villages. In addition to the weaver, each loom required the labor of three people who did the preparatory work, meaning that there were approximately 120,000 individuals involved in production. Wu Zhi selected a sample of 384 households drawn from the whole weaving area for more intensive study.[1] According to his study, 70 to 80 percent of the surveyed weavers were employed in individual weaving households or family-run workshops. The category of "individual weaving households" includes production units in which almost all of the work was done by family labor. Weaving households usually owned only one loom; the men of the household did the weaving and the women and children did the reeling, sizing, and warping.[2] Family workshops developed when individual weaving households reinvested their profits in the purchase of additional looms and hired labor to work alongside family members.

The family compound was the work site for both weaving households and family workshops. Most rural families lived in walled compounds with a main single-floor building at the northern side of a walled courtyard. The loom or looms were placed in sheds on either side of the central courtyard. In good weather, reeling and sizing were done in the courtyard; in inclement weather, the women and children who handled these tasks would work inside on the raised sleeping platform. The iron gear loom needed little in the way of special facilities, but jacquard looms were placed in rooms with pits to accommodate the height of the jacquard frame.

Some of the family workshops had grown into small weaving factories with three to ten or more looms. Some weaving factories were located inside family compounds, others in purpose-built sheds on nearby land. Larger weaving factories were concentrated in the jacquard loom areas, close to town where the factory managers could easily contact the wholesale merchants and dyeing factories that supplied yarn on credit. The village of Xiao-wangguozhuang had a relatively large number of weaving factories that employed 70 to 80 percent of the village's weavers.[3] Villagers in Xiaowang-guozhuang had been among the first to begin weaving using the iron gear loom, and by 1916 most of the village weavers were using dobby devices to produce simple pattern weaves. When jacquard weaving began to develop in the late teens, Xiaowangguozhuang weavers were among the first to take up this specialization. Income from jacquard weaving was relatively high and it transformed the village from one mired in poverty to one where newly prosperous rural families were using their increased income to expand their workshops and build new housing. While weavers from less-prosperous villages transported finished goods to town on wheelbarrows or carrying poles, the villagers of Xiaowangguozhuang used bicycles. By the eve of the war, these villagers owned more than one hundred bicycles, all of them imported from Japan.

Individual weaving households, family-run workshops, and weaving factories were the most common forms of organization of weaving in the prewar period. However, a small number of weavers had joined cooperatives. While cooperatives played an insignificant role in terms of numbers of weavers and total output, they are of interest as forerunners of forms of organization that became important in the postwar period. In the early 1930s there were three basic styles of cooperative organization: cooperative workshops, marketing cooperatives, and cooperative workplaces. In the first, weavers pooled capital and purchased looms; yarn was obtained on credit from a dyeing workshop, and profits and losses were split among the members. In the marketing cooperative, weavers worked independently, joining together to seek better prices for their goods through joint marketing. The third form of cooperative was the cooperative workplace, established by a group of weaving households that lacked space to set up looms. In this style of cooperative weaving households shared a common workplace but worked on their own, independent accounts.

Gender Division of Labor in the Family Workshop

Work time was almost evenly divided between the preparatory stages and weaving, with tasks assigned to family members on the basis of gender and age. Men did the weaving, women and children the reeling and warping. One male member of the family served as the manager (*dangjia*) of the workshop, handling all dealings with the wholesale merchants, including arranging for supplies of yarn and selling the finished fabric.[4] If the workshop had only one loom, the manager was often the chief weaver. If the workshop had two or more looms, then usually the manager did not serve as a prime weaver.

Figure 3.1.   Women Reeling. These women, working in a village collective factory in 1980, are hand-reeling cotton yarn onto spindles in preparation for weaving. As in the 1920s and 1930s, in the 1980s reeling was one of the most important of the preparatory tasks assigned to female labor. (Photo by the author.)

This represented a major reversal of gendered patterns of work in the traditional handicraft-weaving industry. While men had always managed most of the market negotiations, before the introduction of the iron gear loom, textile production in the Gaoyang region—as in most of China—had been women's work.[5] Rural women spun when they were not busy with other work and when enough cotton yarn had been produced, they set up their looms to weave. All of the members of the rural family wore homespun cotton fabrics and surplus cloth could be sold at the local market. By the middle of the nineteenth century, women in many North China rural communities were also producing specifically for the market and the income they earned made a significant contribution to the family budget.

The shift from a women-centered production system to one managed by men, in which men held what came to be seen as the central technical role of operating the loom, was directly associated with the adoption of the iron gear loom and the use of machine-spun yarns.[6] In Gaoyang, peasant weavers purchased iron gear looms. To get a full return on the investment, it was essential to keep the loom in operation as long as there was market demand. During the busiest seasons this often meant that weavers worked from dawn until late at night. Since the women of the household had other responsibilities, including food preparation and child care, it was difficult for them to work uninterrupted for such long hours. Moreover, once weaving became the chief source of family income it seemed natural, within the logic of the patriarchal family system, for the male members of the household to control this new economic enterprise. When weavers in nearby Ding County were asked why women did not weave on the iron gear loom, they answered that women were not physically strong enough to operate the loom or that the loom was mechanically too complicated for women to operate.[7]

Although the shift from a female-dominated system of domestic production of cloth to a male-organized workshop system was common in all of the new rural textile centers in North China, this pattern stood in sharp contrast to the gender division of labor associated with the iron gear loom in Japan and in Yangzi delta region workshops in the 1920s and 1930s. In both of those regions, women were the chief operators of the iron gear loom. One of the crucial differences contributing to this contrast was the question of who invested in the looms. In both the Japanese and Jiangnan cases, workshops owned the iron gear looms and women weavers worked as wage laborers.

In Gaoyang the gender division of labor in which men served as weavers persisted even after the socialization of commerce and industry in the 1950s. In the small weaving workshops set up by rural teams and brigades, men wove while women did the reeling and warping. Even though the shift in the gender division of labor in the late Qing had come as a result of the specific circumstances in which the new technology had been adopted, the new gender-based assignment of roles came to be seen and explained as a result of "natural" differences in physical strength and mechanical aptitude among men and women. Once this new understanding of appropriate gender roles was established, it was very difficult to displace.

Hired Labor and the Weaving Workshop

Philip Huang, in his study of the North China peasant economy, divided North China farmers into two separate strata: a small elite of "managerial farmers," who hired labor to exploit larger land holdings, and a sea of small family farms that were forced to subsidize underemployed family members. The development of rural industry represented one way of dealing with the surplus of underemployed labor that typified much North Chinese farming in the early twentieth century. Rural weaving allowed the peasant family to make more intensive use of its labor power, involving all members of the family in income-generating work. During the first stage of development, most weaving families relied primarily on the labor of family members, re-organizing work so that all members of the family were directly involved in productive labor.

As we have seen, many families reinvested profits from weaving in the purchase of additional looms. In some cases there was sufficient family labor to operate two or more looms; more commonly, families with more than one loom hired labor to assist. The small family workshop that hired labor shared certain similarities with Huang's managerial farmers. Family workshops hired labor in several ways. Male weavers could be hired on a yearly contract that included room and board and a fixed annual wage. The terms were similar to those for hiring long-term agricultural labor, although the wage was higher than that offered for farm work. In other cases, male weavers were hired as temporary workers and paid a piece wage based on output. Rural workshops also hired female and child labor to help with the preparatory work of reeling. Such labor was almost always paid on a daily basis. Huang has shown that hired agricultural labor on managerial farms tended to work longer hours than members of the family, and the same seems to be true of the hired weavers. When the hired weaver was paid on a piece-rate basis, it was in his own interest as well as that of his employers to work long hours at a hard pace to increase earnings.

Hired weavers were drawn from a wide geographical area; the largest number came from nearby counties but some came from far distant provinces. Almost all hired weavers were males in their prime working years, between the ages of sixteen and thirty-six. Half of those who sought employment had previous experience in the weaving industry. Of the other half, 25 percent had previously been employed as agricultural laborers and the other 25 percent had either been involved in other rural industries or had served as apprentices in workshops.[8]

While most households employed only one hired weaver, the owner of the largest family-run workshop in Wu's survey employed twelve weavers. Hired weavers first began to appear during the 1915–1916 boom, when families started to reinvest profits in additional looms. In 1925 hired weavers were paid 60 to 80 yuan a year plus room and board for weaving plain-weave cottons. The slump of the early 1930s brought an across-the-board decline in prices; wages for hired weavers dropped to 40 to 60 yuan a year, with wages in the 40 yuan range most common.

Although the wages were high when compared with the wages offered to agricultural workers, the weaving household was still able to make a substantial profit. The workshop that hired a weaver on a year contract would usually pay the weaver the equivalent of about 40 percent of the value that his labor produced.

WEAVERS AND THE MARKET

In the following discussion of the role of the market in rural weaving, three different concepts of market will be used. On one level, "the market" refers to the temporal rhythm of periodic marketing that played a major role in establishing work schedules. "The market" also describes a physical site, the streets in the town where the merchants had their headquarters for selling or distributing yarn and purchasing or gathering cloth. On the third level, we will use the notion of "the market" to conceptualize the quality of the relationship between the weavers and the production nexus, to think about questions of dependence and independence and how they were seen by participants in the local economy. All three meanings of "the market" are important for understanding the Gaoyang industrial district. Rural weaving was adjusted to the rhythms of the agriculture season, but even more importantly to the rhythms of the market. The system of periodic marketing, based on a ten-day "week," marked out the temporal frame of work. Periodic markets held on the third, fourth, eighth, and ninth days of every ten-day cycle were the main arenas where the weavers met the representatives of the merchant houses who bought finished goods and sold yarn and other raw materials. On market days the narrow streets of town were crowded with weavers carrying bundles of cloth for sale. The market for white goods was held on the fourth and ninth days, with the markets for stripes, checks, and rayon fabrics on the third and eighth days. This produced a five-day cycle that most weaving workshops took as their standard operating period: family managers planned their production so that cloth would be ready for delivery at each of the appropriate market days.

What weavers did when they visited the physical markets in town on one of those periodic market days depended on choices they had made about whether to weave independently or on contract. Independent weavers purchased supplies of yarn and sold finished goods. They were free to choose which merchant house to patronize and whether or not to accept the offered price for finished goods. Contract weavers, on the other hand, had received yarn from one of the merchant houses and were under obligation to turn over the finished goods to that firm. In return they received payment (a "wage" for the work) and yarn for the next period of weaving.

Independent weavers usually earned more per bolt of cloth than contract weavers and as a result contract weaving has often been seen as a more exploitative form of production. Yet while later critics discuss contract weaving as an exploitative form, Gaoyang weaving households and family workshops do not seem to have regarded it in that way. While a weaving household that was working on contract was obligated to return to the contracting merchant all of the cloth woven with yarn that had been advanced, once the work was finished it was possible to switch back to independent weaving. In the same fashion, weaving households that had been independent might choose for some period of time to work on contract for one of the wholesale firms.

The chief advantage of independent weaving, known as *zhi maihuo* (weaving for sale), was the higher profit; the chief disadvantage was the necessity for a larger supply of circulating capital since the weaver had to have sufficient yarn for at least two to three "looms" of cloth, including the goods that were currently in process and yarn that was in the preparatory stages of sizing and reeling.[9] Since market prices for cloth and wages fluctuated from market to market, the independent weaving workshop earned most if it had sufficient capital to delay sale until prices were favorable. Figure 3.2, based on "wages" recorded in the spring of 1923, is an illustration of the fluctuation of wage rates over a three-month period.[10]

For the contract weaver, part of the cost of circulating capital was borne by the wholesale merchant who provided yarn and guaranteed the market for the finished goods. The contract-weaving household or workshop provided the loom, paid its own maintenance expenses, and provided meals for hired employees, as well as paying miscellaneous expenses like sizing and oil for maintenance of the loom. In general, weavers who lived in villages closer to town were in a better position to work independently since they had better access to market information. Weavers in outlying areas were more likely to work on contract, and wages paid to contract weavers de-

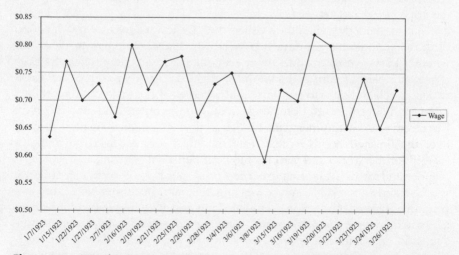

Figure 3.2. Weaving Wages, 1923. (*Source:* Li Feng, "Wushinianlai shangye ziben zai Hebei xiangcun mianzhi shougongye zhong zhi fazhan jincheng," *Zhongguo Nongcun* 1, no. 3 [December 1934]: 69.)

clined the further one moved away from town. In the outlying regions where weavers dealt through middlemen who were working as agents for the Gaoyang merchants, piece-wage rates were as much as 35 to 40 percent lower than those paid to weavers in villages close to town.

Calculations of costs of production were quite similar, regardless of which method of operation the weaving household was using, and many weaving households moved back and forth between contract and independent weaving. Tessie Liu, writing about a similar type of rural weaving in western France, cautions that our modern notions of the differences in these two statuses apply very poorly to the fluid nature of such relations in rural manufacturing.[11] The weaver who, when he and his family were working independently, may seem to be a "petty capitalist," could become a "wage laborer" when he shifted to work on a contract basis. In Gaoyang there were periodic shifts in the balance between contract and independent weaving: contract weavers increased when market conditions were bad, decreased when market demand was high. During the early 1930s depression, more than half of the weavers were working on contract, but when business picked up after 1934, many switched back to independent weaving.[12]

Within the Gaoyang community these differences were rarely regarded as fundamental, and weavers did not see themselves as belonging to hierarchically arranged groups according to their degree of independence. Weaving households that were short of capital or feared fluctuating market prices sought to work under contract, while others who had larger capital reserves or were more willing to gamble to gain the benefits of slightly increased income chose to work through the market.

When weavers made a choice between contract and independent weaving, they had to balance the advantage of slightly higher returns against the uncertainties of the market and the demand for greater investment in circulating capital. Those who wished to work on contract would usually contact a relative, neighbor, or friend who was already working on contract and seek an introduction. Most of the wholesale merchants worked through "master weavers" who acted as their informal agents, introducing prospective weavers and supervising their work.

There was no formal system of apprenticeship among weaving households and the spread of skills among the weavers was left to informal transmission of knowledge. While the term "master weaver" suggests a classification of weavers based on skill acquired through training or experience, this is deceptive. It was commonly assumed that operation of the iron gear loom was so easy to master that one could simply learn by watching others. Boys who grew up in weaving families had usually mastered weaving skills and knew how to set up and repair looms by the time they were fifteen or sixteen years old. The more difficult skills of the trade, particularly the operation of jacquard looms and the setting of the looms for the weaving of more

complicated stripes and checks and patterned weaves, were learned informally from more experienced weavers. Many of the jacquard weavers
worked in small factories under the direction of a manager, who provided
technical leadership and passed on the skills of the trade to those who
worked for him.

Knowledge about and the skills to weave new patterns and kinds of cloth
were developed out of the informal web of personal contacts within which
weaving households operated. In some cases a merchant house would ask
its most trusted weavers to test weave new patterns, often based on copies
of popular foreign designs. After a master weaver had figured out how to
weave the new design the knowledge would be shared with relatives and
friends from the same village. In other cases, weavers with an interest in design created their own new patterns. If the new design met with approval,
the weaver who had developed the design would be paid a small fee for his
design efforts.

The periodic markets, as temporal and physical spaces, were the main arenas for the transmission of news about market demand and new developments in the weaving trade. The thousands of weavers who crowded the
town on market days visited the stalls of many firms, while those who were
working on contract went to their contracting merchant to turn in completed
goods and receive raw materials. Each merchant house inspected the goods
it was purchasing or accepting from contract weavers and quoted a price,
which was based on the market demand for a given kind of cloth as well as
on the quality of the weave that the seller had produced. Older weavers recall that the market days were the best time to learn what goods were in
greatest demand and weavers would go from stall to stall to compare prices
and to get a sense of what goods were most profitable.

This combination of merchant orders and direction and informal exchange
of information in the rural community based on ties of neighborliness and
kinship provided the chief paths for the transmission of information. All of
the information available about the nature of the changing product line suggests that these informal methods of transmission worked well and allowed
weavers to keep abreast of changing fashion and market demand.

NEW SOCIAL RELATIONS: SOLIDARITY AND CONFLICT

The picture we have painted so far is of Gaoyang communities—both town
and village—that were strong in solidarity with little hint of the tumultuous
political struggles that characterized much of Chinese society in the 1920s
and 1930s. It may then come as something of a surprise to discover that in
late summer of 1932, in the midst of the most serious crisis in the history of
the Gaoyang industrial district, the Chinese Communist Party (CCP) chose

the Gaoyang-Li County area as the site for its first attempt to apply the strategy of peasant-based soviet governments to the North China Plain. The uprising, which mobilized a peasant force of between seven hundred and eight hundred, was suppressed within several weeks and dozens of party members and sympathizers were arrested. While the Gaoyang-Li County soviet is of more than passing interest for what it tells us about early CCP organization in North China, what concerns us here is the relationship between the development of the weaving industry, local social change, and the Communist-led revolutionary movement.[13]

E. P. Thompson, in the preface to his classic work *The Making of the English Working Class*, persuasively argues against the notion of class as a thing that can be weighed and measured and whose actions can be predicted. Class is a relationship embodied in real people, he argues, "And class happens when some men, as a result of common experiences (inherited or shared), feel and articulate the identity of their interests as between themselves, and as against other men whose interests are different from (and usually opposed to) theirs."[14] To what extent did the workers in Gaoyang factories, the peasant weavers in the villages, or the merchants and their employees in the town see themselves as members of classes that shared such common experiences and that could act together?

Most of the Communist Party organizers in Gaoyang and throughout the Central Hebei plains region in the late 1920s and early 1930s were young men from rural communities who had been introduced to revolutionary ideas while studying at regional normal schools. Most of the people they recruited were peasants in villages on the periphery of the weaving district; some may have been weavers, but there is no direct evidence to show that they were. No attempts seem to have been made to recruit workers in the town factories, although there is stronger evidence of dissatisfaction among that group.[15]

The CCP organizing committee responsible for the areas east of Baoding sent three party members to work as underground organizers in the region; officially they were sent as teachers to a higher elementary school in the village of Buli.[16] The three organizers joined Zhai Jiaxun, who came from the village of Jianwo and had been expelled from a provincial normal school because of his revolutionary activities. Zhai and his colleagues began to recruit followers, working through family and kinship ties.

Patterns of participation in the uprising reflect the recruitment process. Support for the uprising was very strong in one village, and almost totally missing in its neighbors. While the pattern of recruitment and participation confirms many of our earlier suggestions about the strength of communal ties in Gaoyang villages, it does little to suggest that class issues were involved. Nor do we find much in the official ten-point program announced by the short-lived soviet government that is directly related to the new system of production relations that had emerged over the previous two decades. In no place in that list of demands is there any targeting of the merchant entrepreneurs who controlled the weaving industry; rather, the program demands confiscation of food supplies and the property of landlords and gentry, the end to high interest rates, the burning of contracts, confiscation of church property, and the disarming of landlord and antirevolutionary forces.[17] The closest the program gets to anything related to the social relations that dominated the industrial district was the ninth demand, which called for higher wages and shorter working hours.

The provincial CCP leadership had selected the Gaoyang-Li area as the site for an attempted soviet for two main reasons. First, they were under pressure to take some armed action and felt that organizing had progressed more rapidly in the Gaoyang-Li area than in other possible sites. Second, the provincial CCP leadership was convinced that the crisis in the weaving industry had made local inhabitants receptive to CCP slogans. One of the leaders of the revolt described the situation in Gaoyang in a report for the provincial party journal, *The Northern Red Flag* [*Beifang Hongqi*] in September 1932: "Under this kind of heavy oppression and exploitation the people's livelihood became so bitter that there was no way to endure it. Daily the enthusiasm and demand for struggle heightened. Many of the poor peasants have a very fresh consciousness. This kind of bad year is produced by the Guomindang—we must topple the Guomindang and foreign cloth and goods!'" Support for the revolt came from peasants in villages on the fringes of the weaving district. Those villages, furthest away from the center, had the lowest wages for contract weaving and had been the first to feel the shock of the depression. Party organizers had worked to link the real economic distress that was being experienced by unemployed weaving households to the larger national and international pictures and urged peasants to set up a soviet government and drive out the Nationalists. But real economic distress and stimulus from outsiders to organize do not equal class struggle and class consciousness. Looking at the documents today and recalling the reports of numerous informants, both peasant weavers and town merchants, that they "had heard" about the revolt but were little affected by it, leaves the feeling that the revolt did not grow out of attempts to deal with Gaoyang's specific social relations and problems.

While it is certainly risky to construct a theory on what is missing from the sources, one cannot but be struck by the complete lack of evidence of hostility on the part of CCP organizers, peasants, and workers to the wealthy merchants who controlled the weaving trade. I have found only one reference that even hints at hostility to the merchants. In his memoirs, Zhai Jiaxun recalled that after the defeat of the uprising, when he was fleeing Gaoyang, he stopped to stay in the home of a party member. An employee of the Yang family's Fu Feng had come to visit and Zhai noted that he and his host could not talk freely as long as the guest was there.[18]

While there is little evidence of openly antagonistic relations between workers and merchant entrepreneurs before the Gaoyang-Li soviet, at least one of the entrepreneurs joined in suppressing the leftist political movement. One of Yang Musen's sons reportedly led plainclothes Nationalist forces into the village of Jianwo to arrest Communist Party members in September 1932.[19]

While the youthful Communist organizers had chosen Gaoyang for the uprising because they believed that economic distress as a result of the depression should have made peasants receptive to their organizing efforts, we can identify other factors that made it difficult to organize in the region.

In classic Marxist terms, the workers in the town factories should have been the first targets for party organizing efforts. They worked long hours in what were sometimes unsafe and unhealthy working environments and the occasional disputes that occurred between workers and factory owners suggest a potential for class-based resistance.[20] Moreover, the factories should have been the ideal venues for oppressed workers to become aware of their mutual interests. In spite of that, the young party organizers seem to have made no headway in approaching the workers. We do not know whether they tried and failed, or whether they simply ignored the possibility.

It is easy to see why organizing in Gaoyang factories would have been difficult. Almost all workers lived on the premises of the factory where they worked and were supervised by managers both on and off the job. Many of the workers were not Gaoyang natives; these non-natives tended to work together in a factory where the manager came from their native town, and they shared strong ties with the other workers from their hometown or village. Moreover, in China of the 1930s wages for factory work were comparatively high and employment in a factory was regarded as a good job. Since there was an almost unlimited supply of labor, few who had found factory jobs wanted to risk losing the job because of involvement in political activities. The small, closed community of the factory working environment created what Marxists would consider a "false consciousness" in which native place and kinship ties that cut across class boundaries were more important than appeals to class interests.

In the weaving villages a different dynamic was at work. The years of prosperity brought by the growth of the weaving industry had forged a new sense of household independence and village solidarity that cut across class lines. Weaving using the iron gear loom had not only brought prosperity to Gaoyang villages, that prosperity was spread very evenly across the village community. The general rise in village prosperity had strengthened ties between neighbors. Liang Xihui, the Nankai sociologist who visited the industrial district in the early 1930s, argued that Gaoyang society was characterized by very strong solidarity.[21] When my informants discussed their prewar community, they all spoke with great enthusiasm about the profits they made and about the friendly and cooperative relations within their villages.

The accounts of community and cooperation in the Gaoyang industrial district depict human relations in ways that are very similar to the accounts that have been given for industrial districts in other parts of the world. Competition and cooperation operate side by side, and relations between the proprietors of small firms, their technicians, and the workers are cordial and cooperative. Jonathan Zeitlin's characterization of human relations in Italian industrial districts fits what we know of relations in Gaoyang very well. "Firms in these districts typically combine competition and cooperation in ways that are difficult to reconcile with a pure market model of economic behavior; trust relationships are widespread not only between legally separate enterprises but also between workers and employers; and it is hard to say in many cases where the local community stops and industry begins."[22]

Scattered throughout the reports of the 1930s and through interview data collected in the 1980s are bits of evidence about the web of human relationships that gave life and sustenance to the world of rural weavers. The development of the weaving industry had given rise to new relationships in the villages that facilitated the work of individual households. One clear manifestation of that sense of community could be found in the sharing of some of the tools required in the weaving trade. While all weaving households owned their own looms, they usually shared use of the large wheels used for warping. In most villages, warping wheels were either the private property of a single family or had been bought with funds pooled by two or three families. For example, the villagers of Yentunfu had access to three warping wheels; use of the wheels was shared, on a first-come, first-served basis, by all village households at any time that the owners of the wheels were not using them. Villagers who borrowed this essential equipment were not expected to provide any compensation to the owners of the wheels.

Sharing of such equipment was one of the most visible signs of village solidarity, but there were equally important, if less readily visible, forms of cooperation. Within a village there was frequent visiting back and forth, which provided one of the most common means for the sharing of information, the introduction of new patterns, and the learning of new techniques. Village families often helped each other out; if one family was short of weft yarn to finish a bolt of fabric, it could usually be borrowed from a neighbor with repayment of the borrowed yarn after the finished fabric was sold.

The contract weaving system made use of such friendly relations within the village, working through members of the village community who had established relations with merchant firms. Master weavers, who were often not particularly wealthy or otherwise prominent, introduced their friends to the merchant houses and acted as their informal guarantors. Again, there was no formal system of repayment for such services, either from the merchant who acquired new contract weavers through this system or from the villagers to their sponsor. Often the merchant would express his thanks to a master weaver with a small gift of food at the New Year's holiday season and with a guarantee of work for the master weaver himself even during the periodic slumps. Undoubtedly the greatest reward for a master weaver came in the unspoken but recognized prestige that he earned within the village community.

While village relationships seem to have been eased by the general prosperity that came with the development of the weaving industry, when periodic slumps hit the trade, each family was thrown back on its own resources. There were no formal systems of village social security, and when hard times came, each family had to work longer hours at both agriculture and weaving to acquire sufficient income to survive.

In the early 1930s, the formal appeals to class-based concerns made by the CCP clashed with the established patterns of village solidarity which had taken on new life as the weaving district prospered. For most weavers and workers during the depression of the early 1930s, the main issue was restoration of earlier levels of prosperity. In an industrial district like Gaoyang, where prosperity depended more on the cyclical fluctuations of market demand than on problems of land distribution, the Communist message of rural class warfare against the landlords found little mass support. The CCP would make little headway in Gaoyang until the coming of the war with Japan, when the overriding issues of resistance and national survival would swing popular support to their side.

MAINTAINING COMPETITIVENESS

Gaoyang had gotten its start as a producer of import substitutes for the foreign piece goods that were flooding the Chinese market. In the early years, rural weavers produced shirtings and sheetings, plain-weave fabrics that were at the lower end of the value added scale. Gaoyang weavers had established a reputation for producing good quality fabrics at prices cheaper than foreign imports. By the early 1920s, weavers faced new competition from modern spinning and weaving mills located in Shanghai, Tianjin, and Qingdao.

How did the Gaoyang system survive this competitive challenge? When small-scale, seemingly less-sophisticated rural industry competes successfully with modern industry, our common explanations include a narrative of low wages, self-exploitation of family labor, and rural immiseration. Kathy Walker has argued that something like that scenario occurred in the Nantong weaving district in northern Jiangsu in the prewar period.[23] Gaoyang does not fit that common scenario. In the 1930s wages were not—in either an absolute or a relative sense—lower than those in Tianjin, which was the closest large city with a modern textile industry. Absolute wages were higher in

Gaoyang than in Tianjin, and a comparison of the weight of the wage bill in the overall production costs with estimates of production costs in Tianjin factories shows that the wage bill occupied a higher percentage of total production costs in Gaoyang than in Tianjin.[24] In Gaoyang, wages comprised 9.42 percent of estimated production costs, versus 7.86 percent for the Tianjin factory.[25] Moreover, there is a wealth of statistical and anecdotal information that points to rising levels of prosperity throughout the industrial district. Moreover, weavers continued to invest in looms and expand production. These were not choices that one would expect an immiserated rural labor force to make.

In making comparisons between rural weavers and then-modern urban manufacturing units, it is important to remember that by world standards Chinese modern textile mills were relatively inefficient. Only two of Tianjin's modern spinning mills, Yu Yuan and Heng Yuan, also had weaving divisions; in both factories an average worker in the weaving division was responsible for only 0.58 looms.[26] Reports for 1910 show Chinese mill workers tending an average of 0.48 looms, versus a high for industrial leaders like England, the United States, and Canada of over 2.0 looms per worker.[27] Since the equipment used in modern Chinese mills was virtually identical to that used in England, the difference in efficiency seems to be due to the quality of labor. The important point for our consideration is that although urban mills used power looms which required much heavier investment in fixed capital, their workers were not that much more productive than rural weavers using iron gear looms.

In looking for other factors to explain the continued survival of rural weaving, we need to examine systemic or institutional factors that shaped the competitive playing field, strategies related to the choice of a product line and the structure of investment.

In contemporary China rural industry is again growing at a very rapid rate, faster than the pace of the urban industrial sector that has both technological and scale advantages. In trying to explain why, it is often argued that the "playing field" is not level and that policies favor rural industry. Most commonly cited are lower tax rates. In the 1930s, Tianjin manufacturers made similar claims about their rural competitors, pointing to the factory tax, which was collected from urban factories but not from rural ones.[28] As we will see in chapters four and five, entrepreneurs and their collective organization, the Gaoyang Chamber of Commerce, aggressively fought for special privileges, including tax breaks and lower rail fares in the name of promotion of native industry. While these special privileges alone will not account for Gaoyang success, they did contribute to an institutional environment that provided some protection for rural producers.

The choice of an appropriate strategy based on product mix with higher value added was also a contributing factor. In selecting this particular strategy, Gaoyang entrepreneurs and weavers were following a path that had previously been followed by small-scale producers in England and Japan. In Japan, most of the cotton weaving districts that survived competition with modern mills did so by either adopting low-cost domestically manufactured power looms or by shifting to production of more specialized fabrics. Finally, we need to turn to the question of the structure of investment: the investment burden in the weaving industry was split between the wholesale merchants and the weaving households and factories. Wholesale merchants provided the capital to purchase yarn and buy and market finished goods.[29] Weavers supplied their own looms and workspace and paid the wages of hired weavers. Investment in dyeing and finishing factories was made by still other groups, often in the form of business partnerships that pooled the capital of working partners. This pattern of investment resulted in a system in which wages were competitive, but production costs for the wholesale merchants were held down. Moreover, the system embodied flexibility for both the wholesale merchants and the rural weavers that made it easier for both to survive during business slumps.

How does this compare with the problems faced by the modern urban mills? Most of the Chinese-owned modern spinning and weaving mills were undercapitalized. Chinese mill owners tended to make heavy investments in equipment, leaving them short of circulating capital and forcing reliance on bank loans at relatively high interest rates.[30] H. D. Fong, the Nankai expert on the textile industry, estimates that Chinese mill owners had an average investment of 603.50 yuan per power loom.[31] If we compare that investment with Li Feng's estimates that a putting-out merchant had an investment of 558.70 yuan for each contracted loom, we can see that the investment per loom is roughly comparable. However, in the case of the Gaoyang entrepreneur, the investment was in circulating capital in the form of raw materials, goods in the process of production, and unsold goods in stock. It was much easier for a wholesale merchant to adjust the volume of cloth purchased than it was for large spinning and weaving mills to shift production quotas. While a cutback in output would certainly reduce profits for the wholesale merchant, there were few other costs. This was not the case for the larger mills, where payments on debt, depreciation on machinery, and the costs involved in shutting down and reopening a factory could be quite large.

Weaving households also were more protected from slumps than the urban working class. Although weaving households on average derived 70 to 80 percent of their annual income from weaving, almost all continued to farm. In crisis periods when market demand fell and looms were temporarily idled, farming provided a cushion of security and assured a basic food supply.

NOTES

1. Chapter three of Wu Zhi, *Xiangcun zhibu gongye de yige yanjiu* (Shanghai: Shangwu Yinshuguan, 1936).

2. A large family might have two or three looms and still use only family labor.

3. Wu Zhi's survey indicates that in the two villages where rayon weaving was most developed, Xiaowangguozhuang and Nanyuantou, some 70 to 80 percent of the weavers were working in small factories.

4. The word used for boss was *dangjia*, the same term used for the person who manages the family finances. The choice of this term, rather than *laoban*, which would be used for the boss of a small factory, suggests that the small workshop was seen as an extension of the family.

5. Francesca Bray, *Technology and Gender: Fabrics of Power in Late Imperial China* (Berkeley: University of California Press, 1997).

6. See my article, "Mechanization and Women's Work in Early Twentieth Century China," in *Yanagita Setsuko-sensei koki kinen Chūgoku no dentō shakai to kazoku*, ed. Yanagita Setsuko-sensei Koki Kinen Ronshū Henshō Iinkai (Tokyo: Kyūko Shoin, 1993), 95–120.

7. Zhang Shiwen, *Dingxian nongcun gongye diaocha* (Dingxian: Zhonghua Pingmin Jiaoyu Juojinhui, 1936), 80. In Dingxian, women wove on wooden looms, while all of the weavers using iron gear looms were male.

8. Wu Zhi, *Xiangcun zhibu gongye de yige yanjiu*, 129.

9. Cloth was measured in bolts, but woven in "loom" units. For a plain weave, a single "loom" included six bolts. A single "loom" of rayon fabric included ten one-hundred-foot bolts.

10. The data on wage rates comes from Li Feng, "Wushinianlai shangye ziben zai Hebei xiangcun mianzhi shougongye zhong zhi fazhan jincheng," *Zhongguo Nongcun* 1, no. 3 (December 1934), 69.

11. Tessie P. Liu, *The Weaver's Knot: The Contradictions of Class Struggle and Family Solidarity in Western France, 1750–1914* (Ithaca: Cornell University Press, 1994), 57.

12. Wu estimated that in the early 1930s at most 15 percent of the weavers were weaving independently. My interviews with old weavers suggest that the balance changed after 1934.

13. See my essay "Creating a Northern Soviet," *Modern China* 1, no. 3 (July 1974), 243–70.

14. E. P. Thompson, *The Making of the English Working Class* (London: Penguin, 1968), 9–10.

15. A history of revolutionary struggles in Gaoyang claims that student demonstrators targeted the Li brothers of He Ji in 1926. Zhonggong Gaoyang Xianwei Dangshi Yanjiushi, ed., *Gaoyang xian geming douzheng da shiji* (Xushui: Yazhou Chubanshe, 1992).

16. Buli village had been the site in the late teens for one of the schools set up by the Diligent Work and Study Movement to prepare work-study students to go to France. Many of the graduates later became leaders of the CCP. See Zhang Hongxiang and Wang Yongxiang, eds., *Liufa qingong jianxue yundong jianshi* (Harbin: Heilongjiang Renmin Chubanshe, 1982).

17. The full list of demands is as follows: "1. Confiscate the land of anti-revolutionaries and of Christian churches and divide it among the hired laborers, poor peasants, and middle peasants. 2. Confiscate food supplies and property of landlords and gentry and divide it among poor peasants and refugees. 3. Eliminate severe and excessive taxes. 4. Get rid of high usurious interest rates. 5. Burn all contracts and receipts. 6. Seize the weapons of all landlords and anti-revolutionaries and armed hired laborers. 7. Let the people use local salt and buy and sell it. 8. Eliminate official salt stores and salt patrols. 9. Raise wages and reduce working hours. 10. Establish a soviet government and a Red Army." The list is taken from *Da Gong Bao*, September 12, 1932. See also Kim San and Nym Wales, *The Song of Ariran* (San Francisco: Ramparts Press, 1972).

18. Zhai, a native of Anxin County, was a relative of Zhai Shugong, who was the party secretary for Gaoyang County. Zhai describes Yang Musen, the founder of Fu Feng, as part of the old structure of political power in the county. I have used a mimeographed copy of Zhai's memoir, "Huiyi Gao-Li qiyi," with the author's corrections. I confirmed the story in interviews with Zhai at Nankai University in July 1980.

19. See the biography of Yang Musen in volume three of the *Gaoyang Xianzhi,* Gaoyangxian Difangzhi Bangongshi, 1995.

20. There are few reports of labor-management disputes. The Li brothers of He Ji had a reputation as the harshest taskmasters among the larger factory owners and managers. In 1932, a strike occurred at the factory when the manager tried to claim for himself small sums of money that workers had received from recycling packing materials. Workers went on strike during the peak bleaching, dyeing, and finishing season. Five days into the strike the He Ji manager got a go-between to negotiate with the workers. After the workers returned to their jobs, the manager fired the ringleaders. See Chen Meijian, et al. *Gaoyang zhibuye jianshi, Hebei Wenshi Ziliao,* vol. 19, 1987, 152.

21. Liang Xihui, "Gongshang fazhan yu renkou zhi guanxi," *Da Gong Bao*, March 31, 1937.

22. Jonathan Zeitlin, "Industrial Districts and Local Economic Regeneration: Overview and Comment," in *Industrial Districts and Local Economic Regeneration*, ed. Frank Pyke and Werner Sengenberger (Geneva: International Institute for Labour Studies, 1992), 286.

23. Kathy Le Mons Walker, *Chinese Modernity and the Peasant Path: Semicolonialism in the Northern Yangzi Delta* (Stanford: Stanford University Press, 1999).

24. There is a difference of four years in the period for the wage data. In this case, the four-year difference does not distort the results, but probably underestimates the difference in wage bills. In 1932, Gaoyang was in a depression, and wages were lower. By 1936, Gaoyang wages would have been higher.

25. Quan Guobao, *Zhongguo mianye wenti* (Shanghai: Shangwu Yinshuguan, 1936), 66.

26. Tianjin Shi Fangzhi Gongye Ju Bianshizu, "Jiu Zhongguo shiqi de Tianjin fangzhi gongye," *Beiguo Chunqiu,* January 1960, 96.

27. Gregory Clark, "Why Isn't the Whole World Developed," *Journal of Economic History* 47 (1987), 150.

28. *Tianjin Gongshang Ye,* vol. 1 (Tianjin Tebieshi Shehuiju, 1930), 63.

29. In the early years wholesale merchants loaned funds to weavers to purchase iron gear looms. The loans were repaid by deductions from the payment for cloth. Loans were paid back within a year and the amount of money tied up in such loans was small.

30. Such arguments have been made by Quan in the work cited above, by H. D. Fong in his *Cotton Industry and Trade in China* (Tianjin: Nankai Institute of Economics, 1932); and by C. F. Remer in his classic work *Foreign Investment in China* (New York: MacMillan, 1933).

31. Fong, *Cotton Industry and Trade in China*, 206.

4

Marketing Networks

"In the success or failure of industry, the expansion or contraction of the market is the most important thing," wrote Han Weiqing, head of the Gaoyang Chamber of Commerce, in 1909.[1] From the earliest stages of the development of modern Gaoyang industry, the proprietors of wholesale firms demonstrated a sharp consciousness of the importance of marketing and by the early teens wholesale firms had developed a sales agency system that became a key feature of their operations. The sales agency networks established by each of the major firms not only supported aggressive sales strategies, they also were crucial connections in linking production to market demand. The wholesale outlets promoted sales and provided market information to the head office. None of their major competitors seem to have used similar wholesale marketing systems, giving the Gaoyang merchant firms an advantage over most of their rivals.[2]

This chapter will look at textile marketing in the first three decades of the twentieth century. It seeks answers to two big questions. First, from the perspective of economic history, how were markets for cotton textiles organized? And second, from a business perspective, how did merchants design their marketing strategies to promote goods in those markets?

In recent years there has been much academic interest in the question of foreign penetration of Chinese markets, and studies based on the records of major foreign trading companies have greatly increased our knowledge of the institutional arrangements and business strategies that foreign firms have used to promote their goods.[3] There has been much less study of the ways in which domestic producers have promoted their products. Sherman Cochran has studied the tobacco industry and the campaign by Chinese businessmen to promote "Chinese" cigarettes in competition with the giant

British-American Tobacco Company.[4] Yet while cigarettes were a new product first introduced from the West, cotton textiles had long been major items
in China's domestic trade. Both foreign imports and the output of newly developed domestic textile centers like Gaoyang entered already existing textile markets. Let us then begin our discussion by turning to an overview of
Chinese textile markets in the early twentieth century.

COTTON GOODS MARKETS IN NORTH CHINA

Any survey of China's traditional textile markets must begin by delineating
the basic structure of supply and demand: how big was the demand for textiles and how was it met? By the nineteenth century most of the Chinese population wore cotton garments. Certainly among the upper classes better garments were often made of silk, but for the vast peasant and working classes,
cotton was the first choice for clothes for all seasons. Xu Xinwu made a series of estimates of the market for cotton goods in China between 1840 and
1936.[5] According to his estimate, approximately 45 percent of rural households in 1840 produced cotton textiles. The remaining part of the Chinese
population—that is, 55 percent of rural households, as well as the 5 percent
of the population (non-rural) that were engaged in non-agricultural activities—
purchased fabric.[6]

Weaving households were not evenly distributed geographically. In areas
where climate made it possible to grow cotton, most households were self-
sufficient in the production of cotton fabrics and many also produced sur-
pluses that they sold. Natural geographical features were the first important
factor dividing producing regions from non-producing regions. In general,
cotton was not grown in most of the northeast, areas west of the Sichuan
Basin, and in the southwest, areas outside the Yunnan-Guizhou Plateau. In
addition, there was a second tier of provinces where cotton production was
possible but not well developed. These regions included the northwest border regions (Shanxi, Shaanxi, and Gansu), the southwest border regions
(Yunnan and Guangxi), and the southeast coast (Guangdong, Fujian, and
Jiangxi). The demand for cotton goods in those regions was huge. Liu
Xiusheng has estimated that the population of those provinces stood at over
126,000,000 in 1820, and that if we assume a per person annual consumption
of five to ten feet of narrow "native cloth," annual domestic demand would
have been more than one billion feet of cloth.[7]

During the Ming dynasty, when cotton first became the fabric of choice for
daily wear, the textile districts of the Yangzi delta region supplied a major
share of the market for cotton fabric. Since the climate and soil of the North
China Plain were suitable for growing cotton, during the seventeenth and
early eighteenth centuries rural families in North China produced raw cotton,

which they sold to the textile districts of the Yangzi delta region (Jiangnan). At that time there was little spinning or weaving on the North China Plain, largely because both spinning and weaving were easier to manage in areas with higher levels of humidity. In the eighteenth century North China rural families discovered that the humidity problems could be solved if looms were placed in basement-like rooms that were a meter or so lower than the land surface. This innovation allowed cotton spinning and weaving to spread in the northern cotton-growing regions, and it was not long before northern weavers were selling fabrics in the frontier markets of the northeast and northwest. The old Jiangnan textile districts gradually lost market share in the frontier markets, since their North China rivals were closer to the frontier and had lower shipping costs. While earlier studies often attribute the decline of the Jiangnan textile industry to competition with foreign imports, there is now quite general agreement among Chinese textile historians that the decline began much earlier, and that Jiangnan's loss of market share was the result of competition with other domestic producers. Most would agree that by 1820 this major shift in the domestic market was already well advanced.[8]

When the first foreign imports entered the Chinese market they were entering as competitors in these domestic markets. We can trace the advance of cotton textiles into the Chinese market through a study of the maritime customs figures, which reveal a very clear pattern: foreign piece goods entered markets in the southern part of the country and then slowly began to work their way into markets in the southwest and northeast. Xu Xinwu's estimates suggest that progress was relatively slow, and that foreign cloth reached the peak of its market share around 1913, when approximately 32 percent of the domestic cloth supply came from foreign imports. As domestic mechanized and semi-mechanized weaving industries developed, the foreign share began to fall, standing at 24 percent in 1920 and dropping to just under 12 percent in 1936. While some of the foreign goods were aimed at the small sector of urban consumers who were attracted by the novelty of foreign designs, most of the imported cloth was made from low-count yarns and was relatively thick, designed to substitute for native cloth.[9]

Foreign imports entered as competitors in the traditional textile markets, and most of their early gains in market share were made at the expense of older producers. This is undoubtedly one of the reasons for the large number of complaints in the contemporary press, in which the increase in foreign imports of cotton goods was seen as the opening salvo in a commercial war between China and the West. Most famous of these complaints was the protest of the Qing official Shen Baochen, who lamented the decline of Songjiang textile production. His complaints were echoed by dozens of Chinese social critics. In the north, fears that foreign goods would inundate domestic markets were the openly expressed reason for Yuan Shikai's initiation of rural industrialization policies in the metropolitan province of Zhili.

However, despite the views of contemporary social critics, in the years after the Opium War the market for cotton goods in China was not a zero-sum game. There were a number of changes in the textile market that led to a general rise in the demand for cotton fabric. The chief factors contributing to the expansion in overall demand were a steady decline in the percentage of peasant households producing their own cloth, a slow but steady rise in the per capita consumption of cloth, and an increase in the population.

Changes in the market for cotton cloth were not only quantitative but also qualitative. The opening of the treaty ports and the creation of centers of foreign residence led to the introduction of new lifestyles in the Chinese coastal cities. As time passed, the new styles spread from the small foreign-influenced enclaves into the larger towns of the interior, and from the coastal cities into increasingly smaller cities and towns in the interior. The 1911 Revolution provided a further push to the change in clothing fashion; with the end of the imperial dynasty, the long silk robes which had long been required dress for officials disappeared, to be replaced by more "republican" fashions, including the Western suit or the long traditional gown, the *chang-pao*, now often made of cotton or cotton-wool blends. For women, fashion changes came first for the young who attended modern schools, where uniforms with shorter skirts and gym outfits were the first wave of new, Western-inspired fashion. By the 1920s and 1930s, fashionable women in the cities were wearing the new "native" dress, the qipao, which was a modern adaptation of traditional Manchu costume.[10]

On the demand side there were overall changes, both because of an increase in the population and an increase in the average quantity of individual consumption. There were also shifts in the structure of demand, as changes in fashion led to a shift away from silks toward cottons, wools, rayons, and blends, and to demands for greater variety in color, weight, and design of fabrics.

On the supply side, in addition to the increase in foreign imports, new domestic producers began to replace the older producers of native cloth. Foreign imports had first begun to enter the Chinese market in the mid-nineteenth century and reached a peak in the period immediately before the First World War. During the intra-war years, the development of new rural industrial districts and the growth of modern textile mills, as well as the increasing role of foreign-owned mills in China, led to a general decline in direct foreign imports.

As inexpensive fabrics entered the market, an increasing number of Chinese rural households gave up home spinning and weaving and began to purchase cloth. Xu Xinwu's estimates suggest a slow rise in the percentage of non-weaving households, moving from 55 percent in 1840 to 70 percent by 1936.[11] Again, change was not spread evenly geographically. In the old Jiangnan textile districts, most rural households were still producing and wearing native cloth through the Second World War years, and the final chapter of their story of domestic industry only came in 1958, when home weaving was banned. In other areas the shift came earlier. A survey of cotton cloth consumption in Zhili in the early Republican period (1914) showed that there had been a shift to machine-woven fabrics in the north and northeastern parts of the province, while consumers in other parts of the province preferred the use of "native cloth."

Increases in the total population of China, as well as small increases in the per capita consumption of cloth, further added to total demand. Xu Xinwu's estimates show a steady rise in per capita production from 1.50 bolts (5.45 square yards) per person per year in 1840, to 2.00 bolts (7.27 square yards) per person per year in 1936.[12] Finally, the rise of new domestic suppliers, from both the new textile districts like Gaoyang and the foreign- and Chinese-owned urban mills, changed the structure of the domestic market for cloth. In the early twentieth century most of the markets were for relatively coarse fabrics made with low-count yarns, and both the new textile districts and foreign importers were trying to meet that demand. However, as an increasing number of domestic mechanized mills came on line in the 1920s, both foreign importers and the new textile districts were forced to shift their strategies. In the case of the new textile districts, Baodi, one of the early leaders, went into sharp decline beginning in the mid-1920s. Baodi's production style, which matched the use of iron gear looms with machine-spun yarns, was similar to Gaoyang's, but Baodi producers chose to pursue their original strategy of using low-count yarns to produce shirtings and sheetings that competed primarily on low prices. As the mechanized mills entered the market in the 1920s, their lower costs drove Baodi weavers out of business.

Chinese domestic textile markets in the first several decades of the twentieth century were highly competitive. New domestic producers were engaged in an intense struggle with foreign imports and traditional producers for market share. As the Blackburn Chamber of Commerce survey team discovered during its 1896–1897 tour of the Upper Yangzi basin, regional taste in China varied widely, and successful marketing of textile products depended on more than simply low prices.[13] Matching product to frequently shifting local taste and demand was the key to success. Successful competitors needed very precise market information, and also needed to know how to manipulate the institutional structure to their own advantage. Just as foreign products could attract not only because of lower prices but also because of novel designs, Chinese domestic producers frequently played their own trump card of "national product" status, suggesting that it was a patriotic act to buy domestic products. Let us then turn to a consideration of the ways in which Gaoyang manufacturers developed marketing strategies and look at how they fared in competition with foreign imports.

MARKET EXPANSION

How did Chinese merchants build and expand their markets? The pioneering work of G. William Skinner has shaped our understanding of Chinese marketing systems and the roles they played in social organization. Skinner has provided a classification system that describes a hierarchical structure reaching from the smallest standard marketing communities, up to the largest national marketing centers. In his work, he divides China into a series of macro regions and provides a theoretical framework for conceptualizing the flow of goods, resources, and power within each region and between regions.[14] The data on marketing by Gaoyang merchants allows us to take Skinner's static spatial system and see how merchants worked through a nested marketing structure to promote the sales of their products.[15]

Gaoyang firms used a system of direct wholesale marketing that was one of the fundamental building blocks of their overall production system. In the early years, most firms produced unbleached shirtings and sheetings that they sold to dealers from the northeast and northwest. Beginning in the early teens, they began to diversify their product line, eventually producing small-volume lots of a wide variety of products. One of the keys to the success of that strategy was the development of close links between production and marketing. Each of the larger Gaoyang wholesale firms controlled a distribution network of sales agencies (*waizhuang*) that were located at the nodes of regional marketing systems. In the early 1930s there were more than 170 marketing agencies located in seventy-nine different cities and towns. The marketing agency had two major functions: first, it was responsible for the sale of goods to wholesale and retail dealers, and second, it was responsible for conveying information on market conditions and market demand to the home office.

Each wholesaling firm operated its own network of agencies. In major marketing centers there might have been as many as eight to ten sales agencies of different Gaoyang wholesalers competing for sales. Relations among sales agencies varied from market to market. In some places there was no cooperation among competing agencies, while in other cities sales agents of different wholesalers maintained friendly relations; such cooperation would be expressed in a variety of ways, including the sharing of market knowledge and in some cases the loaning of supplies back and forth if one agency had orders for goods that were out of stock.

Sales agencies were simple establishments. A sales agency might have anywhere from two to ten or more employees who had been dispatched from the main headquarters in Gaoyang; one of the employees served as the sales branch manager. The smaller agencies often operated out of hotel rooms, while the larger sales agencies operated out of rented shop space. The customers for a sales agency were local wholesale and retail merchants who purchased large lots of cloth and either sold them directly in their own retail shops or transported the goods into outlying market centers for sale to city and town retail merchants and to itinerant peddlers who made the rounds of even smaller markets and villages.

The sales agency managers received fabric samples from the head office of their own firm in Gaoyang. They showed these to wholesale and retail customers, who then placed purchase orders. Orders were sent to the head office by telephone or telegraph and goods would be shipped to the agency office for delivery to customers. Speed was essential in sending orders and delivery of goods. Most of the major firms employed staff who had studied English, and who were able to send telegrams to the home office using that language. This was necessary because of the cumbersome method for sending telegrams in Chinese.[16]

The success of a sales agency depended on the ability of its employees to establish and maintain good relations with local customers. One of the advantages of the system of permanent sales agencies was that it allowed the manager and employees of a sales agency to build long-term connections with local wholesale and retail merchants. In many of the cities where sales agencies were located, Gaoyang merchants came to play an important role in local civic life, serving as directors of local chambers of commerce. Such participation in civic activities added to the prestige and name recognition of the employing firm, and helped to promote business in important regional markets. In their day-to-day contacts with customers, Gaoyang agencies also relied on personal connections. Rarely did they wait for potential customers to visit their agency offices. Instead, most of the sales agencies employed runners who visited the hotels and lodging houses where wholesale merchants from outlying marketing centers stayed when they visited the regional marketing center. Runners made daily visits to lodging houses to cultivate ties with visiting merchants, showing samples of their wares and encouraging sales.

Some of the sales branches also had employees known as outside agents (*duanpao*) who would take fabric samples and make a tour of lower-level markets in the region covered by the sales branch. After orders were received, the goods would be shipped from the sales branch to the customers in local marketing centers. As Gaoyang goods penetrated local markets and met with good response, the number of sales branches in a given region was often increased. As we can see from map 4.1, the density of sales branches in a region is one indication of how successful Gaoyang merchants had been in penetrating local markets. The dense concentration of sales branches in Hebei and Henan clearly suggests that Gaoyang cloth was directly marketed by sales agencies not only in major regional marketing centers, but also in central marketing centers. Gaoyang sales methods can perhaps be understood more clearly if we turn to several specific illustrations of the development of marketing areas.

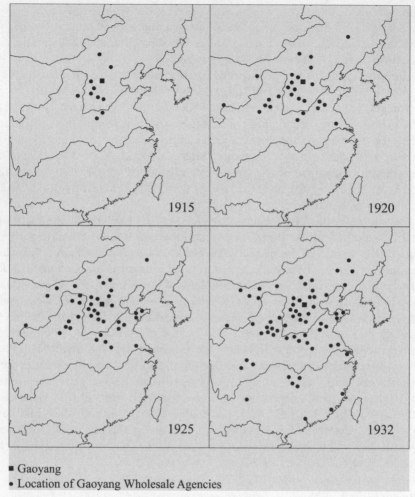

■ Gaoyang
• Location of Gaoyang Wholesale Agencies

Map 4.1.   Expansion of the Sales Branch Network

Patterns of Market Expansion

New-style wide-width Gaoyang cloth first entered the North China market in 1907–1908 and was marketed as a substitute for imported shirtings and sheetings. In the early years, most of the marketing was done locally with wholesalers selling to "guest merchants" who came to Gaoyang. There are some indications that a few of the wholesalers had begun to experiment with sales agencies. A Japanese survey of 1911 reported that Gaoyang whole-salers had agents in Zhangjiakou, Taigu in Shanxi, and Nangong in southern

Hebei. However, the 1910 financial panic led to a temporary withdrawal of most of the sales agencies.[17] The first of the agencies that were still in operation in the 1930s had been opened in 1911 in Xingji and Nangong, both in Hebei Province; these were followed in the next year by the opening of agencies in Beijing and Gaoyi, also in Hebei.

Selection of Xingji as one of the earliest sites for a marketing agency points to an interesting feature of commodity marketing in North China. Xingji, a major wholesale marketing center located sixty-five kilometers east of Shijiazhuang in south-central Hebei, is representative of a type of specialized market that has rarely been discussed in the Western literature on Chinese marketing. Skinner's system is, as he says, based on geographical models designed to explain retail marketing. Skinner extends those spatial models to consider other factors, including administrative centrality and other economic, social, and political functions. He does not include wholesale marketing. By implication it is suggested that wholesale marketing follows similar patterns, with functions concentrating in central places at higher levels in the hierarchy. However, in North China, in addition to the hierarchically structured system of periodic markets, there were also specialized wholesale markets that served wider areas extending across several macro regions. Merchants from all over the country gathered at these specialized wholesale markets to trade in specific commodities.[18] The most famous of the North China wholesale markets was the drug market in Anguo County, which had gotten its start at least as early as the Ming dynasty.[19] Xingji was another important specialized wholesale market, drawing customers from all over the country to trade in leather and leather goods. On the eve of the anti-Japanese war, reports claim that 70 percent of the leather trade in China passed through the Xingji market.[20] Major trading firms from all over the country established agency representatives at such specialized markets. Neither Xingji nor Anguo were particularly convenient locations, since both were some distance from major waterways, and neither was located near rail lines. In spite of those disadvantages, they were able to maintain their primacy as specialized commodity wholesale markets throughout the twentieth century.

In choosing to locate early sales agencies in towns like Xingji, Gaoyang merchants were hoping to display their products at locations where wealthy wholesale merchants gathered. The success of the early sales agencies inspired Gaoyang merchants to expand their marketing networks into major marketing centers across the northern part of China in succeeding years. Map 4.1 shows in summary fashion the spatial expansion of the Gaoyang marketing network.

In selecting the sites for their regional sales branches, wholesale merchants strove to select cities that were at the central nodes of regional marketing systems where wholesale merchants from more distant areas gathered. Since sales agencies were quite simple affairs involving almost no investment in fixed capital, a sales branch office could be opened on a trial basis. In most cases, the first sales branch aiming at a specific regional market would be placed in a regional marketing center. If sales to wholesale merchants from the targeted regional market were good, then further sales agencies might be opened in marketing centers at a level lower on the marketing hierarchy. To understand how this process of market penetration worked, let us turn to a specific example of market expansion.

In 1912, several Gaoyang firms opened marketing agencies in Beijing, presumably intending to sell goods not only to the retail shops in the national capital but also to wholesale merchants from areas outside of the Great Wall who did a major portion of their purchasing through agents in the capital city. The success of the Beijing sales agencies in promoting sales to merchants in the northern frontier regions led in 1915 to the opening of sales agencies in Zhangjiakou, which was a major marketing center for Inner Mongolia, Outer Mongolia, and the regions along the northwest frontier, including northern Shanxi, Shaanxi, and Gansu. The immense success of the Zhangjiakou agencies led to further expansion to more distant frontier marketing centers including Baotou, and Suiyuan. By 1918, Gaoyang merchants were approaching the Shanxi market from two directions, with agencies in Baotou dealing with merchants serving the northern fringes of the Yellow River basin and with newly opened agencies in Taiyuan moving into the same zone from a southerly direction.

As we can see from map 4.1, Gaoyang sales agencies spread from the markets of North China to cover most major parts of the country by the mid-1930s. New products had led to the exploration of new markets. For example, most of the sales agencies south of the Yangzi had been set up after the introduction of rayon fabrics, which were more popular in the warmer climates of the south.

Individual firms adjusted their own systems of sales agencies to the specific mix of the goods they handled. For example, Fu Feng, the largest of the Gaoyang firms, also had one of the largest sales networks, with fourteen sales agencies employing approximately one hundred full-time employees. Fu Feng sales agencies were located in the following cities (with the number of employees in each given in parentheses): Beijing (6), Hankou (5), Xi'an (14), Zhangjiakou (10), Chengdu (5), Pingliang (3), Lanzhou (5), Luoyang (6), Taiyuan (10), Yuci (10), Jinan (4), Nangong (1), Baotou (5), and Chongqing (3). One of Fu Feng's chief rivals, Hui Chang, had a similar system of sales agencies located in thirteen cities. The Hui Chang sales branches were located in Shanghai, Tianjin, Qingdao, Zhangjiakou, Yuci, Xi'an, Kaifeng, Luoyang, Hankou, Changsha, Amoy, Chengdu, and Chongqing.[21] (See map 4.2 for location of the sales branches.)

While some of the sales agencies had been in operation for more than twenty years, turning profits year after year, others were characterized by

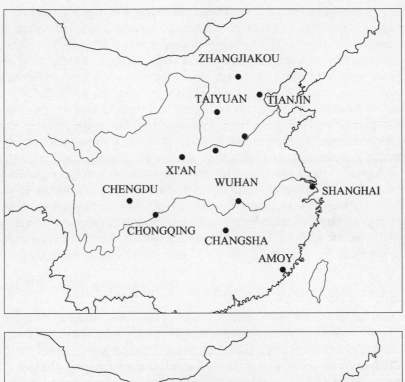

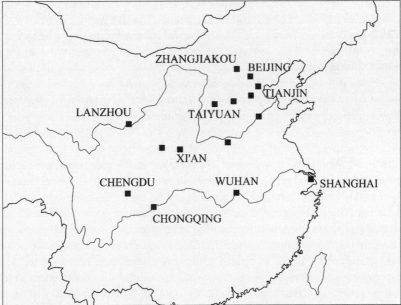

● indicates cities in which Fu Feng sales branches were located.
■ indicates cities in which Hui Chang sales branches were located.

Map 4.2. Location of Fu Feng and Hui Chang Sales Branches

more unstable histories, which reflected the changes in regional markets. For example, Fu Feng's most profitable sales agency in the late teens was located in Kulun (Ulan Batour). The Kulun sales agency was opened in 1914, and its operations differed from Fu Feng's other sales agencies. While most sales agencies were exclusively involved in trade in Gaoyang-produced textiles, because of the special character of the barter trade in Mongolia, the Fu Feng branch in Kulun also dealt in native products, including furs and rare drugs. Cotton goods from Gaoyang were exchanged in Kulun for local products that were shipped for sale in Tianjin, with Fu Feng making profits on both ends of the trade. Annual profits from the Kulun branch exceeded 100,000 yuan in peak years of the late teens. All of this, however, came to an end as a result of political changes in the 1920s; first came the revolution in Mongolia and Mongolia's alliance with the Soviet Union, and then in the late 1920s clashes between the Russian army stationed in Mongolia and troops of the Manchurian warlord Zhang Xueliang. Fu Feng was forced to retreat, withdrawing from what had been one of its most successful sales agencies.[22]

Competition with Foreign Imports—The Case of Zhangjiakou

When Gaoyang fabrics entered new markets they had to compete for market share. While there is no question that there was an overall rise in the total Chinese demand for cloth in the first decades of the twentieth century, the best-documented example of Gaoyang market expansion, the case of Zhangjiakou, clearly indicates that Gaoyang gains were often won at the expense of foreign imports.

The first sales branch in Zhangjiakou was opened in 1915 and within the space of two years Gaoyang cloth had claimed a major share of the market at the expense of goods imported from Japan.[23] Zhangjiakou (known to foreign traders as Kalgan) was a major station on the rail line that linked Beijing to what was then the end of the line at Guihuacheng (contemporary Huhhot) in Inner Mongolia. It was one of the major trading centers for merchants in Inner Mongolia and was also a gathering place for caravan merchants who transported goods into the upper reaches of the Yellow River basin in Shanxi and Gansu. The frontier trade out of Zhangjiakou had grown dramatically in the latter half of the nineteenth century in response to the opening of Tianjin as a treaty port. When foreign trading firms entered Tianjin after 1860, they encountered a major problem. Unlike the southern treaty ports, which had been important trading centers for such traditional export commodities as tea, ceramics, and raw silk, North China had little in the way of export goods. In order to promote the development of Tianjin as a treaty port, foreign trading firms searched for exportable commodities, and eventually strove to develop Tianjin as a center for the export of north and northwest frontier products, primarily wool. While the nomadic tribal groups in the frontier regions had for centuries been involved in a self-sufficient economy centered around the herding of animals, the by-products of their herds only entered the commodity economy on a large scale in the late nineteenth century. Since nomadic herders had little use for cash, almost all of the trade was conducted on a barter basis, with Chinese-manufactured goods exchanged for wool. Steady growth in the wool export trade thus also promoted the expansion of demand for such goods as cotton cloth, and Zhangjiakou and, later, other frontier towns became major centers for the cloth trade.[24] By the early Republican period Gaoyang entrepreneurs had seen the opportunities offered by the frontier markets and begun to aggressively push their products through sales agencies in Zhangjiakou.

Mitsui Bussan, one of Japan's largest trading firms, was an early successful participant in the Zhangjiakou market. When the firm's share of the Zhangjiakou market started to decline, Mitsui, in 1919, commissioned Ishida Hideji to undertake a study of the Zhangjiakou cotton-cloth market to see what was going wrong. At the time of Ishida's report, transport on the Trans-Siberian Railway had been cut as a result of the Russian Revolution and most trade directed at Outer Mongolia and Siberia was being moved through Zhangjiakou and then overland to Kulun and on to Mongolia and Siberia. For Gaoyang merchants, the move into the Zhangjiakou market had marked their first expansion outside of the immediate North China (Hebei, Henan, Shanxi) marketing region. Their tremendous success in the Zhangjiakou marketplace encouraged further pioneering of the frontier zone markets; in 1916 sales agencies were set up in Baotou which had more direct access to northern Shanxi, and in 1917 sales agencies were set up in Hami in Xinjiang.

Zhangjiakou first began to develop as a major trading center for cotton textiles around the turn of the century. In the early years, British and American sheetings and drills had almost complete dominance of the market. Within a few years Japanese began to market in the area. The lower cost of their goods drove out other foreign competitors so that Japanese products came to claim an 80 to 90 percent share of the total trade, which in 1917 had a total value of 1,980,000 taels.

In the years from 1916 to 1919, the market for cloth in Zhangjiakou expanded rapidly as a result of the increased trading area in Outer Mongolia and Siberia, but the Japanese share of the market dropped to under 25 percent as Gaoyang merchants made major inroads in the market. The trading situation had become so dismal for Japanese merchants that Tōyō Bōseki, the leading Japanese trader in the market, closed its sales agency in Zhangjiakou.

In Zhangjiakou Gaoyang cloth was competing head on with both domestic and foreign modern industry. Ishida argued that Gaoyang cloth was more competitive because of lower costs; he argued especially that Gaoyang firms paid less in taxes and transport fees as a result of deliberate state policies to encourage national products. As table 4.1 and figure 4.1 clearly show,

Table 4.1.   Zhangjiakou Comparative Prices

	Sheeting	Drill
Japanese goods	6.7	6.6
Shanghai goods	6.5	5.8
Gaoyang 5.5 jin cloth	4.5	4.5
Gaoyang 7.0 jin cloth	5.0	5.0
Gaoyang 8.0 jin cloth	5.7	5.7

Market prices varied from day to day. These were the quotations on April 18, 1919. The price is in yuan per bolt of cloth.
Source: Ishida Hideji, "Chōkakō menpu bōeki" (Mitsui, 1919).

Gaoyang cloth was underselling both domestic and foreign imports by a wide enough margin to corner the market. In his conclusion, Ishida predicted that the market in Zhangjiakou would continue to grow and warned that if immediate steps were not taken by Japanese producers and importers to counter the Gaoyang advance, the market would be taken over by goods from Hebei weavers.

The experience of Gaoyang merchants in the Zhangjiakou market clearly demonstrates that it was possible for rural workshops to compete with the power looms of modern industry in the period before the 1920s. However, as Chinese domestic production expanded in the late teens and early 1920s

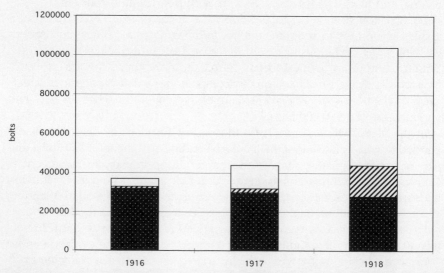

Figure 4.1.   Market Shares in the Zhangjiakou Market. The bottom portion represents foreign imports; the middle portion, Shanghai goods; and the top, Gaoyang goods. (Source: Ishida Hideji, *Chōkakō menpu bōeki* [Mitsui, April 1919], 14.)

and as Japanese investors built more spinning and weaving mills in Chinese coastal cities, the price advantage in low-cost product lines gradually diminished. Throughout the 1920s the increase in supply of machine-spun yarn drove down its price, and with it the price of unbleached cotton cloth.[25] As this happened Gaoyang merchants had to compete not just on the basis of lower costs; they also had to begin to make other appeals. Increasingly they turned to competition in markets for specialty goods and these goods, including checks and stripes, patterned fabrics, and rayon and rayon-mixed weaves came to compose an important part of total output.

In making this shift into competition in the market for specialty goods, Gaoyang goods continued to compete directly with foreign imports. The development of the modern textile industry in China, which proceeded at a particularly rapid pace in the years after the First World War, had led to a significant shift in the composition of textile imports. By the mid-1920s foreign importers had turned their attention from the import of low-count cotton yarns to finished goods, and within the category of finished piece goods from the unbleached shirtings and sheetings which had earlier dominated the import lists to greater stress on dyed and printed fabrics, particularly those made with higher-count yarns. This shift was in response to the greater ability of the domestic textile mills to satisfy the demand for low-count cotton yarns and for the coarser shirtings and sheetings that had earlier been the staples of the foreign trade.[26] Thus as the Gaoyang product mix moved upscale to service specialty markets, most of its competition still came from foreign imports which had also shifted their product mix in the Chinese market.

MARKETING STRATEGIES

In recent years anthropological studies of consumers and consumer choice have made it clear that our earlier notions of an economic man whose consumption choices were determined primarily by a rational calculation of costs and benefits had greatly oversimplified the role culturally influenced factors play in determining the nature of consumption choices.[27] In looking at the marketing strategies used by Gaoyang merchants we are faced with a range of questions, beginning with the technical questions related to the structure and functioning of Chinese marketing systems discussed above, but also touching on the much more difficult questions of taste and of popular appeal. In the Gaoyang case, since the directly controlled distribution system operated only at the wholesaling level, it is almost impossible to know what appeals local retail merchants used when selling Gaoyang cloth to their customers. The best evidence we have comes from product names, brand-names, and packaging techniques, which provide some indication of the markets the merchants were attempting to reach and the appeals that they thought would be most compelling.

As the mix in the composition of Gaoyang goods changed over time, marketing strategies also changed. In the early years, fabrics were marketed primarily as substitutes for more expensive imported shirtings and sheetings. Gaoyang merchants encouraged the appeal of their goods by deliberately marketing their fabrics in ways that made it unclear whether what they were selling was of native or foreign manufacture. It was customary practice among foreign merchants to stamp imported goods with indigo brand-name stamps along the edges of the fabric. Gaoyang merchants had similar indigo trademarks made; each commercial house had ten to twelve different stamps, some of which were copies of foreign trademarks. Foreign piece goods also were packed for shipping in bales that could easily be distinguished from native product. Gaoyang commercial houses began to package their goods in bales identical to those of the imported goods.[28]

When local manufacturers began to market both colored and patterned fabrics, one of the chief sources of design inspiration was goods from foreign and domestic mills. Gaoyang agents would purchase samples of new fabric designs and send them to their firm's headquarters, where managers would commission master weavers to make copies. If the copies were well made it was often very difficult to distinguish them from the original foreign products. For example, an American Department of Commerce publication from 1926 reported that, "These fabrics are of excellent quality, compare favorably with foreign machine-made products, and have an extensive sales in the northern Provinces."[29] In many cases, not only the designs but also the trademarks of the original manufacturer were copied. Such pirating of designs and trademarks was a source of much tension between Gaoyang merchants and the owners of domestic mills and foreign marketing agents. On one occasion, the owner of a Wuchang textile mill who had registered his trademarks Eternal Youth and Racing Horses threatened to bring suit against the Gaoyang merchant community, and the magistrate was ordered to keep a closer check on the activities of the merchants who were suspected of marketing goods under the brand-names registered to the Wuchang entrepreneur.[30]

This use by some Gaoyang merchants of pirated designs and trademarks is very similar to practices that plague the textile industry in our own day. High-fashion design is pirated to produce cheap versions, which are on the market almost as quickly as the originals; imitations of famous brands of clothing, shoes, and bags fill the cheaper stores and markets. Some goods only look like more expensive designs; others claim to be authentic, even when a glance at the materials and workmanship often will show that this is not true. The marketing strategies of some Gaoyang merchants in the early part of the twentieth century can be seen as an early version of these practices. Even while most merchants were proud of their own brand-names, there is no question that one of the attractions of their products was the similarity to imported goods.

In marketing their product as "foreign goods" (*yang huo*) merchants were appealing to the reputation that had been established by foreign brands for good-quality, low-cost cloth. The shirtings, sheetings, drills, and jeans of foreign mills had pioneered the market for such modern fabrics and the Gaoyang merchants then moved into the market with similar goods that could be sold at lower prices. At least through the early 1920s, such appeals were able to win a significant share of the North China market for cotton goods.

In the market for import substitutes, one of the chief problems that entrepreneurs faced was quality control. Since the marketability of domestically manufactured cloth depended on its lower price in comparison with foreign and domestic competitors, merchants were engaged in a constant battle to reduce production costs. Gaoyang merchants could not control the price of yarn, the chief input in weaving. For merchants, the chief area of maneuverability with regard to costs was in the wages paid to weavers. Wages/purchase prices for cotton goods paid to the weavers varied from season to season, with wage bills rising when the market was good and falling when the market was depressed. When new styles were introduced, the wages for those weaves were often quite high, but when competitors moved into the market imitating new products, the merchants would try to reduce costs by cutting wages. One of the few options for weavers under such circumstances was to reduce the quality of their finished goods in an effort to save on the raw materials that they had obtained on contract from a merchant. The small bits of "saved" yarn could then be used to produce additional bolts of cloth that the weaver could sell on the open market, thereby increasing his income. The net result of such techniques was inferior weaves that did not meet the expected standards for density of threads per square inch.

When market conditions were depressed it was not only the weavers who turned to special techniques to maintain their income. Sales agencies throughout the country engaged in "dumping" to encourage sales. In the 1930s it was quite common for sales branch managers to make under-the-table arrangements with their customers which extended the period from delivery of the goods to the settlement of accounts. In good times, merchants expected final payment for goods within one to two months, but during the depression of the early 1930s terms were often extended to six to nine months after the delivery of goods. Sales agents would also lower prices in order to induce customers to purchase more, often cutting the prices to levels that barely met their costs.

Patriotic Appeals

Consumers' choices were influenced by a number of promotional appeals. While in the early years Gaoyang cloth was promoted as a substitute for

foreign imports and marketed in ways that made it difficult to distinguish domestic from imported goods, in the 1930s merchants shifted their marketing
strategy, stressing the native origin of their products. This shift was a direct
response to the growing strength of anti-Japanese nationalist sentiment. In
the years following the 1911 Revolution, the nationalist movement grew in
strength and influence as ever-widening circles of Chinese urban society became involved in the campaign to reduce foreign influence and establish a
strong and independent nation state. From the time of the Twenty-one Demands, much of the force of the nationalist movement was directed to opposing Japan's growing push for influence and control in North China. One
of the chief weapons in the struggle against growing Japanese influence in
China was the boycott of Japanese goods. Boycotts called on merchants to
stop the trade in Japanese products and urged the consuming public to buy
"national products" as a sign of their patriotism. The first great upsurge of patriotic boycotts of Japanese goods came after the publication of the Twenty-
one Demands, when student, worker, and merchant associations all over
China joined in a boycott of Japanese goods, setting up regulations to control trade. Boycotts continued as a popular form of anti-imperialist protest
throughout the May Fourth period and into the 1920s. These were not the
first boycotts of Japanese goods, but were among the first to have a nationwide base of support and a marked effect on Japanese trade with China.[31]
Another big upsurge of anti-Japanese boycotts followed the Japanese invasion of the northeast in 1931. It was during this second round of boycotts,
which lasted throughout the 1930s, that we have clear evidence of Gaoyang
merchants turning to the "national product" appeal in merchandising their
goods.[32]

The roots of the national products movement in North China go back to
the late Qing and the work of Song Zejiu, the manager of one of Tianjin's
leading textile merchandising firms who began to promote native products.
In 1913 Song bought out the formerly government-owned Tianjin Industrial
Products Showroom that had been set up under the auspices of Yuan
Shikai's industrial promotion program. Throughout the teens Song and his
colleagues strove to make the manufacture and trade in national products a
commercially profitable business, offering advice and technical assistance to
producers and carrying out a steady advertising campaign to encourage
mass consumption of goods made in China. Song played an active role in the
anti-Japanese boycotts of the May Fourth era.[33]

As patriotic fervor spread in the 1920s and 1930s, the appeal of "Buy Chinese" campaigns began to influence consumer choice and became a major
selling point for Gaoyang goods. Chinese entrepreneurs began to introduce
patriotic appeals into their marketing campaigns. Many of the Gaoyang firms
began to use trademarks with slogans calling for the restoration of national
rights. (See figure 4.2.) In the boom of the mid-1930s rayon and rayon mixed

Figure 4.2. Tong He Trademark. The banners on the right and left read, "Promote National Products, Restore Chinese Rights." The original trademark is in the collection of the Gaoyang Textile Museum. (Photo by the author.)

weaves were the most important of the new Gaoyang product lines. Most of the raw materials came from Japan, and a large portion of the rayon yarn was smuggled into North China through the Japanese-controlled East Hebei Special Zone. Even such goods were technically considered as "national product" since the final manufacturing was done in China by Chinese workers.[34]

As the demand for national products increased in the mid-1930s, many merchants found that they could not keep up with the demand, and some began to buy up finished goods in Tianjin from both foreign and domestic weaving mills. In some cases, the unbleached cotton and rayon cloth was sent to Gaoyang where it was dyed and had a trademark impressed before being sent to markets in the interior. In other cases, the goods were actually dyed in Tianjin workshops and then impressed with Gaoyang trademarks before being marketed.

Gaoyang's success in winning a significant market share in the highly competitive textile markets of the first three decades of the twentieth century was the result of the aggressive marketing strategies of the textile entrepreneurs. From the very beginning of their endeavors they strove to build systems that made them competitive. Sometimes that required the intervention of government agencies to provide special tax protection. At all times it required the clever choice and manipulation of strategies relating to packaging and trademarks that presented the goods to the public with a certain image. As we have seen, changing products and a changing political and cultural climate required shifts in the choice of appeals. In the early days, when foreign goods had a good reputation in the market, merchants used packaging techniques and trademarks that suggested Gaoyang products were just like foreign goods; in the politically charged atmosphere of the 1930s, Gaoyang products were marketed as prototypical national products.

While the specific product images changed over time, the system of direct wholesale marketing was a crucial link in the production system. Direct wholesale marketing gave the merchant firms control over a nationwide marketing network that also provided day-to-day market information. This allowed merchant firms to quickly adjust their product lines to subtle changes in market demand. As a result, they were able to survive the competition with foreign importers and to gradually expand their marketing network and their profits.

NOTES

1. Tianjin Dang'an Guan, Tianjin Shehuikexueyuan Lishi Yanjiusuo, and Tianjinshi Gongshangye Lianhehui, eds., *Tianjin Shanghui dang'an huibian,* part 1, *1903–1911,* vol. 1 (Tianjin: Tianjin Renmin Chubanshe, 1989),. 225–26.

2. This judgment is based on reports on major rivals, including other rural industrial centers such as Baodi, Weifang, and Nantong. Hokushi Keizai Chōsasho, ed., *I-Ken dofugyō chōsa hōkokusho.* On Nantong, Lin Jubai, *Jindai Nantong tubuye* (Nanjing Daxue Xuebao Bianjibu, 1984).

3. S. Sugiyama and Linda Grove, eds., *Commercial Networks in Modern Asia* (Richmond, Surrey: Curzon), 2001.

4. Sherman Cochran, *Big Business in China* (Cambridge: Harvard University Press, 1980).

5. "Estimates on Chinese Handicraft Production of Cotton Goods, 1840–1936," in *Zhongguo zibenzhuyi fazhanshi,* vol. 2, *Jiu minzhuzhuyi geming shiqi de Zhongguo zibenzhuyi,* ed. Xu Dixin and Wu Chengming (Beijing: Renmin Chubanshe, 1990), 305–32.

6. "Estimates on Chinese Handicraft Production of Cotton Goods, 1840–1936," 313.

7. Liu Xiusheng, "Qingdai mianbu shichang de bianqian yu Jiangnan mianbu shengchan de shuailuo," *Zhongguo Shehui Jingjishi Yanjiu* [Xiamen], no. 2 (1990): 54–61; and Liu Xiusheng, *Qingdai shangpin jingji yu shangye ziben* (Beijing: Zhongguo Shangye Chubanshe, 1993).

8. Both Liu Xiusheng and Xu Xinwu share this view.

9. Kawakatsu Heita, "Ajia momen shijō no kōzō to tenkai," *Shakai Keizai Shigaku* 51, no. 1 (April 1985), 91–125. See also the same author's "The Emergence of a Market for Cotton Goods in East Asia in the Early Modern Period," in *Japanese Industrialization and the Asian Economy*, ed. A. J. H. Latham and Heita Kawakatsu (London: Routledge, 1994), 9–34.

10. Li Yuyi, *Qingmo minchu Zhongguo geda duhui nannu zhuangshi lunji, 1899–1923* (Hong Kong: Chung Shan Book Co., 1972); Zhou Xibao, *Zhongguo gudai fuzhuangshi* (Beijing: Zhongguo Xiju Chubanshe, 1984); Antonia Finnane, "What Should Chinese Women Wear? A National Problem," *Modern China* 22, no. 2 (1996), 99–131; Antonia Finnane and Anne McLaren, eds., *Dress, Sex and Text in Chinese Culture* (Melbourne: Monash Asia Institute, 1998); Henrietta Harrison, *The Making of the Republican Citizen; Political Ceremonies and Symbols in China, 1911–1929* (Oxford: Oxford University Press, 2000).

11. Xu Xinwu, "Estimates on Chinese Handicraft Production," 313.

12. Xu Xinwu, "Estimates on Chinese Handicraft Production," 314.

13. W. H. Burnett, ed., *Report of the Mission to China of the Blackburn Chamber of Commerce, 1896–97* (Blackburn: North-East Lancashire Press, 1898).

14. The most fully elaborated statement of Skinner's conception of Chinese national markets is to be found in the volume he edited, *The City in Late Imperial China* (Stanford: Stanford University Press, 1977).

15. This reconstruction of the Gaoyang marketing structure and networks is based on several sources: Wu Zhi, *Xiangcun zhibuye de yige yanjiu;* Chen Meijian, et.al., *Gaoyang zhibuye jianshi (Hebei Wenshi Ziliao,* vol. 19, 1987); and interviews with former employees of a number of Gaoyang merchant firms.

16. Students at the chamber of commerce–sponsored commercial school studied English.

17. See *Tsūsho Ihō*, August 5, 1911, 47.

18. For examples of wholesale markets, see the brief descriptions in Li Qingwei, ed., *Zhongguo shangye wenhua dazidian* (Beijing: Zhongguo Fazhan Chubanshe, 1994), 1513–1609, and for a treatment of specialized markets in the contemporary period, see Editorial Committee for Zhongguo Nongcun Moshi Yanjiu, *Zhongguo nongcun shichang moshi yanjiu* (Beijing: Xinhua Chubanshe, 1993).

19. Zheng Kecheng, "Anguoxian yaoshi diaocha," *Shehui Kexue Zazhi* 3, no. 1 (March 1932), 94–124; 3, no. 2 (June 1932), 186–233.

20. On Xingji, see *Hebeisheng shangye zhi* (Shijiazhuang: Hebei Renmin Chubanshe, 1988), 659–61; and Qing Ye, "Xingji pimao ming tianxia," *Hebei Wenshi Jicui*, Jingji Juan (Hebei Renmin Chubanshe), 101–9.

21. Data on the location of sales agencies of individual firms can be found in Chen Meijian, et. al., *Gaoyang zhibuye jianshi*, page 72 for Fu Feng and page 99 for Hui Chang.

22. For details, see the Chen Meijian, et.al., *Gaoyang zhibuye jianshi*, 71.

23. All of the data for this section comes from a study of the cotton trade in Zhangjiakou undertaken by Ishida Hideji in 1919. The report, printed privately by the company, is held by the Mitsui Bunko. Ishida Hideji, *Chōkakō menpu bōeki,* Mitsui, April 1919.

24. See my paper "International Trade and the Creation of Domestic Marketing Networks in North China, 1860–1930," in *Commercial Networks in Modern Asia*, 96–115.

25. Kang Chao, *The Development of Cotton Textile Production in China* (Cambridge: Harvard University Press, 1977), 229. On Japanese-owned mills in China, see Takamura Naosuke, *Kindai Nihon mengyō to Chūgoku* (Tokyo: Tokyo Daigaku Shuppankai, 1982).

26. See Nishikawa Hiroshi, *Nihon teikokushugi to mengyō* (Kyoto: Minerva Shobō, 1987); Tōa Dōbunkai, *Shina keizai zensho* (Tokyo: Tōa Dōbunkai, 1907), 547–759; Uchiyama Sei, *Bōeki jo mitaru Shina fūzoku no kenkyū* (1915); Nishikawa Kiichi, *Shina keizai sōran 3: Mengyō to menshi, menpu* (Shanghai: Nihondō Shobō, 1924), pages 363–427 on the Tianjin cotton yarn and cloth trade and pages 429–73 on the trade in Qingdao; Nihon Yushutsu Men Orimono Dōgyō Kumiai Rengōkai, *Naigai shijō ni okeru honpō yushutsu men orimono no gensei* (1929), pages 1–152 on market customs in Tianjin.

27. John Brewer and Roy Porter, *Consumption and the World of Goods* (London: Routledge, 1993).

28. *Tsūsho Ihō,* 1911.

29. Julean Arnold, *China—a Commercial and Industrial Handbook* (Washington: Government Printing Office, 1926), 528.

30. *Hebei Gongshang Yuebao* 1, no. 7 (May 15, 1929), 6–8.

31. Kasahara Tokushi, "Boikotto undō to minzoku sangyō—Shanghai o chūshin ni," in *Kōza Chūgoku kingendaishi*, vol. 4 (Tokyo: Tokyo Daigaku Shuppankai, 1978), 117–47. The collection of materials on the May Fourth Movement in Tianjin edited by the Tianjin Historical Museum and the History Department of Nankai University, *Wusi yundong zai Tianjin* (Tianjin: Tianjin Renmin Chubanshe, 1979), includes a large number of documents related to the boycott movement.

32. Karl Gerth, *China Made: Consumer Culture and the Creation of the Nation* (Cambridge: Harvard University Asia Center, 2003).

33. Jing Rui, "Aiguo shangren Song Zejiu," *Tianjin Gongshang Shiliao Congkan*, vol. 5 (1986), 23–72. Also Rinbara Fumiko, "Qingmo Tianjin gong-shangyezhe de juexing ji quhui guonei yangbu shichang de douzheng," *Tianjin Wenshi Ziliao*, 41 (October 10, 1987), 1–34.

34. The Zhili National Products Support Committee (Guohuo Weichihui) decided that goods manufactured in China with imported raw materials were native products. See Ji Hua, "Guohuo Shoupinsuo shimo," *Wenshi Ziliao Xuanyi*, 31 (July 1962), 224.

5

Communal Resources

Gaoyang firms benefited from a business environment that supported economic growth. The creation of institutions that supported growth did not happen by chance; a group of local businessmen played a central role in guiding development. The organizational vehicle for their efforts was the Gaoyang Chamber of Commerce, founded in August of 1906 by a group of young businessmen who dreamed of reviving the textile industry in their hometown. At the time they were the proprietors of a group of small shops, mostly dealers in imported fabrics and miscellaneous goods, who had little money or experience, but large ambitions. Within the space of a decade they created the best-known rural industrial district of their day and earned prominent positions in provincial and national business organizations.

The young entrepreneurs were inspired by the contemporary national political discourse that called on the business community to work for national salvation through promotion of commerce and industry. This discourse, which also focused on the economic challenges posed by foreign powers, was part of a major intellectual shift in late-nineteenth-century China. For centuries state ideology and practice had privileged agriculture. Faced now with growing foreign influence in the domestic economy and mounting trade deficits, officials began to call for development of commerce and industry.

In the latter half of the 1890s, the Chinese press frequently reported discussions on the foreign commercial challenge, and comprador and theorist Zheng Guanying's collection of essays, *Warnings to a Prosperous Age*, became a best seller, read widely throughout the nation.[1] In that book, Zheng argued that China was faced with a new and serious crisis in the form of "commercial war" with the West. In order to win in the life and death struggle with foreign economic interests, the state needed to take immediate steps to promote commerce and industry, and the energy of private businessmen must be organized to pursue the same cause.

For a Chinese state that had long looked upon the merchants as a somewhat debased and parasitic group whose activities needed to be controlled, the shift to mercantilist policies that encouraged the pursuit of business represented a major shift.[2] Energized by the new and prominent position they were being given in the national polity, businessmen all over the nation responded to the call, forming new organizations like the chambers of commerce and founding hundreds of new enterprises.

There is no way to know precisely when the new ideas first became current among Gaoyang businessmen. In an account of the early activities of the Gaoyang Chamber of Commerce, Li Bingxi reported that a core group of businessmen began to get together for discussions in 1905.[3] At that time Zhili Province was one of the hotbeds of reform as Governor-General Yuan Shikai pushed his new government policies. Yuan and his colleagues sent frequent dispatches to magistrates throughout the province encouraging them to get involved in reform, and the Industrial Institute sent lecture teams into the countryside to explain the new ideas to officials and gentry. Paralleling these official initiatives were actions by concerned groups in Tianjin, who also got involved in promoting reform. Through public lectures, articles in newspapers, speeches at markets, and theater performances they aggressively sought to spread the reform message to all classes of Chinese society.[4]

The businessmen of Gaoyang found it very easy to link their own experiences to the new call for action. Gaoyang's traditional textile trade had declined as a result of competition with foreign products and their own efforts to revive the weaving industry were just what the call for national salvation through promotion of commerce and industry envisioned. Conscious of the need to improve their products and of the necessity to adopt new technology and train men with a new vision and new skills, local businessmen had no trouble applying the language of "commercial warfare" to their own situation. Their reports to the General Chamber of Commerce in Tianjin were generously larded with references to "industrial promotion," "national salvation," and the importance of promoting "national products."

As the Gaoyang Chamber of Commerce actively promoted the textile industry, the new ideas became the common language of a wider group of businesspeople in the local community. One indication of how these new ideas were interpreted can be found in essays written by students from the Gaoyang commercial school in 1915.[5] The students touched on many of the major themes of the new philosophy of the business class.

Liu Guangyuan took up the theme of competition between foreign and domestic products in the Chinese market, writing: "China is like a piece of meat, which the foreign powers are competing to devour." The solution to the problem was to develop commerce. "The twentieth century world is a world of commerce. If commerce is prosperous, then the country is wealthy, if commerce is in decline, then the country is lost. Although the foreigners now control the treaty ports in our country, our China is a land of vast spaces and many products. If we unceasingly devote our energy to the promotion of commerce and industry, create outstanding products, seek both skill and beauty, then we have nothing to fear from the foreigners, and our country's future will be assured."

One of Liu's classmates, Li Xuexiang, took up the question of national products:

Are campaigns to oppose foreign goods the way to promote national products? I do not believe that such campaigns represent a sustainable method. Why? Many national products are not well made, while foreign goods are both cheap and attractive. Can we ask people to give up buying superior foreign products and ask them to buy inferior national products? The better products win, and the inferior products lose. This is the natural process. . . . So how should we promote national products? I say the only way to do it is to promote the development of crafts and industry. Our country's craftsmen are skilled, their raw materials good. If we develop industry, we can make products that are both well made and beautiful. Then we will not need to have campaigns to drive out foreign goods; they will naturally disappear from the market. . . . Our compatriots are born in China. If they see that Chinese products are better than foreign ones, won't they all buy Chinese products rather than foreign ones? The time will come when this will be true.

In both of these essays we can identify the themes of nationalism and commercial challenge that characterized the new ideology. Written in 1915, the essays also express confidence that mobilization of energy and resources can successfully meet the foreign economic challenge. In Gaoyang, that confidence came from the success of the industrial promotion programs undertaken by the chamber of commerce. Let us then turn to look at the organization that created the web of institutions supporting industrial success.

CHAMBERS OF COMMERCE IN LATE IMPERIAL CHINA

The establishment of chambers of commerce was one of the key elements of the mercantilist policies of the late Qing reform movement.[6] Founded by representatives of business interests in the largest cities of China, the chambers were the first voluntary associations to be officially recognized by the imperial court as legal entities with authorized spheres of activity.[7] The chambers were most active as independent organizations in the first two decades of the twentieth century; after 1927, they would find their powers and independence curbed by the Nationalist government.[8]

When most of us envision the activities of chambers of commerce, our attention is drawn to their role in the big cities of China, in Shanghai, Tianjin, Hankou, Suzhou, and Canton.[9] The first chamber of commerce in China was founded in Shanghai in 1902, followed by those in Tianjin and Fuzhou in 1903, and in Nanjing, Xiamen, Chongqing, and Wenzhou in 1904. By 1912 there were 794 chambers of commerce, including 51 general chambers of commerce in the larger cities, and more than 700 branches in smaller county cities and marketing towns. Among those small-town chambers of commerce, the Gaoyang organization was one of the most active.

Writing in 1916, Li Bingxi, one of the early founders of the Gaoyang Chamber of Commerce, had this to say about those early years:

> In 1901 a group of gentry-merchants who wanted to improve the weaving industry jointly donated several hundred strings of cash. They purchased several looms and recruited apprentices to work in a small factory that they set up in a side room of the local academy. They were producing copies of foreign cloth. However, because the looms were not well made, the daily output of the small factory was quite small, and within a few months, they had used up all of the capital and the factory went out of business. Because of this unsuccessful experience, in later years no one was willing to raise the issue again.
>
> In the autumn of 1905 some gentry-merchants in the town including Han Weiqing, Yang Musen, Zhang Xinghan and Li Guiyuan started a primary level commercial school in the Guandi Temple on East Street in the town. Others then began to gather around them. Every time they met, discussions were held about forming a chamber of commerce. They discussed the depression in Gaoyang and its connections to the textile industry. They discussed methods for reform and progress, and recognized the close connections between commerce and industry. If you want to seek a flourishing of commerce, it can't be accomplished without development of industry. And to obtain development of industry, you must have the support of those in commerce. In order to promote this, it is essential to take measures to encourage home industry. . . . At that time we heard that foreign merchants in Tianjin had imported a new style of hand-powered loom. Han Weiqing, Yang Musen, Zhang Xinghan and Li Guiyuan went to Tianjin to investigate.[10]

When we compare this account of the founding of the Gaoyang Chamber of Commerce with those of chambers in the larger cities, we can identify several factors that distinguished the Gaoyang organization from those in the larger centers. First, in almost all of the larger cities chambers were built on the foundations of guild organizations. As Peng Zeyi and others have shown, Chinese guilds underwent significant changes in the years after the Opium War. As foreign goods entered the Chinese market, new guilds were organized among merchants who dealt in the import and export trade.[11] Many of the late-nineteenth-century guilds had already begun to act in more open ways. Where once guild membership was closely linked not only to craft but also to native place of origin, the late-nineteenth-century guilds welcomed into membership all those who wanted to join, and acted on behalf of their members to try to stabilize trade. When Qing government officials came to realize the need for strong commercial organizations to support their modernizing efforts, it was therefore natural that they turned to the guilds for assistance. In Tianjin, Yuan Shikai sought the assistance of guild merchants in recovery efforts after the Boxer Rebellion. Realizing the need for more coordinated efforts, he urged guild leaders to set up a chamber of commerce.[12] In Shanghai, Qing officials sent to negotiate a commercial treaty with the foreign powers were distressed to discover that foreign negotiators were in close contact with the foreign chambers of commerce in Shanghai, and as a result had a better sense of trade problems than did the Chinese negotiating team. Moreover, there was no single organization to which the Chinese negotiators could appeal for advice. Thus did officials come to encourage the leaders of powerful guilds to get together to form a Shanghai Chamber of Commerce, a new organization that would cut across the particularistic interests of the guilds.

In Gaoyang, there were no guilds to serve as the base for the new organization. Rather, a group of concerned merchants got together and started discussions among themselves. Although the Gaoyang Chamber of Commerce was one of the earliest founded in the smaller towns in Zhili Province, by 1911 there were four general chambers and sixty-one branch organizations in the province, covering approximately 50 percent of the county seats and larger market towns. While we only have records on a limited number of the smaller chambers of commerce, at least in Zhili, the initiative in many counties to start chambers came from the local magistrate.[13] The Gaoyang chamber, unlike many of the other small-town chambers, was from the beginning a voluntary activity of the people who were to become the leading merchants of the town.

The founders of the Gaoyang Chamber of Commerce were also different from their big-city counterparts in another way. In most of the urban chambers of commerce, leaders were drawn from the group Ma Min calls "gentry-merchants"—men who had business interests, but who also held degrees, titles, or ranks in the bureaucratic system. For Ma Min, gentry-merchants were a transitional group that appeared in the late Qing; somewhere in-between the classic merchants and gentry, he sees them as the forerunners of the modern industrialist class. While many of the degrees and titles held by the gentry-merchants were obtained through purchase rather than examination, holding of such titles and degrees gave prominent merchants access to bureaucratic channels that were normally closed to merchants who lacked such attributes.[14]

All of the founders of the Gaoyang Chamber of Commerce were men who were to make their fortunes in commerce. Most had received only a few years of private schooling before beginning to work in trade, and what additional polish they had acquired had come through on-the-job training as apprentices in commercial firms. While Yang Musen was proud of the honors he was given by Yuan Shikai for donating money to charitable causes, the more sophisticated urban gentry-merchants saw him as an upstart.[15] While the lack of classical education, degree, and rank may have handicapped Yang and other Gaoyang merchants socially when they sought to take their place on the larger national stage, it may also have been one of their strengths. Unlike other chambers of commerce where the gentry took the lead, criticizing the narrow interests and conservatism of their merchant colleagues,[16] in Gaoyang merchants took the lead and with single-minded determination promoted the local weaving industry.

A third factor that distinguished the Gaoyang chamber from chambers in the big cities was the dominance of members in one trade. The founders of the Gaoyang chamber were determined to revive the textile industry, and as the industrial district grew, managers and owners of textile firms dominated the organization. A 1915 list of officers and directors of the association shows only three who were not involved in the textile trade, and all three were employed by the chamber to handle its business affairs.[17] As a result, the Gaoyang chamber resembled a trade association (*tongye gonghui*). The commercial school established by the chamber was designed to train men for the textile trade, and negotiations with the government were directed to achieving special privileges for the weaving industry. This resulted in a close linking between collective projects and private business goals and gave the Gaoyang chamber a strong sense of cohesion that allowed it to act quickly and decisively and to raise funds to finance various projects.

As the industrial district prospered, many new firms were established to serve the growing town population, and membership in the chamber of commerce also grew. In 1910 there were just 12 member firms in the organization. In 1918, membership stood at 284 firms, and by 1934 membership had grown to 736 firms. Although merchants in other lines of business joined the chamber of commerce, it was still dominated by those in the textile trade. In 1934, the last prewar year for which figures are available, 83 percent of the chamber's budget, which came from membership fees, came from those in the textile trade.[18]

As individuals the directors of the chamber of commerce were owners or managers of firms that competed with each other. At the same time, as members of the chamber of commerce they worked together to build institutions that would nurture their common business interests. In the early years, collective projects focused on three major concerns: transferring new technology, training men with a new vision, and assuring a supportive business environment. Collective institutions included a currency market to stabilize exchange rates, a commercial and technical school to provide training for a new generation of business leaders, a textile research institute to gather and disseminate market and product information, and a set of negotiated agreements with the government that guaranteed preferential tax status.

As it built those institutions, the chamber of commerce gained skill in using the rhetoric of national salvation to promote the development of the industrial district. Leaders of the chamber realized that a close working relationship with government officials and with business leaders in other parts of the country could aid their efforts. Lacking the conventional qualifications that eased access to such circles, they turned to self-promotion as a way of gaining attention for their requests. By the early teens, leaders of the chamber of commerce had begun to promote the Gaoyang experience as a model for rural industrial growth. They also began to play a prominent role in the All China Federation of Chambers of Commerce. Let us then turn to an examination of some of the institutions they built and the roles they played in the growth of the industrial district.

Commercial and Technical Education

One of the first collective acts of the Gaoyang merchant community was the establishment of a night school for apprentices. This school held its first classes in 1905 in rooms attached to the Guandi Temple. It developed from a night school into a full-time secondary-level commercial school and then into a technical school training textile engineers in the late 1920s. The school, which was privately financed by the chamber of commerce, offered tuition-free education to students who the founders hoped would become the new leaders of industry.

Calls for the establishment of commercial and technical schools were a central platform of late Qing reform efforts. During the Hundred Days of Reform in 1898, reform proposals had included plans for industrial and commercial schools, and under the new policy reforms of Yuan Shikai, Zhili Province became one of the chief test points for educational reforms, including the establishment of technical schools.[19] In Tianjin, Song Zejiu, the prominent owner of a fabric wholesale and retail firm, set up a night school for commercial apprentices in 1904.[20] The motivation for organizing commercial schools in Tianjin and Gaoyang were very similar. China was facing a commercial war with foreign powers and needed men with broad general knowledge as well as commercial and industrial skills. While the traditional education provided in private schools and by private tutors taught basic literacy, texts were drawn almost exclusively from a classical curriculum that stressed moral education. The only form of training in the business world combined preliminary study in such traditional schools with on-the-job training provided through commercial apprenticeships.

The leaders of the Gaoyang Chamber of Commerce who had almost all been trained in the traditional way were convinced that a new style of education was necessary for the future: new industries demanded men with very different skills. The night school for apprentices and junior employees was started in 1905; in 1908, the chamber of commerce decided to regularize the school and its curriculum. Merchants donated funds to construct school buildings and housing for teachers. In 1910 the chamber successfully petitioned the Qing government to have the school approved as a junior secondary institution offering a three-year preparatory course and a three-year regular course. Funding for the school was also regularized when the chamber of commerce approved a compulsory surcharge on all cloth sales: firms paid a surcharge of six copper cash per bolt of cloth, which was put into a special fund to support the commercial school. Tuition and housing were provided free of cost, while the student paid for clothing, books, and meals.

A glance at the curriculum presented in 1910 (see table 5.1) shows that students studied a range of courses designed to give them knowledge in eco-

Table 5.1.   Gaoyang Commercial School Curriculum, 1910

Subject	First Year Hours/Week	Second Year Hours/Week	Third Year Hours/Week
Commercial Ethics	1	1	
Commerce	3	3	2
History of Commerce	1	1	2
Commercial Geography	3	3	3
Commodities	2		
Economics	4	3	
Principles of Accounting		2	2
Accounting	1	2	2
Commercial Law		2	2
Chinese Literature	2		
Topics in Commerce		3	3
English	12	6	6
Math for Business	4	4	3
Commercial Strategy			7
Statistics		1	1
Bankruptcy			1*
International Law			2*
Mechanical Engineering		2*	
Physical Education	3	2	

Source: Tianjin Dang'an Guan, Tianjin Shehuikexueyuan Lishi Yanjiusuo, and Tianjin shi Gongshangye Lianhehui, eds., *Tianjin Shanghui dang'an huibian,* vol. 1 (Tianjin: Tianjin Renmin Chubanshe, 1989–1998), 235–36.
Notes, seemingly added later, said that the items marked by * were too difficult and should not be included in the curriculum.

nomics, geography, English, and commerce.[21] The curriculum followed the broad outlines of commercial education in Japan, and the subjects, in slightly different form, are familiar ones in programs of business management in our own day. Foreign language study was encouraged to give the students a more international view, as well as to provide practical skills for dealing with foreign businessmen in the treaty ports and ease in sending domestic telegrams in China.[22]

The curriculum was revised in 1915, when the school was raised in level from a junior secondary school to a senior secondary school. Only one year of preparatory school was kept, and a fourth year of the regular course was added. Under the regulations of 1915, entering students had to be graduates of a senior elementary school. In the revised curriculum, students were introduced to world business history and world geography, and the fourth-year course in Chinese language was devoted to teaching students how to draft business documents and carry on business correspondence.[23] Both the 1910 and 1915 curricula included a practicum for students in their final year of study. The practicum combined laboratory work with on the job training in local business firms. While the graduates of the school were not required to work for local firms, graduates were in demand and many did work for local businesses.

The Gaoyang commercial school was recognized as one of the most successful of the merchant-sponsored commercial schools, and the men associated with it were regarded as experts on commercial education. When the journal of the All China Federation of Chambers of Commerce published a special article on commercial education, it included a photograph of Li Bingxi, principal of the Gaoyang school. Yang Musen also received honors from Yuan Shikai for his efforts in promoting the school.[24]

Although the school had been praised as one of the best in China, managers of the school still ran into problems. The school was funded by a surcharge, paid by the merchants, specifically for support of the school. In 1914 the county government diverted part of the funds for self-government activities. The Gaoyang Chamber of Commerce protested to the Tianjin General Chamber of Commerce, and the Tianjin organization dispatched one of its directors to try to settle the dispute. In an official protest, Yang Musen argued that Ministry of Education regulations specifically banned local government diversion of funds allocated for support of schools.[25] Although Yang and the chamber of commerce had the regulations on their side, they were eventually forced to compromise. The surcharge was raised to eight coppers per bolt of cloth, with six going to support the school and two to self-government activities.[26]

The Gaoyang commercial school continued to prepare graduates for careers in local firms until 1920. In July of that year, the political instability that had grown stronger in North China in the four years after Yuan Shikai's death came to directly affect Gaoyang. War broke out between the Zhili and Anhui warlord factions, and troops under the command of Li Kuiyuan occupied Gaoyang. The poorly provisioned troops began to cause trouble as soon as they arrived in the town, stealing food and extorting money from town residents. In September, representatives from Gaoyang and neighboring counties sent a delegation to Tianjin, asking the Zhili faction head, Cao Kun, to transfer the troops. Cao did not transfer the troops, nor did he pay them. In November the troops mutinied and the Gaoyang Chamber of Commerce was forced to "loan" 35,000 yuan and individual merchant houses 20,000 yuan to temporarily assuage the rioters. When the mutiny was finally put down, the troops were transferred to Baoding; before they left they set fire to the school, destroying a number of the buildings and all of the equipment and teaching materials.[27]

When the school was finally rebuilt in 1928, it took on a new life more in keeping with the demands of a changing industrial structure. When the commercial school was established in the late Qing, the chamber of commerce designed the school to provide business training for prospective employees of wholesale firms. By the late 1920s when the school was rebuilt, there were many mechanized dyeing and finishing plants in the town and the larger firms all recognized a need for employees with technical skills. The new school, renamed the Gaoyang Trade School (Gaoyang Zhiye Xuexiao), had two departments, one specializing in weaving and one in dyeing. The curriculum included courses on mathematics, business and accounting, chemistry, biology, and engineering subjects relevant to the weaving industry. In addition to new classrooms and dormitories, the school had an experimental laboratory equipped with the most modern looms and dyeing and calendering equipment. The chamber of commerce invested 40,000 yuan in rebuilding the school, which was set on spacious grounds on the outskirts of the town. Li Enbo, the owner and manager of En Ji, was first principal of the school.[28] Managers of the largest wholesale firms and factories sat on the board of directors and the teaching staff was recruited from men who had graduated from higher technical schools in China or abroad. Between 1927 and 1937, six classes, including slightly more than four hundred students, graduated from the school. Graduates had no difficulty finding jobs in local firms and factories and their presence contributed to a rise in the technical level of the industrial district.[29]

The original vision of the founders of the chamber of commerce also included provisions for continuing education for people working in the industry. In 1910, when the commercial school was raised to secondary-school status, the chamber also established a Commercial and Industrial Research Institute (Gaoyang Shangye Gongyi Yanjiusuo). Housed in the school, the institute held monthly lectures and discussions, bringing in experts on textile production and commerce, arranging for demonstrations of new equipment, and holding contests and awarding prizes to weavers who produced new designs and products.[30] Through such activities local businessmen were encouraged to improve the variety and quality of goods. That concern for good craftsmanship also won awards from outside the local community. In 1909 the Tianjin Gongyiju (Tianjin Technical Institute) evaluated Gaoyang cloth samples and reported that they were of superior quality, and in 1910, when Yang Musen sent cloth samples to the first Chinese-sponsored international exhibition, the Nanyang Exhibition in Nanjing; the Gaoyang cloth won a gold medal.[31]

The schools and the research institute made major contributions to the growth of the industrial district. They not only provided skilled employees for private firms, but also provided technological knowledge and commercial information to chamber members. As Gaoyang industry moved from the production of low-cost plain cotton weaves into the production of a more complicated product mix, those skills were increasingly important.

Native Cloth, Taxes, and the State

The schools and the research institute were paid for by the Gaoyang merchant community; construction of other collective institutions required outside support. In 1908, when the new textile trade was just beginning to develop, the chamber of commerce started a campaign for preferential tax treatment. At issue were native customs duties. The system of native customs had been established during the Ming dynasty to tax goods in transit. Customs stations were located along the northern frontier, in the Jiangnan region and along the coast, to tax goods that passed through the cities and ports where the customs stations were located.[32] This system of taxation was separate and distinct from the *likin* taxation system, established in the mid-nineteenth century, which also taxed goods in transit.

For Gaoyang merchants, one of the most important markets was the frontier region along the northern borders. Goods destined for frontier markets passed through native customs at customs stations near Beijing. Problems arose because of the different tax rates for goods of domestic and foreign manufacture. Under the treaty provisions, foreign imports paid import duties and a tax equivalent to 2.5 percent of value; the imports were then exempt from all domestic transit taxes. In the case of cotton fabrics, the taxes charged by native customs on cloth of domestic manufacture (*tubu*) were lower than the taxes charged on foreign goods. When the regulations were first established, customs inspectors could easily distinguish the wider, lighter fabrics of foreign manufacture from the narrow, heavy native product. However, Gaoyang goods were made in imitation of foreign goods; they were woven in wide widths and used imported yarns of higher counts. The possibilities for confusion were thus ever present. The situation was complicated by the

fact that some Chinese merchants tried to pass off foreign imports as domestic manufactures to qualify for the lower tax. The first collective efforts of
the Gaoyang Chamber of Commerce to deal with this complex issue were
made in 1908 when Han Weiqing, president of the chamber, sent a letter to
the Tianjin General Chamber of Commerce arguing that Gaoyang people
were working very hard to revive the textile industry and that their efforts
should be rewarded by special tax status. He made no specific proposals and
seems to have received no reply.[33]

Several months later a suggestion from a Gaoyang merchant, Xu Luming,
became the basis for a new round of appeals. Han reported on Xu's experience at the Tongzhou customs station. Xu, in discussions with the customs
officials in Tongzhou, noted that government policy promoted native industry. That being the case, shouldn't native goods be taxed at lower rates? Re-
sponding to the plea, customs agents decided that native cloth should be
charged lower fees. Learning of this discussion, the Gaoyang chamber wrote
to the Tianjin chamber asking for a general ruling. A reply from the supervi-
sor of Tianjin customs agreed that the lower rates were reasonable and
should apply henceforth.[34]

About a year later Han tried a new approach in response to continuing difficulties, offering a new proposal for action. Han began his plea as follows:
"In the success or failure of industry, the expansion and contraction of the
market is the most important thing. Of the transport routes for us, Beijing and
Tianjin are most important. The 'neck' in marketing is at the customs stations."[35] Han then went on to rehearse the efforts of the Gaoyang Chamber
of Commerce to respond to national calls for the promotion of industry,
quoting from an earlier government statement urging that customs give special treatment to native products. While the government had made efforts to
lower taxes on native goods, this had led some merchants to pass off foreign
goods as native cloth. The chamber of commerce proposed that they would
issue certificates to authentic Gaoyang cloth, which would stand as a guarantee that the cloth was of native origin. The initial response from the Ministry of Agriculture and Commerce was negative. "If inspectors carefully examine the cloth, there will be no confusion [between foreign and native
manufactures]."

Dissatisfied with the answer, Han sent off a second appeal, in which he
tried to make an even stronger case for the Gaoyang view. "When we first
began to consider reviving industry, the various merchants got together to do
research on the new machines, and to find some way to support the development of industry that would not require large amounts of capital. We
found a way for poor people to borrow money for the looms and begin
working." He described all of the ways in which the development of
Gaoyang industry had benefited both the weavers and the merchants. "As
you can see, the rise of Gaoyang's weaving industry is just the kind of activ-

ity that is being actively promoted now." He then argued that because the volume of cloth was increasing very rapidly, the customs agents did not have time to examine every bolt. The revised proposal suggested two steps: first, merchants would stamp the dealer's name on the cloth, and would register the dealer's seals with the customs service. Second, they would issue, as suggested before, certificates to merchants, certifying authentic Gaoyang cloth.

The second time around the appeal was approved, and the ministry issued orders to the customs station explaining the new procedures. In order to counter tax evasion, the customs station was ordered to keep records of the volume of Gaoyang cloth that passed through, recorded under the name of the wholesaler. The chamber would send to the tax office regular reports on how many certificates had been issued by each wholesale firm, and the two records were to be regularly cross-checked.

In the end, the persistence of the Gaoyang Chamber of Commerce won not only a guarantee of uniform taxes at the concerned customs checkpoints, but acceptance of their proposal for certificates of authenticity and, finally, the establishment of a system of receipts, much like the *zi kou dan* passes which were given to dealers in foreign goods once they had paid import taxes. In the case of foreign goods, the pass guaranteed exemption from payment of additional transit taxes. In the Gaoyang case, the receipts did not eliminate payment of transit taxes all over China, but did guarantee that once customs fees were paid, no additional taxes would be assessed on goods within the Tianjin customs area, which included Beijing and Zhangjiakou.

The native customs issue reappeared less than a decade later. In the summer of 1917, Gaoyang merchants got caught in the middle of a dispute between the two offices responsible for collecting native customs in Beijing. Chinese merchants from Tianjin and Shanghai—who the Gaoyang merchants describe as "traitor merchants"—tried to pass off imported fabrics as Chinese native product. In retaliation, the customs station at Chongwenmen raised the tax on cotton piece goods fourfold. Almost immediately the increased taxes led to a sharp decline in the volume of Gaoyang cloth passing through the station, dropping from 35,000 bolts a year before the increase, to just 6,400 afterwards.[36]

The Gaoyang complaint in 1917 was just one of hundreds that flooded government offices in Beijing. The national campaigns in 1915 against the Twenty-one Demands and the accompanying boycott movement had given new vigor to the national products movement, and merchants all over the country put increasing pressure on the government to take steps to encourage domestic manufacturers.[37] In December of 1915, and again in April 1916, the national government announced that it was lowering customs taxes on various national products, including certain kinds of cotton cloth.[38]

The new government announcements then touched off a debate about the meaning of "national products." The debate came just at the time when

Gaoyang firms were beginning to shift to higher-value-added products, which were less likely to be included in the "national products" category. The draft regulations, issued in late August 1918, excluded many Gaoyang products, including fabrics made with gassed and other fancy yarns, twills and patterned weaves, and lighter-weight fabrics made with higher-count yarns.[39] Revised regulations were issued in February 1919, adding the provision that "all kinds of cotton goods produced on new style hand looms will be accorded the same treatment [as native cloth]."[40]

In later years, new regulations would attempt to deal with an increasingly complex domestic industrial sector. Regulations drafted in 1928 considered such factors as the nationality of the owners and managers of manufacturing firms, the country of origin of raw materials, and the nationality of the workforce in determining whether products could be considered "national products." Most Gaoyang goods fell in category four, which included products manufactured by firms that were owned and managed by Chinese and that used a native workforce, but that used foreign raw materials.[41]

The customs tax issue is only one example of the campaigns undertaken by the chamber of commerce on behalf of the collective economic interests of its members. Other examples include a special appeal for relief aid in 1917 following a summer of severe flooding all across the Hebei plains region. The Zhili Provincial Chamber of Commerce took the lead in organizing the appeal for relief aid to revive the rural textile industry, which had suffered heavy damage as a result of the flooding. Eventually the provincial government joined with the chambers of commerce to sponsor a program of low-interest–loan guarantees to commercial firms in the cloth trade. Gaoyang firms and weaving households were among the chief beneficiaries of the loan program.[42]

Another instance of collective representation was the campaign to get lower rail rates for shipment. After the establishment of the Nationalist government in Nanjing in 1927, railroads were put under a government ministry that approved rail rates. At first Gaoyang cloth was put in the same category as fabrics produced in modern mechanized mills. The Gaoyang Chamber of Commerce petitioned the government for lower rates, and also sought the assistance of Li Shizeng; as a result of the appeals, Gaoyang cloth was shifted from the second-rate category to the fifth. One former merchant estimated that the shift in category saved firms close to 2,000,000 yuan a year in shipping fees.[43]

In 1924 another tax dispute led to the successful acquisition of land in Tianjin for construction of a guildhall (*huiguan*). In 1924, as in 1917, the late summer brought heavy rains and floods to the Hebei plains region. Transport was disrupted and yarn prices soared. The Tianjin tax bureau decided to take advantage of the rising prices and added a 2.5 yuan surcharge on each purchase of cotton yarn. The Gaoyang Chamber of Commerce, in collaboration with the Zhili Provincial Chamber (whose president was the Gaoyang merchant Zhang Xinghan), protested to the Finance Ministry in Beijing. As a result, the ministry ordered the Tianjin tax bureau to return the funds. The Tianjin tax bureau, lacking ready cash to repay the Gaoyang merchants, gave the Gaoyang Chamber of Commerce a plot of land in the heart of the Santiaoshi industrial district. The chamber of commerce decided to build a hall on the site, which served as a lodging house for merchants and also provided office space for the Tianjin branch offices of many firms.[44]

Not all of the chamber of commerce's plans were brought to fruition. Gaoyang merchants dreamed of turning their hometown into an integrated textile center with its own spinning mills, and in the 1920s they drew up plans to improve access by constructing a branch rail line from Baoding to Gaoyang. In both cases the projects proved to be too costly and had to be abandoned. In the 1930s, under merchant sponsorship, a small electrical power company was established providing electricity for streetlights and illumination in shops in the town. In the mid-1930s, Su Bingzhang, manager of Tong He, took the lead in trying to organize an expansion of the power plant to provide sufficient electricity to run mechanized equipment in the town's factories, which were all independently generating power. Su's plans for the power plant and revival of the railroad construction project were cut short by the start of the war with Japan.[45]

SELLING THE GAOYANG MODEL

Gaoyang entrepreneurs suffered from several disadvantages when they sought to approach government officials. They came from a small county, little known to outsiders, and their representatives lacked the degrees that were common among the urban gentry-merchants who led the chambers of commerce in large cities. Not only did they lack titles, they also had little experience in the social world of the upper class where officials, gentry, and wealthy merchants displayed their common interests through enjoyment of the theater and the arts.

As Gaoyang industry took off after 1908, the owners of the largest firms quickly became wealthy, but wealth did not immediately lead to higher status and acceptance in the world of the influential. Recognizing the problems they faced, the leaders of the Gaoyang Chamber of Commerce waged a publicity campaign to sell the success of their model to others. Their campaign for recognition involved publishing accounts that promoted the Gaoyang model. They also actively participated in provincial and national business organizations.

In 1908, when their efforts to promote the revival of the textile industry had just gotten underway, the Gaoyang Chamber of Commerce began to send reports to the Tianjin General Chamber of Commerce describing their efforts. In 1910 a detailed report appeared in the prominent Tianjin newspaper, the *Da Gong Bao*, written by Li Changsheng of Gaoyang.[46] And after the founding of the All China Federation of Chambers of Commerce, reports on Gaoyang were a regular feature of that association's monthly journal. In 1916 alone there were two articles on Gaoyang success in reviving the textile industry, both written by Gaoyang natives, and a long article on the Gaoyang commercial school including a complete description of the curriculum, rules, and regulations, and selections from essays written by the students.

The publicity campaign was effective, and within several years other areas in Zhili were already pointing to the Gaoyang model. As early as 1909, merchants in Shengfangzhen in Wenan County justified their desire to form an independent chamber of commerce by noting that if Gaoyang could have a chamber of commerce, then they too should be allowed to have their own organization.[47] In 1915 the magistrate of Ding County, in a report on the establishment of a county weaving training center, expressed his hope that Ding County would be able to emulate the success of Gaoyang, which had become a model for the whole province.[48]

Gaoyang ambitions extended well beyond Zhili Province. As efforts to build a national organization to coordinate the activities of the more than seven hundred chambers of commerce developed, Gaoyang merchants began to play prominent roles in the new national organization. While Gaoyang merchants were not present at the first national merchants' meetings in 1907 and 1909, they were on hand for the first formal meetings of the new national association in 1913 and 1914.[49]

The Gaoyang Chamber of Commerce first gained mention in the national press when they requested an emergency meeting of chamber of commerce representatives from all over China to act as mediators between Yuan Shikai and Sun Yatsen's new Nationalist Party in 1913.[50] Individual members of the Gaoyang chamber also began to play a more assertive role in the national organization. In 1914, after the national association had gained formal approval from the new Beijing government, the association began to publish a monthly journal. Yang Musen of Fu Feng was the chief force behind the founding of the journal, and during the first year of its publication each issue carried a notice from the Ministry of Commerce and Industry that listed Yang as the association's representative in negotiating government approval. As we have already seen, the journal of the national association carried numerous reports on Gaoyang activities. Also in 1914, Yang was appointed as one of the secretaries (*ganshi*) of the national association.

Yang's ambitions for even higher office were realized in September of 1916, when he was elected as a vice-president of the national association in a turbulent election that outraged many of the gentry-merchants from the larger cities. Yang and his supporters had carefully laid the groundwork for the presidential election, seeking support from the smaller chambers of commerce in the northern part of the country. When officers of the federation gathered in Beijing several days before the opening of the formal meetings, they found themselves split over the rules for representation and voting. There was general agreement that each provincial delegation should get ten votes, but no agreement on how to treat representatives from what were called "special districts." The special districts included Suiyuan, Chahar, Kulun, and Rehe, all areas where Gaoyang merchants exercised influence over local chamber of commerce affairs.[51] While many of the officers supported a plan that would give five votes each to such special areas, the Gaoyang merchants and their supporters demanded equal voting rights (i.e., ten votes each) for the special areas. Failing to reach a compromise, the issue was put before the general meeting on the morning of September 7, 1916. After much shouting back and forth, the general meeting moved to a vote with the special districts allotted five votes each. When the ballots were tallied, Yang Musen lost the presidency of the federation to Lu Daxian, a prominent Hubei gentry-merchant, by only three votes. Yang and his supporters, disappointed by the results, started shouting and shoving, breaking up the meeting. Feelings ran high as chambers of commerce from all over the country traded telegrams protesting the election. At a second meeting on September 18, Yang and Lai Enpei of the Gansu General Chamber of Commerce were elected as vice-presidents of the association.[52] Zhang Xinghan of Gaoyang was also selected as one of the secretaries of the association.[53]

The election of one of the leaders of the Gaoyang Chamber of Commerce to high office in the national federation was clearly a major accomplishment for men from such a small town. At the same time, the heated protests that broke out over the election reflected the doubts of urban gentry-merchants. Yang was accused of openly campaigning for the election, with suggestions that he had wined and dined influential members of the association to gain their support.[54] Others noted that Yang was merely a counselor of the Gaoyang Chamber of Commerce and did not have the qualifications to represent the national association. His lack of status and education, it was charged, would make it difficult for him to negotiate with government officials.

That Yang and his supporters had carefully plotted out their election campaign is obvious, and Zhang Xinghan and other members of the Gaoyang chamber did all they could to support the effort. Despite the harsh criticisms that followed Yang Musen's climb to power in the national federation, Gaoyang merchants continued to play an active role in national as well as provincial chambers of commerce affairs. In 1918 Zhang Xinghan was elected as one of the vice-presidents of the national organization, only to have his election cancelled because he had been accused of violations of currency regulations.[55] In spite of that, Zhang was later to go on to serve as president of the Zhili Provincial Chamber of Commerce in the 1920s.

CHAMBER OF COMMERCE AND THE COUNTY GOVERNMENT

Associations like the chamber of commerce have been at the center of an on-going debate about the potential for the development of democratic institutions in China. Those debates focus on questions about independent organizations that operate separate from the state. Taking hints from Jürgen Habermas's famous formulation of the rise of the public sphere in European bourgeois society, scholars have debated whether we can identify corresponding developments in China. Some would argue that the weakening of the Qing state and the rise of new-style voluntary organizations in the latter half of the nineteenth century resulted in a shift of control over some activities from the local government to civic organizations. Others, while recognizing the rise of voluntary associations, have argued that the relationship between the authoritarian state and such groups was qualitatively quite different from the arenas for public debate that Habermas has described in Europe.[56] In Habermas's famous analysis of Europe, the development of a public sphere for discourse and action empowered a new bourgeois class that came to oppose the authoritarian state, leading eventually to the creation of a democratic civil society.

Philip Kuhn was one of the first to argue for the devolution of political and administrative power in the late Qing in his study of the militias formed to suppress the Taiping rebellion.[57] His suggestions inspired further work by Mary Rankin, Joseph Esherick, and others, who have plotted the rise of new interest groups in local communities.[58] William Rowe's work on Hankow, particularly the role of various nongovernmental groups and associations in providing services in that city, is a powerful description of the ways in which important administrative tasks were handled by voluntary groups and associations.[59] In her work on the role of charitable and philanthropic associations in Shanghai, Kohama Masako has argued for the central role of the network of associations in the creation of urban society and the fulfilling of public services.[60] Where does the Gaoyang Chamber of Commerce fit in this discourse?

We need to begin our answer by considering the institutional structure within which the chamber of commerce operated. Beginning with Yuan Shikai's new government policies, increasing pressure was put on local administrative units. Not only were they to continue to fulfill their traditional responsibilities, including tax collection, public security and the administration of justice, they also were assigned new tasks, including establishment of modern public schools, building police forces, encouraging economic development, creating a public infrastructure of roads and communications including telegraph and postal services, and undertaking campaigns to eliminate harmful social customs like opium smoking and foot binding. They were also required to answer surveys and write reports on their progress in completing the various tasks.[61] While the list of responsibilities grew, the fiscal resources to pay for the new activities were much slower to come. Local governments were left to find ways to meet the new demands, and they increasingly turned to nongovernmental groups in the local community for assistance.

The local governments we see in the last decade of the Qing and in the Republican period down to the beginning of the war with Japan were thus transitional forms, and like all transitional forms they are difficult to classify. Some elements seem strikingly new, for example the implementation of commercial law codes or the curriculum of modern schools. On the other hand, some practices seem to be remnants of what Chinese scholars often refer to as the "feudal" past, such as the case of the magistrate who, against all written regulations, was able to force the Gaoyang Chamber of Commerce to support self-government activities by seizing school funds and refusing to release them, or that of another magistrate who, as late as the 1930s, was still settling all important legal cases himself, rather than sending them through the courts.[62]

The structure of the local government as well as the communal social configuration shaped, and at the same time constrained, the range of activities of nongovernmental actors like the chamber of commerce. While the merchants were involved in local administration as a way to protect their own interests, that involvement was limited. Formal county administration in the first two decades of the republican period still drew on imperial administrative practice. County magistrates were still appointed from outside—by the 1920s their appointment was usually managed by the warlord governments that controlled the province. Although the rules on avoidance that had stipulated that magistrates could not serve in their own home province were no longer in force, a list of Gaoyang magistrates in the late 1920s and early 1930s shows a parade of outsiders, all of whom served short terms; the longest tenure stood at less than three years and the average at around six months.[63] While the new appointees were now more likely to be graduates of modern administrative training programs rather than holders of traditional degrees, their short terms allowed for little familiarity with local problems. The first experiment with a county-level representative assembly was not even tried until 1936, when an effort was made to extend to North China the rules on self-government in force under the Nationalist government in the central parts of the country. This formal structure of administrative power meant that there were few arenas for open popular discourse at the local level.

A second major factor that shaped the actions of the chamber of commerce was the weakness of competing elite groups in the local community. Before the development of the weaving industry, Gaoyang was a poor county that lacked the wealth to support much in the way of a gentry elite. Gaoyang's location, close to the national capital of Beijing and the modern

treaty port of Tianjin, meant that those who did well on the provincial or national stage usually moved their base of operations to one of the two larger
cities rather than retiring back to their home area. This was true of at least
two locally prominent families, that of Li Hongzao and his son Li Shizeng and
the Qis, whose most famous twentieth-century member was Qi Rushan,
scholar of the Chinese theater and playwright for the well-known actor Mei
Lanfang.[64]

It was within this structure, in which there was little competition from ri-
val social groups and with a county government weakened by lack of funds
and frequent shifts of the top administration, that the chamber of commerce
came to play an important role in both the economic and political life of the
community. In doing so, however, it rarely set itself in opposition to government initiatives. In fact, the 1914 clash over the use of school funds is the
only instance where we can see open confrontation. In most other cases, the
relationship between the chamber of commerce and the county government
seems to have been one of cooperation, with the chamber of commerce investing energy and funds in promoting activities that the government supported but lacked the resources to pursue. In the discussions above we have
looked almost exclusively at chamber of commerce initiatives that were directly related to improving the business environment. In addition to those
activities, the chamber also took on other responsibilities in which it acted as
an adjunct to the county government. For example, in 1908 the chamber of
commerce responded to government campaigns against opium smoking by
helping to sponsor a society to cure opium addicts. And as we have already
seen, in 1920, when warlord troops mutinied, it was the chamber of commerce that stepped in to loan money to pay the troops. These are only two
examples of a larger pattern of chamber of commerce involvement in financing services in the local community.

In the late 1920s, chief taxing power lay with the provincial governments,
which in North China were still under warlord control. The land tax revenues
had been ceded by the national government to the provinces and were used
for provincial expenses, such as financing military units, and certain other
projects, including some educational institutions.[65] The drain of tax funds
away from the local economy was heavy, and few services were offered in
return. In Gaoyang in 1930, of the 65,953 yuan collected in land and miscellaneous taxes, the county government was only able to retain 3,891 yuan for
its own use.[66] To meet its own budgetary needs, the county government had
to make do with a patchwork assortment of surcharges added to provincial
taxes and special assessments.

The chamber of commerce, as the corporate representative of the wealthiest class in the local community, came to play an important role in local government financial activities. Chamber representatives joined with delegates
of the county government and of each sub-county district to form a Zhiyingju

(Management Bureau), which was responsible for arrangements for meeting special expenditures and tax assessments. In Gaoyang the merchants pledged to pay 30 percent of such special assessments, with the remaining 70 percent divided among the villages. Similar systems were in operation throughout most of Hebei, but the Gaoyang merchants seem to have assumed a higher proportional share than the merchants in other counties.[67]

In addition to the questions of taxes and transport fees and some support for local government finances, the main focus of chamber of commerce interest was in the preservation of social order. When that order was threatened in 1929–1930 by the rise of banditry, the chamber of commerce, with county government approval, created a merchant militia which assisted in policing the town. Although the Northern Expedition had officially been completed in 1928, there were a number of major and minor battles in 1929 and 1930. This continuing instability, together with the temporary influx of large numbers of men with military training following the demobilization of soldiers from the national and warlord armies, contributed to a steady rise in banditry in the central Hebei area. Mounted bands roamed the plains, raiding towns and harassing transport routes. In Gaoyang, the tombs of Li Hongzao's family were looted and there were numerous reports of isolated attacks on villages and market towns.[68] In 1929 the banditry had become so serious that it threatened the transport of yarn and finished goods, and the merchants felt that they had to join together to provide defense. Twenty men were recruited to join a "protection force" (*baowei tuan*), which was attached to the county public security bureau. In the following years the force was gradually increased in size and firepower, and its responsibilities expanded from protection of the roads and transport routes to include suppression of popular protest. By the mid-1930s, the annual budget for the protection force stood at 30,000 yuan, with the chamber of commerce pledging 30 percent and the remainder collected from extra taxes divided among the villages.[69]

The Gaoyang experience in the 1920s and 1930s supports the propositions of devolution of political power beginning in the late Qing. A weakened county government turned to the chamber of commerce for assistance with local administration, with technical education, with urban improvement in the town, with tax collection, and finally with public security. In matters related to growth of the textile industry, initiative clearly rested with the chamber of commerce; in those of a more general nature, the initiative usually came from the county government, which sought the assistance and support of a group with large financial resources at its command. Should we see the actions of the chamber of commerce as indications of the presence of a new public sphere for action by independent, intermediary social groups?

Since much of the debate over the public sphere is implicitly linked to questions about the possibility for democracy in China, we need to consider whether the chamber of commerce acted in democratic ways. To the extent that it was established as a formal, legal body with clear standards of membership and regulations for operation it did, at least in a structural sense, carry the possibility for a new kind of communal action. However, when we look at the lists of directors of the chamber of commerce over the years, there is also no question that leadership roles almost always went to the owners and managers of the largest business firms. As for its tactics in pursuing its goals, we again see a mixed picture. In some cases the methods of action of the chamber seem new. For example, in establishing the commercial school the merchants voluntarily agreed to pay surcharges on their business turnover to support an activity that they felt had great value. The content of the school's curriculum suggests a sincere desire to create a new business class with broader, more international interests.

One of the other chief ways the chamber of commerce pressed the interests of the business community was through petitions to the state. A reading of the documents reminds us that the republican state still exercised wideranging control over both public and private activities. Every public and collective project needed government approval—from establishing the chamber of commerce, to setting up the privately funded commercial school, to publishing a journal of the national federation, to seeking tax exemptions. Thus one of the chief jobs of the chamber of commerce was negotiating with the government. That organizations like the chamber of commerce could directly appeal to the government was new in the early twentieth century. Since there had been no formal recognition of such intermediary social organizations before, there was also no language or system of practices for dealing with such groups. Through the 1920s the chambers of commerce continued to address the government in the language of the old imperial court, although they used fewer of the terms that ritually debased the person(s) making the petition. While those petitions frequently refer to the commonly shared goals of economic development, there is little democratic discourse. Nor when their positions were rejected did they turn to other forms of organized political action. While merchants in the larger cities were often involved in the Nationalist politics of the 1920s and 1930s, only once in the early 1930s did the Gaoyang Chamber of Commerce get directly involved in a popular boycott movement, and that with somewhat unhappy results (as we saw in chapter one).

Rather than trying to create an independent space with a new democratic discourse in opposition to government policies, the Gaoyang Chamber of Commerce used traditional political practices. Great stress was placed on building networks of connections (*guanxi wang*) with officials and other businessmen. While they were happy to promote discussions and debates within the chamber of commerce on issues directly related to the textile trades, there is no evidence that they encouraged public debate on other issues. Controlled by the wealthiest and most powerful merchants, the chamber of commerce sought to build a business environment that supported specific collective and private business goals. The institutions and services the chamber created nurtured the industrial district, sustaining it until the beginning of the war.

NOTES

1. Soda Saburo, "Shinmatsu ni okeru 'shōsen' ron no tenkai to shōmukyoku no setchi," *Ajia Seikei Gakkai Ajia Kenkyū* 38, no. 1 (October 1991), 47–78; Sato Shinichi, "Tei Kanei ni tsuite," *Hōgaku* (Tohoku University) 47, no. 4 (1983), 56–106; *Hōgaku* 48, no. 4 (1984), 30–76; and *Hōgaku* 49, no. 2 (1985), 34–89. Sato notes that the book had become a late Qing best seller with more than 100,000 copies in print.

2. Ma Min, *Guanshang zhi jian—shehui jubianzhong de jindai shenshang* (Tianjin: Tianjin Renmin Chubanshe, 1995).

3. *Quanguo Shanghui Lianhehui Huibao* 3, no. 9/10 (1916). I would like to thank Yu Heping for help in getting copies of relevant articles.

4. Li Xiaoti, *Qingmo de xiaceng shehui qimeng yundong, 1901–1911* (Taibei: Institute of Modern History, Academia Sinica, 1992). One of Li's main sources is the Tianjin *Da Gong Bao*.

5. *Quanguo Shanghui Lianhehui Huibao* 3, no. 7 (1916).

6. Ma Min, *Guanshang zhi jian*; and Yu Heping, *Shanghui yu Zhongguo zaoqi xiandaihua* (Shanghai: Shanghai Renmin Chubanshe, 1993).

7. See chapter five of Ma Min, *Guanshang zhi jian*, where he argues that the chambers of commerce were the first voluntary organizations on a national level to be so recognized.

8. The story of the rise and decline of influence of the chambers of commerce is told in Yu Heping's work, *Shanghui yu Zhongguo zaoqi xiandaihua*.

9. Mark Elvin , "The Administration of Shanghai, 1904–1914," in *The Chinese City between Two Worlds*, ed. Mark Elvin and G. William Skinner (Stanford: Stanford University Press, 1974), 239–62; Edward Rhoads, "Merchant Associations in Canton, 1895–1911," in *The Chinese City between Two Worlds,* 97–117; Ma Min and Zhu Ying, *Chuantong yu jindai de erzhong bianzou—wan Qing Suzhou Shang Hui gean yanjiu* (Chengdu: Bazhou Shu She, 1993); Xu Dixin, *Shanghai Shanghui shi, 1902–1929* (Shanghai: Shanghai Shehuikexueyuan Chubanshe, 1991); Hu Guangming, "Lun zaoqi Tianjin Shanghui de xingzhi yu zuoyong," *Jindai Shi Yanjiu*, 1986:4, 182–223.

10. *Quanguo Shanghui Lianhehui Huibao* 3, no. 9/10 (1916). (All translations, unless otherwise indicated, are by the author.)

11. *Zhongguo gongshang hanghui shiliao ji* (Beijing: Zhonghua Shuju, 1995).

12. Hu Guangming, "Lun zaoqi Tianjin Shanghui de xingzhi yu zuoyong."

13. The Tianjin chamber of commerce archives include reports on Li Yinggeng, who served as prefect of Xundefu and later of Zhengdingfu. Wherever he served, new chambers of commerce appeared. See Tianjin Dang'an Guan, Tianjin Shehuikexueyuan Lishi Yanjiusuo, and Tianjin Shi Gongshangye Lianhehui. *Tianjin Shanghui dang'an huibian*, vol. 1 (Tianjin: Tianjin Renmin Chubanshe, 1989),

192–95 on Xundefu; 212–216 on Zhengdingfu. (Hereafter this work is cited as *Tianjin Shanghui dang'an huibian*.)

14. Thirty-seven of the directors of the Suzhou chamber had degrees, of which 86 percent were purchased. All of the directors of the Tianjin Chamber of Commerce held degrees. Ma Min, *Guan shang zhi jian*, 80, 100.

15. *Quanguo Shanghui Lianhehui Huibao* 3, no. 9/10 (1916). In figure 2.1, Yang is wearing all three of the honorary medals he received.

16. This patronizing attitude of the gentry members comes through very clearly in materials from Cizhou prefecture. In a report from the Cizhou Chamber of Commerce to the Tianjin General Chamber, the authors, who were almost all degree holders (*shengyuan*), complain, "The merchants of this town are not seeking after improvement of methods but rather are only thinking of sales." *Tianjin Shanghui dang'an huibian*, vol. 1, 196–97.

17. *Quanguo Shanghui Lianhehui Huibao* 3, no. 5 (1916).

18. *Gaoyang xianzhi*, 1995. The Gaoyang Chamber of Commerce can be found in thirteen of the sections on organizations.

19. Abe Hiroshi, "Shinmatsu gakudo kō—Chokureisho o chūshin to shite," *Bunka ronshu* [Fukuoka Kodai], 1 (1966), 45–88; and Douglas Reynolds, *China, 1898–1912: The Xinzheng Revolution and Japan* (Cambridge: Harvard University Press, 1993). On chamber of commerce involvement in education see chapter five of Yu Heping's *Shanghui yu Zhongguo zaoqi xiandaihua*.

20. Rinbara Fumiko, "So Sokukyu to Tenshin no kokka teishou undo," in *Kyoto Daigaku Jinbun Kagaku Kenkyūjo Kyōdō Kenkyū Hōkoku, Go-shi Undō no Kenkyū*, vol. 2, no. 6 (Kyoto: Dōmyosha, 1983).

21. *Tianjin Shanghui dang'an huibian*, vol. 1, 231–39.

22. In the days before the cybernetic revolution, sending telegrams in Chinese was a cumbersome process. Each Chinese character had to be converted into a four-digit code. The recipient then had to translate the message.

23. *Quanguo Shanghui Lianhehui Huibao* 3, no. 7 (1916).

24. See biography in the *Draft Gaoyang xianzhi*.

25. Yang's report can be found in the Tianjin Shanghui archives, item 3648, Tianjin Municipal Archives.

26. Liang Guochang, *Gaoyang sili zhiye zhongxue yilan*, July 1934.

27. Zhongguo Dier Dang'an Guan, ed., *Beiyang junfa tongzhi shiqi de bingbian* (Nanjing: Jiangsu Renmin Chubanshe, 1982), 175–200.

28. Chen Meijian, et.al., *Gaoyang zhibuye jianshi, Hebei Wenshi Ziliao*, vol. 19, 1987, 165–66.

29. Liang Guochang, *Gaoyang sili zhiye zhongxue yilan*.

30. *Tianjin Shanghui dang'an huibian*, vol. 1, 231–34.

31. *Tianjin Shanghui dang'an huibian*, vol. 1, 1316–1318. Winning a gold medal at the Nanyang Exhibition was a major accomplishment. Products had been selected from all over China, and only sixty-six first class (gold medals) were awarded. Ma Min, *Guanshang zhi jian*, 296.

32. Hamashita Takashi, *Chōgoku kindai keizaishi kenkyō* (Tokyo: Tōyō Bunka Kenkyūjō, 1989), 309–98.

33. *Tianjin Shanghui dang'an huibian*, vol. 1, 1315–16. Communications between branch chambers and government offices were transmitted by the general

chamber of commerce with which they were affiliated. Peng Zeyi, ed., *Zhongguo gongshang hanghui shiliao ji*, vol. 2 (Beijing: Zhonghua Shuju, 1995), 970–77.

34. *Tianjin Shanghui dang'an huibian*, vol. 1, 1318–20.

35. The editors have dated this document to before November 29, 1909; *Tianjin Shanghui dang'an huibian*, vol. 1, 225.

36. Gaoyang Chamber of Commerce, dated July 1, 1917, *Tianjin Shanghui dang 'an huibian*, part 2, 2686–87.

37. For a sample of the appeals, see documents on the national salvation organizations established in 1915 in *Tianjin Shanghui dang'an huibian*, part 2, vol. 4. Zhili Shanghui requests for reduced taxes on native cloth were reprinted in the *Quanguo Shanghui Lianhehui Huibao* 3, no. 11/12 (1916). On the native products movement, see Ji Hua, "Guohuo shoupinsuo shimo," *Wenshi Ziliao Xuanyi* 31 (July 1962), 221–36; and Quanguo Zhengxie Wenshibian, *Zhongguo jindai guohuo yundong* (Beijing: Zhongguo Wenshi Chubanshe, 1995).

38. *Tianjin Shanghui dang'an huibian*, part 2, 3538–41, 3550–51.

39. *Tianjin Shanghui dang'an huibian*, part 2, 3555.

40. *Tianjin Shanghui dang'an huibian*, part 2, 3556–57.

41. *Tianjin Shanghui dang'an huibian*, part 3, vol. 2 (1928–1937), 1480–81.

42. Tianjin Shanghui archives: er lei, 886; san lei, 3648. Tianjin Municipal Archives.

43. Interview with Han Xianghui, former manager of the Tianjin *waizhuang* (branch) of one of the major Gaoyang firms, May 28, 1980.

44. *Draft Gaoyang xianzhi*. Also, Chen Meijian, et.al., *Gaoyang zhibuye jianshi*, 162–63.

45. Su Bingzhang and Li Futian, *Jiangnan shiye canguan ji* (Gaoyang: Privately published, 1936).

46. *Da Gong Bao*, May 24, 1910.

47. *Tianjin Shanghui dang'an huibian*, part 1, 247–52.

48. Reports dated November 22, 1915, and December 11, 1915. The second report expresses the hope of the Ding County magistrate that the new training center will set Ding County on the same successful route as Gaoyang. These reports are included in a set of several thousand note cards copied from the Ding County archives in the mid-1930s. The cards are in the collection of the Institute for Economic Research, Nankai University.

49. Yu Heping, *Shanghui yu Zhongguo zaoqi xiandaihua*, chapter 2. For Gaoyang participation in meetings, see *Tianjin Shanghui dang'an huibian*, part 2, 526–27. For a list of delegates at the meetings in 1912 and 1914, see Suzhoushi Dang 'anguan, "Zhonghua Quanguo Shanghui Lianhehui diyici daibiao dahui," *Lishi Dang 'an*, January 1983, 44–50.

50. Yu Heping, *Shanghui yu Zhongguo zaoqi xiandaihua*, chapter 5.

51. Two of the officers of the Zhangjiakou Chamber of Commerce, Wang Jiguang from He Ji and Song Yunlu who represented Guang Yu, were from Gaoyang. *Tianjin Shanghui dang'an huibian*, part 2, 519–20.

52. *Da Gong Bao*, September 8, 1916, plus documents in the *Tianjin Shanghui dang'an huibian*, part 2, 544–52. Correspondence between Tianjin delegates and the Tianjin Chamber of Commerce are in the Tianjin Shanghui archives, disanlei, file 195.

53. *Tianjin Shanghui dang'an huibian*, part 2, 552.

54. The Tianjin General Chamber of Commerce was in the forefront of the protests against Yang Musen, and there are suggestions that leaders of the Tianjin General Chamber were hoping one of their own members would be elected. On the 1918 election, see reports in *Shen Bao* on June 8, June 10, and June 25, 1918. For Bian Yinchang's use of money politics, see the report on "Current Situation of the Tianjin national association meetings," in *Shi Bao*, April 29, 1918.

55. *Shen Bao*, June 8 and June 18, 1918.

56. William Rowe, "The Public Sphere in Modern China," *Modern China* 16, no. 3 (July 1990), 309–29; "Symposium: Public Sphere/Civil Society in China?" *Modern China* 19, no. 2 (April 1993), entire issue.

57. Philip Kuhn, "The Development of Local Government," in *The Cambridge History of China*, ed. John K. Fairbank and Albert Feuerwerker, vol. 13, part 2 (Cambridge: Cambridge University Press, 1986), 329–60.

58. Joseph W. Esherick and Mary Backus Rankin, *Chinese Local Elites and Patterns of Dominance* (Berkeley: University of California Press, 1990).

59. William Rowe, "The Problem of 'Civil Society' in Late Imperial China," *Modern China*, 19 (April), 1993, 139–57; Frederic Wakeman, "The Civil Society and Public Sphere Debate: Western Reflections on Chinese Political Culture," *Modern China* 19 (April), 1993, 108–38.

60. Kohama Masako, *Kindai Shanghai no kōkyōsei to kokka* (Tokyo: Kenbun Shuppansha, 2000).

61. Tianjin Academy of Social Sciences has a manuscript for a survey of Wuqing County done in the last days of the Qing.

62. *Gaoyang xianzhi*, 1995.

63. *Hebei Yuekan* 3, no. 1 (January 1935).

64. See Liu Fenghan and Li Zongtong, *Li Hongzao xiansheng nianpu*, 2 vols. (Taibei: Zhongguo Xueshe Zhucuo Jiangzhu Weiyuanhui, 1969); and Qi Rushan, *Qi Rushan huiyilu* (Taibei: Zhongyang wenwu gongyingshe, 1956).

65. Li Rui, "Hebeisheng gexian nianlai zhi junshi zhiying," *Da Gong Bao, Jingji Zhoukan*, September 20, 1933.

66. *Gaoyang xianzhi*, 1932, 134–38

67. Reports from Shenze County, southwest of Gaoyang, report a 12–88 percent split between merchants and the general population. Mantetsu Hokushi Jimukyoku Chōsabu, ed., *Kahokusho zeisei chōsa hōkoku* (1938).

68. Nagano Akira, *Dōhi, guntai, kosokai* (Toko: Shinmondai Kenkyūjo, 1931), 120–21. *Da Gong Bao*, July 29, 1932.

69. *Draft Gaoyang xianzhi,* in the section on military affairs.

6

Wartime Collapse

From the beginning of its rise as an industrial district, Gaoyang industry was enmeshed in a web of finely intertwined relationships that linked rural producers to suppliers, markets, and financial institutions outside the local community. Modern textile mills supplied the yarn, finished goods were marketed in a nationwide market, and accounts were settled through Tianjin native banks. The Japanese invasion in the summer of 1937 ripped apart this web of relationships and brought production in the industrial district to a sudden halt. Although it would not have been immediately obvious to contemporary observers, in hindsight we can see that the war also marked the end of Gaoyang industry under the direction of the relatively large firms whose growth we have followed in the earlier chapters. When industry entered a second phase of growth, after the Japanese surrender in 1945, a system based partly on socialist prototypes and partly on small-scale, locally generated workshop capital would play a central role. In this chapter we will look at the collapse of the industrial district as a result of the Japanese invasion, the wartime attempts to revive production, and what those processes reveal about the internal dynamics of the Gaoyang system of production.

The Japanese armed invasion of China was triggered by the well-known clash at the Marco Polo Bridge outside Beijing in July 1937, and the first brunt of the Japanese attack fell on the central Hebei plains. The plains region became one of the focal points of struggles between the Japanese occupying armies and the Chinese Communist Party–organized resistance. The first of the wartime anti-Japanese base areas, the Shanxi-Chahar-Hebei anti-Japanese base area (Jin-Cha-Ji), was created in this area in 1938; Gaoyang was in the center of the central Hebei base, which was a subregion of the Jin-Cha-Ji anti-Japanese base area. The first headquarters of the central Hebei anti-Japanese resistance was set up in Gaoyang and throughout the war years the former weaving areas were part of the core of the resistance zone.

The war was bitterly fought, as Japanese forces struggled to gain political and economic control over the strategic plains, and losses were heavy on both sides. By the early 1940s Gaoyang was garrisoned by regular Japanese forces and their Chinese puppet allies who had built six strong points in the county and had troops in fortified watchtowers in more than twenty villages.[1] More than twenty-five hundred people in Gaoyang lost their lives as a result of active participation in the wartime resistance struggles; this number does not include those who were victims, but not active members of the resistance.[2] Although this chapter will touch only tangentially on the political and social issues related to the resistance struggle, it is important to keep them in mind as the background to the other changes that took place.[3]

As Japanese armies began their swift advance south from Beijing and Tianjin in the summer of 1937, moving down the major rail lines that cut across the North China Plain, local governments dissolved. Magistrates, local government officials, and members of the local police forces retreated before the advancing armies. In Gaoyang the owners and managers of firms hastily boarded up their shops and factories, shipping their inventories of finished goods to safer cities. Some of the entrepreneurs fled to the safety of the international concessions in Tianjin, others to Japanese occupied Beijing and Baoding, and still others to unoccupied regions further south. Operations in almost all factories, workshops, and wholesale companies were suspended, and many of the factory workers, shop clerks, and hired weavers joined in the flight, taking refuge with their relatives in the countryside or heading for larger cities where they hoped to find employment.[4]

Two basic patterns emerged from the chaotic conditions that seized central Hebei in the summer of 1937. In some counties, members of the local elite organized Peace Preservation Committees (*Zhian weichi hui*) that maintained order until the Japanese arrived. Peace Preservation Committees were later converted into collaborationist governments. In other counties, and Gaoyang fits this pattern, the sudden departure of the county government and most of the local business elite paralyzed those who remained. The departure of organized security forces left a vacuum, opening the door to banditry, and the rise of banditry led to the organization of self-defense forces. The Japanese could gain control only by placing military forces in such counties. The resistance was stronger, and there was much greater loss of life and property.

Control of the Gaoyang region shifted hands several times in the early years of the war. The Japanese army briefly occupied the town in October 1937 during their first southern advance. Resistance forces under the former Nationalist officer Lu Zhengzao arrived in November 1937; they set up a temporary headquarters in the city and then left. In April 1938 Lu's forces returned, driving out the Sakagaki division of two hundred fifty men and beginning a nine-month period in which the resistance built an infrastructure of administrative and popular organizations to support the anti-Japanese struggle.[5] In January of 1939 Japanese forces returned to the Gaoyang area, garrisoning the town and building fortified outposts in many villages and marketing towns. Resistance forces were pushed to outlying villages. The Japanese would continue to garrison the town for the remaining war years, holding it through the summer of 1945, when CCP attacks launched in early September freed the city from Japanese occupation.

The bitter struggles in the central Hebei region made revival of rural industry impossible. During the early war years (1937–1941) most of the wholesale firms that had played a central role in creating the industrial district were either destroyed or transferred out of the region.[6] The marketing structures that had been carefully built and nourished over the years were pulled apart as North China cities, which were occupied by the Japanese, were separated from the rural resistance zones under the leadership of the CCP. Raw materials no longer entered the rural industrial district, and, following the disastrous floods of the summer of 1939, impoverished weavers were forced to sell their looms in exchange for cash.

In looking at the collapse of Gaoyang weaving during these years, we can thus see a massive disinvestment in the material base of production: machinery was sold off or moved to other places, the entrepreneurs who managed the system left, and the weavers who possessed skills and equipment could not operate without the wholesale firms and finishing factories which had supplied raw materials and guaranteed markets.

ENTREPRENEURIAL CAPITAL DURING THE WAR

While the early entrepreneurs began their firms with small investments of capital, by the 1930s the Gaoyang system was dominated by a number of large firms that had extensive systems of sales branches all over the country. As we saw in chapter three, the largest of the firms had capital holdings well over 1,000,000 yuan, with the largest group of firms owned by the Yang family passing 2,000,000 yuan. There were two separate categories of Gaoyang firms: the firms that began as commercial enterprises and the firms that grew out of workshops. These two forms of capital met very different fates during the war years. Almost all of the wholesalers lost their fortunes by the middle war years, while many of the workshop-based firms transferred their bases of activities to the occupied cities of Beijing, Tianjin, or Baoding, and were able to survive the war years with some of their capital intact.

Fu Feng, the flagship of the Yang family firms, was bankrupted by a series of miscalculations by its managers between 1938 and 1941. Yang Musen was

seventy-three in 1937 and had already stepped back from day-to-day management of his firms. In July 1937 Yang's managers and senior employees
packed up their inventories of fabric and shipped them to their Beijing
branch, which now became the Fu Feng head office. Yang retired to his
home village of Nanbianwu. There he recruited a private defense force to
protect his property, refusing all invitations to join in the anti-Japanese resistance. Yang died in his hometown in 1939, at the age of seventy-five.

Fu Feng began trading in Beijing in 1938, initially surviving off the profits
from sales of existing stocks. Since the Gaoyang production system had been
shut down, managers realized that their inventory would soon be exhausted;
if they did not take steps to reinvest, rising inflation would consume their
capital. The managers also realized that there were fortunes to be made in
wartime China. The disruption of trade and production had produced shortages of many goods in the unoccupied areas. As Japanese control in Beijing
tightened, the Fu Feng managers decided to shift their base of activities to
Nationalist-controlled areas to the south. All the branch offices in North
China were ordered to sell remaining inventories and transfer funds to the
Beijing headquarters. The managers in Beijing invested the capital in goods
that were in demand in the interior and made plans to ship the goods to the
town of Shangqiu in eastern Henan Province, which was near the line dividing the occupied and unoccupied zones. Arrangements were made to pay
off puppet troops so that the goods could be transported across the lines.
The convoy transporting the goods, however, ran into a Japanese patrol.
When inspectors discovered a large volume of nationalist currency in the
shipment, the Fu Feng employees were arrested and the goods confiscated.
In late 1940, efforts to close out the southern branches of Fu Feng and transfer assets to the interior also failed.

Not all Yang family efforts were failures. Yang Mingchen, eldest son of
Yang Musen, moved from Beijing to Luoyang in 1940, where he set up a National Products Improvement Society. He recruited workers from Gaoyang
who worked to improve old-style looms by adding flying shuttles. He also
set up a fabric-printing workshop to process cloth woven by local weavers.
Mingchen's nephew, Yang Yuetan, joined him in Luoyang and set up a
leather factory. Almost all of the managers and technicians in the Yang family's new enterprises in Luoyang had worked for Fu Feng, Da Feng, or Yuan
Feng in Gaoyang. The new companies continued their operations in Luoyang until the Japanese occupied that city in 1944.[7]

Most of the other large Gaoyang wholesale firms had similar experiences
during the war years. In almost all cases, their proprietors transferred inventories out of Gaoyang and used profits from their sale to create funds for
other trading ventures. However, few found success. It is perhaps not surprising that Fu Feng and other Gaoyang firms were not very successful in
their wartime speculative ventures. The success of Gaoyang wholesale firms

had been based on the careful construction of business networks and the accumulation of commercial knowledge that were specific to the textile trade. When these textile entrepreneurs branched out into the highly speculative business of wartime trade, where success depended on very different skills and networks, they were no better equipped than other novices. The size of the capital they had to invest only made their losses more dramatic. By the end of the war, the large wholesale firms that had led the first cycle of development in Gaoyang had all gone bankrupt, their fortunes dissipated by wartime losses and inflation.

The proprietors of the firms like He Ji and Tong He that had grown out of workshop capital survived the war years much more successfully. Entrepreneurs with technical skills had established these firms. Such firms had much heavier investments in fixed capital resources—machinery and buildings—that could not be moved and reinvested so easily. At the beginning of the war the factories were closed. Most entrepreneurs left Gaoyang, delegating the task of guarding their factories and equipment to workers. During the war years some of the equipment was sold off and some appropriated by the occupying army or the resistance forces; only a small proportion of the original material base was left at the end of the war.

The proprietors of the workshop-based firms, like those in the wholesale trade, scrambled to make a living in their new locations. However, since they had technical skills, it was easier for them to start over again, establishing new enterprises. Li Enbo, the proprietor of the En Ji mechanized dyeing and calendering factory and principal of the Gaoyang Trade School, moved to Beijing, taking along more than forty of his workers. He set up a headquarters in En Ji's Beijing branch office, and in 1938 established a small bleaching and dyeing factory. In 1939 Li's factory got a contract from the Japanese army. Li's new venture flourished and he continued to operate the factory in Beijing until the socialization of commerce and industry. In 1955, his factory was incorporated into the Kuanghua Dyeing Works. Li was retained as chief engineer.[8]

The textile industries in both Beijing and Tianjin benefited from the input of Gaoyang capital and technical skills during the war years. The foundations for Beijing's modern dyeing industry were laid during the early war years, with the lead taken by Gaoyang men like Li Enbo.[9] In Tianjin there was a similar influx of workshop capital from Gaoyang, and Gaoyang entrepreneurs established many new weaving and dyeing workshops there during the early war years.[10]

WEAVERS DURING THE WAR YEARS

While most of the larger entrepreneurial families left Gaoyang, most of the rural weavers stayed at home and struggled to survive in the hostile environment of the resistance war. Their fate was directly influenced by the economic strategy of the Japanese occupation forces. Japanese strategy in North China was based on the premise that North China could be profitably integrated into a larger Japan–Korea–Manchuria–North China economic bloc; agricultural products and natural resources would be exchanged for industrial goods from Japan and Manchuria.[11] Although the plan was phrased in terms of integration, in fact the role envisioned for the North China region was that of a colonial dependency which would supply crucial raw materials for Japanese industry and serve as a market for Japanese manufactured goods. In the North China plains region, the most important raw material was cotton. In the prewar years North China had been a major supplier of raw cotton for the export markets; in the 1930s North Chinese cotton was traded through the port city of Tianjin and the chief buyers were Japanese. Chinese cotton was exported to the Japanese home islands or processed in Japanese-owned spinning mills in Tianjin, Qingdao, and Jinan. Thus, in drawing up their plans for expansion of the textile industry, the Japanese were hoping to build on this prewar base, planning to expand production and strengthen their control over the market.[12]

Cotton was also of crucial importance to the Chinese weaving industry. In the immediate prewar years the Gaoyang region was involved in multiple ways in the cotton industry: as an exporter of raw cotton, as an importer of yarn, and as an exporter of finished piece goods. For some years grain production had been only a supplementary occupation for most families, whose level of prosperity was determined instead by the cash income derived from weaving. As we have seen earlier, some 70 to 80 percent of the average family income of rural households in the region came from the weaving industry, and Japanese administrators after 1939 realized that economic and social stability was impossible without some effort to restore the base of rural family income.[13]

When the Japanese occupied Gaoyang in January 1939, they found a region that had suffered heavy losses in the first two years of the war. Most of the local elite had fled and there were few local collaborators willing to join in a Japanese puppet administration. The Japanese-appointed magistrate and all of his subordinates came from other parts of Hebei; the magistrate was a graduate of the Japanese military academy.[14] A census conducted in 1941 showed a drop in the county population of over 20 percent, from 180,408 recorded in a 1935 census to 140,264 counted in 1941. Some of the most obvious losses of population were in the town. When the Japanese occupation forces arrived in January 1939 the town had for all practical purposes been abandoned by its residents; the first of the Japanese garrison forces found a town population of only 500, mostly beggars, in a town that had once been a bustling commercial center of 15,000. As order was restored, the population gradually increased so that by late spring of 1939 the town population had risen to 3,000. Most of those who returned were the poor who were living off handouts from the Japanese-sponsored government.[15] The thick brick-faced walls that had once surrounded the town had been torn down in 1938 to ease the movement of resistance forces, and factories and shops were shuttered and the streets were almost deserted. In the countryside those who had been employed as hired weavers had left, since there was no employment once the wholesalers and factories shut down. Many rural weaving households, pressed to desperation by the lack of food, had been forced to sell their looms; the looms were broken apart, with the wooden frames burned as fuel and the iron gears sold as scrap metal. By the end of the war years there were less than 1,800 of the prewar total of 30,000 looms still in existence.[16]

Japanese administrators made an effort—largely unsuccessful—to restore the weaving industry. In reviving weaving, policies of economic recovery were combined with social control in a system that put the industry under Japanese management. Weavers in the town were invited to join a Japanese-sponsored weavers' association that was controlled by the New People's Association (Shinminkai), a Japanese organization that was given the task of providing civilian assistance in pacification efforts. In order to join the weavers' association a candidate had to have a guarantee letter and had to agree to move his loom into the town, which was garrisoned by the Japanese military. A villager from Nanyuantou, near the town, reported that he had participated in the Japanese-run weaving program. He and his five-member family had moved into town, taking their loom. He recalled that twenty families from his village participated in the program and members of the twenty families had provided guarantee letters for each other. With the population of the town greatly reduced, it was not difficult to find cheap housing; fees paid for weaving were stable until the last year of the war and prices in the occupied town were also fairly stable. The supply of yarn for weaving was handled through a rationing system managed by the weavers' association.[17]

The weavers' association operated under the supervision of a Japanese trading firm that supplied the yarn and purchased the finished piece goods. The Kitazawa Yanghang arrived in Gaoyang in April 1939, just after the reoccupation of the town, and began operations in January 1940. Kitazawa soon ran short of capital and in May 1940 sold out to one of the giants of the Japanese textile industry, Tōyō Menka, a branch of the giant trading firm Mitsui Bussan. Tōyō Menka continued to operate in the Gaoyang area until the end of the war.[18]

Encouragement of indigenous business was one of the goals of the Japanese administration and a Japanese-sponsored chamber of commerce was established in 1939,[19] but the Japanese firm's monopoly of the supply of yarn from Japanese-owned spinning mills in Tianjin made it difficult for Chinese firms to enter the trade. Throughout the war years raw cotton and yarn were in short supply and were rationed through an industry-wide association, which gave first priority to the mechanized weaving mills in Tianjin. The small trickle of yarn reaching Gaoyang—only some 4 percent of the 1934 level—was insufficient to induce a revival in the weaving industry.[20]

Given the extreme shortage of raw cotton and cotton yarn and the inability of Japanese mill operators to keep their factories operating at even a fraction of their capacity, it is not surprising that the effort to revive rural weaving failed. What is surprising is that the attempt at restoration was made at all. Tōyō Menka seemed to have almost nothing to gain by diverting supplies of rationed yarn to rural weavers. The dyeing and finishing factories that had played a major role in creating the distinctive characteristics of Gaoyang cloth were almost all closed. Synthetic fibers were no longer available and, according to the reports of both Japanese investigators and weavers who participated in the program, all of the output was of unbleached cotton cloth. Transportation was difficult over land and water routes that were harassed by guerrilla attacks. With the prewar marketing system in a state of collapse, the output of Gaoyang looms was absorbed into the Tōyō Menka system: cloth was dyed and finished in Tianjin factories and marketed under the Tōyō Menka brand name. It is not surprising that even with a monopoly Tōyō Menka had difficulty making a profit on the Gaoyang trade. Investigators from the research department of the South Manchurian Railroad who studied the Gaoyang economic situation in 1942 advised that the industry should be returned to Chinese control in hopes that indigenous operators might be more successful in putting the industry on a profit-making basis.[21]

REFLECTIONS ON THE INDUSTRIAL
DISTRICT MODEL OF DEVELOPMENT

The war destroyed the prewar Gaoyang system of production, and neither the Japanese nor the resistance forces had much success in trying to revive it.[22] The patterns of collapse of the industrial district during the war years remind us of the factors that made the district so successful during the first three decades of the twentieth century. Production in the Gaoyang industrial district was linked to national markets for raw materials and finished products. Similar to many export-oriented industrial districts in our contemporary world, Gaoyang producers in the early twentieth century imported raw materials from urban factories and from abroad for rural processing and then exported the finished goods for sale in a national market.

During the war years many entrepreneurs, technicians, and weavers left the Gaoyang area and migrated to Tianjin, Beijing, and other cities, where they set up new workshops and factories. This spatial relocation was motivated by several considerations. First, the cities, although under Japanese occupation, were more secure. Second, the cities—particularly Tianjin—were home to modern spinning mills, which meant that it was much easier to acquire raw materials. Finally, it was much easier to find customers in the urban regions than in the far-flung marketing areas in frontier regions and smaller towns.

This wartime relocation of the entrepreneurs and weavers raises questions about the original location of the industrial district in Gaoyang. If ready access to the source of raw materials was an advantage during the war years, why was it not so in the earlier decades of the century, when Gaoyang weavers had so successfully competed with the small weaving factories of Tianjin? This question, in a broader sense, applies to the whole Chinese experience with rural industrial districts, not only in the early twentieth century, but also during the postwar recovery and in the reform era. What are the dynamics that allow rural industrial districts to survive and grow in highly competitive market systems, and why have their urban rivals, with seemingly more advantageous locations, not experienced the same level of success? Let us briefly reflect on what the prewar Gaoyang experience has to say with regard to these questions.

We can identify four factors that are crucial to an understanding of why the industrial district developed. First, the small core of merchants who set out in the first decade of the twentieth century to revive industry in their hometown aggressively promoted the textile industry. Yuan Shikai's industrial promotion policies created conditions favoring the development of the weaving industry and the Japanese export promotion campaign made raw materials available on relatively generous terms. We might think of this side of the equation as the "push" factors providing the technology and raw materials. What determined whether that "push" would stimulate production, and, if it did, where, was action by regional merchant communities. Some communities, because of their own internal dynamics, took advantage of the opportunities offered by the new initiatives.[23]

The second and third factors that shaped the development of the industrial district grew out of the decision to promote the local textile industry. Gaoyang's continuing success across three decades was the result of the creation of a business and marketing infrastructure that supported the local production system. Here the gradual development of the system of sales agencies with their important information-gathering functions was a crucial step. The sales agency system allowed Gaoyang firms to adapt creatively to changing marketing conditions presented by the development of the modern textile industry in the coastal cities. When modern mills began to move into the markets for low-cost fabrics, Gaoyang producers were able to shift to a strategy of flexible production of a wide variety of goods in part because they had a well-developed marketing network that provided information on demand in regional markets.

The fourth factor contributed at this point: the concentration in one region of people with both business and technological skills. As the product mix was diversified, the attention to dyeing techniques and textile design were increasingly important. The technical school trained people for the industry, but equally important was the creation of a group of business leaders who had respect for technology and innovation and were willing to pay relatively high salaries to engineers and skilled workers.

The re-creation of a rural industrial system in Gaoyang in the immediate postwar period and then again in the reform era is testimony to the initiative of rural entrepreneurs, as well as to the vitality of the rural industrial district as an organizational form.

NOTES

1. Gaoyang County Communist Party Committee and the Gaoyang County Archives, ed., *Hebei Sheng Gaoyang Xian zuzhi shi ziliao, 1930–1987* (Shijiazhuang: Hebei Renmin Chubanshe, 1992).

2. There is a list of revolutionary martyrs in the biographical section of the new *Gaoyang xianzhi*, 1995. The list includes the names of 2,879 people who died in revolutionary activity; 95 percent of them died between 1937 and 1949.

3. My Ph.D. thesis, "Rural Society in Revolution: the Gaoyang District, 1910–1947," completed in 1975 at the University of California, Berkeley, is concerned with the war years and the social and economic changes induced by the wartime resistance struggle. Among the recent publications that deal specifically with the Gaoyang experience during the anti-Japanese war are Gaoyang Party History Editorial Committee, *Gaoyangxian geming douzheng dashiji* (Yazhou Chubanshe, 1992); Baoding CCP Propaganda Bureau and the Baoding Party History Research Office, ed., *Baoding kang-Ri zhanzheng lishi ziliao huibian* (1995); Gaoyang Party History Research Office, "Xin guomin yundong dui Gaoyang renmin de zanhai," *Hebei Wenshi Ziliao Xuanyi* 15 (1985), 101–5. For short essays written by participants in the struggles see Jizhong Yiri Xiezuo Yundong Weiyuanhui, *Jizhong yiri*, originally published in 1942 and reprinted in 1959.

4. "Kōnichi seiryoku no shokōsaku to shin seiken no katsudō jōkyō chōsa hōkoku—Kahokusho seitei oyobi Kōyō-ken ni okeru," *Rikushi Mitsu Dai Nikki* 46, April 1939, 118. The *Rikushi Mitsu Dai Nikki* is a chronological compilation of original documents held by the War History Office of the National Self-Defense Forces in Hiroo, Tokyo. This account was confirmed in interviews with local residents who had worked for wholesale firms at the beginning of the war. Su Bingjie of Tong He joined the forces resisting the Japanese invasion. Su died of illness during the resistance war, while one of his employees went on to become a general in the People's Liberation Army. Interview with former Gaoyang merchants, May 1980.

5. Chen Kehan, *Mofan kangri genjudi Jin-Cha-Ji bianqu* (Chongqing: Xinhua Ribao, 1939), 17.

6. During the Japanese occupation only two factories continued in operation. Longdetang was a jacquard-weaving factory, located at the East Gate of the town with

fifty jacquard looms. The proprietor worked on contract to a shop in Baoding. The other factory was a weaving and fabric-printing workshop in Beiquantou village. Chen Meijian, et.al, *Gaoyang zhibuye jianshi, Hebei Wenshi Ziliao*, vol. 19, 1985, 33.

7. Chen Meijian, et.al., *Gaoyang zhibuye jianshi*, 74.

8. Chen Meijian, et.al, *Gaoyang zhibuye jianshi*, 146–47.

9. Zhongguo Renmin Daxue Gongye Jingjixi, ed., *Beijing gongye shiliao* (Beijing: Beijing Chubanshe, 1960), 314.

10. The archives of the Tianjin trade organizations include registrations for many small workshops whose proprietors are listed as natives of Gaoyang, Li Xian, or Renqiu.

11. Kobayashi Hideo, *Daitōa kyōeiken no keisei to hakai* (Tokyo: Ochanomizu Shobō, 1975).

12. Jerome Cohen, *Japan's Economy in War and Reconstruction* (Minneapolis: University of Minnesota Press, 1949), 34, notes that 87 percent of Japan's total investment in China was in the cotton industry. Tōyō Bōseki, *Tōyō bōseki nanajunen shi* (Osaka: 1953), 422, shows Japan's rising dependency on cotton from China and Korea.

13. Hu Rengui, *Youjiqu jingji wenti yanjiu* (Shanxi: Huanghe Chubanshe, 1939), 82.

14. "Kōnichi seiryouku no shokōsaku to shin seiken no katsudō jōkyō chōsa hōkoku," 120.

15. Ōshima Tadashi and Kabayama Yukio, "Jikenka ni okeru Kōyō shokufugyō," *Mantetsu Chōsa Geppō*, 1942, 21–62.

16. Gaoyangxian Renmin Zhengfu Caizheng Jingji Bangongshi, "Gaoyang xian 1954 nian shougongye diaocha gongzuo zongjie," October 1954, mimeographed copy held by the Gaoyang County archives, 4.

17. Interview with former weavers, May 1980.

18. Ōshima and Kabayama, "Jikenka ni okeru Kōyō shokufugyō," 52.

19. Wang Tianzhai, who served as head of the collaborationist chamber of commerce, was executed shortly after the liberation of Gaoyang in 1945.

20. Ōshima and Kabayama, "Jikenka ni okeru Kōyō shokufugyō," 52.

21. Ōshima and Kabayama, "Jikenka ni okeru Kōyō shokufugyō," 61–62.

22. The resistance had greater success with the more primitive handicraft spinning and weaving in some nearby counties. Central Hebei Administrative Office, "Jizhong fangzhi ye," handwritten report, November 1948.

23. Tanimoto Masayuki suggests the "push" and "pull" factors approach. In Tanimoto's Japanese cases, the actions of local merchants who aggressively took advantage of imported raw materials were crucial in determining the location of industrial districts. Tanimoto Masayuki, *Nihon ni okeru zairaiteki keizai hatten to orimonogyō—shijō keisei to kazoku keizai* (Nagoya: Nagoya Daigaku Shuppankai, 1998).

II

The first part of this book examined the prewar development of the Gaoyang industrial district, looking at management forms, production, marketing, and the development of collective resources by the business community. The second part of the volume will explore the development of the Gaoyang industrial district over the last half of the twentieth century and to the present, a period in which China first created a socialist economy, and then introduced market-oriented reforms. During this period, small-scale industry in Gaoyang experienced two periods of rapid growth. The first, from 1945–1953, coincided with the postwar recovery of the Chinese economy, and the second, from 1978 to the present, has taken place under the economic reform policies that have introduced market principles and allowed private enterprises to develop. Sandwiched between these two periods of small-scale industrial growth were more than two decades of high socialism, which created a system in which all major economic decisions were shaped by the national economic plan. During those two decades small-scale industry in Gaoyang virtually disappeared. In its place was a state industrial sector that had been built on the foundations laid by the private firms. In the town, a group of state-owned factories produced cotton and rayon fabrics, towels, and printed specialty items like sheets and tablecloths. In the countryside, a small number of individuals were employed in the single workshop that each village was allowed to operate. Since employment opportunities in the weaving industry were limited, most of the rural population devoted their working hours to agriculture. That division of labor prevailed until the early 1980s, when the economic reform policies allowed Gaoyang industry to enter a new era of growth.

The second part of this book will explore the development of the Gaoyang industrial tradition as it interacted with the socialist economic system. Chapter seven traces the process of the postwar revival and the subsequent banning of private trade and household weaving during the campaigns for the socialization of commerce and industry. Chapters eight and nine analyze the revival of small-scale industry during the era of the economic reforms. Our central question with regard to both phases is how small-scale industry, which was seemingly destroyed—once during the wartime period and then a second time during the socialization of commerce and industry in the mid-1950s—was able to make such strong comebacks. How did entrepreneurs use the Gaoyang tradition to aid in the building of new factories and firms? How do contemporary firms compare with those created during the first phase of growth? What does the dynamic pattern of small-scale industrial districts like Gaoyang tell us about the Chinese economy as it enters the twenty-first century?

ENTREPRENEURIAL LEGACIES

Growth in Gaoyang small-scale industry in both the second and third phases of growth was strongly influenced by entrepreneurial legacies from the prewar period. In part two of this book we will examine the ways in which the institutional and entrepreneurial legacies of the first phase of growth were adapted to fit the changing economic and political environment over the last fifty years, and the role they played in small-scale industrial growth.

Let me begin by offering a simple definition of what I mean by "entrepreneurial legacies." I use this term to describe the repertoire of business practices, interfirm relationships, and entrepreneurial spirit created in the Gaoyang industrial district during the first phase of growth. The first generation of entrepreneurs, including the wholesale merchants, the owners of small factories and workshops, and the weavers, collectively created the industrial district. While these pioneers drew on practices that had long been used in traditional commerce and handicraft industry, they adapted those traditional practices to meet the demands of changing textile markets and the developing economic and institutional systems. As was demonstrated in part one, the institutional framework adapted to work with new forms of transportation, interfaced with a modern banking system, was affected by the movement for economic nationalism, took advantage of new technical and business training schools, and much else.

When a new generation of entrepreneurs in the postwar period set out to revive the Gaoyang industrial district, they did not begin with a blank sheet, but rather with the legacies provided by their predecessors. Those entrepreneurial legacies provided guidelines in a number of different ways. First, they provided knowledge of business practices: how to organize a business partnership, methods for pooling capital to support a business, ideas about how to set up marketing networks, and much more. Second, they provided a handbook of knowledge specific to the textile trades. Third, they provided assurance, based on past history and experience, that small-scale industry could produce prosperity for a large number of individuals in the local community. Finally, the entrepreneurial legacies of the first generation created a large body of individuals with a willingness to take economic risks. They created an entrepreneurial spirit that was commonly shared not only by those who had the funds to set up factories and wholesaling firms, but also by the members of thousands of rural weaving households, who dreamed of building their family workshops into larger enterprises.

Gaoyang was certainly not the only region in China with this kind of local entrepreneurial tradition. During the late imperial period powerful cliques of merchants from Huizhou and Shanxi dominated China's domestic long-distance trade. In other regional markets, locally based cliques of merchants dominated trade in certain lines of goods. In regions where such entrepreneurial traditions were strong, it was much easier for a young man to enter a commercial apprenticeship, a step that was often the beginning of an entrepreneurial career. In such communities there was a critical mass of individuals with skills and connections in the business community who kept alive the commercial tradition, passing down entrepreneurial practices from generation to generation.

While the socialization of commerce and industry in the mid-1950s seemed to mark the end of the private business culture, the rebirth of private businesses in the 1980s and 1990s has shown that local entrepreneurial traditions were not so much dead as only temporarily displaced. As scholars have turned to the study of China's new entrepreneurial class, they have found in community after community strong connections that link prewar entrepreneurs to the new entrepreneurial class.[1] Ivan Szelenyi, the sociologist who investigated similar phenomenon in socialist Hungary, asked how bourgeois or entrepreneurial traditions were passed on from one generation to the next in the absence of private property.[2]

In the Chinese case, efforts were made to root out such entrepreneurial traditions after the revolution. At the time of land reform in the late 1940s, every individual was assigned a class status, and children and grandchildren inherited those class statuses.[3] Classification as a member of the former capitalist class attached a stigma to an individual and his family. In addition to constant ideological pressure, former "capitalists" were often subject to criticism during mass campaigns. Moreover, state pressure was sometimes exercised in more direct ways. One illustration of this was a show trial held in Gaoyang in 1963. Massive floods had hit the central Hebei plains in the summer and fall of that year. In order to protect Tianjin from destructive flooding, dikes that should have protected the Gaoyang region were deliberately breached, heightening the impact of the flooding on the plains. In Gaoyang, the flooding only added to the misery from lowered living standards in communities that had only just begun to recover from the Great Leap Forward. Two weavers in the village of Liguozhuang who still owned their own looms started weaving without official permission. Accused of violating national regulations and displaying an unacceptable petty capitalist spirit, they were given show trials and sentenced to prison terms of fifteen and twenty years.

In spite of such government efforts to extirpate the entrepreneurial tradition, the spirit survived to serve as inspiration for a third phase of growth beginning in the 1980s. In the Hungarian case, Szelenyi identified what he called an "embourgeoisement trajectory" in rural society that was passed down in families who had made the transition from peasant to entrepreneur farmer or rural manufacturer. Under socialism, he also identified what he called "parking orbits," which were positions in society that allowed entrepreneurially inclined individuals to preserve skills that could be used when the market economy was reintroduced.

In the Gaoyang case we can also identify practices that led to the preservation of entrepreneurial legacies, although that was clearly not the intention. One crucial aspect of the Gaoyang industrial tradition was the sharing of knowledge and skills specific to the textile industry. Those skills and knowledge were preserved in two important ways. First, a crucial core of trained individuals was transferred out of Gaoyang in 1954, when the region was stripped of approximately twenty-five hundred skilled workers and technicians who were assigned to work in newly constructed state textile factories in Baoding, Shijiazhuang, Tangshan, and Handan.[4] This cadre of Gaoyang workers and managers, who had spent several decades working in state-owned textile factories, could be called on to provide technical and managerial skills when private capital was again allowed to develop. State-sector factories in Gaoyang also provided positions and training to a new generation of textile workers and engineers. The second way in which skills were preserved was through management of village industrial activities. Although almost all village factories during the era of high socialism were small and quite primitive, the individuals running them were able to develop skills that would serve them well when the collectives were disbanded and free trade was again allowed.

Another factor that acted in Gaoyang's favor was the relatively short span of state socialism. Men who had been weavers in their youth remembered what life had been like during the first and second phases of growth. It was they who could provide the inspiration to family-based economic endeavor, which inspired many households to take the risks to invest in equipment and begin rural industry in the late 1940s and again in the 1980s.

NOTES

1. See the work of my colleague David Wank on the business class in Xiamen. David Wank, *Commodifying Communism* (Cambridge: Cambridge University Press, 1999). Much of the work on Wenzhou development suggests very similar processes.

2. Ivan Szelenyi, *Socialist Entrepreneurs—Embourgeoisement in Rural Hungary* (Madison: University of Wisconsin Press, 1988).

3. The system of assigned class status has gone out of use. But from the early 1950s to the early 1980s, coming from a "bad" class background, which meant coming from the prewar elite, was a stigma that could blight a career, education, and marriage chances.

4. While local interests would have been better served by state investment in modern factories in Gaoyang, that was not to be. Gaoyang's inconvenient location and distance from important transportation routes may have been the reason why it was not chosen to be one of the new textile centers. It is clear that none of the North China cities that were chosen had the kind of trained personnel that were present in Gaoyang. See the brief sketches of Handan, Shijiazhuang, Baoding and Tangshan in Xu Junxing, *Hebei chengshi fazhanshi* (Shijiazhuang: Hebei Jiaoyu Chubanshe, 1991).

7

From Market to Plan:
The Second Phase of Growth

There are many different ways to organize the production and sale of consumer goods. In the first part of this book we examined one of those ways,
the industrial district, and the industrial and commercial system that grew up
around it in rural Gaoyang in the early twentieth century. The industrial district developed within an institutional structure characterized by a relatively
weak state that placed few extra-economic restraints on independent firms
and actors. There were major changes in the institutional setting during the
war years, most importantly the Chinese Communist Party's creation of
strong party and state organizations in the anti-Japanese resistance bases.
When Gaoyang industry entered its second phase of growth after 1945, it
was within this radically changed institutional environment, and state organizations came to play a major role in the recovery of the weaving industry.
In the 1950s, decisions by the party and state organizations brought an end
to small-scale industry in rural Gaoyang.

This chapter will trace the shift from production mediated by the market
to that mediated through the plan, and the consequences of that shift for
weaving households and entrepreneurs. The story of Gaoyang in these years
is one small part of the story of the socialization of the Chinese economy. In
the account that we will present here, the story of the dramatic changes in
economic organization that took place in the early 1950s will be told in a way
different from that of the standard texts. Most accounts of the socialization
process have been presented from the perspective of policies and state actors, including the government and party officials who designed and implemented the policies that are collectively referred to as "the socialization of
commerce and industry."[1] In this account we will look at the "socialization"
process from the bottom up, using our case study of one industrial district to

examine the ways in which policies acted on a rapidly changing local industrial system. The historical records from those years present a story of
stops and starts, of plans initiated and then aborted, of multiple, simultane-
ous movements that interacted in complex ways.

Before turning to the complex record of events, let us begin with a simple
summary of the issues that came into contention during the second phase of
growth. The decade between 1945 and 1955 saw a contest between the prewar model of the industrial district, with its private firms and actors, and a
new model of industrial and commercial organization that traced its origins
to experiments in the anti-Japanese base areas during the resistance war.
This alternative, which provided part of the model for China's socialist economy, introduced two new forms of organization: rural production cooperatives and state-run firms. Both eventually came to play important roles in the
transformation of the industrial district. These two new organizational forms
were closely linked to government initiatives through a strong state apparatus that had gained legitimacy through its leadership of the wartime resistance to Japan.[2]

While the beginning of state planning in China is usually associated with
the adoption of the first Five Year Plan (1953–1957), government economic
planning on a regional level had been important in the many anti-Japanese
base areas during the war years.[3] Government-centered economic initiatives
were continued in the newly liberated areas between 1945 and 1949. While
the degree of state intervention in the economy intensified in later years,
even in the immediate postwar period, when the economy was still funda-
mentally based on market principles, government policies and organizations
played a significant role.

State intervention in economic development during the civil war and reconstruction periods of the early 1950s took a number of forms. Party authorities at the base-area–level formulated economic goals for each year and
used a combination of financial incentives, administration regulations, tax
laws, and mobilization through mass campaigns to push development in the
directions they wished to encourage. In the early years, the chief forms of
government intervention included the provision of low-cost loans to commerce and industry to encourage and stimulate private investment, lower tax
assessments on income from targeted industries, and provision of technical
assistance.

Alongside this encouragement to essentially private enterprise was the
growth of a state-controlled sector in the form of state-owned trading firms
and small factories. Many of the state-owned commercial enterprises traced
their origins to the state firms that had been set up in the resistance base areas during the war.[4] In the early stages of development, the business operations of public trading companies differed little from private commercial
firms, and in most cases their personnel was drawn from those who had

gained experience in prewar private firms. Managerial responsibility, however, rested with state cadre assigned by the base area government, and profits went to the state organization that had provided the capital. During the transitional period from 1949–1952, state-run wholesale firms were given an enlarged role, including a monopoly over the supply of yarn, and in 1952 they were incorporated as the local branches of the state monopoly firm, the Huashabu Gongsi (Cotton, Yarn and Cloth Trading Company). In addition to the new state commercial firms, there was also a group of state-operated factories in Gaoyang. All of the state-owned factories traced their origins to the liberated area government's much disputed assumption of control over private factories that had been "abandoned" by their former owners.

The transition from government guidance and encouragement to state control was not always smooth. State policies were often contradictory. On the one hand, the party wanted a rapid economic recovery, and on the other hand it had promised relief to the poor. The clashes between the conflicting goals were very apparent in the Gaoyang region and resulted in struggles over the control and development of industry. The Chinese Communist Party had long prized its role as the representative of workers and peasants and strove to establish more equitable relations between capital, weavers, and the workers in the small workshops and factories. Yet while seizing property from capitalists or promoting shorter working hours and higher wages played well to this peasant and worker audience, it did little to promote efficient production or encourage entrepreneurs to risk their capital in new ventures. Caught in the contradictions between economic efficiency and broader social and political goals, local governments enacted policies that showed an ambivalence toward private entrepreneurs that ran counter to publicly stated national policies on the protection and encouragement of private capital.

A second major change in the postwar setting was the absence of an independent, organized voice to represent the interests of the entrepreneurial class. Where entrepreneurs of an earlier generation had created the Gaoyang Chamber of Commerce to support their business interests, entrepreneurs during the second phase of growth were excluded from the formal policy-making process. Although the three-story edifice of the chamber of commerce was still the most prominent building in town, businessmen no longer gathered there to make the decisions that would shape the development of their industry. The center of action had shifted to the county government, which had taken over the old government offices that had been used by the imperial and republican county governments. When government officials wanted to communicate with the owners of firms and factories, they called them together to receive lectures on policy changes from local government cadre. Although there were no formal bans on independent, voluntary alliances among businessmen, the party-supervised Federation of Commerce and Industry (Gong-Shang Lianhe Hui) was the only collective body for the business community. It had been created after the war, following the pattern of all party-directed mass organizations, which were designed to transmit and assist in the implementation of government policies.

PERIODIZATION OF THE TRANSITION

The nine years of the second phase of growth can be roughly divided into two periods distinguished by the nature of the political regime and the degree of economic integration between the rural and urban economies. The first period, from 1945 to early 1949, included the civil war years. During these years, North China was divided into two administrative zones: the liberated zone, controlled by the Chinese Communist Party, and the Nationalist zone, controlled by Chiang Kaishek's government. The Nationalist zone included the major cities of Beijing, Tianjin, Baoding, and Shijiazhuang. Gaoyang, liberated from Japanese control in September 1945, was under stable Chinese Communist Party control throughout the period. The modern spinning mills, which supplied yarn, the essential raw material for weaving, were located in the zone occupied by Chiang Kaishek's government. While the administrative split resembled the situation during the resistance war, with the Nationalists replacing the Japanese, the Nationalist government was never able to extend its control out into the county towns. When hostilities between the Nationalist and Communist forces intensified after 1946, Communist forces initiated an economic boycott, blocking movement of goods between the two zones and creating serious problems for the development of Gaoyang industry.

During the second period, from mid-1949 to 1953, China was politically reunified and economic policies were designed to bring agriculture and industry to prewar levels of production. For Gaoyang, the most important difference between the civil war period and the early 1950s was the reintegration of rural production with coastal industry. As the supply of machine-spun yarns increased, the private sector expanded rapidly between 1950 and 1952, leading in 1953 to an intense struggle between private capital and state-controlled enterprises.

The postwar recovery of Gaoyang industry began with the Japanese surrender and the subsequent expansion of the central Hebei base area to include almost all of the rural counties of the Hebei plains region.[5] Once political control was assured, restoration of industry was one of the primary goals for base area planners in 1946.[6] Base area policy makers were determined to revive Gaoyang industry for several reasons. First, China's cotton textile industry had suffered heavy losses during the latter years of the war as the production of raw cotton in rural areas fell to less than one-third of the prewar peak.[7] The shortage of raw materials meant that spinning mills were operating well below capacity.[8] At the same time, there was a huge demand for cotton fabrics of all varieties for both military and civilian use. One of the goals of the production campaigns was to satisfy this demand. Equally important, however, was improvement in the livelihood of rural residents. In the prewar period, most rural weaving households drew 70 to 80 percent of their household income from weaving, and improving income required a restoration of this industry.

Three major obstacles stood in the way of revival of the weaving industry. First, during the war most weaving households had been forced to sell their looms as scrap to buy food to survive. Second, yarn was in short supply. Third, the merchant entrepreneurs who had built Gaoyang industry had fled at the outset of the war and few had returned. Thus there was need for organizational restructuring to create new firms and factories to handle production, processing, and trade.[9]

Government officials tried to create policies in 1946 and 1947 to deal with all three problem areas, although Communist Party cadre were undoubtedly most comfortable with policies that were directly related to improving the livelihood of their peasant supporters. Wartime practices in the base areas had given them experience in conducting rural production campaigns, and their first efforts in Gaoyang were targeted to aid poor weavers by helping them purchase looms.[10] By 1948 there were almost 3,500 iron gear looms in operation. If we assume a prewar total of roughly 9,000 in Gaoyang County alone, this would be 38 percent of the prewar level. Fuller restoration came after the end of the civil war. By 1952, more than 8,900 looms were in operation, close to prewar levels.[11] A loan program sponsored by the central Hebei government had facilitated this rapid increase in looms.[12] While the process we can observe here was similar to that in the first phase of growth, it is important to note the source of low-cost loans. During the first phase of growth, private entrepreneurs had devised the loan schemes; in the late 1940s, it was the base area government that took the initiative and provided the funds.

While the loans helped, market demand also played an important role in encouraging investment in looms. As with the loans, the pattern of market incentives in 1946–1947 was very similar to the patterns we noted during the first phase of growth. At the beginning of this second phase of growth, there is no question that market conditions favored weavers. There were general shortages of goods throughout North China and demand had been multiplied by the reopening of the northwest frontier markets, which had been starved for consumption goods throughout the war.[13] Demand for cloth skyrocketed and traders reported making super profits, with a single bolt of cotton cloth trading for a price equivalent to that of a horse.[14]

In spite of the heavy demand, expansion of production followed a stop-and-start pattern in response to political and macro-environmental changes.

There were two periods of rapid expansion. In the first, between late 1945 and late 1946, the number of looms increased from almost 0 to 3,000. Shortages of yarn then halted expansion until 1949. The end of the civil war and establishment of a unified central government removed economic barriers, and reopened links between urban spinning mills and rural weavers. The second expansion boom, between 1949 and 1953, saw the number of looms in the county triple, approaching levels close to those of the prewar weaving industry.

To better understand the complicated processes of change in the late 1940s and early 1950s, let us first turn to examine the individual actors—wholesale merchants, weaving households, and processing factories.

NEW MANAGERIAL STRATEGIES—PRIVATE AND STATE FIRMS

In the prewar period, the largest and most prestigious firms in Gaoyang had been the large yarn and cloth wholesalers, like Fu Feng and Hui Chang, with their hundreds of employees and far-flung networks of marketing agencies. The large wholesalers were bankrupted during the early war years. During the second phase of growth, two different types of firms provided wholesaling functions. The first group was made up of private wholesaling firms that were created by men who had been accountants, salesmen, technicians, and submanagers in the prewar wholesale firms. Working with a model based on their prewar experiences, these men used their knowledge of the business and their personal networks of connections to find similarly minded friends with whom they could create new partnerships. Moving quickly, they reestablished relations with yarn merchants in Tianjin and began to supply machine-spun yarns to rural weavers. Working in both the yarn and cloth trades, they purchased finished cloth in Gaoyang and transported it to markets like Zhangjiakou, where the cloth could be sold for very high profits.

The second group of new businesses included state-owned wholesaling firms. In this period, the category of "state-owned" firms included businesses that were created by various branches of the government in the liberated areas that provided the investment capital. Some of these firms were owned by the county government, others by subbranches of the county or district governments, or by branches of the army or by government trading companies. There were three larger state-run commercial enterprises in Gaoyang: Yuan Feng, Zhong Xing, and Hua Feng. All three were established in early 1946.[15] Government units supplied the capital for each of the state firms, and the chief manager of each firm was a cadre from the administrative network. Since the cadre who served as manager generally had little business experience, most of the daily operations were handled by experienced personnel who had been hired locally. Although these publicly owned wholesale firms were considerably smaller than the large yarn and cloth wholesalers of the prewar period, averaging ten to twenty employees each, their sphere of activities was similar to that of the larger prewar wholesale firms. The state firms supplied cotton yarn, purchased finished goods, contracted for printing or dyeing and finishing of fabrics, and sold cloth through a distribution system. The marketing networks for the state firms used the state store network throughout the North China liberated areas. State firms also purchased cloth for use by the military and civilian governments.

While the managers of the new private wholesale firms worked with a model based on prewar experience, in which wholesalers worked in both the yarn and cloth trade, it was not long before events intervened to disrupt the smooth development of the private firms. During 1945, the United States tried to mediate hostilities between the Communist and Nationalist forces. American mediation failed and the two sides moved closer to civil war. It was within that context that the Chinese Communist Party in North China initiated an economic boycott, touched off by a Nationalist government decision to import American raw cotton for the urban spinning mills. The prices of the imports made it impossible for domestic producers to compete.[16] Communist Party leaders decided that the only way to defend the base area economy against cheap American imports was to declare an economic boycott of all imported goods. For Gaoyang that meant that machine-spun yarns could no longer be used by local weavers.

Boycott measures drafted by the local government, in cooperation with the state-owned firms, were designed to deal with two problems: the purchase of fabrics already in production using the now banned machine yarns, and development of cooperatives to supply homespun yarns to the weaving industry. The boycott, which began in December 1946, led to extreme shortages of essential raw materials.[17] Even before the boycott began, machine yarns had been in short supply and weavers had experimented with the use of a mixture of homespun and machine-spun yarns to produce "two-corner cloth," which used a homespun warp with a machine-spun weft. During the boycott, party organizations launched a campaign to increase the supply of handspun yarn by organizing rural women to spin.[18]

The hand-spinning campaign played a major role in shaping the development of Gaoyang industry by giving a special advantage to the state-owned trading firms. Although the three state firms had official backing, until the beginning of the boycott they had simply been players along with the private wholesalers. As the boycott began, the local government decided to use the state firms as the mechanism for implementing the boycott. The state firms were assigned two roles: first, they were made the exclusive agents for purchase of cloth already in production that had been woven using the now banned machine-spun yarns; second, they were given exclusive access to supplies of raw cotton, making them the chief source of supply to the spinning cooperatives that were set up in almost every village.[19]

The first open clash between private wholesalers and the state-owned firms came over the procedures for purchase of cloth that had been woven using machine yarns. Since there were more than three thousand looms in operation at the time, and most were using machine yarns, almost all of the weaving households were affected by the procedures the government set up. The central party directive mandating a boycott arrived in Gaoyang on December 10, 1946. Party officials held a meeting on December 25 and decided that cloth made with machine-spun yarn could not be sold after January 10, and that two-corner cloth could not be sold after January 15.[20] They further directed that all stocks on hand were to be sold to the three state firms at 80 percent of current market value.[21]

Although the state stores had been assigned the task of buying up existing stocks, their capital resources were insufficient to accomplish this task, even at the discounted price.[22] Meanwhile, private firms were outraged at the decision, which gave monopoly rights to the state firms, and weaving households were unhappy with the discounted price since it would reduce their income. Moreover, the government regulations had set a very short time span for compulsory sales and had not specified when and where transactions were to take place.

Faced with growing dissatisfaction, the county government called an emergency meeting of the managers of the state firms to devise new tactics on January 9. Under the new measures two smaller state firms were added to the three larger ones and each was assigned responsibility for one of the five districts of the county. In the end, the only real losers in the transition period from machine-spun to homespun yarn were the private wholesalers who held stocks of machine-spun yarn. Following the declaration of the boycott and the ban on production of two-corner cloth, the price of factory yarn dropped, leaving dealers with yarn stocks that could no longer be sold.[23] The revised boycott measures found a way of dealing with the immediate problems of the boycott that seems to have been regarded by the weaving households as reasonably fair. However, the protests showed strong popular support for the market system and competitive prices.

The second decision made at the time of the boycott was to encourage hand spinning as a way of producing a substitute for machine-spun yarns. Building on its experience of organizing cooperatives during the war years, the base area government set out to mobilize rural women to join spinning cooperatives. The campaign to encourage women to spin was aided by market incentives that came from the high prices for yarn.

The government plan called for the state firms to play an active role in the spinning promotion campaigns, serving as agents for the distribution of raw cotton to spinning cooperatives. The government plan called for state stores to control the supplies of raw cotton and yarn. However, even though the number of spinning groups under contract to the state-run firms increased rapidly in 1947, they were not able to meet the full demand for yarn, and lively yarn markets appeared in the town as well as in village periodic markets. Independent women spinners who sold yarn at the markets used the income from the sale of yarn to purchase raw cotton. Although prices in the markets fluctuated, the overall shortage of yarn made the market essentially a sellers' market.[24]

Although Gaoyang weavers had to make do with homespun yarns, the cloth they produced still could be distinguished from the homespun "native cloth" that was being produced by rural weavers in other parts of North China. Since the Gaoyang weavers used iron gear looms, they were able to produce wide-width cloth in many stripe and check designs. Calling on their long history in mechanized dyeing and finishing, processing factories put out a finished product that only experts could distinguish from goods of factory manufacture. As a result, the market for Gaoyang cloth held steady even during the difficult years of 1947 and 1948.[25]

However, from the beginning of the boycott in December 1946 until the liberation of Tianjin in January 1949, profits earned by the weavers were reduced by the high cost of yarn.[26] In spite of that, households that had already purchased looms continued to weave because there were few alternatives. Farming still provided only limited income. Land reform, which had been completed in November 1946, had adjusted some inequalities in land distribution but had made little headway in rectifying the technological problems that had led to low agricultural productivity.[27] Bad weather, including major floods in 1948 and 1950, complicated matters.

In summary, one of the most significant changes during the boycott years was the strengthening of the state firms at the expense of the private wholesalers. During the boycott, state firms were given preferential access to supplies of locally grown raw cotton, which they distributed to the spinning cooperatives. This gave the state firms access to supplies of yarn, which they distributed to contract weavers. While the weaving households could earn more by selling to private wholesalers, in a situation characterized by a shortage of raw materials, many weaving households opted for the security of guaranteed yarn supplies. Private firms were unable to compete because of their inability to gain supplies of yarn. While there was a lively trade in yarn at the periodic markets, there were too many small sellers to make it feasible for the wholesalers to gain control over the market. Thus the boycott gave a clear advantage to the state firms that played a dominant role in the yarn supply system. While private firms were able to regain a significant share of the cloth trade in the early 1950s, they were not able to reenter the yarn trade, leaving wholesalers with a diminished role.

During the boycott and in several later clashes, the private firms presented themselves as the defenders of the weavers' interests, willing and able to pay fair market prices for finished cloth. State firms, on the other hand, were put in the position of acting as government agents, forced to sacrifice the rural weaver's interests to achieve political goals. In later years, as the central government moved step-by-step toward a state monopoly on commerce, official propaganda would depict the private traders as individuals engaged in speculation and market manipulation to increase their own profits at the expense of common public interest; however, as we can see in this case, it was the private merchants working through the market who were compelled to offer competitive prices to producers in order to insure their share of the market. As a result, throughout the years from 1945 to 1953, there was often an unspoken alliance between the thousands of weaving households and the private business firms. State firms, meanwhile, often found themselves in the difficult position of having to fill two often conflicting roles at once: one as the agent for the implementation of government policy, and the other as commercial firms striving to maximize profits in a competitive market.

LAND REFORM, WORKSHOP CAPITAL, AND THE DYEING AND FINISHING SECTOR

Many of the prewar owners of the weaving, dyeing, and finishing factories survived the war years by moving their bases of operation to the Japanese-occupied cities of Beijing or Tianjin. Unlike the owners of the large wholesale firms who had risked and lost their capital in wartime speculation, they were thus in a position to return to Gaoyang and restart their factories and workshops after 1945. However, records show that few of them did return; of those few who did, almost none remained after land reform in 1946–1947. What were the circumstances that made so few of these entrepreneurs willing to return?

Conflicts involving the dyeing and finishing factories began almost as soon as Gaoyang was liberated from Japanese control. During the war years, most of the factory managers had left for the safety of the larger occupied cities, but not without taking precautions to leave trusted employees to guard factory property. Although some equipment was confiscated by the occupying Japanese army and some by resistance forces, most of the factory buildings and some equipment survived. As soon as Gaoyang was liberated, local government officials rushed to begin the process of rebuilding industry. One of their first acts was to take over "abandoned factories." Little attention was given to property rights and no records were kept of what was confiscated, what put under "protection," and why properties had been classified in a certain way. When government officials tried to review the process and adjudicate disputes in early 1948, they found a confusion of accounts that was impossible to untangle.[28]

Basically, if owners were not on the spot to begin operating their factories, the local government took them over. Once a factory was taken over by the government, decisions would be made about what to do with the property and equipment. In some cases the factories were operated as joint state-private ventures. Under this form of management, operation of the factory was turned over to a government-appointed manager, with a percentage of the profits earmarked for payment to former owners or shareholders if they should appear. In other cases, especially those in which there was some suspicion that the owner of a factory was a supporter of the Nationalist Party, equipment was confiscated and divided among competing military and civilian units in need of boilers, generators, and other kinds of machinery.[29] Such practices obviously discouraged entrepreneurs from returning to aid in the rebuilding of Gaoyang industry.

He Ji, owned by Li Shuliang and his brother, was one of the few factories to be reopened by its original capitalist. While Li Shuliang had started a factory in Tianjin and did not personally return to Gaoyang, he sent a new manager to look after his interests. When rumors about land reform spread in the fall of 1946, the manager, Zhang Xiangting, fled, and in January 1947 He Ji was confiscated by the government and reorganized as the Jian Hua Dyeing and Finishing Factory. In the following years other private factories were taken over by the state and merged with Jian Hua, creating what was to become Gaoyang's largest state enterprise, the Gaoyang Dyeing Works. Through the process of mergers, the factory grew to employ fourteen hundred workers in 1952.[30]

While most of the prewar dyeing and finishing factories fell victim to confiscation practices in the late 1940s, not all of the dyeing and finishing trades fell under control of the state. At the same time that many of the prewar factories were being taken over by the state, new workshops and factories were being founded. Despite the social and economic dislocation associated with the civil war years, consumers still had an interest in fashion. There was little imported fabric available in the markets and urban factories were not producing fashionable fabrics. To meet this new demand, beginning in the late 1940s workshop entrepreneurs in Gaoyang began to produce hand-printed fabrics. The technology for this new process was quite simple. Fabric-printing workshops used simple stencils and dyes to hand-print designs on fabric. There were already thirty-five fabric-printing workshops in operation when the first survey was conducted in 1950, and by 1954 the number had grown to eighty-nine. Fabric-printing workshops were small-scale operations, often started by three or four workers who joined together to set up a small workshop. As the fabric-printing industry flourished, the number of workers employed in fabric printing steadily rose, reaching a total of close to five thousand by 1954. All of the early fabric-printing workshops were privately owned. Most were organized as worker's partnerships, similar to some of the prewar workshops we examined in chapter three. Fabric-printing workshops, like the prewar dyeing and finishing factories, worked both on contract to wholesale dealers or state firms and on their own account. When they worked on contract to an outside firm, they received processing fees; when they worked on their own account, they bought cloth on the market, printed it, and then sold it to wholesalers who handled marketing. Again, like the prewar dyeing and finishing factories, the printing workshops did not develop their own distribution networks.

In the early 1950s the fabric printing, dyeing, and processing sectors were a new arena for competition between public and private firms, a competition that the state firms usually lost. Jian Hua, the large state dyeing factory, competed with small privately owned dyeing firms as well as with the fabric-printing workshops. This was a competition in which we would expect Jian Hua to have a strong advantage, since the state had taken over the most technologically advanced of Gaoyang's former private factories. However, in spite of the fact that the state-owned firms were technologically more sophisticated, their managers ran into numerous problems. We can see this very clearly in the fact that in the early 1950s almost all of the private firms in Gaoyang were making profits, while state ventures often showed losses. Frank discussions in an internal government report showed that county government officials, assigned the task of improving the performance of state firms, believed that the problem lay in the fact that the state firms were not operating like enterprises but rather like bureaucratic organizations.[31] A comparison between the costs of production at Hong Ji, a state firm, and Wei Jinpo, a private firm, gives some indication of the reasons for the lower profits of state firms. A survey of the time showed that production costs were higher at the state firm: it cost four hundred yuan/bolt more to process cloth in the state firm than the private firm. The main reasons for the difference in cost were lower levels of worker productivity as a result of overstaffing in the state firm, higher non-wage benefits, and less intensive labor. Workers at the state firm worked ten hours a day and at the private firm twelve hours a day. Both factories provided meals for their workers: 25 percent of the grain supplied at the state firm was wheat flour, while private firm workers were served higher-quality grains only twice a month. The state firm had more workers and many more apprentices, but had fewer looms in operation. Finally, the government survey team concluded there was no "spirit of hard work" at the state firm. In order to improve the poor performance of the state firm, the survey team recommended that state firms adopt the piece-rate wages used in private firms to provide greater incentives for better performance.[32]

In summary, we can see that the conversion of dyeing and finishing factories from private to state ownership took place in the confusion of the immediate postwar period, long before the Chinese Communist Party laid out plans for the socialization of commerce and industry. While the government assumed control over "abandoned" assets with the intention of putting them to productive use, the state-owned firms experienced difficulty in competing with privately owned firms. Moreover, the seizure of privately owned factories discouraged the participation of prewar entrepreneurs. Even such progressive entrepreneurs as the Su brothers of Tong He had property seized. During the first round of land reform, villagers in Beishawo claimed that the Su brothers were landlords and confiscated and divided the looms in their factory. When government officials finally got around to a review of the case two years later, there was no way to reclaim the looms that had been removed, even though government officials agreed that the seizure had not been justified.[33]

By the early 1950s the situation in Gaoyang had stabilized. Land reform had been completed and the liberation of Tianjin in late 1948 had reopened links between the urban spinning mills and rural weavers. The state had reorganized the factories in Gaoyang that had been seized, and those state firms were competing in the market with the newly founded fabric printing and dyeing firms. While the confused processes that had led to many seizures in the immediate postwar period and during land reform had led many prewar entrepreneurs to abandon their interests in Gaoyang, a lively new group of petty entrepreneurs had risen to take their place.

TRANSITION TO SOCIALISM

The final completion of the socialist transformation of Gaoyang industry was an unusually complicated process because of the nature of the industrial district that linked together household-based weaving with workshop-based fabric printing, factory-based dyeing and finishing, and independent marketing and distribution. Government policies for socialist transformation were designed to deal with single-sector activities, not with the complexities of industrial districts. In the countryside, there were models for setting up rural cooperatives, primarily for agricultural activities. In towns, there were collectivization programs to reorganize handicraft workers. For commerce and industry, there were policies to implement a shift from private ownership to state or collective ownership. Rural industrial districts that were engaged in market-oriented mass production bridged the separate categories and, as the Gaoyang experience suggests, socialist transformation directives were ill equipped to deal with the conflicts that resulted from transformation at different paces in different sectors.

Local administrators were thus faced with a very complicated situation in the transitional period. Perhaps we can best begin to understand their policy initiatives by outlining the goals they were trying to meet and how those goals matched with the interests of different sectors of the local community. In the early 1950s expansion of production was a major goal, one that served both national and local interests. Let us begin with the question of changes in the national textile industry and the position of rural industrial districts in the overall structure. We can start by observing that in the first half of the 1950s demand for cotton textiles still exceeded supply; as a result, even in the eyes of planners who were committed to a shift to large-scale production, rural industrial districts still had an important role to play in supplementing the output of urban mills.

There were major changes in this national picture beginning in the early 1950s. Between 1950 and 1952, urban factory production rapidly recovered from wartime damage. Weaving mills that had been working at only 61 percent of capacity in 1949 were up to almost 90 percent of capacity by 1952. During that same period, the state invested almost two hundred million yuan in the cotton textile industry. During the years 1950, 1951, and 1952, investment in cotton textiles annually comprised between 55 and 60 percent of total state investment. By 1951, production of cotton cloth had already surpassed production from the highest prewar year, 1936. As planners moved toward launching the first Five Year Plan, further investment in cotton textiles was slated, bringing a great expansion in modern factory facilities.[34] Even with the continuing expansion of modern textile facilities, market demand consistently exceeded supply, and concurrent with the establishment of the national cotton textile monopoly in September 1954, a nationwide system of cotton rationing was established to assure a relatively equitable distribution of textile products.[35]

Throughout the early 1950s the chief block to the continued expansion of the Gaoyang weaving industry was a shortage of raw materials, as Gaoyang had to compete with the large urban mills for supplies of yarn. While in the prewar period mechanization of spinning had greatly outpaced the mechanization of weaving, the new investment in the 1950s was concentrated in the construction of integrated spinning and weaving mills. This greatly increased the capacity of the mechanized sector of the weaving industry and made allocation of supplies of yarn to rural weaving systems much tighter. This, in turn, led to a growing gap between local interests, which demanded continued expansion of rural industry, and national planning targets, which sought the most efficient allocation of raw materials.

For Gaoyang weavers, rural industry continued to be the prime source of income. Land reform and early collectivization efforts had contributed little to improved agricultural production. The basic problems of land insufficiency and the poor quality of the land left most rural dwellers heavily dependent on non-agricultural income for survival. Records for the five years between 1949 and 1953 show that the agrarian sector always fell way below projected production targets.[36] Peasant households, as in the prewar period, had little choice but to rely on weaving to survive. A central work team reported in 1954 that 90 percent of rural households were involved in rural industry, most of them in some branch of the weaving industry. They cited the experience of the village of Yanfucun, which had a population of 1,454 at the time of the survey. The village's total income from agriculture in 1953 was valued at 50,217,000* yuan, while income from weaving totaled 577,960,000 yuan; agriculture was supplying less than 9 percent of the village's income. While Yanfucun may have represented an extreme case, it would seem that by 1953 a rural income pattern closely resembling that of the prewar period had emerged in which income from rural industry was significantly more important than agricultural income. Given this situation, any contraction in the weaving industry posed a major threat to the household economy.

At least through 1953, expansion of weaving production was the overriding rubric in administrative guidelines for the Gaoyang region's economy, and most government policies were designed to achieve that goal while also adjusting for certain problems in the market. The second major goal was market stabilization; the aim was to assure relatively constant output at stable prices. During the transitional period, inflationary pressures in the national economy were still strong, and local administrators attempted to intervene in the market in ways that would help stabilize prices as part of the effort to slow inflation. A third consideration was the assurance of fair wages to weavers. In trying to achieve this goal, state firms often found themselves in competition with private wholesalers for control of the output of the weaving households. State firms, which were also assigned the task of stabilizing prices, often were at disadvantage since the two goals (i.e., fair wages and stable prices) could not always be achieved simultaneously. The fourth major concern was with quality control. Quality control, as we have seen in the chapters on the prewar textile industry, had been a problem almost as long as the industry had been in existence. Although the attempts to achieve quality control in the early 1950s were more successful than similar attempts during the prewar period, this was again an area in which there were often conflicts between state and private firms.

THE EARLY 1950S EXPANSION

Whether we measure expansion in terms of the number of looms or the number of commercial firms involved in the wholesale cloth trade and in the

---

* Inflation began during the war years and continued into the postwar period. When currency reform took place, the old currency was converted to new at an exchange rate of 10,000 to 1. Thus, as a rough rule, early 1950s numbers can be divided by 10,000 to get a value in standard yuan.

printing and dyeing industries, Gaoyang industry underwent very rapid growth in the years between 1949 and 1953. (See figure 7.1 and table 7.1.) High profits were made in both the cloth wholesale trade and in the fabric printing business. A 1954 survey of Gaoyang industry cited the example of two firms, the Qing Chang printing workshop and the Tian Cheng wholesaling firm. The former company, with a capital investment of 30,000,000 yuan, had a trade turnover in the first six months of 1953 of 810,000,000 yuan, on which the firm made a profit of 70,000,000 yuan—or more than double its capital investment. The wholesaling firm, which had a capital investment of 36,000,000 yuan, had in the same period done a business turnover of 640,000,000 yuan, on which its profits were 50,500,000 yuan. These figures give some indication of the profits that could be made in the early 1950s and explain why newcomers were inspired to invest in the industry, giving rise to the very rapid growth rates.

During the early 1950s most of the weaving households were involved in contract or semi-contract weaving for the public firms. By 1950 a new state firm, the local branch of the nationwide Huashabu Gongsi, had replaced the state-owned wholesalers and was the chief supplier of machine-spun yarn. Weaving households could weave on contract for the Huashabu Gongsi, for the state-owned dyeing factories, or for the newly created cooperatives, or, if they were willing to accept the risks, they could operate as independent weavers buying raw materials and selling finished goods to state-owned companies or private wholesalers. The fabric-printing workshops generally worked on subcontract to the state firms or the private wholesalers, undertaking work on a fee basis.

As the number of looms increased and output rose, there was also a significant expansion in the geographical areas covered by marketing networks. Both the public firms and the private wholesalers began to send sales agents into more distant regional markets. In 1949 sales agencies were located in nearby cities like Shijiazhuang, Yixian, and Bozhen, a major regional marketing center on the Grand Canal. By 1950 there were sales agencies in

Table 7.1.   Growth of Workshops and Factories, 1950–1954

	Fabric Printing		Dyeing		Weaving	
Year	Firms	Weavers	Firms	Workers	Firms	Workers
1950	34	1,560	13	206	29	
1951	83	3,120	23	408	33	
1952	79	2,026	22	404	35	198
1953	91	3,947	23	504	40	196
1954	89		23	489	2	

Source: Central Work Group, "Gaoyangxian jingji de jiben qingkuang: Jiefanghou Gaoyang xiang shougong zhibuye zhong de siren ziben," Manuscript, 1954.

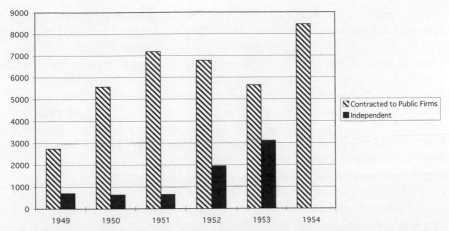

Figure 7.1.   Competition between Public Firms and Independent Weavers, Early 1950s. (Source: Central Work Group, "Gaoyangxian jingji de jiben qingkuang: Jiefanghou Gaoyang xiang shougong zhibuye zhong de siren ziben," Manuscript, 1954.)

Beijing, Taiyuan, Handan, Zhangjiakou, Zhengzhou, Loyang, and Jinan; and 1951 saw further expansion to Kaifeng, Xuchang, Xuzhou, Xi'an, Baotou, and Shenyang. By 1951 entrepreneurs had thus made major progress in reestablishing agencies in many of their traditional marketing regions in the north, northwest, and northeastern parts of China.

THE FINAL TRANSITION

Although I have not been able to find any declaration outlining state plans for the socialization of Gaoyang industry, a study by a central work committee dispatched to the region in the fall of 1954 allows us to make at least a partial reconstruction of the final transformation process and its problems. It would seem that state encouragement for private industry in the Gaoyang industrial district was still strong in 1950 to 1952. Private firms were seen as important supplements to the state-owned firms that were assigned the leading role. During this period, private wholesale firms were encouraged to play a major role in marketing. Since most of the private wholesale firms were owned by or employed men who had worked in the industry before the war, it was assumed that their experience and connections gave them an advantage over the newly organized and still poorly developed state-marketing outlets. As we have already seen, the private wholesalers were very successful in their efforts to reestablish connections in many of the prewar marketing centers.

While much of the marketing of finished goods was left to private wholesale dealers, the state firms worked to establish their control over production. This was accomplished in the case of weaving through the establishment of contract relationships between the state firms and private weaving
households and in the case of dyeing and finishing through the establishment of contract service relationships between the state firms and the dyeing and fabric-printing workshops. Thus while the small production units, including both weaving households and fabric-printing workshops, were still
privately owned, coordination and control of the overall production process
was in the hands of state firms. We can imagine that local authorities envisioned a process in which privately owned production units would be incorporated into cooperatives, leaving only cloth wholesaling in private
hands. Isolated from the production system, it would then be relatively easy
to convert the private wholesale firms to some form of cooperative or state
ownership.

Clearly the smooth transition envisioned by state authorities did not occur.
The private sector grew very rapidly from 1950 to 1952, and by 1953 it was
involved in a struggle for dominance with the public firms. The central work
committee report places a major part of the responsibility for the bitterness
of the struggle on miscalculations by personnel in the state firms. The report
contends that inexperience led to errors that opened the way to private capital. The first round in the battle began when the state firms took steps to enforce quality control standards. The shift from contract weaving for private
firms to contract weaving for state firms had not resolved the problem of irregular goods.* The early 1950s represented a boom period in which demand
consistently outstripped supply. Under those circumstances, many private
dealers did not penalize weavers for irregular goods. When the state firms
decided to enforce new quality control regulations, the private merchants
continued to buy up irregular goods at high prices. Some weavers went so
far as to take yarn on contract from state firms and then sell the finished cloth
to private merchants.

Not only were the private firms willing to buy irregular goods, overall they
offered higher prices than state firms. The 1954 work team report showed
that the market price to a weaver for a bolt of plain cloth stood at 19,233
yuan, while the cooperatives were paying 8,933 and the Huashabu Gongsi
was paying only 6,602. At the same time, a bolt of striped cloth would bring
in profits of 21,270 yuan on the market, but only 10,564 on contract for the
Huashabu Gongsi. Private firms were able to pay higher prices and still keep
their profit ratios high because of very high demand. From 1950 to 1952, a

---

* Quality of textiles was measured in several ways, including overall size (width and length)
and density of the weave. Often what the state regarded as "irregular goods" were bolts of cloth
that were shorter than the officially proscribed length.

bolt of printed fabric would bring a profit of 40,000 yuan. Following the 1952 quality control movement which improved the reputation of Gaoyang cloth, the same cloth sold in Zhengzhou brought a profit of 55,100 yuan, and by 1953 even plain white cloth was bringing a profit of 70,000 yuan a bolt when sold in the northeast.

The second major arena for competition between the state and private firms was the field of design. In the prewar period much of the Gaoyang reputation had been built on higher-value-added products, including yarn-dyed and figured fabrics. Merchants had developed a strong interest in design and had kept their market share by keeping abreast of the latest changes in fashion. The fabric-printing workshops continued that tradition in the early 1950s. Most of the fabric-printing workshops had gotten started doing work on a contract basis for the state firms. The state firms offered fixed fees per bolt of fabric, however, and the workshops quickly developed ways of operating on their own account which were much more profitable. One way was to print different designs for state contract and for private trade. For example, in 1953 they printed a medium-sized pattern on fabrics contracted by the state firms while printing a more popular small pattern on fabrics they were producing on their own account. When the state decided to switch over to the more popular design, the workshops would then design new patterns for work done on their own account. In this manner they tried to stay one step ahead of the state, competing in the market by producing goods that were in higher demand.

The struggle between state and private capital—over both price and design issues—reached a crisis in 1953. In the first half of 1953, the Huashabu Gongsi found its warehouses overstocked and it temporarily suspended cloth purchases. This opened the door to private dealers, whose capital resources had increased between 1950 and 1952. When the Huashabu Gongsi tried to reenter the market in August, it was only able to fill 65 percent of its purchase quota of forty thousand bolts of cloth.[37] Also at this time, local authorities were making a major push to organize weaving households into producers' cooperatives, and the activities of the private merchants threatened to undercut the cooperatives (which were the first stage in the process that would end private weaving).[38] By the summer of 1953 the local government had planned to have most weavers organized into cooperatives working under contract to the Huashabu Gongsi.

In the government view, the activities of the private merchants encouraged "capitalist thinking" among the masses, and in some cases had led weavers who had joined a cooperative to withdraw from the cooperative, to weave on their own account. Since cooperativization of weaving was the central concern in the creation of a rural socialist economy in Gaoyang, this challenge to the organization of weaving cooperatives met with swift state action. In August the Huashabu Gongsi got the assistance of the government and called together representatives of the state and private organizations to consult about changes in the cloth marketing system. Since the state companies, at least officially, had a monopoly over the supply of yarn, they decided to institute a system of exchanging yarn for cloth in which cooperatives would only be able to obtain new supplies of yarn when they turned over the finished cloth woven with the previous supply of yarn. This official declaration of policy made little headway while it was still more profitable for weavers to sell finished goods on the market. Cloth peddlers, who could make very high profits even on small-scale trade, began to go out to the villages to buy finished cloth directly from weaving households. The situation worsened in early October, when the Huashabu Gongsi announced price changes that effectively raised the price of yarn and lowered the price of finished cloth. Since this policy was only implemented within Gaoyang county, weavers took their finished cloth to markets in neighboring counties where they could sell for higher prices. This flight from the Gaoyang market was clearly reflected in the volume of cloth trade: at the October 3 market preceding the price change, 5,071 bolts of cloth were collected, while at the October 11 market the trade volume was only 3,662 bolts of cloth.

The Huashabu Gongsi, finding itself in a losing battle with the private merchants, sought assistance from the Hebei provincial finance committee; in late October the committee banned the private sale of yarn and cloth in Gaoyang and neighboring counties and issued a public order banning private cloth wholesale merchants in the central Hebei region. By the end of 1953 private wholesalers had almost completely disappeared from the Gaoyang market and trade in cotton cloth was in the hands of the Huashabu Gongsi.

This socialist transformation of the Gaoyang weaving industry took place almost a year in advance of the establishment of a national monopoly in the cotton textile industry. It would seem that the impetus for the early completion of the socialization process was the threat to rural collectivization. With the state firms unable to meet their purchasing targets and with the threatened collapse of the newly formed weavers' cooperatives, local and provincial officials took swift action to ban private commerce.

In comparing what happened in Gaoyang with what we know of the socialization of commerce and industry in other areas of China, one of the striking differences is the absence of any preliminary move against private commerce during the *wu-fan* (five antis) campaign of 1951–1952. In many parts of urban China this campaign, which included among its targets tax evasion, cheating on government contracts, and private speculation, signaled the first step in the socialization of private commerce.[39] None of the work committee reports make any mention of the *wu-fan* campaign, despite the fact that they mention extensive tax evasion among private entrepreneurs.

Since Gaoyang private entrepreneurs had been little affected by the *wu-fan* campaign there had been few curbs on the methods and techniques that they used in competing with the state firms for control of the cloth trade. Thus when the government made its move in the fall of 1953 to socialize the textile trade, the swiftness of that action had a shock effect on the overall industry, with consequences that were very damaging to Gaoyang in the following years.

The final end to the second phase of small-scale industrial growth came in 1954 and 1955, with two government decisions that directly shaped future development. First, the Huashabu Gongsi, which supervised contract weaving, ordered weaving cooperatives to switch to production of unbleached, plain white cotton fabrics. This decision reversed a half-century of Gaoyang experience with the strategy of flexible production and marked the beginning of the end for rural weaving. Rural weavers could not compete with large state textile mills in the production of standardized products, and weaving would continue only as a form of state relief. The second major decision was to strip Gaoyang of skilled personnel; they were transferred to new textile factories in the larger cities. More than twenty-five hundred workers were transferred out of Gaoyang by the end of 1955, leaving only skeleton crews at the mechanized dyeing and finishing factories in the town. While the Gaoyang factories would rebuild in later years, the links between rural household weaving and the sophisticated dyeing and processing in town factories had been irreversibly severed.[40]

STATE PLANNING AND THE SMALL-SCALE INDUSTRIAL MODEL

While there is theoretically no reason why small-scale industry could not have thrived under a system of socialist central planning, in the Chinese case it did not.[41] When we begin to consider why that was the case, we first notice that in the early stages of socialist planning, rural industrial districts like Gaoyang were included in the category of "handicraft industry."[42] State planners in China shared the views of many mainstream Western economists who were convinced that "handicraft" was a backward form of production that should eventually be replaced by factory-based mass production. During the first Five Year Plan, the Chinese state put heavy investment into the cotton textile industry, building many new integrated spinning and weaving mills. Raw cotton production did not expand at the same rapid pace, leaving a shortage of raw materials. Under those circumstances state planners believed that the most efficient use of resources could be obtained by allotting scarce resources to large state firms engaged in the mass production of standard products. Moreover, in the mid-1950s the state planning apparatus was quite primitive, lacking the necessary means to gather and process large volumes of data. Effective planning required a simplification in both production and distribution networks. As we have seen through our exploration of production in Gaoyang, the prewar Chinese textile industry had produced a vast array of goods designed to satisfy demand in many local and regional markets. Thousands of intermediate dealers had worked in the marketing networks, researching local demand and finding and marketing suitable products. State planners could not envision a system that would control the activities of that army of distribution specialists in an efficient way, and so they elected to simplify both production and distribution. Their decisions led to a shift to mass production of a relatively limited number of standardized products. In the textile industry, concern for fashion waned as stress was placed on volume. The new system limited the variety of products, which were then marketed through a state-marketing system with a greatly reduced number of distribution channels. By the time the socialization of commerce and industry was completed, distribution channels had been reorganized into regional blocks, and within each regional block there was only one wholesale channel for the distribution of each category of goods. Where in the past there had been dozens of dealers in every market selling slightly different products at competitive prices, by the late 1950s all dealers carried the same standard products, which were sold for the same state-fixed prices. To deal with the problem of excess or unsatisfied demand, a rationing system was put in place that fixed individual allotments of goods that were in short supply.[43]

On the supply side, production units were reorganized as subunits of larger state organizations. Thus the small village workshops in Gaoyang were put under the control of a county organization that was the local branch of the state monopoly firm that controlled the supplies of raw cotton and yarn. The factories in town were also attached to various state organizations, which had the responsibility for negotiating their output targets and providing political and economic protection. The largest factories were under the wing of the national textile ministry and its Hebei provincial branch, while smaller factories were associated with different offices of county or subcounty government units. Planning was done down the vertical lines of authority, with no horizontal coordination at the local level between units that were attached to different administrative lines.

Almost everything about this system stood in direct opposition to the classical Gaoyang pattern of small-scale industrial production. As we have seen, during the first phase of development Gaoyang production was characterized by a system of flexible specialization, producing small volumes of a large range of goods designed to satisfy demand in different regional markets. Wholesale merchants acted as the coordinators of the production and marketing systems, seeking out new markets and designing products for each. In each market prices were influenced by the degree of competition. In this system, there was a close linking between peasant weavers, town processing factories, and the wholesale dealers who provided raw materials and bought up finished products. Information about new products, technology, and market conditions flowed freely between the various actors.

This description of the basic logic of planning in the textile industry from the mid-1950s on has about it an inevitability that is not so obvious when we examine the historical record of development in the postwar period. From the end of the war in the late summer of 1945 until the early 1950s, former employees of the wholesale firms, textile technicians, workers, and peasant weavers, with the backing of the Communist Party, worked to rebuild the Gaoyang industrial district as an essential part of China's textile industry. As a result of those efforts production was restored to levels approaching those of the prewar period. But in the early 1950s government decisions to socialize commerce and industry led to the collectivization of weaving and a ban on the private wholesale trade. Within the space of several years, the industrial district was on the point of collapse. While Gaoyang industry was weakened, the rapidly expanding state sector in other areas had a shortage of skilled workers. In 1955 more than twenty-five hundred skilled workers were reassigned to new state textile factories in cities like Shijiazhuang and Handan. When the Great Leap Forward began in 1958, weavers who still owned looms were put under very strong pressure to "donate" the iron gears of their looms to the "backyard furnace" projects to produce steel by "native" methods.

While the Gaoyang industrial district came to an end in the mid- and late 1950s, the modern state industrial sector in the town, which had been built on the foundations of the mechanized dyeing and finishing factories, continued to hobble along, processing fabrics that were allotted from state mills in the larger cities. As time went on, some of the state firms were able to expand their production capacity and to take on new workers, creating a small working class in the town.

This pattern continued to prevail through the turmoil-filled years of the 1960s when the town and countryside were torn apart by the struggles of the Cultural Revolution. Finally, in the early 1980s, reform policies were enacted to dismantle the structures of rigid state planning. Within a few years the face of Gaoyang was transformed, as thousands of individuals and families began to build small home-weaving workshops once again. It is to the account of the third phase of growth that we will turn in the remainder of this book.

NOTES

1. Dorothy Solinger, *Chinese Business under Socialism: The Politics of Domestic Commerce, 1949–1980* (Berkeley: University of California Press, 1984). I have also consulted the Tianjin and Hebei volumes of the series Zhongguo Zibenzhuyi Gongshangye de Shehuizhuyi Gaizao Ziliao Congshu Bianjibu, *Zhongguo zibenzhuyi gongshangye de shehuizhuyi gaizao* (Beijing: Zhonggong Dangshi Chubanshe, 1991).

2. While technically there should be distinctions between state and Communist Party roles, they are difficult to discern and I have generally treated them together under the rubric of the state.

3. Kubo Tōru has argued that one of the other major contributing streams to socialization was the creation of a state industrial sector in the urban areas under Guomindang control from 1945–1949. Postwar confiscation of "enemy" property—i.e., Japanese assets—provided the base for large conglomerate-like companies in different industrial sectors. See Kubo Tōru, *Chūgoku keizai 100 nen no ayumi* (Tokyo: Sōken Shuppan, vol. 1, 1991; vol. 2, 1995).

4. For accounts of a number of such state-operated commercial enterprises, see Shangyebu Shangye Jingji Yanjiusuo, ed., *Geming genjudi shangye huiyilu* (Beijing: Shangye Chubanshe, 1984).

5. The official Japanese surrender on August 15, 1945, coincided with the launching of a major offensive by resistance forces throughout the central Hebei area. In the space of three months, CCP forces liberated all but the largest cities of Beijing, Tianjin, Baoding, and Shijiazhuang. A siege of Gaoyang was the last major military engagement in the northern part of central Hebei. Kusano Fumio, *Chūgoku sengo no dōtai* (Kyoto: Kyōiku Shuppansha, 1947), 166–68.

The elimination of Japanese and puppet forces in September 1945 made central Hebei a secure base area. Zhangjiakou was captured by the Communist forces in August 1945 and remained under their control until October 1946. Zhangjiakou was "reliberated" in December 1948. Frontier markets were open until October 1946 and then again from early 1949. Xu Junxing, ed., *Hebei chengshi fazhanshi* (Shijiazhuang: Hebei Jiaoyu Chubanshe, 1991), 221–47.

6. *Jinchaji Ribao*, January 26, 1946.

7. According to a study by the Hebei Provincial Bank, there were more than thirteen million *mu* of land planted in cotton in the province in 1937; this fell to a low of just over 3,200,000 in 1945, and made a slow recovery in 1946 and 1947. *Hebei Sheng Yinhang Yuekan* 1, no. 3, March 31, 1948.

8. State Statistical Bureau, *Woguo gangtie, dianli, meikuang, jichi, fangzhi, zaozhi gongye de jinxi* (Beijing: Tongji Chubanshe, 1958), 150–52.

9. "Gaoyang gongshang ye de chubu diaocha," handwritten report prepared by the Gaoyang County Government, 1948.

10. The Gaoyang county government focused on two crucial factors: production of the machines and supply of funding for purchase of looms. On November 1, 1945, workers' representatives established a Gaoyang County Workers Congress. Production campaigns mobilized workers for a full-scale attack on local industrial production. *Jiefang Ribao*, November 11, 1945.

11. Since looms were in households and small workshops, it was very difficult to get accurate counts. Prewar estimates run as high as 100,000 looms for the whole weaving area, but this figure seems too high. I have used Wu Zhi's estimate of 30,000 for the whole weaving district. Postwar figures come from two reports. The estimates for 1948 come from a report on "Central Hebei Textile Industry" prepared by the central Hebei administrative office, dated November 1948. Figures for the 1950s come from Central Work Group, "Gaoyangxian jingji de jiben qingkuang: Jiefanghou Gaoyang xiang shougong zhibuye zhong de siren ziben," October 20, 1954. Manuscripts held by the Gaoyang County Archives.

12. *Jiefang Ribao*, June 3, 1946.

13. In 1946 the Communist Party took control of Zhangjiakou, one of the gateways to the frontier markets. During the year that they held control of the city, before they retreated in the face of the Nationalist forces, goods flowed from North China into the northwest frontier markets.

14. The Central Hebei textile industry report states that in the immediate postwar period, a bolt of native cloth could be exchanged for two *dou* of grain, but that a bolt of Gaoyang cloth which had been dyed and finished in a mechanized factory would sell for one *dan* one *dou* of wheat (Central Hebei Administrative Office, "Jizhong fangzhi ye" [manuscript, 1948]).

15. The three firms were under the administrative supervision of a publicly run commercial organization for the whole central Hebei base area, Yuan Xin, which had its headquarters in Wurenqiao, in Anguo County to the south of Gaoyang.

16. In cotton spinning, raw materials occupy a significant percentage of total production costs. According to H. D. Fong, writing in the 1930s, approximately 80 percent of the total production cost of yarn was the cost of the raw materials (H. D. Fong, *Cotton Industry and Trade in China* [Tianjin: Nankai Institute of Economics, 1932], 87). The American cotton was so cheap in the late 1940s, however, that the raw materials made up only 30 percent of the production costs. Most of the major coastal mills had shifted to the use of imported cotton (State Statistical Bureau, *Woguo gangtie, dianli, meikuang, jichi, fangzhi, zaozhi gongye de jinxi*, 148–50). In 1948 the situation changed as a weakening of the Chinese currency made cotton more expensive. At the same time, pent-up consumer demand had been partially satisfied. While the price of finished goods continued to rise, it rose slower than the price of cotton. See Teng Maochun, "Lun hua-sha-bu guanli zhengci," *Gongye Yuekan* 5, no. 4 (April 1, 1948), 4–5.

17. The shortages were not restricted to yarn. There was also a severe shortage of dyes and chemicals used in the dyeing industry. In the prewar period most dyestuffs had come from Germany; in the postwar years the dyestuffs were largely American and were also subject to the boycott.

18. In early 1947, there were more than three thousand iron gear looms in Gaoyang. Local experts estimated that a minimum of ninety thousand spinners would be required to supply yarn to those looms. However, there were only thirty thousand spinning wheels. In order to deal with the yarn supply crisis, the government cadre pushed women to spin and organized rural technicians to develop improved spinning wheels. A local newspaper reporter who visited the market at Xinqiao found the market crowded with women of all ages who were selling yarn and buying cotton. One yarn purchaser told the reporter that he didn't care what price he had to pay as long as the yarn was well spun (*Jizhong Daobao*, March 5, 1947). Another calculation suggested that for home spinning to produce sufficient yarn, 14 percent of the population needed to spin full-time (Central Hebei Administrative Office, "Jizhong fangzhi ye").

19. Hand spinners were urged to improve their techniques to produce higher-count yarns; a graduated pay scale rewarded women who improved their skills.

20. Normally when homespun and machine-spun yarns are used in combination, the machine-spun yarn is used for the warp. All printed reports on two-corner cloth report that it used a machine-spun weft and a homespun warp. The former weavers I interviewed could not remember why the normal pattern was reversed.

21. The party gave little attention to the need for a public education campaign to explain the boycott.

22. The government estimated that there were approximately twenty thousand bolts of cloth in various stages of the weaving process. At the discounted price, the state firms would pay one hundred thousand yuan per bolt, or a total of two billion yuan, a sum that greatly exceeded their capital resources.

23. Liang Zhao, "Gaoyang dizhi meihuo jingyan," *Jizhong Daobao*, February 15, 1947.

24. Despite the aggressive campaigns to encourage women to spin, yarn demand exceeded supply. In order to increase the supply of yarn, local technicians developed several types of improved spinning wheels and small workshops in Gaoyang started to produce an eighteen-spindle spinning wheel that could produce a minimum of a pound (*jin*) of yarn per day. *Jizhong Daobao*, March 27, 1947.

25. See Central Hebei Administrative Office, "Jizhong fangzhi ye."

26. While the costs of production had risen due to the high cost of yarn, the price of cloth had risen more slowly. To remain competitive, weavers had to accept lower returns. One 1948 estimate suggested that weaving income had fallen to 64 percent of the prewar level of return per bolt of cloth. Central Hebei Administrative Office, "Jizhong fangzhi ye."

27. On land reform, see *Jizhong Daobao*, December 9, 1946; February 19, June 21, and August 25, 1947; and April 10, 1948.

28. See the report "Dui Gaoyang gongchang jiqi chuli baoguan yijian," handwritten report prepared by the Central Hebei Administrative Office, November 1948, held in the Hebei Provincial Archives. According to the report, the property of nine factories was improperly confiscated.

29. In almost all cases, workers had been assigned to guard the factories; while there were some losses during the Japanese occupation, there was much usable equipment left at the end of the war.

30. This section is based on a series of government reports, mostly written in 1948, when efforts were made to try to sort out what had happened and to return property that had been improperly confiscated. See "Dui Gaoyang gongchang jiqi chuli baoguan de yijian." The document is dated November 1948 on the title page, but there are references in the text to events that took place in 1950. It may have been incorrectly dated at the time of filing, since the title cover and letter do not seem to be in the same handwriting. See also "Jiqi tonji biao," October 22, 1948, which was prepared by the Central Hebei Administrative Office. It provides lists of the equipment that each factory originally had, and shows how much still remained. See also Central Hebei Administrative Office, "Jun Zhong Xingshu guanyu Gaoyang You Ji Gongchang chuli yijian," handwritten draft July 1949, held in the Hebei Provincial Archives; and Gaoyang County Government, "Gaoyang gongshang ye de chubu diaocha" (manuscript, 1948).

31. Information on the pattern of mergers comes from the "Gaoyang Ranchang Changshi," mimeograph, March 1988. Handwritten additions include production data through 1993.

32. There is a frank discussion of the problems with the textile industry in Gaoyang County Government, "Gaoyang gongshangye de chubu diaocha," 42.

33. Other equipment had been turned over to a state-run factory that had taken over the factory buildings. Eventually the state-run factory was ordered to make arrangements with the Su family on payment for lost property rights, but the whole affair left the former owners embittered and unwilling to invest in Gaoyang.

34. Their analysis can be found in Gaoyang County Government, "Gaoyang gong-shangye de chubu diaocha."

35. State Statistical Bureau, *Woguo gangtie, dianli, meikuang, jichi, fangzhi, zao-zhi gongye de jinxi*, 154–55 and 173. New textile factories could be constructed easily, with the average plant requiring only thirteen months for construction. If operated at full capacity, profits from a textile factory would cover the investment costs within a year.

36. The Central Work Group 1954 survey reported the following figures: in 1949, county agriculture production reached 60.8 percent of the target; 1950, 31 percent; 1951, 52.3 percent; 1952, 69.9 percent; and 1953, 51 percent. In terms of output per person, in 1952, the best year, grain per person, after payment of taxes in kind, was 343.8 *jin* per person.

37. There were problems with both wholesale and retail trade. On the retail side, private merchants were underselling the state firms; when the state stores charged 3,500 yuan per foot of cloth, the private merchants would sell for 3,400 yuan.

38. The first weavers' cooperatives were established in Gaoyang in October 1951, at the time of a visit by a Soviet expert; the real push for cooperativization did not come until late 1952, when steps were taken to collectivize agriculture. The early weavers' cooperatives acted as the intermediary bodies between the Huashabu Gongsi and the individual weaving households; yarn was put out through the cooperatives to weavers who worked in their own homes. In some cases some of the preparatory work, including sizing and warping, was collectivized, but in most cases the early cooperatives acted simply as administrative organizations to manage contract weaving and assure an equitable distribution of yarn.

39. The chronology given in the draft county gazetteer notes the beginning of the *san-fan* (three antis: anti-corruption, anti-waste, anti-bureaucratism) campaign that preceded the five antis campaign in most parts of the country. The three antis campaign was carried out during 1951 in the town, and 1952 in the countryside. The only mention of anything that resembles the five antis campaign is to be found in references to a two-month-long campaign against tax evasion that took place from May 1 to July 4, 1953. There is no reference to this being part of the five antis movement. In interviews with entrepreneurs in a rural market town in Songjiang, outside Shanghai, all the informants described the *wu-fan* period as the real beginning of socialization of commerce in their town.

40. The reconstruction of the state sector will be dealt with briefly in the next chapter. Survival of the state sector is probably more a tribute to bureaucratic inertia than anything else.

41. During the Cultural Revolution and into the 1970s there was much discussion of the "five small industries" in China. This kind of small industry was different from the kind of small-scale industry that flourished before 1953 and after 1978. The forms of rural industrial production that were together referred to as the "five small industries" provided inputs to agriculture on a local level. They were run by collective units

and had little relationship to market production. Almost all of these industries, which included the production of fertilizer, food processing, and so on, were done on a commune level and were intended for local consumption.

42. In 1954 a national survey of handicraft industry included Gaoyang in this category, along with a number of other rural industrial districts. See Beijingshi, *Yijiu-wusinian quanquo geti shougongye diaocha ziliao* (Beijing: Sanlian, 1957).

43. For example, in the textile industry rationing was introduced in the 1950s and remained in place until 1984. Under the cloth rationing system, people needed both money and ration tickets to buy cotton goods. The amount of cotton rationed per individual varied over time. In 1954 to 1957 the individual allotment was over twenty feet of cotton cloth a year. During the early 1960s, the ration fell as low as three feet per person per year. It rose to sixteen feet of cloth per person from the late 1960s to the early 1980s. These figures are averages, and there were differences in the allotment between urban and rural residents. Shangyebu Fangzhipin Ju, *Xin Zhongguo de fanzhipin shangye* (Beijing: Zhongguo Shangye Chubanshe, 1989), 174.

8

From Plan to Market: The Third Phase of Growth

Gaoyang natives associate the beginning of the third phase of growth with the national policies for economic reform that were first announced in December 1978. According to county officials, the reform initiatives "broke the fetters of leftist policies" and opened the door for individuals and groups to start thousands of new businesses.[1] By 1995, after a little more than a decade of growth under the economic reform policies, there were more than 11,000 registered rural enterprises in Gaoyang County, employing more than 50,000 workers. The value of their total output stood at 2.38 billion yuan.[2] While most of the enterprises were small, family-based operations, there were 340 larger firms with more than 100,000 in registered capital. Sixty-five of these larger firms had registered capital holdings of over 1,000,000 yuan, and there were 7 very large firms with over 5,000,000 yuan in registered capital.[3] Almost all of these firms, from the smallest family workshops to the largest wool-spinning firm that employed three thousand workers, were privately owned.

This chapter will analyze the mechanisms that contributed to explosive growth of the small-scale industrial sector. We will consider the creation of a new institutional environment as a result of the economic reform policies and the ways local entrepreneurs took advantage of the opportunities it created. Running through our discussions will be questions about the Gaoyang entrepreneurial tradition and how it has shaped contemporary industrial practices.

ECONOMIC REFORM POLICIES

In December 1978, when the Central Committee of the Chinese Communist Party officially launched the reform initiatives, few envisioned the radical changes that the reforms would bring. The "political logic" of the Chinese economic reforms, as Susan Shirk argues, was essentially to begin with reform of those sectors of the economy where political opposition was likely to be weakest.[4] There was no master plan in 1978, only the results of some experiments with agricultural reforms that seemed promising and that were to be taken as the starting point. While planners did not have a clearly worked out master plan, they did share a perception of the major problems in the Chinese economy. Thirty years of socialism had produced major improvements in the economy; this could be seen in the fact that extreme poverty, which had been so obvious in some parts of China on the eve of the Communist revolution in 1949, had largely disappeared. Food supplies were sufficient to feed a population that had doubled since the revolution, and campaigns against disease, the spread of a basic health system, and a more equitable division of resources had led to steadily rising life expectancy. Agricultural output per unit of land also had increased, as a result of improved seeds, better systems of water control, more intensive use of land, and increased use of modern inputs like chemical fertilizers. By the late 1970s, however, the increases in output per unit of land seemed to have reached a ceiling, and while agricultural output was sufficient to assure the physical survival of the population, it was not adequate to bring real prosperity. If the Chinese Communist Party, which was just emerging from the disastrous ten years of the Cultural Revolution, wanted to solidify its base of support, it needed to show that it had policies that could bring more dramatic improvements in the standard of living. Since 85 percent of the people lived in rural areas, that put rural reform at the top of the agenda.

While it has become customary to refer to all of the economic policy changes that were implemented after December 1978 as "the economic reforms," this term includes initiatives that were implemented at different times and at different paces in various parts of China. Our concern here is with the policy changes that directly created the windows of opportunity for local entrepreneurs in Gaoyang. We can identify five separate "reforms" that contributed to the windows of opportunity for rural industry:

- Organizational reforms that eventually broke up the commune as an economic unit and freed rural labor
- Reforms designed to provide incentives for increased production in state-run manufacturing firms, which opened up access to raw materials
- Reforms that allowed non-state firms to share in the benefits of semi-monopoly prices, creating market incentives for rural output

- A decision to increase investment in the state textile industry, which provided access to improved equipment
- Early reforms that raised rural incomes, thus increasing purchasing power and demand for the products of rural industry, which contributed to the creation of a "virtuous cycle."

As can be seen, these policy changes do not represent a coherent single package of "rural industrial reforms." Rather, each of the individual reform initiatives was targeted at some other problem. Local actors in Gaoyang, and in many other rural communities, seized the opportunities presented by the policies to create new industrial systems.

THE REFORMS AND THE GROWTH OF RURAL INDUSTRY

Freeing the Supply of Labor. The first stage of the reforms called for economic incentives to motivate rural dwellers to increase farm output. The first step was to assign responsibility for agricultural work to individual households. Rural families very quickly realized that farm work on their small assigned plots used up only a small portion of their total labor time. Freed from working on assigned labor teams, individual peasant families began to use surplus family labor to engage in sideline activities. The reopening of rural markets in 1979 provided many opportunities for sale of agricultural goods and the products of sideline industries. Some individuals took up occupations as rural craftsmen or as petty traders or brokers in the markets. As peasant families began to earn cash income from these activities, the demand for consumer goods began to rise. The reforms in agriculture contributed to the new opportunities in several ways. First, individuals now had time to engage in non-farm activities. Second, income earned from non-agricultural activities put money in the hands of rural families, creating an increased demand for all kinds of consumer goods and at the same time providing small amounts of capital for investment in other non-agricultural activities.

Opening Access to Raw Materials. One of the chief ways in which the state had controlled the development of rural industry during the period of high socialism had been through its monopoly control over the supply of raw materials. In the case of the textile industry, in the mid-1950s the state had established a monopoly over the supply of raw cotton and had put all spinning and weaving mills under the state plan, which meant that they could only deal with designated suppliers and customers. The small village cooperative factories, which were all that was left of a once vibrant Gaoyang weaving industry, had been reorganized under this state monopoly and were allotted raw materials within the state plan. The reform that opened a window of opportunity by providing access to raw materials was not originally designed to aid rural industry, but was initiated in an effort to improve the efficiency of state firms. The state plan—with its allocation of raw materials, output targets, and fixed prices—provided few incentives for efficient production. Under this reform, if state firms exceeded the target figure for output, the commodities over the target could be sold at a bonus price to customers of the firm's own choosing. While the initiative was intended to provide incentives to state factories, it had the happy result of making inputs like yarn available to non-state actors. This reform, together with the first, which freed labor, created the possibilities for the development of small-scale industry. Individuals now were legally authorized to engage in non-collective activities and could legally acquire the raw materials and machinery needed to begin production.

Market Incentives. The first two reforms created the potential for small-scale industrial growth. The third factor, the creation of market incentives for individual action, was an unintended consequence of the early reform period. During the period of high socialism, years of shortages of consumer goods had created a vast, pent-up demand for goods of all kinds. As the reforms started in the early 1980s, new consumer goods manufactured by rural industry began to enter the market. Consumers, long conditioned by an economy of scarcity to buy anything, quickly bought up commodities at relatively high prices. The ease of sales served as an important incentive to producers to undertake more investment. The market incentives, which came from experience with an economy of shortages, were the result of a peculiar feature of the early reform economy in China. During the years of high socialism, the state plan had carefully controlled the allocation of goods through a system of state-assigned prices that often had little to do with the actual production costs. When Gaoyang weavers first entered the market, demand still greatly exceeded supply and rural producers were able to make high profits in part because they were able to gain a share of state monopoly profits. Barry Naughton argues that this situation was true for much of rural industry in the early reform period.[5] High profit margins had been allotted to state firms by the state's commodity price structure. In the textile sector in 1980, sectoral profit rates stood at 69 percent, third highest in the whole Chinese economy. While increased competition and the gradual movement away from a dual price system eventually drove profits down to lower levels, in the early years shortages of goods combined with a price structure that had been set to benefit monopoly producers worked to the advantage of non-state firms.

Access to Improved Equipment. In the early stages of the reforms, rural industry was able to gain customers because of the great pent-up demand for consumer goods and the explosive growth of disposable income in the hands of rural families. However, if rural industry was to move beyond competition only on price, to competition on quality and variety of products, it needed to acquire modern machinery that was capable of producing better products. Ironically, in the textile industries it was a state decision to invest heavily in the modernization of the state-owned factories that changed the terms of competition between state and small-scale private industry. As the national government moved to put new investment into state-owned firms, the state firms decided to sell their decommissioned equipment to used equipment dealers. Brokers bought the machinery and resold it to rural factories, which very quickly began producing more sophisticated products at prices the state firms could not meet.

Creating a Virtuous Cycle. The reform process, by chance rather than by design, created a virtuous cycle in which rural reforms freed the labor supply and increased purchasing power, industrial reforms opened access to raw materials and machinery, and the two working together created large, competitive markets which drove up demand, providing incentives that overcame the investment risks.

With this rough sketch of the major steps in the national process of reform, let us turn to examine development in Gaoyang.

BEGINNINGS OF REFORM IN GAOYANG

In the Gaoyang area the reforms also began with agriculture. Between 1958 and 1978 massive investment in agriculture had improved the ecological balance in the region, but had not resolved the problems of basic poverty. As we saw in chapter one, an agricultural crisis in the late Qing had provided much of the initial motivation for the development of rural industry. After the forming of People's Communes in 1958, local government bodies mobilized manpower to change the basic ecological environment. Dams were built in the mountains to the west of the Hebei plains to help prevent flooding, and a water control system was constructed that linked the surrounding plains into a drainage system centered on the Baiyang lake region. This water control system, which stretched across the Gaoyang region, allowed for both irrigation in times of drought and for drainage after heavy rains.[6] The investments in agriculture began to pay off in the early 1970s as per capita grain output rose from 157 kilograms in 1972 to 180 kilograms in 1974. Then factional struggles associated with the latter stages of the Cultural Revolution began to take their toll and output fell back to earlier levels, standing at 131 kilograms per capita in 1976 and only 120 kilograms per capita in 1977.[7] The poorer villages and those most directly affected by ecological problems found themselves regularly dependent on state grain relief.[8]

Despite the investment in agriculture, which had improved the productivity of the land, the absence of rural industry meant that local living standards were little better than during the prewar period.[9] Per capita purchasing power had stagnated at the level of 30 to 40 yuan per person, per year, and this was reflected in consumption patterns. Most of the new housing constructed between 1958 and 1978 used sun-dried, rather than kilned, bricks, and sample surveys showed that only 10 to 15 percent of rural households had accumulated enough in savings to purchase even one bicycle.

Since the Gaoyang region had clearly suffered a relative decline in standards of living under the collective economy, with its stress on production of grain, we might expect that the local government would have eagerly seized the opportunities offered by the economic reform policies. Counter to that expectation, county government officials were slow to respond. This was largely due to the fact that there were two contradictory traditions in Gaoyang in the early 1980s. The first was the rural industrial tradition, tracing its roots back to the late Qing period, which valued technological skills and entrepreneurial initiative and rewarded individual economic endeavor. Opposing the rural industrial tradition was a mass mobilization tradition that traced its roots to the anti-Japanese resistance war; this tradition had gotten a new infusion of energy during the recently ended Cultural Revolution. The mass mobilization tradition stressed the importance of class struggle and promised collective rewards that would lead to a more egalitarian society. This tradition directly challenged the fundamental principles of the rural industrial tradition, denying legitimacy to entrepreneurial initiative and the differential economic rewards that accompanied it. The bitter struggles of the Cultural Revolution had tipped the balance in favor of the mass mobilization tradition.

Even after the Cultural Revolution ended, local cadre hesitated to take any action that might raise suspicions about their support for socialism. We can see this very clearly in the suppression of private industry that took place in the village of Liguozhuang in the spring of 1981, several years after the national reform policies had begun. Residents of the village, using the name of the village-owned collective factory, had revived household-based weaving and were earning good profits. When reports of their activities reached the county government, officials came to the village, put seals on the looms, and fined the village seventy-five yuan per loom.[10] These events took place at a time when rural industry was already starting to develop in neighboring counties.

County officials in Gaoyang finally decided to encourage the development of small-scale industry in late 1983.[11] Successful implementation of the responsibility system in agriculture in 1981 and 1982 had marked the first step away from a rigidly controlled rural economy. While the agricultural reform brought some improvement in income, county government officials realized that changes in agricultural policy alone could not significantly improve rural living standards in a place like Gaoyang, with its relatively poor land and high population density. Spurred on by state directives that urged local officials to promote rural industry and reassured by the success of nearby counties, local officials decided to encourage a revival of rural industry: Gaoyang would return to its historical tradition and develop the textile industry.[12] County officials called meetings of village cadre, urging them to take the lead in organizing rural industrial activities in their villages. They were encouraged to participate as a way of assuring the population that it would not be censured for pursuing market production.

Almost overnight rural industry took off. In 1983 there were 168 registered village enterprises, or 1 small collective enterprise per village in Gaoyang County. By the end of 1984, more than 12,000 enterprises were registered, most of them privately owned, and more than thirty thousand individuals were employed in rural industrial activities.[13] By 1995, rural industry employed most of the county's labor force and was responsible for 85 percent of the total agricultural and industrial output.[14]

DEVELOPMENT TRAJECTORIES

The third phase of growth can be roughly divided into two periods differentiated by the institutional structures that shaped patterns of competition between state and non-state firms. During the early reform period (to 1989), rural enterprises primarily produced goods that the state sector had neglected, while during the second period (beginning in 1990), rural firms began to compete directly with state firms. In the first few years after the beginning of the reforms, most industrial activity was concentrated in the field that Gaoyang natives knew best: weaving. While this choice was influenced by familiarity and experience, it was also the result of the institutional framework that prevailed at that time. The first hesitant steps toward reform had given private firms limited access to the raw materials that were the essential inputs for household weaving. But although the non-state sector began to develop, the low raw-materials prices and guaranteed markets available to state firms gave these firms a commanding position in the textile industry and made direct competition difficult.

The Gaoyang strategy of development in the early reform period made use of flexible production technologies. Local producers searched for niches in the market that were not being served by state firms and designed new products to fill them. In most cases the niches were for products that were at the lower-value-added end of the product chain. Some were for products that state firms had neglected, some had originally been supplied by collective factories that had collapsed in the early stages of the reform, and some were for new products that the large state firms, with their relatively inflexible plans, had not yet moved to fill.

During this early period, from 1983 to 1989, China's textile markets went through explosive change. As the reforms in agriculture increased rural

income, domestic demand spiraled upward. At the same time, China's reen-
trance into the world economy led to dramatic increases in the export demand as well.[15] In the state sector, a major shift in investment policies had
funneled funds to the long-neglected light industrial sectors, including textiles, causing a growth spurt in the early 1980s.[16]As the supply of textile products increased, the cloth rationing system was abandoned in December of
1984 and market demand and prices came increasingly to control production
and sales. Per capita consumption of textile products rose steadily: total fabric consumption per capita jumped from 11.51 meters in 1978 to 17.73 in
1994, and in the knitting yarn industry, which Gaoyang entered in the late
1980s, per capita consumption increased nine and a half fold between 1978
and 1994.[17]

Concurrent reforms in the market system and the increasing number of
production units led to changes in the dual price system. Where once state
firms had first allocated in-quota output to business partners specified in the
plan, the incentives for sale on the market increased. Gradually the gap between in-plan and out-of-plan prices—both for intermediate goods like yarn
and for finished consumer items—narrowed and then disappeared.

As a result of these changes, rural enterprises began to compete directly
with state firms. For the state textile firms in Gaoyang, 1989 marked the peak
of their post-reform profitability. Industrial reforms introduced to aid state
firms during the credit crunch of 1989 to 1990, brought on in part by the high
inflation rates that preceded the Tiananmen demonstrations, had unintended
consequences, pushing state firms into decline.[18]

In Gaoyang, the shift to the second period, characterized by direct competition between rural and state enterprises, can be seen most directly in the
production of toweling. Until the early-1990s, the Gaoyang Towel Factory
was one of the region's most successful state enterprises. Started in the 1950s
as a small cooperative workshop owned by several villages, it had been
taken over by the county in 1970 and came under national ownership in
1978. In the 1980s it was a major exporter of toweling, primarily to Japan.
The firm's success had led to an increase in state investment, which was just
coming on line in 1990, when the workforce was increased from eight hundred to twelve hundred workers. In 1989 the Gaoyang Towel Factory was
one of fifteen state-owned towel factories in Hebei Province; by the spring
of 1995, it was the only state-owned towel factory in the province that was
still operating, and it was only able to produce at about 50 percent of capacity. In 1996 the towel factory began a joint venture with a Korean partner
as a new survival strategy. While competition from rural enterprises was not
the only factor effecting the competitiveness of the state-owned textile firms,
clearly it played a significant role in the troubles that state factories all over
China were experiencing in the early 1990s.

At the same time that the province's state-owned factories were floundering, rural industry continued to grow, increasing the pressure on state firms. After 1990 state and non-state firms purchased raw materials in the same markets, at common prices. In many cases they used similar equipment and produced similar products. In the three years beginning in 1993, raw materials prices rose 2.6 times, while the sales price of finished toweling rose only 1.9 times. The resulting squeeze on profits fell much more heavily on the state-owned enterprises, which had much heavier commitments to worker welfare, including the payment of pensions to retired workers and welfare benefits to current workers.[19] The state firms had also long been used by local labor bureaus as depositories for surplus labor, meaning that the Gaoyang state firms, like state firms in other parts of China, employed more workers than were really needed to carry out the assigned tasks.[20] The experience of the Gaoyang Towel Factory is just one example of the common experiences of state textile firms that came into competition with non-state enterprises after 1990. National statistics show that by the end of 1993, the rural enterprise sector was producing 44 percent of the total output value in the textile industry for all of China.[21]

Thus, in little more than a decade, Gaoyang's new rural enterprises moved from household-based production of low-cost, low-quality items that state industry had been unwilling to manufacture, to production of a much broader range of goods, many of which were in direct competition with products manufactured by state-sector firms. In setting up the thousands of new enterprises that had begun to compete successfully with the state firms, Gaoyang's rural entrepreneurs and firms drew on a network of connections in the Chinese textile industry that gave them an advantage over rivals in communities that did not have entrepreneurial traditions. Let us then turn to examine the ways in which the Gaoyang tradition aided development during the third phase of growth.

ENTREPRENEURIAL LEGACIES AND THE THIRD PHASE OF GROWTH

Gaoyang's long history in the textile industry gave local entrepreneurs an advantage in the uncertain markets of the mid-1980s. Foremost among the advantages was the network of connections to individuals who worked in the textile industry all over China. A tally done by the Gaoyang Textile Museum in the early 1990s claimed a total of 5,383 natives of Gaoyang working in the textile industries in various parts of China. (See table 8.1.) This Gaoyang network had been created by three major exoduses of trained personnel from the region. The first had come at the beginning of the anti-Japanese war, when many factory and workshop owners had moved their operations to Beijing or Tianjin; most of those whose businesses survived the war continued in their new locations after the war. While the original proprietors and technicians had long since retired, their children had often inherited their positions and took on the task of offering assistance to firms in their native place.[22] The second outflow of Gaoyang natives had come at the end of the civil war, when cadre from the North China base areas moved into Tianjin and the larger cities of Hebei Province to take over the administration of those cities. While many of the cadre who were transferred at this time did not have technical skills, some of them were to rise to important positions in the economic ministries of major North China cities.[23] The third and largest exodus took place in 1955, when skilled workers were transferred to staff new textile factories all over North China.

Table 8.1.   Gaoyang Natives Working in National Textile Industry

Place	Number	Place	Number
Beijing	373	**Sichuan**	
Tianjin	187	Chengdu	161
Hebei		Chongqing	86
Shijiazhuang	603	**Gansu**	
Baoding	447	Lanzhou	104
Tangshan	168	Tianshui	41
Xingtai	48	**Shanxi**	
Handan	156	Taiyuan	92
Zhangjiakou	67	Yuci	64
Henan		**Hunan**	
Zhengzhou	142	Changsha	102
Anyang	157	Hengyang	46
Xinxiang	63	**Inner Mongolia**	
Luoyang	174	Baotou	102
Nanyang	48	Huhhot	13
Kaifeng	63	**Others**	
Xuchang	52	Changchun	94
Shandong		Hangzhou	24
Jinan	134	Xuzhou	91
Qingdao	52	Pengpu	19
Dezhou	31	Wuhan	64
Liaoning		Xi'an	172
Shenyang	103	Kunming	41
Jinzhou	122	Xining	166
Dalian	61	Yinchuan	46
		Urumuchi	21
		Taibei	16

Source: Data comes from a tabulation made by the Gaoyang Textile Museum of what it describes as incomplete data, 1995.

Guanxi xue, the study of how personal networks have been constructed and used in contemporary China in the private business sector, has become a hot subject in recent years.[24] Often the use of *guanxi* has been seen as primarily instrumental, with those seeking special favors making use of gifts to establish preferential relations with officials in a position to provide direct benefits to the petitioner. In the Gaoyang case, while gifts were certainly used to build relationships, appeals also were made to the native-place ties that have long been regarded as one of the important elements of personal identity, especially for those living away from their place of origin.

We can identify three specific ways in which the Gaoyang network of native-place loyalties assisted private firms during the third phase of growth: connections were used to gain access to raw materials, to provide training in use of new technology, and to provide market information. In all three of these areas, native-place connections were particularly important during the early reform period, a time when markets were just emerging and the institutional supports for private industry were not yet in place. Let us begin with an examination of the use of *guanxi* in acquiring raw materials.

In the early 1980s, Chinese planners created a dual price system to provide greater performance incentives to state firms. This system made it possible for rural entrepreneurs to acquire raw materials for industrial activities. However, even when customers were willing to pay bonus prices, raw materials were often in short supply; it was difficult to get market information and competition for bonus price goods was stiff. Being able to call on native-place ties could ease access. Most useful were ties to people in the accounting and sales divisions of large state factories, as well as people in the state marketing agencies. Fellow "natives" might offer goods at slightly discounted prices or make it easier for Gaoyang dealers to move to the front of the queue for goods that were in short supply.

While the use of native-place ties to gain access to raw materials was quite common in the 1980s, by the mid 1990s it had virtually disappeared. As state regulation eased, the markets for intermediate products matured and the gap between the lower state allocation price and the bonus price narrowed and then disappeared. Today, while connections may still help in gaining market information and small discounts, special connections and lavish gifts are no longer prerequisites for working in the yarn wholesale trade. Although successful wholesalers still work to build relations of trust with their regular trading partners, the openness of the market has changed the quality of the relationship.[25]

The second way in which native-place networks contributed to growth in Gaoyang was through the provision of technical training. As entrepreneurs moved from household-based weaving using relatively simple technology to the establishment of factories with more sophisticated equipment, they found that they needed to bring in textile engineers to train their workforce.

When local entrepreneurs wanted to hire engineers, they most commonly sought to hire Gaoyang natives who were working in or soon to retire from large state firms. Some entrepreneurs went through their own family or village connections to find skilled engineers, while others sought introductions through the county government's Township and Village Enterprise Bureau.

Local firms had to pay competitive wages to hire those with advanced engineering skills, but the native-place connections gave Gaoyang entrepreneurs access to a large pool of trained personnel who were more willing to take on the jobs because of their ties. In a highly competitive business where improvements in quality could greatly strengthen competitive position, access to skilled personnel played a very important role in the growth of individual firms. At the same time, it bred a more general respect for quality control that continues to influence production decisions of local producers.[26]

The third way in which native-place ties aided the third phase of growth was through provision of market data and information. In addition to the Gaoyang natives who worked in textile factories all over China, there were other native sons and daughters who worked in marketing and distribution organizations. Such individuals were called on to aid in finding markets. While most of the work of acquiring market information still depended on the initiative of the individual firm, introductions to Gaoyang natives who served as purchasing agents for regional marketing organizations often led to contracts. As in the case of markets for raw materials, these personal connections were most important in the early reform period. Once firms had established a reputation in the market and begun to build relations with a set of regular customers, past performance was more important than personal connections. But at the outset, when producers were just feeling their way, connections played an important role.

CONTEMPORARY GAOYANG INDUSTRY

Gaoyang's contemporary textile industry includes four large subdivisions: the weaving sector, which produces toweling; the fine-wool–spinning sector, which produces knitting yarns; the coarse-wool–spinning sector, which produces carpet yarn; and the wool-weaving sector, which produces more than one hundred kinds of woolen and wool-blend fabrics and blankets. In addition there are many firms that service the four main lines of production, including raw materials wholesale dealers, dyeing factories and workshops, trading firms, and transport firms. Since the technological requirements and patterns of development of each of the four main sectors of the textile trade are different, we will consider them separately.

Weaving Industry

The third phase of growth began with weaving. Since large state factories dominated the market for production of standardized types of cloth, weavers began by producing niche goods that state firms had neglected, including cotton gauzes used for covering the cotton padding of bedding; lining fabrics for furniture, shoes, and bags; plastic screening, which was used for a variety of purposes, including screening for windows and the nets used in fish-raising ponds; and toweling. Today the largest division of the weaving trade is the production of toweling. In 1994 county weavers produced toweling with a value of 500 million yuan, which represented 35 percent of the total output value of Gaoyang's rural industry. By the early twenty-first century, Gaoyang had become one of China's largest producers of toweling for domestic and export markets.[27]

When we compare the contemporary situation with that of the past, there is no question that it is the weaving sector that most closely resembles organizational forms of the first two phases of growth. Production is concentrated in small, family-based workshops, located in more than fifty villages scattered throughout the county. Although the family workshop is the most common form of organization, by 1995 more than two hundred firms had grown to a size where they were classified as factories, a classification given to firms with more than six power looms.[28]

Beiquantou village specializes in the production of toweling. In the spring of 1995, the village had a population of 1,586 native residents, in 395 households, and their workshops operated 550 power looms. In addition to the native population, more than 2,000 non-native workers from provinces as distant as Sichuan and Ningxia were employed in the village, split almost equally between men and women. Most of the village's small weaving workshops had been set up within family resident compounds. Looms operated twenty-four hours a day, with workers split between two twelve-hour shifts. Most of the workshops used a combination of family and hired labor, and day and night the clacking sounds of the shuttles could be heard in almost every village lane.

While the weaving sector of contemporary industry seems closest to "Gaoyang roots," it has also undergone rapid technological change since the beginning of the third phase of growth. When private weaving first got started in 1984, most weavers used either old iron gear looms that had been "mechanized" by the attachment of a leather belt hooked up to a small engine, or a simple power loom known as the GY 42-inch loom, which was manufactured by the county's textile machinery factory.[29] The situation changed in the late 1980s, when a surge of investment in state-owned textile firms led their managers to scrap old equipment. The used machinery was sold to brokers, who resold the power looms to rural weavers at relatively low prices. In Gaoyang, weavers began to switch to two power looms (the

44-inch 1511 and the 75-inch 1515), which were considerably more efficient than the 42-inch Gaoyang loom.[30] While a single worker could tend two 42-inch looms, one worker could watch four of the 1511 or 1515 looms.[31] The number of power looms in use in the county steadily rose, reaching eight thousand by 1990 and standing at fifteen thousand in the spring of 1995.

Use of the improved power looms contributed to a shift in the product mix as rural weavers were no longer restricted to the production of only low-value-added niche products. Access to the improved equipment leveled the playing field between state and private factories. Thus the stage was set for direct competition between state factories and private workshops.

Organization of Production

By the early 1990s, the scale of workshop production was very similar to that during the first and second phases of growth, but the overall organization of the weaving industry was quite different. During the first phase of growth, wholesale capital dominated Gaoyang industry; large wholesalers had built integrated firms that controlled production and sales. In the third phase of growth, no firms have yet been able to create the same integration of production and marketing. In contemporary Gaoyang, independent firms are responsible for the supply of raw materials, bleaching and dyeing of yarns, weaving, and marketing of finished products. While individual weaving workshops have established regular business relations with yarn wholesalers, dyeing workshops, and the jobbers who manage marketing, each of the separate processes takes place in an independent firm that acts on its own account. Let us then consider the organization of the wholesaling and processing ends of the trade.

Yarn Wholesalers. In the mid-1990s there were approximately sixty yarn wholesale dealers supplying raw materials to the thousands of weaving workshops.[32] The earliest wholesale firms were started in 1984. Originally many dealers worked out of their rural homes, but by the mid-1990s most had offices in the new three-story commercial buildings that lined the main streets on the north and east of the town. First-floor shop rooms were piled to the ceiling with bundles of yarn and handwritten signs in the windows listed types of yarn and prices. On a good day, one of the medium-sized dealers would sell four to six tons of yarn.

Most of the yarn wholesale firms were created as business partnerships. When yarn wholesaling first appeared in 1984, a firm needed about 100,000 yuan in working capital. The capital for wholesaling usually came from savings and loans from friends and relatives. Most of the firms were organized as partnerships (*hegu*), with each working partner holding a share (*gu*). Wholesalers searched for yarn supplies in mill towns all over North and northwest China, in cities like Zhengzhou and Anyang in Henan, Xi'an in

Shaanxi, Yuci in Shanxi, Lanzhou in Ningxia, Baotou in Inner Mongolia, Shijiazhuang, Handan and Baoding in Hebei, and Tianjin and Beijing. Business relationships built during those days continue to sustain the wholesale trade today.

As weaving has grown, so has the scale of the wholesale firms. An average wholesale firm in 1995 had capital of 1,000,000 to 2,000,000 yuan. As before, most were organized as business partnerships. While the prewar wholesale trade was the beneficiary of various forms of credit, contemporary yarn wholesaling relies almost exclusively on cash. Yarn suppliers are rarely willing to sell on credit. When wholesale firms are short on cash they seek short-term loans from banks near supplying factories. Since interest rates on short-term loans are relatively high, wholesale dealers seek fast turnover of their stock and rapid repayment of loans. Success in wholesaling depends on building relations of trust with managers in factories supplying the yarn and with customers in rural weaving workshops. While workshops are not tied to particular wholesalers by contract relations as in the past, most workshops do most of their business with only one or two of the wholesale dealers and will seek supplies elsewhere only when their regular dealer is unable to provide the required quality or quantity of yarn.

Figure 8.1. Drying Yarn. Small rural workshops dyed yarn for the production of towels. While modern equipment was used for bleaching and dyeing, the dyed yarn was dried on outside racks. (Photo by the author.)

Dyeing Workshops. All of the yarn used in the production of toweling has to be either bleached or dyed before weaving. The most commonly produced toweling in Gaoyang uses striped designs that required a combination of bleached white yarns and dyed yarns. Most of the dyeing workshops that process yarn for the weaving factories are concentrated in two or three villages that have specialized in dyeing for several generations.

Yarn-dyeing workshops are small operations set up by partners who pool funds and labor.[33] Dyeing workshops usually work to the order of customers who supply the yarn. In this highly competitive business, speed is important: in 1995 average turnover time from receipt of yarn to delivery to the customer was four days. Since workshops offered almost identical services at almost identical prices, customers usually established a working relationship with one, or at most two, dyeing workshops. Once a working relationship was established, trusted customers could keep running accounts with a final settlement before the Lunar New Year.

Marketing. Direct wholesale marketing of goods was one of the distinctive features of the classic Gaoyang system of production. Sales agencies (*waizhuang*) set up in major commercial centers sold Gaoyang fabrics to local wholesale and retail outlets and collected information on market demand. In the mid-1980s there were some attempts to create a new system of sales agencies in important regional markets, but few survived into the 1990s. The high costs of maintaining the agencies, the fact that most of the toweling was not designed for specific markets, and the convenience of new regional wholesale markets has led to a different approach to marketing. Sixty to 70 percent of the approximately 650,000,000 towels Gaoyang producers sold in 1994 passed through the state-regulated wholesale marketing network, with the remainder going directly to customers on contract.[34]

The village of Liguozhuang organized the first specialized wholesale market in September 1983.[35] When I visited the market in September 1988, the market was relatively simple: sellers lined the main street of the village, each with piles of cotton gauze cloth to sell. By later standards, the volume of individual sales was small. Most of the sellers operated home workshops and transported goods to market on the back of bicycles.[36]

While small-lot sales had not totally disappeared in the mid-1990s, a new marketing system had emerged which moved larger volumes of goods over longer distances. In 1992 the County Bureau of Industry and Commerce decided to construct a new wholesale market near the northwest corner of the county town. In 1995, 60 to 70 percent of the toweling passed through this wholesale market, which drew up to 60,000 dealers on a busy day.

There are two types of sellers in the wholesale market. About 60 percent of the permanent wholesale establishments are factory outlets. While family workshops with only one or two looms are not able to support such outlets, small factories with six to eight looms often do have their own wholesale

Figure 8.2. Liguozhuang Market. Rural weavers selling cotton gauze at a periodic market established in the village of Liguozhuang in the late 1980s. (Photo by the author.)

outlet. The wholesale outlets display sample products and take orders. Factories that do not have their own outlets market through wholesale specialists whose shops display goods from several small workshops. Sales through such wholesale specialists are on commission.[37]

Most of the goods purchased at the Gaoyang wholesale market are shipped to one of four large regional wholesale markets located in Zhejiang (Yiwu), Shenyang (Wuai), Wuhan, and Harbin. Large regional specialized wholesale marketing centers like these are a relatively new phenomenon in

Figure 8.3. Transporting Goods to Market. Rural weavers transported finished cloth to the Liguozhuang market by bicycle in the late 1980s. (Photo by the author.)

Figure 8.4. Textile Trading Center. The county government constructed this textile trading center, where small factories market goods. (Photo provided by the Gaoyang County government office.)

China. From the 1950s to the early 1980s marketing in China was handled by bureaucratic organizations that created single marketing channels for each category of good in each regional area.[38] As the economic reforms developed, the state loosened control over the distribution system and in 1984 lifted the last controls on wholesale marketing. State and private actors could now move freely across administrative borders. As goods became more freely available, new wholesale centers began to develop. At first many of those centers were like the towel market in Gaoyang that was close to a production center. Most of the new marketing centers were established with the encouragement of local governments, which helped acquire land and raise funds for construction of basic facilities. While some of the new wholesaling centers were located near rural industrial centers, others were established primarily to serve as distribution centers. Yiwu in central Zhejiang Province followed the second pattern. Yiwu has become famous for its wholesale trade in daily-use items. In 1994 annual trade volume in this one regional distribution center exceeded ten trillion yuan.[39] Towels produced in Gaoyang are sold to wholesale dealers at the Gaoyang towel market; they are then shipped to Yiwu and sold there to wholesale and retail dealers who move the goods into regional and export markets.

Comparisons. The weaving sector most closely resembles earlier Gaoyang industrial patterns. Production is centered in small, family-based production units spread out over more than fifty villages. Yet while the organization of production in the cotton-weaving sector strongly resembles earlier patterns, the overall industrial structure is different, since there are no integrated firms that manage production from the import of raw materials to the export of finished goods. Let us take a moment to consider why that is so. Prewar yarn and cloth wholesaling firms started as yarn importers and then added on direct marketing networks, contract weaving, and mechanized finishing and dyeing factories. None of the yarn dealers in contemporary Gaoyang has yet made a move to expand its activities beyond yarn wholesaling. Most of the contemporary Gaoyang yarn wholesalers began as pick-up arrangements between three or four friends who pooled their resources and went into business. Today, many of the firms have quite substantial resources, but quite simple organizational structures. Most commonly, all of the partners are active participants in the business, with two or more of the partners handling the "outside" work of purchasing yarn from factories all over North and northwest China, while the remaining partners man the Gaoyang store where they deal with local customers. There are no sources of easy credit of the kind that allowed the late Qing wholesale dealers to get a start. When loans are needed, they are almost always short-term bank loans at relatively high interest rates. Most of the capital of contemporary wholesalers is invested in yarn stocks and few have the extra resources to engage in credit sales to customers. Moreover, in most periods, demand for yarn has been sufficiently high that wholesale dealers have not had to offer credit in order to find customers.

A second factor may be the scattered location of suppliers. In the prewar period almost all yarn was either imported from overseas or purchased from Tianjin and Shanghai spinning mills. One branch office in Tianjin could handle the purchase of raw materials and manage credit with local wholesalers and native banks. Today yarn suppliers are scattered over much wider territory and wholesale firms have to expend more energy to gain market information and arrange purchases. There is little indication that any of the yarn wholesalers have any desire to turn their firms into integrated operations that combine production with sales.

The middle actors in the production chain, the weavers and dyers, are organized in small-scale units that lack the resources to even consider expansion into integrated firms. While the larger of the weaving factories have set up their own wholesale outlets, none have yet moved beyond that stage. As long as the largest weaving factories have a maximum of thirty looms, the situation is not likely to change.

As for marketing, sales arrangements are more complicated than they were in an earlier day. Goods move much more swiftly, transported by rail and highway, and marketing specialists use modern communication, including mobile telephones and pagers, to keep in touch with swiftly changing market demand. From the beginning of the third phase of growth, petty traders have played an active role in the wholesale markets. One of the characteristics of the wholesale trade is heated competition among dealers. Competition has worked to the advantage of small Gaoyang producers: commission fees are low and competition inspires the wholesalers to work hard to gain sales. The seller's market conditions that prevailed throughout the mid-1980s provided little incentive for Gaoyang producers to undertake their own wholesaling, and by the time market pressures might have made it advantageous for producers to consider setting up sales agencies, the system of independent wholesale dealers was already in place.

One of the interesting features of the wholesale trade is the gender division of labor. Most yarn wholesaling is done by partnerships that are exclusively male, while women do most of the wholesaling of finished goods. Two factors seem to contribute to this division of labor: capital and work location. Yarn wholesaling requires larger sums of capital and travel outside the local community. Cloth wholesaling is done locally and requires much smaller amounts of capital. This gender division of labor was established quite early. In the mid-1980s one often saw women in their thirties and forties peddling Gaoyang cloth on the streets of the larger North China cities. The prominence of women in the cloth wholesale trade would seem to be a continuation of this pattern.

Growth of Wool Spinning and Weaving

Most of the larger firms in Gaoyang today are involved in the wool indus-try, a new line of production introduced during the third phase of growth. The Gaoyang region was not a traditional producer of woolen products; the first wool-spinning factories were established in Gaoyang in 1984. A decade later, in 1995, spindle capacity stood at 20,000 spindles for spinning fine yarns (*qingfang*), 25,000 spindles for coarse yarn (*sufang*), and weaving ca-pacity stood at 11,000,000 meters of cloth.[40] While the Gaoyang firms are rel-ative newcomers to the wool industry, growth has been rapid and the vari-ous sectors of the wool industry have become major producers. In 1995 Gaoyang firms produced roughly 23,000 tons of knitting yarns, which was approximately 6.3 percent of China's total national production of knitting yarn. While wool weaving output stood at roughly 2.6 percent of the na-tional total, capacity was rising rapidly in the mid-1990s.[41]

Wool spinning and weaving is done only in factories, producing economic and social relations that are quite different from those in the cotton-weaving industry. Initial investment requirements are much larger and in order to gather the necessary capital to start a firm, entrepreneurs form partnerships (*hegu* or *hehuo*) in which a group of individuals pool labor and capital to set up a firm. The workplace is separated from the home and there is little use of family labor. The smallest factories employ at least twenty workers and the county's largest wool-spinning firm employed three thousand workers in 1995. The wool factories have given rise to a rural working class that draws on both local and immigrant labor; in the spring of 1995 there were more than ten thousand registered non-native workers in Gaoyang, the vast ma-jority of whom were young, unmarried women working in the wool-spinning mills.

In order to understand the explosive growth of wool spinning and weav-ing we need to briefly consider the overall development of the Chinese wool industry in the 1980s and 1990s. Although the Chinese wool industry has grown faster than other sectors of the textile industry since the beginning of reforms in 1978, per capita consumption of wool is still relatively low, at roughly one-third of a kilogram of wool per person per year.[42] The rapid ex-pansion of the wool spinning and weaving industry has been largely the re-sult of the dramatic development of the rural industrial sector. In the early 1990s there were approximately three thousand wool-spinning firms in China, and two thousand of those were rural enterprises. State firms pro-duced only about one-third of the total output of wool yarn in 1995, with the rest coming from rural firms.[43] In Gaoyang, as in the wool industry at large, some of the rural enterprises were using decommissioned equipment from state factories that was at a relatively backward technological level, while other rural enterprises were using advanced technology, including computer-controlled open-end spinning equipment.

The rapid growth of the wool industry is the result of changes in both domestic and export demand. Although per capita consumption of wool products is still relatively low, it is now more than nine times higher than it was in the pre-reform period. Demand for wool products displays high income elasticity in China, and as income levels have risen, domestic consumption of woolen products has also risen.[44] Rural businessmen are now much more likely to wear Western-style woolen business suits and tailored winter coats are popular with an increasingly broad segment of the urban and rural populations. Fashionable sweaters are also replacing the padded jackets of an earlier era. On the export side, China's export of clothing includes a large volume of wool and knitted goods, as well as vast quantities of wool carpets and blankets. All have contributed to the dramatic growth of wool-processing industries in recent years.

A second factor that has contributed to rapid growth of the rural wool-processing industries has been changes in government policies with regard to raw materials. Before the launching of the economic reform programs in 1978, China's wool spinning and weaving industries were largely self-sufficient, with 93 percent of the raw wool they consumed coming from domestic sources.[45] The reform policies affected the wool industry in many ways. Privatization of the herds, together with a rising demand for mutton, upset the domestic wool production system, leading to problems with both quality and quantity of production. At the same time, the number of consumers of raw wool increased as collective and private spinning and weaving mills were established. The Chinese government's response was to enter the world wool market, dramatically increasing imports of raw wool. State control over the wool marketing system was loosened and despite the launching of "wool wars" over control of the domestic supply of raw wool, state monopolies were never re-imposed. For raw wool consumers, including the newly established rural industrial firms, this meant access to supplies of both domestic and imported raw wool at openly determined market prices. The result has been a rapid increase in the use of imported raw wool. In 1994, Gaoyang was the largest single Chinese regional consumer of New Zealand wool, taking a total of 15,000 tons. While competition has driven up raw wool prices in recent years, none of the surveyed Gaoyang firms have expressed any difficulty in acquiring raw materials.[46]

Wool Spinning

Gaoyang's first wool-spinning factory, Red Flag (Hong Qi), was established in 1984 in the village of Zhaoguanzuo. In that year, the village's collectively owned weaving factory, which had only eight looms, was on the point of bankruptcy. A group of young men in the village, led by Gao Yankai, decided to pool their labor and savings to set up a new firm that contracted to take over the village factory. From the beginning they intended to set up a wool-spinning factory. At the time neighboring Li County was experiencing a boom in growth, led by spinning factories that spun synthetic fibers into knitting yarns. A large market in Li County supplied raw materials and offered a market for finished goods. Zhaoguanzuo village was located in the southern part of Gaoyang County bordering Li County, and many of Gaoyang's spinning factories were started there in direct imitation of the Li County model.[47]

As Gao Yankai tells the story, he and his partners intended to set up a factory to spin knitting yarn, but knowing little of the industry they mistakenly purchased equipment that could only spin coarse yarns. They soon discovered that there was a very high demand for the kind of coarse yarn that is used in making carpets. Thus was born Gaoyang's first carpet-yarn factory.

The story of the development of the Gaoyang carpet-yarn industry parallels the tale of the cotton-weaving industry, illustrating again the direct competition between small-scale rural industry and large state firms, a competition in which rural industry has emerged victorious.[48] High-quality wool carpets have been a major North China export since the 1920s, when European entrepreneurs set up the first Tianjin handicraft factories, producing for an export market. From the 1950s to the early 1980s, several large state factories in Tianjin and Beijing dominated the industry, steadily raising the quality of their products and making the Tianjin brand-name famous in international markets. While production was under state control, sales were also closely regulated, with the foreign trade bureaus dealing only with a carefully restricted list of established foreign agents. The opening of China to the outside world under the economic reform policies stimulated production in China's traditional export industries, and after the United States granted China Most Favored Nation status, American demand for Chinese carpets exploded. Foreign trade bureaus began to welcome new trading partners, and as the demand for carpets grew, the famous factories of Tianjin and Beijing began to set up branches in outlying areas, particularly in Wuqing, one of the counties attached to Tianjin Municipality. At first the parent firm trained workers for the branch firms, supervised production processes, and provided all of the raw materials, including the carpet yarn. It was not long before the rising demand for raw materials exceeded the capacity of the spinning mills attached to the parent firms.[49] It was at that point that rural firms like Gaoyang's Red Flag got their start, working on contract to foreign trading bureaus, which acted as intermediaries between the rural spinning mills, the urban carpet factories, and the Wuqing branches.

By the late 1980s the branch firms that had been set up in Wuqing, desiring to gain a larger share of the profits, began to operate independently of the parent firms and to compete directly with their original sponsors. New private firms were set up in imitation of the former branch firms, adding to the number of competitors of the old state firms. This explosive growth of the carpet industry created a vigorous market for carpet-yarn spinners. While the yarn produced by Gaoyang factories was often below the standards set by Tianjin's most famous state factories, it had a huge advantage in terms of price. For example, in the 1990–1991 period, when carpet yarn from a state producer was selling for twenty-three yuan per kilogram, Gaoyang producers were selling their product for twelve to thirteen yuan. The acquisition of lower-price raw materials allowed the Wuqing factories to undersell Tianjin's established factories by a large margin.[50] By the early 1990s, the well-established Tianjin factories were being forced to close down and today almost all Tianjin carpets are produced in the rural factories of Wuqing.[51]

In the spring of 1995 there were more than fifty carpet-yarn factories in Gaoyang, and the region had become a major supplier of this specialized product. While the scale of most of the factories was small, with the average factory producing about two hundred tons of yarn a year, the concentration of so many small factories in one area made the Gaoyang region the major North China supplier of carpet yarn. Belonging to an industrial district worked clearly in the region's favor. Customers seeking carpet yarn gathered in Gaoyang and as a result, when carpet-yarn factories in other areas went out of business, entrepreneurs bought equipment at discount prices and moved it to Gaoyang to start new factories.

In the mid-1990s the international market for Chinese carpets was relatively strong, and demand for carpet yarn continued to sustain Gaoyang firms. In the spring of 1994 alone, some thirty new carpet-yarn factories were founded to serve this market. In 1994 Gaoyang County spinners produced nearly twenty thousand tons of carpet yarn.[52]

The carpet-yarn factories stand at the low end of the technological continuum of the wool industries. Most of the firms use decommissioned equipment from former state factories and quality control standards are not rigidly enforced in many firms. An average carpet-yarn factory processes approximately one ton of wool yarn a day and employs three shifts of workers in factories where working conditions are often quite primitive. Fiber waste clings to the walls and ceilings of the dimly lighted production sheds, as workers move back and forth removing full spindles and reattaching broken threads. While the Gaoyang carpet-yarn spinners' product is not always of the same high quality as the yarn that was produced by the state factories when they were at the peak of prosperity, in the years ahead stiff competition between the dozens of carpet-yarn spinners should result in gradually rising technical standards.

Fine Spinning

One of the key features of Gaoyang industry during the first phase of growth was a pattern of meeting crises by introducing new products and technologies. In the contemporary industry, we can identify similar patterns in which some firms have moved from production of relatively simple products to the production of higher-value-added goods that require more sophisticated technology. The standard technological trajectory in contemporary Gaoyang has been to move from coarse spinning, often using used equipment, to fine spinning using newly purchased equipment. Some of the pioneers, like Red Flag, which started the coarse-spinning business, have added on fine-spinning lines of production. Some factories that once produced coarse yarn have converted completely to the production of knitting yarns, and some new factories have been founded that from the beginning have engaged in production of knitting yarns. By the end of 1994 there were forty-one fine-wool–spinning factories in the county, with a combined capacity of about twenty thousand tons of yarn a year.

Most famous of Gaoyang's fine spinning mills is San Li, a firm established by Wang Kejie in the early 1980s. In 1982 Wang quit his job at a state factory in the provincial capital of Shijiazhuang and returned to Gaoyang, where he bought two knitting machines and set up a home workshop knitting

Figure 8.5. Spinning Mill. Women workers in one of the wool-spinning mills. Some spinning mills produce knitting yarn, while others supply yarn for the production of woolen cloth and blankets. (Photo provided by the Gaoyang County government office.)

sweaters. As others in his native village of Jilang began to copy his success, Wang began a new business in 1985, knitting wool scarves. The profits from these early activities were invested in his first spinning factory, founded in 1986. While Wang's firm experienced difficulties in 1989–1990, when government policies tightened credit and drove down raw materials prices, he weathered the storm and continued to expand his factory. In 1996 the San Li industrial group included several factories with a total of ten thousand spindles and employing three thousand workers. San Li's annual production capacity stood at ten thousand tons of yarn, which put it in the category of a large-scale enterprise.[53] The San Li brand-name was becoming increasingly well known all over China, thanks to an active advertising campaign that included spot advertising on national television, and Wang continued to pursue his dream of surpassing the famous Tianjin yarn spinner Dongya. San Li and a number of the other larger fine spinning mills had also added on dyeing equipment, completing the technological trajectory which gave them control over all stages of production.[54]

Wool Weaving

The third section of Gaoyang's wool industry is wool weaving, which is also a new business started during the third phase of growth. In 1995 there were forty-three enterprises engaged in the weaving of wool fabrics and they jointly had an annual capacity of 11,000,000 meters of wool fabric. Scale of production and investment varies widely in the wool-weaving industry. The larger of the wool-weaving factories are integrated production units, which card and spin the wool and then weave it into finished fabric. Some of the factories also dye the finished fabrics, while others send the fabric to specialized fabric-dyeing firms. The smallest factories have six to eight looms and the carding and spinning equipment needed to supply that many looms. At the other end of the scale are factories that use computer-controlled open-end (*qiliu*) spinning machines. One "set" of open-end spinning equipment produces enough yarn to supply forty looms. The first Gaoyang firm to use open-end spinning equipment was established in 1992, and during its first year of operation the firm earned profits exceeding 1,500,000 yuan. The notable success of this firm inspired others, and by 1995 there were thirteen similar factories.

In less than a decade, Gaoyang's wool-weaving firms developed very rapidly. Starting first with used spinning and weaving equipment, they produced fabrics that were at the lower-value-added end of the product range. At the beginning, most of the firms had only mastered spinning and weaving technology and the finished fabrics were shipped to other areas for dyeing. In 1992, the addition of open-end spinning technology marked a major leap forward, with the most advanced firms moving from the bottom of the product chain to a position that represented much higher value added. As the most advanced firms shifted to the new technology, they also started to use better, but more expensive, raw materials. More use was made of imported raw wool, often imported from Australia.[55] The larger firms also began to add on their own dyeing operations, giving them control over the whole production process. Today Gaoyang's largest wool-weaving firms are located in modern buildings with highly trained staffs to supervise the operation of the computer-controlled spinning equipment.

Wool Industry: Some Comparative Issues

While the coarse- and fine-wool–spinning industries and the wool-weaving industry each have followed distinct patterns of development, they share certain characteristics that sharply distinguish them from the cotton-weaving industry. The first difference is the size of investment. Even the simplest carpet-yarn factory required a minimum investment of 150,000 yuan in fixed capital assets, and the more sophisticated, computer-controlled equipment used for open-end spinning can go as high as several million yuan.

A second characteristic of the wool firms is a pattern of production that must adjust to high seasonal differentiation in demand. Wool yarns and fabrics are produced throughout the year, but sales are concentrated in the period from late August to February.[56] Thus for almost half of the year, from March to mid-August, Gaoyang firms produce goods that are stored in their warehouses awaiting sales during the busy season. The natural result of this pattern is a high demand for circulating capital. The average factory using open-end spinning equipment has one line of spinning equipment that is able to produce roughly one ton of yarn a day. If we assume consumption of one ton of raw wool per working day, the raw material costs alone in 1995 came to 20,000 yuan per day.[57] We then need to add wages, which in 1995 were approximately 10 yuan per worker per day, and overhead costs. Wool sector factories thus have heavy demands for short-term circulating capital, and many turn to bank loans to supply capital during the off-season, when expenses are high but there is little income. When financing is hard to find, some firms stop production for one to two months during the slack season and others switch to synthetic fibers, which are cheaper than wool. There is no question that this pattern of seasonal differentiation in demand presents real challenges to Gaoyang's small, privately owned firms. Successful managers must devote some of their time to building ties with local bankers and others who have access to loan funds that will allow the firms to continue production during the slack season.

Thus while the profits to be made from the wool industries are higher than those in the cotton-weaving trade, the capital demands and the risks are also higher. The family-based production units which are so common in the cotton-weaving trade have no place in the rapidly growing wool spinning and weaving industries. In the next chapter we will turn to examine management strategies in these larger firms, and to consider the social consequences of the differing patterns of investment and production in Gaoyang's contemporary cotton and wool industries.

NOTES

1. Almost every explanatory meeting I have attended in Gaoyang since the mid-1980s has included this formulation.

2. Briefing by Gaoyang county officials May 6, 1995.

3. By 1996, the number of larger firms had again increased. In that year there were 689 firms with more than 100,000 yuan in registered capital. Among the largest firms, there were 102 with over 1,000,000 yuan in registered capital, and ten with over 5,000,000. Briefing by Gaoyang county officials on August 29, 1996.

4. Susan Shirk, *The Political Logic of Economic Reform in China* (Berkeley: University of California Press, 1993).

5. Barry Naughton, "Implications of the State Monopoly over Industry and Its Relaxation," *Modern China* 18, no. 1 (January 1992), 14–41; the theme is also developed in his book, *Growing out of the Plan—Chinese Economic Reform 1978–1993* (Cambridge: Cambridge University Press, 1995).

6. After the drainage system was constructed, fields were converted into "platform fields." This involved digging drainage ditches, roughly two meters deep, around blocks of land. Alkaline salts drain into the ditches, rather than rising to the surface of the fields; as the alkaline salts are removed, the productivity of the land is improved. *Gaoyang xianzhi*, 1995.

7. See information provided in the section on people's livelihood in the *Gaoyang xianzhi*, 1995. The chronology included in the *Gaoyang xianzhi* also includes other comments on the economic situation at this time. For example, an entry for November 29, 1972, reports the beginning of the "Study Dazhai" campaign and notes that there had been false reports that the county had "Crossed the Yellow River," that is, achieved output levels equivalent to those richer areas south of the Yellow River. In fact, according to the report, agriculture had gotten worse. And a report for 1975 notes that this year marked the last year of the fourth Five Year Plan, and that total county output at the end of the year was 12 percent less than in 1970.

8. Interview with officials of Liguozhuang, 1988.

9. While most official Chinese comments on the situation argue that the policies of the 1960s and 1970s were not successful, they always add that life was better than before the revolution. There is no question that there had been significant improvement in health conditions and a much more equitable division of income. However, in terms of the cash economy, there was considerably less improvement. Clearly the standards of living of the mid-1930s, when peasants were able to support a whole family with one active loom and when prosperous households could purchase imported bicycles, indicate much higher levels of cash income than during most of the 1960s and 1970s.

10. Chen Meijian, interview notes on a visit to Liguozhuang, March 3–4, 1984.

11. The breakup of collective agriculture had come slowly, starting in the spring of 1981. Tentative experiments with a limited version of the responsibility system moved, by the end of 1982, to full implementation of the responsibility system, which transferred control over agricultural production to the individual household. Rural markets were reopened in 1980, providing stimulus for greater diversity in agriculture; and as rural incomes rose, there was increasing demand for other goods. By 1983 most villages had disbanded collective factories. In some cases they divided equipment among village households, in others they contracted out collective resources to villagers. Information on the timing of changes and results can be found in the sections on agriculture in the *Gaoyang xianzhi*, 1995.

12. Important documents on rural policy issued in 1980, 1981, and 1982 permitted rural households to engage in private economic activities. In the Baoding area, neighboring Li County was one of the first counties to aggressively promote rural industry. Thanks to more open-minded local officials, the county got an early start in setting up spinning factories to produce polyester yarns and also set up a large specialized market for polyester yarns. Rapid growth in Li County, and the failure of provincial officials to move against it, encouraged Gaoyang officials to take their turn at encouraging reform.

13. These numbers come from records of the Gaoyang County Township and Village Enterprise Bureau. Chris Wong has argued that changes in statistical recording methods make statistics on small-scale rural industry for this period particularly unreliable. It was only in 1984 that the state statistical bureau started counting household enterprise activities. In Gaoyang, the decision by the local government to finally encourage rural industry corresponds very closely in time to the shift in statistical collection methods. Thus, while there may have been more rural industry in 1983 than is reflected in the statistics, in fact the major increase in household-based weaving does date to 1984. Christine Wong, "Interpreting Rural Industrial Growth in the Post-Mao Period," *Modern China* 14, no.1 (1988), 3–30.

14. Data on the number of workers and share of industrial output comes from the Township and Village Enterprise Bureau; a review of Gaoyang's overall performance can be found in *Hebei jingji nianjian 1995* (Beijing: Zhongguo Tongji Chubanshe, 1995), 734, 736.

15. Estimates of China's growth between 1980 and 1985 suggest annual growth of 9.8 percent a year, and during the same period textile exports grew from roughly US$2 billion in 1979, to US$4.6 billion in 1986. In 1986, 33.6 percent of China's total exports were textiles and clothing. See Kym Anderson, *New Silk Roads: East Asia and the World Textile Markets* (Cambridge: Cambridge University Press, 1992), 75. General statistics on textile expansion can be found in the Chinese textile yearbook, *Zhongguo fangzhi gongye nianjian* (Beijing: Zhongguo Fangzhi Chubanshe, 1994). Chinese industrial statistics are compiled by type of firm ownership. So while this almanac reflects production in China's state sector, it does not consistently include the non-state sector, which is included under Township and Village Enterprises. As a result, statistics compiled after the rapid rise of rural industry are incomplete, and it is difficult to determine what has and has not been counted in different estimates.

16. For a discussion of the shift see Dorothy Solinger, *From Lathes to Looms: China's Industrial Policy in Comparative Perspective, 1979–82* (Stanford: Stanford University Press, 1991).

17. *Zhongguo fangzhi gongye nianjian*, 1995 edition, 171.

18. For a general discussion of these issues, see Barry Naughton, *Growing out of the Plan: Chinese Economic Reform, 1978–1993*. Chapter 8 discusses the post-Tiananmen retrenchment, and its impact on the profitability of state firms. Earlier changes had already had an impact on profit rates. According to Naughton's calculations, sector profits in the textile industry had dropped from 69 percent in 1980 to just 15.8 percent in 1989 (238). The 69 percent profit rate had made textiles the third most profitable sector on his list, after the tobacco industry, with profits rates of 326 percent, and refining, where profits stood at 98 percent.

19. As Dic Lo argues, state-owned enterprises during the period of high socialism were not allowed to retain profits and as a result did not create savings as contributions to pension funds. When the administrative and budgeting systems were changed in the reform era, they were thus forced to pay pensions—which should have been the obligation of the state organizations that had absorbed their profits—out of current funds. Dic Lo, "Reappraising the Performance of China's State-Owned Industrial Enterprises, 1980–1996," *Cambridge Journal of Economics* 23 (1999), 693–718.

20. Data on the Gaoyang Towel Factory comes from a brief history of the factory included in the *Gaoyang xianzhi* (1995), and from interviews with factory managers. The most recent data comes from an interview on May 7, 1995. While the towel factory was not doing well in 1995, one could not but notice the vast amount of new housing that had been constructed for workers of the factory.

21. This percentage has been calculated from figures given in the 1994 *Zhongguo fangzhi gongye nianjian*. The figure for total value of output for the national textile industry can be found on page 115, and for the rural industry contribution in a "supplement" on page 140. Both have converted prices to 1990 constant prices. The position of rural firms was even stronger in the fast-growing wool industry. State firms produced only about one-third of the total output value in the wool-spinning industry in 1994.

22. Job assignments in China were often influenced by a parent's employment.

23. For example, in the late 1980s one of the vice-mayors of Tianjin was a Gaoyang native, as was the head of the commerce bureau for Beijing.

24. See David Wank, *Commodifying Communism* (Cambridge: Cambridge University Press, 1999) on private business in Xiamen. See also Mayfair Mei-hui Yang, *Gifts, Favors and Banquets—the Art of Social Relations in China* (Ithaca: Cornell University Press, 1994); Yunxiang Yan, *The Flow of Gifts: Reciprocity and Social Networks in a Chinese Village* (Stanford: Stanford University Press, 1996); Yunxiang Yan, "The Culture of Guanxi in a North China Village," *The China Journal* 35 (January 1996), 1–25; Thomas Gold, Doug Guthrie, and David Wank, *Social Connections in China: Institutions, Culture and the Changing Nature of Guanxi* (Cambridge: Cambridge University Press, 2002).

25. The use of *guanxi* to gain access to raw materials was limited to the first years of the third phase of growth. Contemporary factory managers place a high value on building long-term relations with their raw materials suppliers but at the same time a high percentage of the firms in our survey sample (85 percent) reported that they rely primarily on the market for supplies of raw materials and do not need to use special connections.

26. In addition to the technological input into individual firms, Gaoyang has also been able to draw on native-place ties with researchers in such institutions as the Tianjin Textile Research Institute and the Tianjin Institute of Textile Science and Technology, who have run training courses in Gaoyang; the local government has also sponsored a number of joint projects with both institutions. Wang Kejie, one of Gaoyang's most successful entrepreneurs, has funded scholarships at the Tianjin Institute of Textile Science and Technology.

27. County officials claimed that Gaoyang produced one-third of China's total towel output in 2004.

28. The weaving sector seemed to favor small-scale production; the largest weaving factories rarely exceeded twenty to thirty power looms. Among the thirty-four firms included in the sample survey of larger firms with over 100,000 yuan in registered capital, there was only one weaving factory, a towel factory with thirty looms that had been established by a retired vice-director of the state-owned Gaoyang Towel Factory.

29. The GY 42-inch loom was the first choice of most households in the early 1980s. This loom was essentially an iron gear loom with a metal frame, which was powered by a small engine. Manufactured in large numbers by the local textile machinery factory, the loom sold for 700 to 800 yuan. Output on the looms was roughly equivalent to that on an old iron gear loom—one bolt of cloth in a single shift of ten to twelve hours—but labor productivity was higher than with an iron gear loom since a single worker could normally tend two looms. One indication of the speed with which technology had changed is the fact that the textile machinery factory, which was doing very well in 1988, went bankrupt by 1995. The factory went out of business because its chief products—the GY 42-inch loom and jacquard devices to use with it—lost their markets. In the early 1980s, as rural industry first started to develop, machinery was in short supply and many rural producers chose the GY loom, which was relatively cheap and sturdy.

30. For a consideration of the state strategies for reinvestment in the textile industries, see Dorothy J. Solinger, *From Lathes to Looms*.

31. In 1988, used power looms sold for about 1,000 yuan; by 1995, the effects of inflation and increased demand had raised the price of a 1515 to 7,000 to 8,000 yuan, and a jacquard device for weaving towelling cost an additional 5,000 yuan per loom. A single loom was almost guaranteed to earn its owner an annual profit of at least 10,000 yuan. A large market for used equipment was set up on the outskirts of the village of Liguozhuang.

32. Some of my informants suggested the number may have been as high as eighty.

33. I visited a dyeing workshop that had been established by eight partners in 1985 with only 1,000 yuan in capital. At first all work was done by hand; by 1991 capital had grown to between 50,000 and 60,000 yuan, and each partner was earning 7,000 yuan a year. At that time, the workshop used a combination of mechanized and handicraft methods.

34. Trade statistics were provided by the County Bureau of Industry and Commerce. However, the statistics only cover the part of the trade that passed through government-regulated wholesale markets. In 1994 that was 450,000,000 towels, which they believe represented between 60 and 70 percent of total volume traded.

35. After gaining approval from the County Bureau of Industry and Commerce, the village set up a market for the sale of yarn and cloth which met according to the traditional periodic market schedule; at first the market met two days out of the ten-day cycle; later, as business increased, it began to meet four days out of ten.

36. Buyers were wholesale dealers who purchased cloth and transported it to regional markets for resale. Many of the buyers were petty operators who traded in relatively small lots. While the larger operators hired local transport companies to ship their purchases, smaller dealers packaged their purchases in small bales that were transported on the roofs of the buses that provided regular highway service. Although most of the towelling now goes through the wholesale market in the town, the Liguozhuang market continues as a market for specialized products. In 1995 there were twelve hundred 1515 power looms in the village producing screening and netting, and village leaders claimed that Liguozhuang weavers produced 70 percent of the national supply of this category of goods. I have not been able to check this claim for accuracy. Data on Liguozhuang comes from two visits, one in September 1988, and the second in May 1995.

37. In 1995, the standard commission on towels was 5 to 7 cents (*fen*) per towel; on larger items like sheets, the commission would be 1 yuan on an item that had a factory price of 16.50 per unit.

38. On the early reforms in commerce, see Dorothy Solinger, "Commercial Reform and State Control: Structural Changes in Chinese Trade," *Pacific Affairs* 58, no. 2 (Summer 1985), 197–215.

39. For a brief description of Yiwu as a marketing center, see *Zhongguo xiangzhen qiye nianjian 1995* (Beijing: Zhongguo Nongye Chubanshe, 1995), 361–62.

40. Unless otherwise indicated, statistical data comes from the Gaoyang County Township and Village Enterprises Bureau, provided in interviews in May 1995.

41. Statistics on China's total national production are difficult to acquire, and not necessarily reliable. Estimates of Gaoyang production were provided by the county's Bureau for Township and Village Enterprises. They are measures of capacity rather than of output, but since the industry was working at close to full capacity during 1995, they are presumably also reasonable estimates of total output. Estimates of national output come from two sources, Prof. Yang Suoting of the Tianjin Institute of Textile Science and Technology, and from the Tianjin office of the Textile Ministry. The rapid rise of small-scale rural industry has made statistical collection very difficult. National publications of the Textile Ministry, like the annual textile industry *Almanac,* provide statistical data on the state-owned units. It does not cover the rapidly growing rural industries, which are owned by lower-level cooperatives (township and villages) or the vast number of privately owned factories. It is this latter category of enterprises—which includes almost all Gaoyang firms—that is most likely to be left out of the counting. Even when county statistical bureaus make an attempt to grasp production at this level, statistics are inaccurate. Enterprises, fearing that they will be pressured to pay more taxes, underreport output and profits. Thus, at the local level, the most accurate estimates are estimates of capacity.

42. Background information on the wool industry comes from the work of a group of Australian economists centered in the Chinese Research Unit at Adelaide University. Christopher Findlay, ed., *Challenges of Economic Reform and Industrial Growth: China's Wool War* (Sydney: Allen & Unwin, 1992); Andrew Watson, Christo-

pher Findlay, and Du Yintang, "Who Won the 'Wool War'?: A Case Study of Rural Product Marketing in China," *China Quarterly* 118 (June 1989), 213–41; Zhang Xiaohe, Lu Weiguo, Sun Keliang, Christopher Findlay, and Andrew Watson, "The 'Wool War' and the 'Cotton Chaos': Fibre Marketing in China," Working Paper no. 91/14 from the Chinese Economic Research Unit, University of Adelaide, October 1991; Academic Committee of the Chinese Association of Textile Engineers, ed., *Fangzhi gongchang "ba.wu" keji fazhan zhanlue yanjiu* (Beijing: Fangzhi Gongye Chubanshe, 1990), 63–78.

43. New wool spinning and weaving industrial districts have appeared in Zhejiang and Jiangsu, as well as Shandong.

44. Ray Byron, "Demand for Wool Products in China," chapter two in Christopher Findlay, ed., *Challenges of Economic Reform and Industrial Growth: China's Wool War.*

45. Watson, Findlay, and Du Yintang, "Who Won the 'Wool War'," 215.

46. Gaoyang's spinning factories that produce yarn for hand knitting use New Zealand wool: New Zealand is the world's largest exporter of "strong wool," which is suited for spinning into knitting yarn. Some of the wool-weaving factories use Australian wool.

47. Gaoyang officials admit that the Li County government was much faster to respond to the economic reform initiatives than was Gaoyang.

48. Information on the development of the North China carpet industry was provided by Mr. Li Linpan, general technologist for the Tianjin Carpets Corporation. All of the statistics and estimates in the discussion below were provided by Mr. Li in an interview on September 4, 1996.

49. According to Mr. Li Linpan, at the peak of production, the Tianjin carpet factories' total spinning capacity was approximately 6,000 tons of yarn a year. We can see something of the growth of this sector in the fact that Gaoyang firms were producing more than 20,000 tons of carpet yarn in 1995.

50. Prices at the time were approximately sixteen yuan per square inch for carpets produced by the state firms, ten yuan per square inch for those produced by their rural competitors.

51. The victory for the small, non-state factories was aided by decisions taken by the Tianjin Foreign Trade Bureau, which controlled the Tianjin carpet trademark of Fengquan. This trademark had earned a worldwide reputation for high-quality carpets. When the Tianjin state factories first started subcontracting part of the production work to rural branch factories, the final cutting and finishing of the carpets was still done by the parent firms, and all of the carpets were sold under the Fengquan brand-name. As the demand for carpets rose, the Foreign Trade Bureau allowed the small, non-state factories to ship their goods under the same brand-name, even after they had become independent from their parent firms. One of the results has been a sharp fall in quality control, which in 1995 had begun to affect the demand for "Tianjin" carpets.

52. I have been unable to find data on the Chinese carpet industry that would allow an estimate of the share of Gaoyang production in the industry.

53. According to Shen Fandeng, *Fangzhi gongye jingji guanli* (Beijing: Fangzhi Gongye Chubanshe, 1989), 47, wool-spinning factories with over 10,000 spindles were counted as large scale, 5,000–10,000 as medium size, and under 5,000 spindles as small.

54. In the case of 100 percent wool yarn, the wool is dyed after spinning. In the case of synthetics, fiber is dyed before spinning.

55. Firms carefully choose the wool that they use in the production process. In general, the longer staple of Australian wool is preferred for wool weaving, while New Zealand wool works very well for spinning knitting yarns. Carpet-yarn firms generally use domestic wool.

56. Carpet-yarn factories do not experience the same seasonality in demand. Since carpet yarn is an industrial raw material, demand is more or less even throughout the year.

57. The example here has been greatly simplified and makes no attempt to compensate for losses during the spinning process or any other raw materials inputs or upkeep on the machines.

9

Entrepreneurial Legacies in Contemporary Firms

In 1983, Gaoyang County leaders urged village party cadre to take the lead in organizing rural industrial activity. In village after village, collectively owned workshops were disbanded and looms were divided among villagers who used them to set up small family workshops.[1] It was not long before ambitious villagers began to dream of establishing more technologically sophisticated factories. Realization of those dreams required larger sums of capital, and in the mid-1980s neither state banks nor rural savings and loan cooperatives loaned money to peasant entrepreneurs. Moreover, the land reforms of the late 1940s and the subsequent decades of collectivized agriculture had effectively leveled income among rural households; there were no rural rich to turn to for investment funds. To overcome this capital shortage, Gaoyang entrepreneurs created the shareholding partnership to mobilize capital for industrial activities.

In the 1990s almost all of the larger textile firms were shareholding partnerships.[2] The shareholding partnership combines elements from three traditions of Chinese economic practice: traditional commercial partnerships (*hezi*); voluntary cooperatives of workers (*hehuo*), which were common in handicraft; and socialist practices, used in collectively owned industry. Rural manufacturing firms in contemporary Gaoyang have adapted traditional business practices in innovative ways, creating a new style of business partnership that almost always involves the pooling of capital and labor. While the contemporary shareholding partnership draws on both the joint partnership and joint labor traditions, it is most commonly described using the term for joint labor, *hehuo*. The partners in contemporary firms not only work in the firm as members of the managerial team, they also have invested significant sums of capital. The preference for describing such partnerships as joint labor (*hehuo*) rather than joint capital (*hezi* or *hegu*) is undoubtedly related to the socialist heritage, which can more easily accommodate notions of cooperative labor than of joint capital, which has more ambivalent meanings.[3]

While the contemporary business partnership draws on entrepreneurial legacies from the past, there are some significant differences between contemporary firms and those of an earlier period. All of the firms are manufacturing firms with significant investment in fixed capital assets. This distinguishes them from the prewar wholesale firms that started as trading firms with most of their investment in circulating capital. In the past, partnership contracts were drawn up for three years, with partners free to withdraw at the end of the term. While such short-term agreements were workable when investment was in circulating capital, the same principles do not apply to investment in manufacturing firms. There are no time limits on partnership agreements in contemporary firms; while most partnership agreements allow individual investors to withdraw, contracts protect the interests of the firm.

The contemporary shareholding partnership has proven to be an effective vehicle for organizing rural industry in an environment characterized by shortages of investment capital. The combination of investment and managerial participation by the shareholders has created strong commitment to the long-term interests of the firm; this has led to high levels of reinvestment and rapid growth rates very similar to those of the first two phases of growth. However, the shareholding partnerships also have certain characteristic weaknesses. Since the partnership is based on voluntary cooperation, disagreements can lead members to withdraw their assets from the firm. Thus partnership firms are potentially unstable. The second weakness of the partnership firm is one it shares with the traditional Chinese family-owned firm. Since managerial roles are assigned to investing partners, there are limits on the pool of managerial talent.

This chapter will examine the origins of partnership firms, financial arrangements, organizational structures, development strategies, problems of continuity, and questions of labor-management relations. The primary data for this examination of current Gaoyang business practice comes from a survey of 34 firms conducted in May 1995. The 34 firms were randomly selected from a list of 194 textile firms that had registered capital of over 100,000 yuan.[4] Other sources of data include qualitative and quantitative data provided by the county's Township and Village Enterprise Bureau during visits in 1988, 1990, 1991, 1995, and 1996, and visits to and interviews with the entrepreneurs and workers of a number of firms over the same time period.[5]

SHAREHOLDING PARTNERSHIP FIRMS

Shareholding partnerships are the dominant form for organization of rural enterprises in contemporary Gaoyang. The vast majority of firms with over

100,000 yuan in registered capital fall in this category, and all thirty-four of the firms in our survey began in this way. The Gaoyang-style shareholding firm is a limited partnership of friends, relatives, or fellow villagers who pool capital and skills to establish a new firm. Each of the partners in the firm holds only one share and most also work in the firm, usually as a member of the management team. While the participants describe their investment in terms of shares (*gu*) and refer to the partners as shareholders (*gudong*), shares cannot be sold or traded. Seventy percent of the thirty-four sample firms had explicit regulations banning the sale or transfer of shares; although transfer of shares is officially permitted in the remaining firms, there had been no cases of transfer. When partners have disagreements they cannot resolve, the shareholders in the majority buy out the interests of those in the minority.[6]

There are two noteworthy features of this arrangement: first, each shareholder or partner holds an equal investment, and second, the shares cannot be transferred to individuals who were not part of the original partnership. Both of these were common features of prewar voluntary cooperatives and are a direct link to the long tradition of work cooperatives that were a common organizational form for small manufacturing workshops.[7] The first shareholding partnerships appeared in 1984. Most of the partners had accumulated small sums of capital from non-agricultural activities. The two most common sources of capital accumulation were profits from weaving or other household-based workshop production or profits made in trade. Three of Gaoyang's largest contemporary firms all had such modest beginnings. Dong Feng, one of the larger wool-spinning mills, began in 1982 as a small workshop producing industrial felt out of waste from state textile mills. San Li, Gaoyang's largest wool spinner, began as a workshop that knit sweaters; and the capital for Zhen Hua, the largest wool-weaving mill, came from profits in the wool trade. While the seed capital came from commerce or workshop activities, it was widely dispersed in the local community. No individual investor had sufficient funds to pay for the equipment to start a spinning or weaving factory.

Gaoyang shareholding firms can be divided into two groups distinguished by the size of their shareholding bodies. Most of the firms have less than ten shareholders; however, a small number of firms have a larger number of shareholders. (See table 9.1.) Since one of the main aims of the shareholding firm is to gather savings to invest in new business enterprises, it might seem that recruiting a large number of shareholders would raise more capital. Records show, however, that in firms with a large number of shareholders, the value of each share is typically smaller.[8]

Closer examination shows that the distinction between the two types of firms, at least in terms of the number of investors as distinct from shareholders, is not as clear-cut as the above description suggests. The largest number of the firms in our sample (ten) had an initial share value of between 10,000

Table 9.1.   Shareholding in Sample Firms

Firm #	Founded	# of Shares	Value of Share When Founded	# of Shares 1994	Value of Share 1994
1	1987	15	20,000	15	50,000
2	1985	15	10,000	12	240,000
3	1993	5	400,000	5	500,000
4	1991	17	50,000	13	150,000
5	1988	8	100,000	4	not reported
6	1986	15	20,000	13	60,000
7	1990	5	100,000	1	1,200,000
8	1990	3	100,000	1	2,000,000
9	1984	18	30,000	6	not reported
10	1991	13	60,000	13	48,000
11	1992	10	50,000	10	50,000
12	1991	1	1,000,000	1	1,000,000
13	1987	7	10,000	4	50,00
14	1985	1	50,000	1	3,000,000
15	1983	3	30,000	3	2,000,000
16	1989	2	50,000	2	100,000
17	1986	4	100,000	4	200,000
18	1984	3	100,000	3	250,000
19	1988	3	50,000	3	200,000
20	1992	2	200,000	2	400,000
21	1992	1	400,000	1	600,000
22	1989	5	40,000	1	120,000
23	1984	20	10,000	3	150,000
24	1990	9	20,000	9	29,000
25	1980	4	5,000	8	120,000
26	1988	6	15,000	3	100,000
27	1988	3	20,000	1	200,000
28	1987	8	50,000	10	100,000
29	1988	7	20,000	1	1,000,000
30	1990	29	10,000	29	60,000
31	1989	7	40,000	4	73,000
32	1987	6	100,000	6	500,000
33	1982	84	4,000	210	30,000
34	1982	3	50,000	3	150,000

Source: Survey conducted in 1994.

and 50,000 yuan. In the mid- and late 1980s, when most of the firms were founded, these were substantial sums in a rural community where per capita income was still quite low. How did so many investors acquire such large sums of capital? Questioning revealed a complicated system of layered investment in which several small investors contributed funds for one share in a new firm. The shares represented in the partnership are known as large shares (*dagu*), and the contributions from the friends and relatives who loaned funds are known as small shares (*xiaogu*). The person who is listed as the owner of the large share and thus a partner in the firm is often the representative of a block of smaller investors who had contributed funds for the share. Since the companies only register the large shares, there is no formal record of small shareholders and responsibility for reporting to the small shareholders rests with the partner who is the owner of the large share.

This pattern of large and small shares is commonly used throughout the Gaoyang region as a local substitute for the traditional credit associations (*hui*) that have been described in much of the literature on southern China and Taiwan.[9] The Gaoyang practice differs from the traditional credit association in several important ways. First, in a credit association the members of a credit group take turns receiving the funds gathered from the members; in the Gaoyang case, the pooling of funds for a large share is a one-time deal. While individuals may put up funds for small shares in more than one enterprise, each transaction is a separate act. Second, unlike the complicated methods for calculation of interest that are common in the traditional credit association, in Gaoyang practice the central figure in the relationship—the person who holds the large share and is a partner in the firm—calculates profits and interest and reports to those who loaned the funds. In some cases the small shareholders receive interest on a periodic basis; in other cases the large shareholder uses profits to pay off the small shareholders, returning the funds that were originally loaned together with interest, so that after several years he holds the large share outright.

This complicated pattern of shareholding and sub-shareholding in contemporary firms has created new webs of associations between village households. In many villages, virtually every household has some financial interest in at least one of the village-based firms. This pattern of investment has had two consequences: it has proven to be a very efficient system for gathering and using capital for industrial investment, and also means that more members of the community may have a share in the profits of rural firms than is indicated by the listed numbers of shares.

Some firms have chosen a different strategy and recruited funds from a larger number of shareholders. In those firms, share value is kept low and all who wish to work in the firm are required to invest funds as a condition for employment. One of our sample firms, founded in 1982, originally had 84 shareholders, all of whom worked in the firm. In 1992, when the firm wanted to expand its capital base, workers who had joined the firm after 1982 were encouraged to purchase shares. The newly issued shares had a value of 30,000 yuan, and there are now 210 shareholders.

In this form of shareholding the factory is owned by its workers; this creates a work environment that resembles collectively run enterprises. Many Gaoyang firms have been troubled by high rates of labor turnover; firms in which most of the workers are shareholders have been the exception to this pattern.

FINANCING RURAL FIRMS

Prewar rural industry floated on a sea of credit that made it relatively easy for entrepreneurs to run businesses with quite limited investment. As we saw in chapter two, in most periods importers and producers sold yarn, dyes, and other raw materials on credit, thus supplying part of the capital for the operation of yarn and cloth wholesale merchants. Contemporary firms face a much more difficult credit situation. First, the initial investment required for purchase of equipment is much larger and consumes a larger share of capital. Second, the rapid growth in rural industry has created a huge demand for raw materials, which are, as a consequence, in relatively short supply. This has created a sellers' market; few producers or dealers provide raw materials on credit. Moreover, for fine-wool–spinning and wool-weaving firms, the seasonal nature of demand requires larger capital outlays to sustain production during the slack spring and summer periods.

The demand for operating capital in contemporary rural industry is thus very high. At the same time, state financial institutions are reluctant to lend to non-state enterprises and entrepreneurs are wary of becoming dependent on state banking institutions. In the years since the initiation of the economic reform policies, state policies on lending have changed frequently: when the economy overheats, one of the first responses of the national government is to try to rein in credit—and the first target is almost always credit to non-state firms.[10] In 1989–1990, when the first round of spiraling inflation since the early 1950s contributed to public disaffection, the government tightened credit. Many Gaoyang firms experienced difficulties at that time. Rural entrepreneurs have learned that it is risky to rely too heavily on state financial institutions. Most prefer to meet their capital needs through high rates of reinvestment and through loans from non-bank sources. Many of the measures they use to finance their firms are similar to those used in the prewar period.

Traditional Chinese commercial firms accepted deposits from employees and from other individuals, paying interest on the deposits. This practice was widely used in the prewar period, in part because of the weak development of the indigenous banking system. Contemporary Gaoyang firms have revived this practice. Funds deposited with firms come from three primary sources. First, many shareholders deposit the dividends they have earned on their investment. Most of the thirty-four sample firms (84 percent) used this practice and had acquired significant funds through its use: in 1995 the firm with the largest deposits had 6,000,000 yuan and the median across all of the firms was 600,000 yuan.

Employees of the firms also deposited funds. Our sample firms were split almost evenly between those that allowed this practice (seventeen) and those that did not (sixteen).[11] Among those that did not, it was usually because the managers believed it was too much trouble to keep track of deposits and withdrawals and to calculate interest on small deposits.[12]

The third source of funds deposited with firms came from depositors who held no shares but were friends of one of the partners. Twenty-two of the thirty-four firms (64 percent) allowed deposits of this type and seventeen firms reported that they currently had deposits of this type. Among those seventeen firms, average deposits stood at 100,000 yuan per firm, although the firm reporting the highest level of deposits had 2,000,000 yuan. Deposits from individuals who were not participants in the partnership can be viewed in several ways. For the managers of the firm, the deposits functioned as a private loan. For the individuals who offered the loans, it was a form of investment that strengthened the personal relationship between the person who provided funds and his friend or relative who was a partner in the firm. In each of the firms that used these deposit systems internal rules specified interest rates—which were competitive with bank interest rates—and the terms for withdrawal of funds. Almost all firms required prior notification for withdrawal, with waiting periods of anywhere from several days to several months, depending on the size of the withdrawal.

Most of the capital that has been raised in these ways has been drawn out of savings accumulated by rural families in industrial and commercial activities. Wages earned from work as part of a managerial team as well as profits earned on shares are often reinvested in the enterprises. The result was a very rapid spurt of development at the beginning of the growth cycle. We can see this very clearly from the increase in share values for our sample firms. (See table 9.1.)

PATTERNS OF ENTERPRISE GROWTH

Present-day Gaoyang is a specialized industrial district, and the patterns of growth of most firms have been closely linked to the benefits that come from location in a regional production center. Most small firms specialize in one stage of the production of a commodity. Independent firms handle distinct stages of the production process; relations between firms are mediated through the market or arranged through subcontracting (*jiagong*). Only the very largest of the contemporary firms have moved beyond single-stage production processes to integrate all stages of production and sales within a single firm. Since the technological possibilities and constraints on development differ in the separate sectors of contemporary industry, let us begin by first considering the technological ramifications of the different types of products.

Carpet-yarn factories present the simplest form of organization and also have the least possibilities for development. Their product is standardized and carpet yarn is almost always sold in its unbleached form; weaving factories dye yarn to meet their own design needs. Given these parameters, there is little possibility for development in carpet-yarn factories except for expansion in scale. Increasing scale does not seem to have much impact on the overall profitability of a firm; greater volume does not significantly lower per unit production costs, or bring other benefits of scale. As a result of these constraints on growth, firms with more aggressive leadership have shifted from carpet-yarn to fine-yarn spinning, an area where there is more room for diversification. The first commonly observed pattern of firm development is the move to more technologically demanding forms of production.

Many of Gaoyang's largest firms are in the fine-spinning business and they have shown a pattern of development that does represent both technological and organizational growth. Integrated production in the fine-spinning field does depend on increases in scale. Most fine-spinning firms began with one set of spinning equipment with roughly three hundred spindles, producing unbleached yarn that was either sold in that form or dyed on commission by independent dyeing factories. As firms developed, some added on additional equipment, increasing their daily output volume, and eventually built their own integrated dyeing workshops. Such large firms as San Li, Red Flag, and Dong Feng have all moved in this direction.

In the third sector of the wool industry, wool weaving, technological diversity is more marked than in the wool-spinning industry. The wool-weaving industry includes firms that only weave, often in small factories with less than ten looms, and it also includes large, integrated mills that do their own spinning, weaving, and dyeing. The boom in founding of integrated spinning and weaving factories in the mid-1990s is an indication that ambitious entrepreneurs are deliberately selecting this line of endeavor because it seems to offer the most sophisticated technological and organizational possibilities.

The big leap in the wool-weaving industry came in 1992, when the first factory to use the open-end spinning process was founded. While open-end spinning equipment was more expensive than standard spinning equipment, it has been widely used in rural industry in Gaoyang because it shortens the production process. Standard spinning equipment uses a two-stage spinning process, moving from coarse spinning to fine spinning; open-end spinning combines the two stages, simplifying production and supervision. The largest of the wool-weaving mills have also added on their own dyeing facilities, producing both yarn-dyed fabrics and fabrics dyed after the weaving is completed.

While the long-term trend in both the fine-spinning and wool-weaving sectors is to create an at least partially integrated firm, there are technological and financial constraints that limit the ability of smaller firms to move in this direction. In the 1920s and 1930s the fully integrated Gaoyang firm did possess its own dyeing facilities, manned by skilled technicians who had been trained in higher technical colleges. In the 1990s a firm that wished to add dyeing facilities needed to invest in equipment and also had to find experienced technical personnel. Several of the firms that made this leap sought outside help. For example, when Red Flag added dyeing facilities, the dyeing unit was established as a joint venture with a Tianjin firm that provided the technical expertise; when Fei Zhou, one of the largest integrated woolen mills, decided to do its own dyeing, it hired technical experts who had previously worked in the Yangzi delta region.

While the processes of development we have described so far may seem quite similar to what we saw with the development of the integrated firm in the prewar period, there are key differences. In the prewar pattern mechanized dyeing facilities were not set up as divisions within the original firm but as related firms, sharing the same capitalist but organized as independent firms. Such firms processed goods for the parent firm, but also processed goods on a fee basis for all comers. The scale of the parent firm was thus not an important concern, since the related dyeing factory worked on both a subcontracting basis for the parent firm and as an independent accounting unit. Almost all of the contemporary firms that have moved to more integrated production have set up dyeing facilities as subdivisions of the parent enterprise. Since time constraints in the wool industry make it much more difficult for subdivisions to take in work from outsiders on a fee-paying basis, the parent firm must have reached a significant scale before it can even contemplate setting up a dyeing division. In the fine-wool–spinning sector, the timing of demand for services plays an important role. During the spring and early summer months the spinning mills produce and store stocks in their warehouses, awaiting the beginning of the fall sales season. Almost all of the stock is stored in an undyed state. In late August when the market begins to pick up, agents of wholesale and retail firms check color samples and place orders. Once the order is received, the dyeing workshops dye, dry, and pack the yarn. The largest firms with their own dyeing facilities are able to process the orders quickly, giving them an advantage. However, because of the concentration of work during the busy season (from late August to the following Lunar New Year), the large firm's dyeing facilities are too busy processing their own orders to take on subcontracting from smaller firms. At the same time, the small firm is hesitant to entrust its competitive position in the market to the subdivision of one of its larger rivals. Only the largest firms have sufficient spinning capacity to make dyeing facilities economically profitable. Smaller firms rely on subcontracting relations with independent dyeing factories.

Integration of production processes represents one direction of firm development. Organizational innovations designed to increase the scale of pro-

duction represent a second growth trajectory. In Gaoyang, this push for organizational innovation can be seen in the formation of industrial groups (*ji-
tuan*), which bring several companies together under common direction.
The rapid growth of the rural wool industry after 1985 drew the attention of
government planners, who were distressed by the chaotic nature of the markets and the often cutthroat competition between the small firms that were
struggling to establish themselves in the market. Wishing to gain some control over this new industry, the Hebei provincial government urged small
firms to join a government-sponsored industrial group that would incorpo-
rate all of the wool spinners under a coordinated management system. Managers of the private firms showed no interest in the government's proposal,
preferring to maintain their freedom and take their chances with the competitive market.

While the private firms rejected these efforts of bureaucratic control, some
of the larger private firms have organized their own industrial groups. In
1995, an enterprise that wished to found an industrial group had to include
at least several factories linked together by a common managerial structure.
By merging several production units under common management, private
entrepreneurs hope to gain by the economies that come with larger scale of
production. Larger scale should reduce transaction costs, since raw materials
can be purchased in larger volume and marketing can be more easily
brought under the control of the firm. The larger scale of production also
spreads the cost of technical services, including the salaries of engineers and
managers, over a wider base, making it easier and less costly to strive for
higher standards of quality control.

San Li was the first Gaoyang firm to set up an industrial group. This move,
which clearly had the backing of both the county and provincial governments, was marked by a ceremony attended by several hundred individuals
in the spring of 1995. San Li's owner and manager, Wang Kejie, argued that
there were essentially two main motivations behind the establishment of the
San Li Industrial Group. The first aim was to improve San Li's corporate image. Wang Kejie was the first of Gaoyang's contemporary entrepreneurs to
stress corporate image and advertising. San Li's major product was fine wool
for knitting sweaters. Sold in retail stores all over North China and in the
northeast, brand-name recognition was an important factor in sales. Wang's
strategy called for competition on two lines: price and quality. By the mid-
1990s, San Li had ten thousand spindles with an annual spinning capacity of
three thousand tons of yarn, which in the fine-wool–spinning industry put it
into the category of a large-scale production unit. Unlike the smaller firms
that competed primarily on price, San Li wanted to directly challenge China's
most famous wool spinners. San Li claimed that it could produce quality yarn
that sold for lower prices than its competitors. The firm proudly advertised
quality awards won in national competitions and valued its designation as a

"Famous Chinese Product" (*Zhongguo mingpai*). The move to form the San Li Industrial Group added to the image of the firm as a forward-looking industrial leader. The San Li Industrial Group began to sponsor regional sporting events, bought advertising spots on national television, and established scholarships at various universities.

The second aim of San Li in establishing itself as an industrial group was to stabilize its customer base. Regular customers were invited to join the San Li Industrial Group. Wholesalers who joined the group made commitments with regard to annual purchasing targets; in exchange, group members were given access to trade information, offered preferential treatment in purchasing, and given guarantees that San Li would not offer the same easy terms to their closest regional competitors.

The formation of the San Li Industrial Group served as a spur to several other large firms, which followed in San Li's footsteps in 1996. Dong Feng, Gaoyang's second largest fine-wool spinner, was registered as the Dong Feng Industrial Group, and the Red Flag group of firms registered as the Shuang Yang (Twin Sheep) Industrial Group.[13] The shift in name of the Red Flag group represented an interesting commentary on the rapid changes that had taken place in just over a decade. When Red Flag was established in 1984, it chose a good revolutionary name, locating it within a revolutionary rhetoric that neatly obscured its ownership affiliation. The newly chosen name, Twin Sheep, and the accompanying trademark that bears the authorization by the International Wool Board was designed to appeal to other audiences—stressing international quality, the appeal was more directly targeted at contemporary customers.[14]

In the mid-1990s, competition in all of the sectors of Gaoyang's rapidly growing textile industry was sharp, and county officials expected that competition would lead to a sorting out of firms; those with higher-quality products and better managerial teams were likely to survive, while marginal firms were likely to go out of business. While weaker firms may fail, there is no reason to assume that the overall structure of the industrial district, with its mixture of large and small, integrated and task-specific firms, will change. If the prewar structure of industry can serve as a guide, there should continue to be room within the industrial district for both larger integrated firms and for the smaller specialized firms.

RECRUITING MANAGERIAL TALENT

In the prewar period, most firms employed individuals who had gained professional managerial skills through commercial apprenticeships or through study at the commercial school. As Gaoyang industry has entered the third phase of growth, one of the major problems it faces is the lack of professional managerial personnel. The traditional system of managerial training, the commercial apprenticeship system, was targeted as a "feudal practice" and abolished during the campaigns for the socialization of commerce and industry in the mid-1950s. With the end of the traditional commercial apprenticeship system, most professional managerial training came to an end. While newly established technical schools provided instruction in specific skills like accounting, more broadly defined managerial training disappeared. In most factories and firms, managerial posts were given to Chinese Communist Party members. While engineers and technicians were given formal training, formal training in managerial skills was neglected. Thus, as rural industry began to develop in the 1980s, there was no pool of trained managers.

The second factor that has strongly shaped the recruitment of managerial staff has been the shareholding partnership. In contemporary firms, the vast majority of those who work in managerial positions are also shareholders. In our sample firms, 69 percent of those who were managers were also shareholders; in all but six firms, the vast majority of managers were shareholders.[15] The remaining six firms can be divided into two groups: in three of the firms, the general manager was a shareholder while all of the remaining managers were employees; in the other three firms, all the managerial staff were employees. The practice in these six firms most closely resembles the prewar practice, in which investors employed managerial staff. However, in the prewar firm, hired employees were selected for their experience and skills in the textile trade. In our contemporary firms, there is no significant difference in the backgrounds of the managerial staff of those six firms and of the managers in the other twenty-eight firms who were also shareholders. Overall, more than 70 percent of the managers were peasants before they joined their current firm.[16] Of the remaining group, about equal numbers had been workers or cadre and a smaller contingent had been students or served as shop-floor supervisors.[17] Many of the former workers and shop-floor supervisors had worked in Gaoyang's state textile factories. While only a small percentage of the managers had experience in the textile industry, they were on average better educated than their rural neighbors. A full one-third of the managers had graduated from high school, an additional 6 percent had post–high school education, and most of the remaining individuals were graduates of junior middle school. While these figures may not seem very impressive, it is important to note that junior high school education only became compulsory in the 1990s.[18]

Prewar firms whose investors were not Gaoyang natives often employed managers who came from the hometown of the chief shareholder. In the contemporary firms studied, virtually all of the managerial staff (190 out of 194) were Gaoyang natives. In the 1920s and 1930s many of Gaoyang's dyeing and finishing factories employed full-time engineers and technicians who had graduated from the leading technical schools in Tianjin. In the 1990s that practice was almost unknown, not because local firms were unwilling to hire outside talent but because the educational system had drawn talented youth out of the rural areas. Few rural youth who had obtained higher education and urban residence status were interested in returning to the countryside to work.

These factors have limited the ability of Gaoyang firms to recruit and hold full-time professional managerial staff. The only major exception to this has been the employment of highly skilled engineers who have worked for the firms for relatively short periods of time. While factory managers are convinced that their staff can master managerial skills through short-term courses and on-the-job training, they are willing to pay premium prices to hire those with technical skills. The majority of our sample firms (21 out of 34) had at some time hired engineers to provide technical assistance. Engineering help was expensive, with salaries running as high as 2,500 yuan a month plus room and board, and most firms had hired the engineers for short periods.[19] Some firms repeated this process, bringing in professional engineers to train their staff when they introduced new equipment, while others kept engineers on their staff as part-time consultants.

County government officials believe that one of the most serious problems is the problem of managerial talent. Since most of the firms draw their managers from their pool of shareholding partners, there is a natural limit on managerial skills very similar to the limits that are often described as a major problem for the Chinese family firm. By restricting the pool to shareholders, the firm reduces its options for finding men of talent. Certainly some of the partnerships were formed with these problems in mind, and efforts were made to include partners who contributed different skills. In spite of those efforts, however, many of the firms experience a shortage of adequately trained personnel. Efforts to hire college graduates have been mixed: while a few firms have been able to hold on to their well-educated recruits, other recruits have left their employers to establish their own independent businesses. The Bureau of Township and Village Enterprises has worked to overcome these managerial handicaps by running training courses for rural industrial managers, offering short-term courses and sponsoring a lecture program. Some entrepreneurs have used more personalized strategies for recruitment, offering scholarships to students at higher technical training schools and training their own children as successors by investing heavily in their educations.[20] By the summer of 1996 some of the larger firms had also started to build modern family housing units for their managerial and technical staffs as a way of luring young, professionally trained personnel.

As enterprises have grown in size and complexity, managerial problems have become much sharper. Increasing competition puts continuous pressure on firms to improve the quality of their products while maintaining competitive prices. Better quality control depends on closer supervision, but most firms find it difficult to reach beyond their partners to recruit high-level managers. This problem is a side effect of the joint labor (*hehuo*) tradition that was originally used in organizations that were smaller and less complex. In traditional *hehuo* forms, partners pooled labor and capital and worked basically as equals. The scale of most workshops was such as to demand little in the way of supervision or long-range planning. The attempt to adapt this form to larger-scale manufacturing enterprises with more than one hundred workers has revealed strains that in some cases have led to the breakup of partnerships.

STABILITY OF BUSINESS PARTNERSHIPS

The great strength of the shareholding partnership is its ability to pool scattered capital holdings for investment in enterprises. While the managerial pool is limited by the nature of the partnership, working partners do have an unusually high commitment to the firm since they share the profits. The great weakness of the shareholding partnership is an inherent instability. The firm is created by a voluntary alliance of individuals. Although all of the partners have an equal financial commitment, one of them plays the leading role in directing the firm's development. Partners do not always agree with the decisions of the chief manager and disputes among the investing partners can lead shareholders to withdraw.

The prewar wholesale firms were faced with similar problems; one of the characteristics of the wholesale trade was the relatively easy entry and exit from business. At that time, since most of the capital was held in stocks of raw materials and finished goods, it was quite easy to dissolve a firm and create a new firm with more congenial partners. For contemporary firms, the danger of disagreements among the partners still remains, but since most of the investment is in manufacturing it is more difficult to dissolve business partnerships. When crises occur within a firm, the partners who stand on the majority side are forced to buy out the interests of the partner(s) who is (or are) in the minority. Often this process may take a year or more; all partners must first agree on the current evaluation of the assets of the firm and work out a plan for buying out the partner/partners who wishes/wish to leave. This may leave the firm short of capital, since the remaining partners often have to withdraw the funds they deposited with the firm to buy out those who leave. The resulting increase in debt is thus a reflection not only, perhaps, of new investment in fixed resources, but also of a greater reliance on outside capital, forced by the withdrawal of some of the original shareholders.

Even though most firms had been in existence for less than ten years at the time of the survey, half (seventeen out of thirty-four) had already had some of their founding partners withdraw. The most commonly cited reasons for the breakup of partnership agreements were disputes over managerial strategy, the desire to found new factories, and dissatisfaction with profit rates. (Table 9.2 provides data on each of the seventeen cases.) Let us examine a few cases to see what caused the breakup of firms.

Partners in some of our firms (such as firms #2 and #4) withdrew because of disputes over expansion. In almost all cases in this category, expansion of the firm involved a shift to production requiring a higher level of technology. Expansion of the firm thus involved a significant increase in fixed capital investment and often also a much heavier burden of debt. Since the firms were profitable, some of the partners were unwilling to assume the new risks and decided to withdraw. In the case of firm #2, three of fifteen partners withdrew when the firm switched from the production of carpet yarn to fine spinning. The shift required an increase in fixed capital investment from 1,800,000 to 3,000,000 yuan. Those who left feared that the firm lacked experience in the new line of business. In the case of firm #4, a partnership of seventeen shareholders was reduced to thirteen only two years after the founding of the firm. The firm was originally involved in wool weaving on a contract basis. A shift from wool weaving to fine wool spinning in 1993 involved an increase of 1,000,000 yuan in fixed capital investment and a rise in outstanding bank loans from 300,000 yuan to 2,550,000 yuan.

The most frequently mentioned reason for changes in partnerships was the desire of one or more of the partners to establish an independent firm. This practice was a reflection of the very strong entrepreneurial spirit in Gaoyang. Although partners were theoretically all equal, as a shareholding partnership developed one partner usually came to play a dominant role in the management of the firm. The chief manager often treated the firm as his own private property and often members of the community refer to factories by the name of the dominant partner. Since other partners were members of the managerial team, we can think of the partnership as a training ground in entrepreneurship. Participation in a partnership provided on-the-job training and experience; partners were also able to accumulate capital that could be used as a nest egg for a new partnership.

A similar entrepreneurial spirit and practice had characterized the prewar textile industry as many employees of wholesale firms later established their own businesses, building on the training they had gained and the capital they had accumulated while working for larger wholesale firms. For chief managers, this practice was problematic. The manger of a leading spinning firm lamented the difficulty of keeping trained and experienced staff; as soon as young employees learned the trade and built up a network of connections they left the firm and set up on their own. This was the result of the "everyone can be his own boss" spirit that pervades Gaoyang, he argued.

Table 9.2. Changes in Business Partnerships

Firm	Year Founded	Year of Change	Nature of Change	Reason
2	1985	1990	3 of 15 shareholders withdrew	Shift from coarse to fine spinning
4	1991	1993	4 of 17 shareholders withdrew	New debt for expansion of production
5	1988	1994	4 of 8 shareholders withdrew	Withdraw to start new firm
6	1986	1992	2 of 15 shareholders withdrew	Shift from coarse to fine spinning
7	1990	1991, 1993	4 of 5 shareholders withdrew	Personal conflicts
8	1990	1991	2 of 3 shareholders withdrew	Unspecified
9	1984		12 of 18 shareholders withdrew	To set up a different business
10	1987	1990	3 of 7 shareholders withdrew	To set up a new factory
22	1989	1994	4 of 5 shareholders withdrew	Disagreement over production strategy
23	1984	1985, 87, 89, 91, 94	17 of 20 shareholders withdrew	To start new factories
25	1989	1992	1 shareholder left, new shareholders added	To start a new factory
26	1988	1992	3 of 6 shareholders withdrew	To invest in other business
27	1988	1989	2 of 3 shareholders withdrew	Withdrawal in response to 1989 credit crunch
28	1987	1993	2 shareholders added	Need new capital to expand production
29	1988	1989	6 of 7 shareholders withdrew	1989 credit crunch
31	1989	1993	3 of 7.3 shareholders withdrew	Profits too low; seek other investment opportunities
33	1982	1992	shareholders increase from 84 to 210	Expand production need new capital; new workers invest

Source: 1994 survey

Another commonly cited reason for the withdrawal of shareholders from partnerships was the failure of firms to produce acceptable profits. Almost all of the withdrawals in this category took place in the aftermath of the student movement in Beijing in 1989. The sharp contraction of credit ordered by the central government to reduce the inflation that had been one of the factors contributing to the student movement had a strong impact on some firms, reducing profits and forcing some firms to temporarily halt production. Stagnating sales and uncertain future profits led some shareholders to withdraw from firms at that time.

While more than half of our firms have seen changes in the numbers of their shareholding partners, the firms have overcome the difficulties and continued to develop. This has not been true in many other parts of China. The Chinese literature on the shareholding partnership argues that the partnership form of business organization is subject to frequent failure because of the problem of disputes among shareholders.[21] The Gaoyang tradition also talks of the frequency of failure of partnership but with a more positive interpretation. One local folk saying remarks, "Gaoyang folk join together easily and also split apart easily," implying that the natural breakup of business partnerships leaves no hard feelings. While the breakup of business partnerships has caused temporary crises for individual firms, depleting their capital holdings and forcing them to turn to bank loans, there is no indication of any decrease in the enthusiasm for this form of business organization. The advantages in terms of raising capital seem to outweigh the inherent problems of such forms of partnership in the eyes of Gaoyang residents, who turn to the shareholding partnership as a good way to organize new firms.

LABOR-MANAGEMENT RELATIONS

The contemporary shareholding partnership shares features from three traditions: commercial partnerships, the cooperative workshop, and the socialist commune. So far we have looked at elements that trace their origins to the first two traditions. An examination of labor-management relations shows the influences of the socialist tradition.

Contemporary Gaoyang enterprises are private firms operating in a socialist market economy. In many cases, partners in the firms are members of the Communist Party who were once, and in some cases still are, village cadres. Although the managers may be village cadre, the factories do not belong to the collective. The partners employ fellow villagers as well as outsiders, including those who come from nearby villages and distant provinces. Many of the private factories have Communist Party branches with party secretaries appointed to look out for the political education of employees, and both managers and local leaders see the private firms as the mainstay of the village and regional economies.[22]

As this brief description suggests, the shareholding partnerships are a hybrid form that straddles the line between private and collective and there has been much debate about how to classify them. Some argue that rural shareholding enterprises are a form of collective ownership, citing the constitutional provision for rural cooperatives. Others argue that rural shareholding firms must be seen as a part of the private economy.

Such disputes over classification are more than an academic issue in contemporary China, where both party theorists and the entrepreneurs themselves are feeling their way toward an understanding of what "socialism with Chinese characteristics" permits. During the Cultural Revolution Gaoyang was torn apart by factional struggles that pushed political debate to the extreme left. As a result the county was slow to initiate economic reform and remained sensitive to political charges about the pursuit of capitalism. In the early 1980s, when the economic reformers had just begun to recognize the legitimacy of private enterprise, state guidelines said that private entrepreneurs should not employ more than seven workers: to take on more would involve exploitation. As the economy grew and private manufacturing flourished, firms have become much larger and the restrictions on the number of employees have faded. This does not mean that the question of exploitation has completely disappeared.[23]

One reflection of the continuing sensitivity to such issues is the confusion as to how to categorize the shareholding partnerships. When firms register with the government, they must state the category to which they belong: private (*geti*), partnership (*hehuo*), or collective (*jiti*). Although all of the sample firms were business partnerships, some were registered as partnerships while others were registered as collectives. None of the firms registered as "collective" were actually owned by collective units. Moreover, there was no clear pattern suggesting why firms were registered in a particular category.[24]

The attempt to disguise the categories of collective and private was in part a product of the process that gave birth to the earliest factories and in part a reflection of the ideological environment. In the early years, many of the factories were partially owned by collective units. For example, Red Flag got its start when a group of young men contracted to run an existing village factory. In exchange for use of land and buildings and access to electricity and water, the village government was given several shares in the enterprise. As Red Flag prospered it outgrew the old buildings. Negotiations were undertaken with the village for land and the factory moved to a newly designated "industrial zone" on the outskirts of the village.

The agreements that gave villages shares in firms like Red Flag in exchange for use of land and other resources have now been renegotiated almost everywhere in Gaoyang. Most villages now have industrial zones, and land in these districts is rented to enterprises at fixed rates. This new system, which replaces the earlier system of granting shares to local government bodies, has spread throughout the Gaoyang region and village governments no longer hold a direct interest in partnership firms.

Although almost all of Gaoyang's shareholding firms are now truly private enterprises without government shareholders, this does not mean that the influence of party and ideology has disappeared. One telling illustration of this can be seen in the terminology that is used to refer to the leaders of the new enterprises. When county government officials address the managers of firms on formal occasions, they almost always refer to them as entrepreneurs (*qiye jia*), using a phrase that carries a sense of individuals who have created something new and beneficial to the community. The term that is used more informally when officials refer to managers, or when workers themselves refer to the manager of a factory, is boss (*laoban*), a term that was also used in the prewar period to refer to managers. While the word "boss" in English has quite strong class implications, in contemporary Gaoyang all parties regard boss as an acceptable term to describe the person who manages a factory.

On one occasion, when talking informally with a group of factory managers, I referred to them as "capitalists" (*zibenjia*), and I discovered very quickly that that was not seen as an acceptable word for their role. While the academic literature and popular press outside China often discuss China's booming rural manufacturing enterprises as if they were capitalist enterprises, none of the parties in Gaoyang see what they are doing in those terms. Just as the slogans painted on the walls that surround rural factories stress the links between rural industrialization and national salvation, so the businessmen involved choose to see their own efforts as designed to develop the local community, rather than as the simple pursuit of personal wealth.[25]

This sensitivity to reference terms, the claim that while managers are bosses they are not capitalists, is a reflection of a broader ethic of labor-management relations that can be seen in labor management practices of contemporary firms. Although many of the "bosses" are in fact shareholders in the firms who receive differential benefits for their work, every effort is made on a formal level to disguise this and to put a benevolent face on the ways in which companies treat their workers. In order to understand how this operates, we need to first take a brief look at work in Gaoyang factories.

Working conditions varied quite dramatically among the thirty-four factories studied. In 1995 the largest of the factories employed 370 workers, while the smallest employed only 17. Working hours also varied greatly. In most of the larger factories, including most of the spinning mills, work time was divided into three eight-hour shifts, with workers rotating from shift to shift on a weekly basis. In some of the smaller factories, work time was divided into two twelve-hour shifts, again with rotation on a weekly basis. Almost all of

the factories provided free dormitories for their workers and subsidized cafe-
terias; the richer factories had multistoried dormitories with modern con-
veniences, while the poorer factories provided simple one-story buildings,
with workers sleeping on traditional heated sleeping platforms.

Most of the workers are first-generation workers who are just learning to
adjust to the discipline of regular factory labor.[26] Like textile factories in
many parts of the world, the factories employ a large number of young
women, most of them unmarried daughters of peasant families. The young
women working in the factories are not well educated: roughly half have
only a grade school education, while the rest are graduates of junior high
school. Among the workers are many who are not Gaoyang natives; in our
sample factories, on average only half of the workforce was recruited locally.[27] Factory regulations are designed to deal with this workforce that is
young and not very well educated. Factory rules are simple and are usually
printed on blackboards throughout the factory. Penalties for infractions of
the rules and for absence from work or tardiness are almost always in the
form of reduction of pay. There is no "iron rice bowl"—or guarantee of life-
time employment—protecting the rights of workers in the factories and there
is also little loyalty among the workers to their employer. Workers change
jobs frequently, moving from factory to factory in search of slightly higher
wages or better working conditions, or simply seeking to work in a factory
with colleagues or friends from the same village or native region.

In an effort to retain their workers, factories compete with each other by
paying relatively high wages. When I conducted a survey of women workers in 1991, average take-home pay was 170 yuan per month. By 1995, the
combination of increased prosperity and inflation had driven the average
wage up to 355 yuan per month for women and to 367 yuan per month for
men, with jobs that were regarded as "dirty" or which required higher skills
bringing wages of up to 520 yuan per month for women and 610 yuan per
month for men. In both periods wages were at least equal to—if not higher
than—those earned by average workers in China's larger cities.[28] The relatively high wages were the result of an intensification of work: the factories
all used wage systems that combined a low basic wage with bonuses based
on piece-work quotas. This method of calculating wages was designed to
encourage higher levels of productivity among the workers. Work floors always seemed to be busy and there was little of the idling about that was
common in state-owned factories. During an eight-hour shift, workers got
only one thirty-minute meal break, and even then the machines did not stop;
workers took their breaks in shifts, covering for those who were temporarily
absent.

While wages in rural factories were relatively high, workers received few
other benefits. There was little job security and a company could fire or lay
off workers whenever it chose to do so.[29] Yet not all factory managers were

ruthless in pursuit of their goals and most tried to provide work during secular downturns. For example, one spinning factory shifted from spinning wool to spinning synthetic fibers during the summer months, since the lower cost of the synthetic fiber allowed the factory to operate throughout the summer months without laying off workers.

None of the factories had pension systems and health insurance schemes paid medical benefits only for on-the-job injuries. Health care for all other diseases or injuries had to be paid for by the individual worker out of pocket.[30] None of the factories had clinics or health professionals on call. Despite the fact that roughly 60 percent of the workforce was made up of young women, none of the factories provided nurseries for young children and only ten out of the thirty-four factories offered even limited maternity leave benefits.[31]

As this brief description makes clear, working conditions in Gaoyang factories were a long way from a socialist vision of acceptable working conditions. Unlike the state factories, which provided generous social benefits, regular systems of promotion, and a welfare system that looked after workers and their families even after retirement, the rural factories offered a simple economic exchange: wages in return for work during the contracted working hours, with little in the way of extra benefits or long-term guarantees. On the surface there seems little to suggest socialist influence on labor-management relations.

Managers of the rural factories surveyed read the situation in a different way. Although most managers were also shareholders, they presented themselves to outsiders as though they were just like any other worker in the factory. Unlike the bureaucratic managers of state firms who rarely got their hands dirty by intervening in the production process, it was not unusual to find a rural factory manager with his hands covered in grease from helping to repair machinery. Managers were working managers who spent much of their time on the shop floor and had a good understanding of the technical production process. They worked long hours, often ten to twelve hours or more a day. Like other workers in the factory, managerial personnel received a monthly salary in return for their labor, and managerial salaries were almost always pegged very closely to the average salary of the workers. In 1995 the vast majority of managers (75 percent) received salaries below 500 yuan a month.[32]

This practice of paying managers nominal salaries that were little higher than those of their workers was deliberately designed to maintain an appearance of equality within the work unit. Most Gaoyang bosses believed that they were benevolent employers, and the lack of wage differentials was one sign of this. Other marks of managerial benevolence were seasonal bonuses and special gifts of tea, fruit, and other specialties at the Lunar New Year and on other festive occasions. Sensitive to questions of exploitation, such practices were designed to disguise the great gaps in wealth that are one of the side products of the factory building boom.

The new generation of factory managers also recognized the special needs of rural industry. All of the native workers' families continued to farm and most factories suspended production for several weeks during the busy agricultural season so their workers could assist with farming. Some village factories had gone one step further and started to assist in farm work. Taokoudian was the village where this assistance was most developed. In the mid-1990s the village had fifteen factories. Communist Party members had founded many of the factories and the village party committee included the managers of the seven largest factories. Close coordination between the village government and the factories led to a novel experiment. When village land had first been divided after the dissolution of the commune, land assignments had been based on work team units. Now that almost everyone worked in or owned shares in one of the factories, land was reassigned so that the fields were organized according to factory affiliation. Each of the factories made arrangements to mechanize plowing, planting, and harvesting for all of its workers. Thus the burden of farm work was reduced and less time was lost to allow workers to help in the fields.

While the Taokoudian system represents the most organized version of factory assistance in cultivation, other factories with large numbers of native workers had purchased agriculture equipment to plow and harvest their workers' fields, either for free or for minimal fees.

All of the practices described above—the paying of low wages to managers, the giving of seasonal gifts, the involvement of the factory in organizing agricultural work—were designed to reinforce the image of the managers of the firms as benevolent actors. Just as the new generation of managers did not want to think of themselves as capitalists, they wanted to see themselves as contributing to communal welfare. Some of these practices may have been designed to deflect the criticism of those who were jealous of the newly wealthy, but some came from more fundamental commitments to rural communal values.

THE FIRM, THE VILLAGE, AND THE LOCAL STATE

One of the distinctive features of the prewar system was the creation of collective resources that supported the growth of Gaoyang as an industrial district. The chamber of commerce had played the central role in building the collective resources that promoted local economic growth. The visitor to contemporary Gaoyang can see the transformation of the town and countryside that has accompanied the construction of new collective resources in the 1980s and 1990s. Paved roads now link village industrial zones to the major county roads and highways, there are bypasses around the town, and a new six-story building at the northeast corner of the town houses restaurants, meeting rooms, hotel rooms, and offices for many of the county's textile firms, as well as the offices of the Bureau of Township and Village Enterprises. Newly constructed marketing complexes serve as centers for the wholesale trade in towels and other textiles. All are visible signs of the growing infrastructure that collective institutions and resources have created to support the contemporary industrial district. Other forms of infrastructure are less visible, but just as important. The modernization of the telephone system in the early 1990s greatly improved communications with suppliers and customers outside the local community. Where in the late 1980s it could take hours to get a telephone call through to Tianjin, modernization of the system has brought rapid service. The Bureau of Township and Village Enterprises has vigorously promoted technological progress through its lecture series on new products, market trends, and business management practices. In late August every year, the county government organizes a textile festival that coincides with the beginning of the sales season in the wool industry, drawing potential customers and investors to Gaoyang.

While the creation of collective resources shares some similarities with the patterns identified during the first phase of growth, the processes involved have been very different, reflecting very different relations between the firms and the various levels of the local government. During the late Qing and Republican periods, when the chamber of commerce played such a central role in organizing local economic endeavors, the local state apparatus was weak. Magistrates served only short terms in office, the county government staff was small, and links between the county bureaucracy, subdistricts, and village were underdeveloped. Thus there was much room at the county level for an organization like the chamber of commerce to take the initiative in organizing projects that served the interests of business groups. While local leadership brought with it an obligation to make financial contributions to a wide range of projects, not all of which were directly related to business interests, in the economic sphere the initiative was most commonly taken by the chamber of commerce.

In contemporary Gaoyang a different institutional setting has created a different balance between firms, village governments, and the state.[33] More than fifty years of Communist Party rule have created a large and vigorous county bureaucracy with strong links between county government, the party, and the corresponding organizations at the township and village level. One of the consequences of this has been the elimination of nongovernment civic organizations. When the CCP created a county-level Federation of Commerce and Industry (Gongshang Lianhe Hui) in December 1945, the federation effectively usurped the role that the older chamber of commerce had played. It replaced the voluntary organization with a state organization, which was given the responsibility of supervising commerce and industry.[34] County organizations responsible for supervising, organizing, or in some other way administering commerce and industry today include the federation, which is in theory a mass organization, as well as two bureaus with direct supervisory functions, the Bureau for Commerce and Industry (Gongshang Ju) and the Bureau for Township and Village Enterprises. In recent years there have been some attempts to create associations (*xiehui*) for entrepreneurs in the major sectors of Gaoyang's textile industries, but since the initiative comes from the county government and leaders of the associations are designated by county government officials, these organizations cannot be seen as truly representing the independent interests of businesspeople.[35] Government and party-sponsored organizations have thus constituted the formal institutions that articulate interests in the local community, leaving little room for independent collective initiative on the part of the entrepreneurs themselves. Busy with the tasks of managing their own firms, few entrepreneurs have shown any interest in directly challenging this state-party monopoly. Some individuals have been co-opted into the state-sponsored "mass organizations" and assigned roles as industry spokesmen, but most have simply chosen to ignore the organizations except when the organizations directly impinge on their private business interests.[36]

This institutional environment has created a set of practices in which state and semi-state organizations take the initiative in determining what collective resources are needed. However, the collapse of the collective industry and the decline of the state industrial sector have weakened the fiscal position of local governments at village, township, and county levels, draining them of the resources to implement their plans. Simultaneously, the rapid growth of the private industrial sector has enriched individual entrepreneurs, giving them control over the major source of funds for both private and public investment. In the 1980s and 1990s, a symbiotic relationship slowly developed between local government officials at all levels and the new industrial entrepreneurs, in which local officials took the initiative in defining goals and drafting plans and the entrepreneurial community was asked to provide the financing. To understand how this new symbiotic relationship works we need to begin with a consideration of the points at which official and private interests meet.

Entrepreneurs and local government officials share a common interest in promoting rapid economic growth. For the entrepreneurs the benefits are obvious: economic growth increases individual personal wealth and at the same time brings status and respect within the local community. For officials the rewards are also attractive, if somewhat more complicated. At the county level, government leaders can be divided into two major groups. The first, relatively small, group includes higher-ranking cadre in the party and county government who are non-natives assigned to the county for relatively short terms of office. The county's first party secretary as well as the chief magistrate and some of their immediate subordinates fall in this category of nonnative career bureaucrats. Most of these career bureaucrats are natives of Hebei Province who have moved out of their native counties into the provincial bureaucracy.[37] Periodically reassigned from one county to another, their careers depend on regular evaluation of their accomplishments in each posting. In reform era China, administrative success is often judged in economic terms. One of the fastest ways for career bureaucrats to earn promotion is by demonstrating their ability to take initiatives that lead to economic growth, which is measured in higher output and raised per capita income.[38]

The second major group of county government officials includes natives who have worked their way up within the local government system without entering the outside career path. Most of the clerical staff and ordinary office workers in county government offices fall in this category, but so do some of the highest-ranking county officials, including the party vice-secretary and several of the vice-magistrates as well as members of the standing committee of the party. The interests of the native officials are more complex than those of the outside career bureaucrats. While native officials also have an interest in rising up the bureaucratic ladder, their ambitions are within their native community where they plan to spend their whole career and where they plan to retire. They have more complicated networks of connections within the local community and are inclined to see things from a local point of view. Some of the rewards they receive for a job well done are in the form of increased prestige in the local community, while some may come in the more material form of gifts and favors exchanged.

County government officials cannot realize their ambitions without the cooperation of members of the local business community who help to finance the projects that officials will proudly point to when they face promotion reviews. Thus is born a symbiotic relationship between officials and the entrepreneurs who run the private firms. One side holds the economic resources, the other political power. Only when the two come together is there effective investment in collective resources that can promote communal development. Needless to say, there are often differences of opinion on the relative benefits of various proposals, and the unequal status and power of the two groups involved further complicates the picture. Entrepreneurs often find it difficult to say no to requests, even when they are convinced that few benefits will result. To understand why that is so, we need to turn briefly to the ways in which money is extracted from the entrepreneurial groups.

Financing local government has been a persistent problem in China for centuries. During the late imperial period, land taxes provided the core of government revenues. Collected by county government offices, most of the revenue was destined for national government coffers, leaving provincial and county officials to fund their activities from an assemblage of special assessments and surcharges.[39] After the 1911 Revolution, the new republic took over major parts of the Qing fiscal system, including its neglect of local finance. As Prasenjit Duara has shown, this led to "state involution," a process in which "the formal structures of the state continued to grow simultaneously with informal structures—such as tax farmers and mercenary soldiers." On the local fiscal front this created a county government dependent on extra-statutory tax-raising methods that put a heavy burden on rural communities in the form of *tankuan*, irregular assessments apportioned among the villages in accordance with the demands of the local government.[40] After 1949, the People's Republic of China solved its revenue problems with a fiscal system based in a combination of agricultural taxes and revenue from state-owned enterprises.[41] While the results can hardly be seen as a rationalized system of revenue sharing between different levels of government, since the various levels of government were able to control the state industrial sector through an elaborate dual system of party and administrative control, the revenue base was generally assured. At the local level, collectives could be called upon to invest unpaid labor in major public works projects, also easing the fiscal burden on local government bodies.[42]

The reform policies of the 1980s have shaken the base of Chinese public finance. Village collective industries were dissolved, and subsequent changes in the state industrial structure have greatly reduced the profits of state industry, forcing many enterprises into debt and others to close. As a result, state revenues as a share of national income have steadily dropped and hard-pressed national and provincial bureaucrats have pushed the fiscal burden for the construction of infrastructure off on local government units, which are left to find their own revenue sources.[43]

In Gaoyang, entrepreneurs have been one of the chief targets of local government efforts to gather funds, and over the last decade they have been asked to contribute to a vast array of projects by county, township, and village governments. Since most rural industry is privately owned, profits belong to the shareholders or owners of the firms, not to government units. Government claims on the income generated by rural enterprises comes in the form of fixed taxes on industrial production, plus taxes on income. In order to keep their taxes as low as possible, most firms in China—whether publicly or privately owned—try to evade taxes. Commonly a firm will keep two or more sets of books, one for use in reporting to state authorities, a second and sometimes a third that gives a more realistic reflection of the actual financial state of the firm.[44] Officials in the county tax office know what is going on but in most cases are not able to collect the full taxes due. This practice of under-collecting taxes puts individual firms in debt to the local tax office and vulnerable to pressure from county government officials for "donations" for various projects. Firms find it difficult to plan for the demands for "donations" and special contributions, but resistance is reduced since the funds are used for projects in the local community. It is difficult to know how heavy the burden of such special assessments is: county officials claim that the combined total of taxes and special donations is less than the amount firms would owe the state if all taxes were collected fully according to the official tax rates. Entrepreneurs, on their side, complain of the requests for donations, but pay. Since both sides disguise the sums involved, it is impossible to make an accurate estimate of what is actually owed and actually collected.

On one level, the process involved in financing county government projects is not unlike that in use in the 1930s, when merchants also bore a significant portion of the burden for financing local government projects. However, there is one very significant difference. In the prewar period the chamber of commerce was able to represent the interests of its members, giving them a much stronger voice and a stronger negotiating position. In contemporary Gaoyang individual firms must negotiate with government offices on their own. While the largest and most prosperous firms stand in a fairly strong position vis à vis the county government, average-size firms are in a much weaker position.[45]

The informal systems for funding county government investments that have developed over the last few years can be seen as a form of extralegal revenue sharing devised by local government officials who are under great pressure to perform, but have been given few fiscal resources. By turning a blind eye to the under-collection of taxes on private enterprises, they have been able to ensure cooperation when they seek contributions for local infrastructure.

PRIVATE FIRMS AND THE VILLAGE

Almost all of the private manufacturing firms today are located in villages rather than in the county town. When we consider relations between firms and the "local state," it is also necessary to look at the pressures and requests that come from village governments. When entrepreneurs want to establish a new enterprise, the first problem is finding a site. Land in rural China is not for sale and the only way to obtain use rights is to gain permission from the village that controls them. Most villages have designated "industrial zones" which include land that has been taken out of agricultural use and set aside for building factories. The factories are an important part of the village community: at least some of the partners in a firm will be natives of the village, linked by complicated ties of kinship to many of their neighbors. Many of their employees are likely to be fellow villagers and the factory owners will be expected to contribute to village life.

While most villagers who are not partners in firms believe that their richer fellows have an obligation to contribute to the collective well-being, not all village governments have dealt with this expectation in the same way. The Gaoyang villages that I have visited can be divided into three types, based on the ways in which the relationship between private firms and the village community are handled. In one group are villages where weaving workshops predominate. In weaving villages, investment is relatively evenly dispersed throughout the village community and villagers have seen an across-the-board increase in standards of living. With no big players to consider, the village party committees have been able to work out an equitable assessment of fees for village projects. In one weaving village, the original pattern of assessment was based on the number of power looms a workshop owned; later the village shifted to a calculation based on electricity consumption. Since such villages have been able to spread the financing requests evenly over a large portion of the village population, they have little trouble reaching agreement on projects and how to fund them.

Type two and type three villages are those in which there are a smaller number of relatively larger operators who are the employers of much of the village labor force. In these villages there is not the same equitable division of income and the village government has to find ways to get contributions from the wealthiest members of the community. While most entrepreneurs are willing to make contributions for projects, many of them believe that their increased wealth is the result of hard work and they resent the fact that poorer neighbors think they should bear the burden for all public investment. I have divided these villages into two groups, based on differences in the way in which they handle this question. In type two villages, there has been a blending between the village government and the entrepreneurial community. This blending is in some senses the natural outcome of the process by which industrialization began. In the early 1980s local party cadre were told to take the initiative in starting rural industry as a way of assuring ordinary peasants that entrepreneurial activities were legitimate. Many of the factories started by village cadre have prospered and their managers have continued to wear two hats, one as village cadre, one as factory manager. In at least one village the whole party committee is made up of factory owners. In villages where part or all of the village party committee is made up of entrepreneurs, it is usually easier to gather funds for investment projects, since the entrepreneurs who will be asked to make significant contributions are part of the decision-making body. Once the cadre/factory managers take the lead in volunteering contributions, it is easier to induce others in the community to follow.

The greatest tension between entrepreneurs and village cadre exists in villages where there are a smaller number of large factories and the owners are not members of the party. In these villages entrepreneurs tend to be less willing to contribute to village projects, not because they are less cooperative, but because they have less say in what projects are necessary. In such villages party cadre find it harder to operate, since ordinary villagers are not willing to contribute unless the wealthy are willing to pay their share. As a consequence, while these villages have been able to put in basic infrastructure that is clearly in the interests of private firms—for example paving roads and improving the electricity supply—they have been slower to build new schools and undertake other investments of a more general nature.

Whether the village is type one, two, or three, at the village level local cadre have little of the leverage that is exercised by county government officials to persuade wealthy entrepreneurs to "contribute" funds for public projects. They must rely on the ties of kinship and neighborliness to persuade entrepreneurs to part with some of their profits for public projects. At all levels of the local political scene, the new entrepreneurial class has yet to establish its own voice or to articulate its own visions of the future. While collective resources are being created, they have been created under the leadership of party and state bureaucrats without a formal voice from the people most directly involved. Busy today with building their own businesses, few seem interested in challenging the state monopoly on power, but the day may come when the informal structures of revenue sharing put too heavy a burden on private industry, and at that point their representatives may seek a more active voice.

NOTES

1. In many villages there were not enough looms to go around; those who did not get a loom received a cash payment.

2. On the county list of more than 190 textile firms with more than 100,000 yuan in registered capital, 103 (52 percent) were registered as *hehuo* (joint partnership) firms. Another 52 (27 percent) were registered as collective enterprises (*jiti*). In some villages 75 percent of the firms were listed as "collective" even though they were business partnerships.

3. In recent years, the term *hezi*, which in earlier times was used to describe partnerships, has come to be used almost exclusively for joint ventures with foreign partners.

4. I have compared the characteristics of the larger list with the 34 firms in the sample. The two groups are similar in most characteristics.

5. Jia Jianhua, *Cuican de Qunxing* (Haikou: Hainan Chubanshe, 1994). This is a collection of reportage on Gaoyang firms and their managers.

6. Even in the case of the death of one of the partners it is more common for the remaining partners to buy out the heirs than to transfer shares to a new generation.

7. The operations of small workshops described in chapter three used this same principle of organization, as do many of the small dyeing workshops in contemporary Gaoyang.

8. In firms with two to nine shareholders the initial value of a single share was 50,000 yuan, while in firms with more than fifteen shareholders, the median value of the share was 10,000 yuan. In firms with ten to fifteen shares, the value of the share at the time of firm founding stood at 20,000.

9. Wang Zongpei, *Zhongguo zhi hehui* (Zhongguo Hezoushe, 1941), and Yang Ximeng, *Zhongguo hehui zhi yanjiu* (Shangwu Yinshuguan, 1934).

10. This situation was worsened in the early 1990s by the problem of "triangular debt." State-run export firms delayed payments to state textile firms. The manufacturers in turn could not repay their debts to their suppliers—the producers of fiber and yarn. Since rural industrial firms got their supplies of yarn and fiber from the same state firms, pressure for cash dealing was heightened. During the 1990–1991 credit crunch, local officials estimated that small firms needed 30,000,000 yuan in loans; during the first quarter of 1990, the state quota for loans in the county stood at 200,000 yuan. Background provided in discussions with the Township and Village Enterprises Bureau in 1990 and 1991.

11. The answer of one firm is unclear.

12. In prewar firms, the practice of paying *hongli* to senior employees as a bonus at the end of the accounting year may have contributed to this practice. In contemporary firms, *hongli* as part of salary is less common.

13. Gao Yankai, the manager of Red Flag, joined together the firm he managed with two independent firms managed by his younger brothers in the new industrial group.

14. As of September 1996, the Dong Feng Industrial Group had not changed its corporate name; Dong Feng, or Eastern Wind, was a commonly used symbol from the revolutionary days.

15. Firms provided data (age, educational level, former employment) for all members of their managerial staff.

16. The occupational category of "peasant" (*funong* or *nongmin*) is a very slippery term in contemporary North China, as I discovered when conducting fieldwork in Luancheng County in central Hebei Province. During the daytime there were very few men in the village and yet family members repeatedly said they were "peasants." Only after much questioning did we learn that anyone independently employed or engaged in private commerce was considered a "peasant."

17. The breakdown by former occupation showed 73 percent (139) as peasants, 7 percent (14) as workers, 6 percent (12) as cadre, 2 percent (4) engaged in commerce, 2 percent (4) as shop-floor supervisors, 10 percent (6) as students, and smaller numbers of handicraftsmen and village cadre.

18. Gaoyang educational standards are difficult to judge. The county's two high schools have produced large numbers of graduates who have gone to the best national universities. Overall figures, however, show somewhat lower levels of average education. There has been a marked improvement in recent years.

19. The mean period of service of outside technical personnel was 15.95 months, with the shortest term of employment 1 month and the longest period of service 48 months. Salaries ranged from a low of 300 yuan a month to a high of 2,500 yuan a month, with a median at roughly 800 yuan per month. Some of the firms provided room and board.

20. This investment in the education of children has been made easier by the changing situation in Chinese higher education. Where once examination success was the only way to obtain entry into prestigious universities, many universities now accept students with lower scores; the trade-off is higher tuition fees.

21. Xiao Weizhao, Wang Minsheng, and Liu Qing, "Hehuo siying qiye cunzai de wenti ji yindao duici," *Gaige yu Lunli* 6 (1990), 34–35. The authors argue that there are five main reasons for failures: unclear contractual agreements become a source of friction; too great demands are put on the firm; backward management leads to a low level of efficiency; a complicated mix of blood and local-place ties leads to splits when trouble comes; and finally, the tendency of *hehuo* firms to look only at short-term interests.

22. The party branches in the private firms differ significantly from those in state-run enterprise. In state firms the party secretary almost always outranks the manager, while in private firms the manager clearly is in charge.

23. Zhongguo Shehui Kexueyuan Nongye Jingji Yanjiusuo, ed., *Nongcun gugong jingying diaocha yanjiu,* 1983.

24. There was no correlation by founding date and the only pattern that can be identified was a tendency for some villages to register most enterprises as "collective" or as "partnership."

25. A very common slogan is "Promote rural industrialization, build a strong China."

26. There is still psychological resistance to working in factories. Young women interviewees in Hebei and Shandong villages expressed ambivalent feelings about factory work. Those who have chosen to work in factories find it more interesting than staying at home, where very little happens. Those who do not work outside the home often have negative images: one young woman described a factory as being like a cage without any windows.

27. The percentage of non-native workers varied, reflecting different management strategies. Firms with large numbers of shareholders employed a higher percentage of native workers. Average age for workers showed little variance. In most factories the average age of women workers was twenty and almost all were unmarried.

28. The 1991 survey compared nominal and real wages of women working in the rural factories with women textile workers in a state factory. Even after adding on all of the subsidies and other hidden benefits to the salaries of state workers, the rural workers' average wages were higher.

29. While this happened frequently in the 1980s, by the 1990s layoffs were not so common. The last great wave of layoffs came in 1989–1990, in the aftermath of the national attempt to slow down an overheated economy.

30. Many of the factory managers did claim that if a worker had unusual medical expenses the factory would donate money to help cover the expenses and fellow workers would also make voluntary contributions to help out. In the mid-1990s government leaders were encouraging non-state firms to join government-sponsored insurance and pension systems, but since such programs were not compulsory, very few rural enterprises had joined.

31. The only factories that offered maternity leave were the spinning factories that have had more difficulty finding and holding women workers. Even then, only three

of the ten reported that they paid wages during maternity leave. Of those three, each paid a portion of the basic wage, ranging from 30 percent to 100 percent. However, since most of a worker's income came from the per-piece calculations part of the wage, even paying 100 percent of the basic wage would leave a worker with roughly one-third of normal income. Labor protection was beginning to break down in state factories in the mid-1990s as the result of increased competitive pressure from private industry. For a description of this in the textile industry, see Minghua Zhao and Theo Nichols, "Management Control of Labor in State-Owned Enterprises: Cases from the Textile Industry," *The China Journal* 36 (July 1996), 1–21.

32. This was only a little more than the average worker's salary. A full 60 percent of the managers received less than 400 yuan per month, which put them almost equal with the average worker. The major exception to the principle of low managerial salaries was hired managers who did not hold shares in the company for which they were working; their salaries were usually considerably higher.

33. There is a large literature on local government institutions in China. Among the books that I have found useful are the essays in Vivienne Shue, *The Reach of the State: Sketches of the Chinese Body Politic* (Stanford: Stanford University Press, 1988); Edward Friedman, Paul G. Pickowicz, and Mark Selden, *Chinese Village, Socialist State* (New Haven: Yale University Press, 1991); and Marc Blecher and Vivienne Shue, *Tethered Deer: Government and Economy in a Chinese County* (Stanford: Stanford University Press, 1996).

34. There was a wartime chamber of commerce that collaborated with Japanese occupation forces. None of the core members of the prewar chamber of commerce had anything to do with the puppet organization, but the use of the organizational name made it easier for the CCP to discredit voluntary organizations. There is a brief description of the activities of the federation in the section under popular organizations in the *Gaoyang xianzhi* (1995).

35. While there have been moves in other parts of China to create truly voluntary organizations led by private entrepreneurs, the picture in Gaoyang is much closer to that described in Jonathan Unger's study of Beijing commercial organizations, "Bridges: Private Business, the Chinese Government and the Rise of New Associations," *China Quarterly* 147 (September 1996), 795–819.

36. Conversations with businessmen suggest that many entrepreneurs see the new organizations as more show than function.

37. Liu Fei was first party secretary in Gaoyang in 1995. He had served as a financial officer in Anguo County, home to North China's largest traditional drug market. Success there led to his appointment as a magistrate in Li Xian and success there to appointment as first party secretary in Gaoyang.

38. In the mid-1990s one of the standards was *xiao kang* status, a designation given to areas that had achieved across-the-board improvement in standards of living as measured by per capita income.

39. Madeleine Zelin, *The Magistrate's Tael: Rationalizing Fiscal Reform in Eighteenth-Century Ch'ing China* (Berkeley: University of California Press, 1984).

40. Prasenjit Duara, "State Involution: A Study of Local Finances in North China, 1911–1935," *Comparative Studies in Society and History* 29, no. 1 (1987), 132.

41. Christine Wong, ed., *Financing Local Government in the People's Republic of China* (Hong Kong: Oxford University Press, 1997).

42. To greatly simplify the pre-reform era situation, we can begin with a model in which county revenues were derived from county-owned enterprises. Counties were assigned a quota of their revenue that had to be forwarded to higher levels of government. In the Baoding district, there were twenty-four counties, only six of which (including Gaoyang) were required to turn over funds to higher levels of government. The other eighteen counties, with weak industrial bases, were net recipients of funds generated by their wealthier neighbors.

43. While some have seen this as a "decentralization" that will give greater freedom to local government units, I am inclined to agree with Christine Wong's assessment that what we see is an unintended dysfunctional outcome of the reforms. See Christine P. W. Wong, "Central-Local Relations in an Era of Fiscal Decline: The Paradox of Fiscal Decentralization in Post-Mao China," *China Quarterly* 128 (December 1991), 691–715, and "Between Plan and Market: The Role of the Local Sector in Post-Mao China," *Journal of Comparative Economics* 11 (1987), 385–98; for a more optimistic evaluation of the impact of the reforms on local government, see Jean Oi, "The Role of the Local State in China's Transitional Economy," *China Quarterly* 144 (December 1995), 1132–49, and the same author's "Fiscal Reform and the Economic Foundation of Local State Corporatism in China," *World Politics* 45 (October 1992), 99–126.

44. Deceptive calculations and false statistical reports are pervasive among Chinese business and government organizations. Firms as well as local government units make false reports of their economic status. Where once it was fashionable to over-report production statistics as a way of gaining praise, today underreporting is also common. One village leader bragged that he and his colleagues had underreported their village's total income by a factor of roughly ten. In the mid-1990s most villages underreported per capita income out of fear the county government would use higher figures to claim more in donations. See Thomas G. Rawski, "What's Happening to China's GDP Statistics?" paper prepared for the *China Economic Review*, December 2001. (Web version available at http:www.pitt.edu/~trawski/papers2001/gdp912f.pdf.)

45. A review of two incidents from the mid-1990s gives some indication of the symbiotic relationship between prosperous entrepreneurs and local government officials. In one case, the wedding of the only son of one of the largest entrepreneurs, virtually every local official above the clerk level made a point of visiting and leaving a red envelope with a cash gift; in the second case, the funeral of the father of another large entrepreneur, more than 200,000 yuan was spent on the funeral; virtually all county officials turned up to pay their respects.

Conclusion

This study has examined the development of the Gaoyang industrial district over almost a century, from its origins in the early twentieth century to the 1990s. I have argued that the Gaoyang style of growth represents a particular form of an industrial revolution in China during the long twentieth century. In this concluding chapter I will consider how and why the industrial district model, which arose as part of the first wave of industrialization in late nineteenth- and early twentieth-century China, has taken on a new life in the economic reform era. What factors in the transition from high socialism to reform led to the flourishing of industrial districts in China? How were legacies from pre-socialist Chinese business practice adapted to meet new institutional needs? And where does this form of industrial organization fit in our overall understanding of Chinese modern economic growth patterns?[1]

The contemporary Gaoyang industrial district developed as part of the transformation process of China's socialist economy. Conflicts between market and plan as principles for organizing economic activity were at the center of reorganization and reform movements that shaped the region's development over the last half century. They continue to play a significant role in the reform economy of contemporary China. While some economists see market and plan as incompatible principles of organization, others are attracted by Chinese experiments that seem to be creating a new developmental state model in between the polarities of market and plan.[2]

Whether centered on market or plan, there is no question that the rapid growth of rural industry has been an important element in China's "economic miracle" of the late twentieth century. While commentators often speak of "rural industry" as a single phenomenon, case studies of rural industrialization in different regions of China discuss a number of local growth

261

models characterized by widely differing structural arrangements. It is now clear that macro-level economic reform initiatives invited different responses at the micro level. As local communities took advantage of the opportunities presented by reform initiatives, they developed a wide range of approaches to organizing rural industrial activity involving different combinations of free market initiatives and local state control. Although case studies use the common term "rural industry," they describe organizational forms that can be placed at many points on a continuum whose poles represent state control and market autonomy.[3] At one end are communities that organize enterprises on the basis of collective organizations under the leadership of the Communist Party and at the other are communities where private enterprises play the leading role. Andrew Walder and Jean Oi argue that the two patterns—one a government-centered corporatist model and the other an entrepreneur-centered model—trace their origins to different resource endowments at the beginning of the reform process. Communities that follow the corporatist model almost always inherited team- and brigade-operated rural industries, while those where entrepreneurship is stronger usually began with weaker collective bases.

Jean Oi has developed the analysis of what she calls "local state corporatism," based on areas where collective activities are still important. Oi argues that the process of fiscal reform strengthened the power of the "local state," creating new corporate bodies at the local level. In Oi's model, the waning of the planned economy did not lead to a free market economy, but rather to the creation of a new system of organization in which economic control has been shifted downward to the level of the county or township. "The state responsible for much of this growth is *local* governments that treat enterprises within their administrative purview as one component of a larger corporate whole. Local officials act as the equivalent of a board of directors and sometimes more directly as the chief executive officers. At the helm of this corporate-like organization is the Communist Party Secretary."[4]

Oi's model of local state corporatism stands at one end of the continuum; the Gaoyang model stands close to the opposite end of the continuum, representing a local development pattern in which the state plays a relatively limited role. The Gaoyang model is the product not only of the entrepreneurial legacies we discussed in earlier chapters but also of the particular arrangement of economic activity in the period of high socialism and of the way in which the socialist system was transformed.[5]

THE GAOYANG MODEL AND THE LEGACY OF HIGH SOCIALISM

When we compare Gaoyang with regions where state corporatism is strong, one of the first things we notice is that in most of those places local governments at the township and village level built on collective industry that had developed during the period of high socialism. Although Gaoyang had been *the* leading prewar model for rural industrialization, the collectively owned (that is, village, commune) rural industrial sector during the era of high socialism was surprisingly weak. In explaining why this was so, we can identify four factors that contributed to this situation; some of these factors are related to the macroeconomic environment and pattern of state control, some have more to do with local politics and economy.

Let us begin with the legacies of the process by which private industry was converted to state ownership. As we saw in chapter seven, various segments of the industrial district were treated in different ways: private wholesalers were driven out of trade, modern dyeing and finishing factories were converted into state-owned enterprises, and household weavers were organized into weaving cooperatives. The new state-owned enterprises were then cannibalized, with their cadre of experienced managers and technicians reassigned to state textile factories all over North China. At the same time the state strengthened its monopoly over the textile industry and began to expand production by building spinning and weaving mills in larger cities in cotton-producing regions. As output levels in the new textile factories rose, state planners no longer needed rural weaving to meet demand. As a result, weaving cooperatives lost out in the competition for raw materials. Over time the remaining cooperatives were confined to production of low-value-added goods and pathways to development were blocked. By the early 1960s most of the village-sponsored weaving and dyeing cooperatives were being maintained as a form of relief by the state, rather than as profit-generating economic units.

There were one or two exceptions to this grim picture. Several of the small cooperative workshops set up in the early 1950s were able to escape this trap and move into the production of higher-value-added goods. Successful units did not remain independent for long; success almost always led to incorporation by the state, so that the village (brigade) or commune that had developed the factory was not able to benefit from the continuing profits a factory produced.

For communes and brigades rural industry served several purposes. It was, of course, designed to produce useful products that fed into the local economy. It was also assigned the task of generating profits that could be pooled with the income from agriculture to raise the cash value of the "work points" that were earned by collective members. Finally, rural enterprises provided an important source of jobs for collective members, jobs that not only increased income but also provided important job training and skills. When a collectively owned factory was taken over by the state, the collective received a payment. However, it lost the industrial enterprise as a source of jobs since state enterprises recruited their employees through the state labor bureau, which drew on a labor pool that included those with urban residence status.

The experience of the Gaoyang Towel Factory provides an illustration of the process. In 1958 three villages had started a weaving cooperative. At the beginning this small weaving factory employed forty villagers who worked on twenty iron gear looms. They began to experiment with the production of towels and were able to catch the interest of the Tianjin foreign trade bureau, which encouraged the experiment and provided assistance in acquiring raw materials. In 1961 the cooperative bought its first power loom, and in 1964 it was able to refit its small workshop with power looms originally manufactured in the 1920s, which had been decommissioned by a state mill in Shijiazhuang. The towel factory's success attracted the interest of higher-ranking organizations and in September 1970 it was taken over by the county. The county paid its commune owners 1,000,000 yuan in compensation.

Through processes like those that affected the towel factory, successful collective units were taken over by the state, leaving only weak and backward units under the control of communes or brigades. As a result, the collective sector in Gaoyang was weak at the beginning of the reform era, providing little base on which to build. In 1983, when the county party committee began to aggressively promote rural industry, most collectives decided to shut down their small factories and divide the equipment among members. At that point villages chose individual and family-based initiatives, rather than collective or corporatist ones. This turn toward private and family-based endeavors was influenced by developments during the high socialist era. During the Cultural Revolution (1966–1976) fierce ideological struggles had torn the Gaoyang community apart, with villages splitting into hostile factions that waged armed struggles. By the time peace was finally restored in 1976, more than three hundred individuals had lost their lives and more than three thousand had suffered injuries. This heavy toll had diminished the willingness of individuals to participate in collective activities. When the reforms made it possible to begin non-agricultural activities, most families wanted to work on their own or join together with small groups of relatives or friends whom they could trust.

When the reform initiatives began in the early 1980s, small village factories were dissolved and families and small groups of friends began to operate small workshops. While party members often played a leading role in encouraging their fellow villagers to begin weaving, assuring them that they would not be punished for undertaking independent economic ventures, the state played only a limited role in the developments. At this time, the state-sector factories in town were the major concern of county-level economic bureaucrats. The late 1980s saw the last great boom in state-owned textile firms, and the small rural workshops, which had begun to produce low-value-added goods, seemed to be a minor sideshow. While cadre associated with the new Township and Village Enterprise Bureau were well aware of the challenge that the rural enterprises might eventually pose, no one predicted the reversal in fortunes that soon overtook the mighty state textile industry. By the time the local state realized what was happening, the system of private ownership of small- and medium-scale firms was already well established and the local state was left to search for a new role and function in the emerging institutional structure.

PRIVATE ENTREPRENEURS AND THE STATE IN THE REFORM ERA

Contemporary industry in Gaoyang has been built almost exclusively by the investments of private individuals. While village governments made contributions during the early days and villages were sometimes granted shares in factories in payment for the use of land and energy, by the late 1980s collective involvement in the direct management of factories had almost completely disappeared. It was replaced by the payment of land rent and fees for services provided. In the Gaoyang model, political units—township and village governments, or the party at the township and village levels—have no direct control over economic enterprises. Local officials do not sit on the management boards of private firms unless they, as individuals, have invested in the firm. Profits of the firms are divided among shareholders, with the local government lacking any legal claims other than those authorized by tax regulations. In spite of this lack of direct influence over the management decisions of individual firms, there is no question that the local state has played a significant role in the development of the contemporary industrial district, and because of that involvement, the Gaoyang model can be seen as a different version of local state corporatism. In contemporary Gaoyang the local state is providing many support services, services similar to those that in the prewar period were provided by the chamber of commerce. Chamber of commerce members supported their organization's activities by voluntarily paying a surcharge on their business turnover. In contemporary Gaoyang, local state organizations have taken over the role of promotion of industry and provision of services to private entrepreneurs. The funding for these services comes through a complicated system of taxation and "donations" that is full of ambiguity and has the potential to generate rent-seeking behavior on the part of state officials.

Local state corporate bodies operate on several levels in the industrial district and we need to distinguish their range of activities. One set of actors includes the cadre in county government bureaus and offices who have taken on a variety of tasks in support of the textile industry. Major infrastructure in the county—roads, improved telephone service, and construction of specialized markets—are part of this effort. Equally important are publicity and marketing efforts, including the textile fair, as well as efforts to build links with higher-level government officials.[6] In this way one can see county government officials performing some of the functions that chamber of commerce officials provided in the prewar period, seeking patronage and support from relevant governmental organizations at provincial and national levels. Unlike the officials of the chamber of commerce, county officials derive their source of power from office, not from a base of support in the entrepreneurial community.

Village leaders, who are the other important group of actors, are closer to the enterprises than county leaders and operate in a much more ambiguous status. When the economic reform policies were first announced, Communist Party cadre were urged to take a leading role in starting new economic activities in order to assure the population that there had been a real change in policy. As a consequence, many village party leaders are also entrepreneurs, and many village-level party leaders hold shares in private firms or have kin who are shareholders or managers of industrial enterprises. Village governments have also provided services to the industrial firms, including offering land at reasonable rents, organizing the building of paved roads, and improving the supply of electricity. Funds to pay for these services are usually supplied by the enterprises.

Within the village, cadre and enterprise managers and villagers are linked together in a web of overlapping relationships that includes such links as village leader and villagers, employer and employee, kinsmen, classmates, neighbors, fellow party members, fellow shareholders, and former members of the same work team. Village community is the sum of the complexity of these links and it is very difficult to draw lines around the economic sphere and separate it from the social or community sphere. Although there is no formal system of village investment in local enterprises in contemporary Gaoyang, there is a kind of village corporate community. There are major differences between this style of local corporatism and the local state corporatism analyzed by Jean Oi. In Oi's examples, the local government unit owns the rural industrial units and local government cadre act as part of the managerial team. While some of the results are similar, such as funds generated by rural industry are used to improve infrastructure and provide social services, the method of management and control of the funds differs. In the Gaoyang model, enterprise funds flow from the privately owned firms to village and county governments through regularized taxation and through irregular forms of contribution and donation. The latter, as we saw in chapter nine, share certain similarities with the practice of assessment of irregular taxes (*tankuan*) that was so common in pre-revolutionary rural North China. Both forms of corporatism run the risk of rent seeking by government officials who may use their positions to extract bribes or other fees for access to services and both of them operate in a world in which the division between private and collective interests is often difficult to discern.

The Gaoyang model, like many of the other Chinese growth models, clearly is not able to block corruption and rent-seeking behavior, but the high sustained growth rates also show that the system has been able to provide sufficient incentives to draw the support of both private and public actors. Great wealth has been generated in a very short time and enough members of the community share in that wealth to encourage continued private investment and to encourage public actors to exert energy to provide the necessary supporting services.

THE INDUSTRIAL DISTRICT MODEL IN CONTEMPORARY CHINA

Having briefly examined the logic behind the formation of the contemporary Gaoyang model, with its combination of private investment and a corporate local state, I now want to turn to the third part of the industrial district structure, the concentration of small firms in a single line of business, and consider how this fits into the contemporary Chinese economic structure. Gaoyang, like most of China's rural industrial regions, is involved in small-scale manufacturing that could be located in many different places. Like much rural processing industry, it brings together a vast supply of underutilized rural labor with readily available technology and readily available raw materials. Once a pioneer demonstrates the viability of an industrial model, it is not long before success leads to imitation, with other entrepreneurs and regions flocking to copy the original model. The result is over-investment and over-capacity, increased competition for raw materials and markets, pressure on profits, and the collapse of many of the enterprises that entered the competition. Lance Gore argues that this process is in part the legacy of the mechanisms created under the planned economy that had driven regions to claim resources for investment even when the results were far from optimal.[7] Gore's estimates for 1995 show low levels of capacity utilization rates in almost all areas of light manufacturing industry that point to the persistence of this problem of imitation and over-investment. In reform era China, competition among regions and communities has brought a continuation of the over-investment mechanisms created during the era of high socialism. One of the results in the early twenty-first century has been intense competition, low prices, and the threat of deflation in many countries where Chinese exports hold a strong position in the market.

In this bitter struggle for survival among competing small-scale rural manufacturers, organization in an industrial district can provide an edge that will aid the survival chances of all members. As we have seen throughout this

volume, small firms that are part of an industrial district receive many benefits from belonging to a center for specialized production. Shared technology, manpower pools, industrial knowledge, and much else can aid firms in
designing better products, better advertising messages, and better marketing
strategies. It is easier to find skilled technicians and to develop product and
management innovations. As we have followed the history of the development of the textile industries in Gaoyang, we have seen again and again this
process at work. Competitive challenges have led to product and management innovations that have allowed firms to survive and prosper. In contemporary China, small rural manufacturers have been able to reach and
capture both domestic and international markets in part because of the concentration of firms in industrial districts. While no single Gaoyang manufacturer of towels, or wool yarn, or carpet yarn, or blankets is alone strong
enough to attract the attention of domestic and international marketing
agents, the combined strength of dozens—in some lines of business, hundreds—of small firms has made Gaoyang one of China's largest manufacturers of towels, of blankets, and of wool yarns.

NOTES

1. A glance at any of the industrial atlases of contemporary Chinese industry will
show hundreds of industrial districts. Some of these districts have gained some
prominence in English writing about China—for example the Wenzhou district with
its concentration on production of plastic goods, Daqiuzhuang with its small-scale
iron and steel manufacture, etc. On the marketing side, specialized wholesale markets also dot the Chinese landscape and serve as important interfaces between Chinese producers and the international market. To just mention a few, there are the
huge wholesale markets in daily-use commodities held in Yiwu and Zhejiang, and
the traditional drug market in Anguo, Hebei.

2. See a forum on gradualism in China that appeared in the January 1999 issue of
The China Journal. Wing Thye Woo argues that the success of China's economic reforms can be explained by the standard principles of neoclassical market economies,
while Thomas Rawski argues for the success of China's various economic experiments which he believes cannot be explained only by neoclassical principles.

3. Jean Oi and Andrew Walder, *Property Rights and Economic Reform in China*
(Stanford: Stanford University Press, 1999), 13.

4. Jean Oi, "The Role of the Local State in China's Transitional Economy," *China
Quarterly* 1132. The links between the fiscal reforms and local state corporatism are
explored in the same author's "Fiscal Reform and the Economic Foundations of Local State Corporatism in China," *World Politics* 45 (1992).

5. This section has been influenced by the work of David Stark and László Bruszt
on the transition in East European economies after the collapse of socialism. Stark
and Bruszt argue, "Actors who seek to move in new directions find that their choices
are constrained by the existing set of institutional resources. Institutions limit the field

of action, preclude some directions, and constrain certain courses. But institutions also favor the perception and selection of some strategies over others." Stark and Bruszt, *Postsocialist Pathways: Transforming Politics and Property in East Central Europe* (Cambridge: Cambridge University Press, 1998), 82–83.

6. The Gaoyang County government now contributes to several websites that provide information on local industry. One of these goes by the name of "Gaoyang hotline" (www.gyinfonet.cn) and another, which describes itself as an internet marketing center, promises "unlimited commercial opportunities" (www.gaoyang.gov.cn).

7. Lance L. P. Gore, "The Communist Legacy in Post-Mao Economic Growth," *The China Journal*, no. 41, January 1999, 25–54.

Bibliography

Abe Hiroshi. "Shinmatsu gakudo kō—Chokureisho o chūshin to shite" [An examination of late Qing modern schools—the Zhili case]. *Bunka ronshu* (Fukuoka Kodai), 1 (1966): 45–88.

Abe Takeshi. *Nihon ni okeru sanchi men'orimonogyō no tenkai* [The development of Japan's cotton weaving industrial districts]. Tokyo: Tokyo Daigaku Shuppankai, 1989.

Academic Committee of the Chinese Association of Textile Engineers, ed. *Fangzhi gongchang "ba.wu" keji fazhan zhanlue yanjiu* [Studies on scientific development strategies in the textile industry during the eighth Five Year Plan]. Beijing: Fangzhi Gongye Chubanshe, 1990.

Anderson, Kym. *New Silk Roads: East Asia and the World Textile Markets*. Cambridge: Cambridge University Press, 1992.

Arnold, Julean. *China—a Commercial and Industrial Handbook*. Washington: Government Printing Office, 1926.

Asheim, Bjorn T. "Industrial Districts: The Contributions of Marshall and Beyond." In *The Oxford Handbook of Economic Geography*, edited by Gordon L. Clark, Maryann P. Feldman, and Meric S. Gertler, 413–31. Oxford: Oxford University Press, 2000.

Bao Juemin. "Jiefang qiande Nankai Daxue Jingji Yanjiusuo" [The Economic Research Institute of Nankai University before the war]. *Tianjin Wenshi Ziliao Xuanyi* 19 (March 1982): 97–111.

Baoding CCP Propaganda Bureau, and Baoding Party History Research Office, eds. *Baoding Kang-Ri zhanzheng lishi ziliao huibian* [Collection of materials on the history of the anti-Japanese war in the Baoding area], 1995.

Beijingshi, ed. *Yijiuwusinian quanguo geti shougongye diaocha ziliao* [Materials on the 1954 national investigation of handicraft industry]. Beijing: Sanlian, 1957.

Berger, Suzanne, and Michael Piore. *Dualism and Discontinuity in Industrial Societies*. Cambridge: Cambridge University Press, 1980.

Bergere, Marie-Claire. *The Golden Age of the Chinese Bourgeoise, 1911–1937*. Cambridge: Cambridge University Press, 1989.

Blaug, Mark. *Economic Theory in Retrospect*. Fourth ed. Cambridge: Cambridge University Press, 1985.

Blecher, Mark, and Vivienne Shue. *Tethered Deer: Government and Economy in a Chinese County*. Stanford: Stanford University Press, 1996.

Bray, Francesca. *Technology and Gender: Fabrics of Power in Late Imperial China*. Berkeley: University of California Press, 1997.

Brewer, John, and Roy Porter, eds. *Consumption and the World of Goods*. London: Routledge, 1993.

Brook, Timothy, and Hy V. Luong. *Culture and Economy: The Shaping of Capitalism in Eastern Asia*. Ann Arbor: University of Michigan Press, 1997.

Brusco, Sebastiano. "The Idea of the Industrial District: Its Genesis." In *Industrial Districts and Inter-Firm Cooperation in Italy*, edited by Frank Pyke, Giacomo Becattini, and Werner Sengenberger, 10–19. Geneva: International Institute for Labour Studies, 1990.

——. "Small Firms and the Provision of Real Services." In *Industrial Districts and Local Economic Regeneration*, edited by Frank Pyke and Werner Sengenberger, 177-196. Geneva: International Institute for Labour Studies, 1992.

Burnett, W. H. *Report of the Mission to China of the Blackburn Chamber of Commerce, 1896–97*. Blackburn: North-East Lancashire Press, 1898.

Byrd, William, and Lin Qingsong. *China's Rural Industry: Structure, Development and Reform*. Oxford: Oxford University Press (for the World Bank), 1990.

Byron, Ray. "Demand for Wool Products in China." In *Challenges of Economic Reform and Industrial Growth: China's Wool War*, edited by Christopher Findlay. Syndey: Allen & Unwin, 1992.

Bythell, Duncan. *The Handloom Weavers*. Cambridge: Cambridge University Press, 1969.

Central Hebei Administrative Office. "Dui Gaoyang gongchang jiqi chuli baoguan yijian" [An opinion on the measures for settlement and protection of machinery and factories in Gaoyang]. Manuscript, 1948. Held by the Hebei Provincial Archives.

——. "Jiqi tonji biao" [Statistical table on equipment]. Manuscript, 1948. Held by the Hebei Provincial Archives.

——. "Jizhong fangzhi ye" [The central Hebei textile industry]. Manuscript, 1948. Held by the Hebei Provincial Archives.

——. "Jun Zhong Xingshu guanyu Gaoyang You Ji Gongchang chuli yijian" [Central Hebei Administrative Office recommendations on how to settle the matter of the You Ji Factory in Gaoyang]. Manuscript, 1949. Held by the Hebei Provincial Archives.

Central Work Group. "Gaoyangxian jingji de jiben qingkuang: Jiefanghou Gaoyang xiang shougong zhibuye zhong de siren ziben" [Basic economic conditions in Gaoyang County: Private capital in the Gaoyang handicraft weaving industry since liberation]. Manuscript, 1954. Held by the Gaoyang County Archives.

Chan, Wellington K. K. "The Organization Structure of the Traditional Chinese Firm and Its Modern Reform." *Business History Review* 46 (Summer 1982): 218–35.

Chandler, Alfred C., Jr. *Scale and Scope: The Dynamics of Industrial Capitalism*. Cambridge: Harvard University Press, 1990.

———. *Strategy and Structure*. Cambridge: Harvard University Press, 1962.

Chao, Kang. *The Development of Cotton Textile Production in China*. Cambridge: Harvard University Press, 1977.

———. "The Growth of a Modern Cotton Textile Industry and the Competition with Handicrafts." In *China's Modern Economy in Historical Perspective*, edited by Dwight H. Perkins, 167–201. Stanford: Stanford University Press, 1975.

Chen Kehan. "Mofan kangri genjudi Jin-Cha-Ji bianqu" [The model anti-Japanese base area, Jin-Cha-Ji]. Chongqing: Xinhua Ribao, 1939.

Chen Meijian, et al. *Gaoyang zhibuye jianshi* [A short history of the Gaoyang weaving industry]. *Hebei Wenshi Ziliao*, vol. 19, 1987.

Chen Weiwei, ed. *Zhongguo fangzhi kexue jishu shi—gudai buben* [A history of textile technology, ancient period]. Beijing: Kexue Chubanshe, 1984.

Chen Yaoting. "Gaoyang buye de yenge ji tedian" [History and characteristics of the Gaoyang weaving industry]. *Zhongguo Jindai Fangzhishi Yanjiu Ziliao Huibian* 10 (1990): 23–25.

Chu, T. S., and T. Chin. *Marketing of Cotton in Hopei*. Beijing: Institute of Social Research, 1929.

Clark, Gregory. "Why Isn't the Whole World Developed? Lessons from the Cotton Mills." *Journal of Economic History* 47 (1987): 141–73.

Clark, W. A. Graham. *Cotton Goods in Japan and Their Competition on the Manchurian Market*. Washington: Government Printing Office, 1914.

Cochran, Sherman. *Big Business in China: Sino-Foreign Rivalry in the Cigarette Industry, 1890–1930*. Cambridge: Harvard University Press, 1980.

Cohen, Jerome. *Japan's Economy in War and Reconstruction*. Minneapolis: University of Minnesota Press, 1949.

Dai Nippon Bōseki Rengōkai Geppō [Monthly review of the Japanese Association of Cotton Spinners].

Ding Shixun. "Tianjin miansha pifa shanghe shilue" [A short history of Tianjin yarn wholesaling business]. *Nankai Xuebao*, no. 4/5 (1981): 47–54.

———. "Yijiusansi nian zhi yijiuxijiu nian de Gaoyang buye" [The Gaoyang weaving industry from 1934–1949]. *Nankai Xuebao*, no. 1 (1981): 24–35.

Duara, Prasenjit. "State Involution: A Study of Local Finances in North China, 1911–1935." *Comparative Studies in Society and History* 29, no. 1 (1987).

Editorial Committee for Zhongguo Nongcun Shichang Moshi Yanjiu. *Zhongguo nongcun shichang moshi yanjiu* [A study of models for Chinese rural markets]. Beijing: Xinhua Shudian, 1993.

Elvin, Mark. "The Administration of Shanghai, 1904–1914." In *The Chinese City between Two Worlds*, edited by Mark Elvin and G. William Skinner. Stanford: Stanford University Press, 1974.

Emmanuel, Arghiri. *Appropriate or Underdeveloped Technology?* Chichester: Wiley, 1982.

Esherick, Joseph W., and Mary Backus Rankin. *Chinese Local Elites and Patterns of Dominance*. Berkeley: University of California Press, 1990.

Fang Xianting. *Lun Huabei jingji ji qu qiantu* [On the future of the North China economy]. Nankai Jingji Yanjiusuo.

———. "Zhongguo mianfang zhiye zhi weiji" [The crisis in China's cotton textile industry]. *Jingji Zhoukan* 8, *Da Gong Bao*, April 19, 1933.

——. "Tianjin zhibu gongye" [The Tianjin weaving industry]. *Gongye Zongkan.* Tianjin: Nankai Daxue Jingji Yanjiusuo, 1931.

——. "Zhongguo xiangcun gongye de chulu" [The future of China's rural industry]. *Da Gong Bao* (February 27, 1935).

——. "Zhong-Ri jingji tixie yu Huabei" [Sino-Japanese economic cooperation and North China]. *Shangxue Huikan* 5 (1937): 1–12.

Fang Xianting and Bi Xianghui. "You Baodi shouzhi gongye guancha gongye zhidu zhi yanbian" [Perspectives on Chinese handicraft industry based on observations from the handloom weaving industry of Baodi]. *Zhengzhi Jingji Xuebao* 4, no. 2 (January 1936): 261–329.

Feng Huade. "Hebeisheng Gaoyangxian de xiangcun zaizheng" [Rural finance in Gaoyang County, Hebei]. *Da Gong Bao* (November 29, 1933).

Feuerwerker, Albert. "Economic Trends in the Late Ch'ing Empire, 1870–1911." In *The Cambridge History of China*, vol. 11, edited by John H. Fairbank and Kwang-ching Liu, 1–69. Cambridge: Cambridge University Press, 1980.

——. "Handicraft and Manufactured Cotton Textiles in China, 1871–1910." *Journal of Economic History* 30, no. 2 (1970): 338–78.

Findlay, Christopher, ed. *Challenges of Economic Reform and Industrial Growth: China's Wool War.* Sydney: Allen & Unwin, 1992.

Finnane, Antonia. "What Should Chinese Women Wear? A National Problem." *Modern China* 22, no. 2 (1996): 99–131.

Finnane, Antonia, and Anne McLaren, eds. *Dress, Sex and Text in Chinese Culture.* Melbourne: Monash Asia Institute, 1998.

Fong, H. D. [Fang Xianting] *Cotton Industry and Trade in China.* Tianjin: Nankai Institute of Economics, 1932.

——. *The Growth and Decline of Rural Industrial Enterprise in North China.* Industry Series. Tianjin: Nankai Institute of Economics, 1936.

——. *Rural Industries in China.* Industry Series of the Nankai Institute of Economics. Tianjin: Nankai Institute of Economics, 1933.

Friedman, Edward, Paul G. Pickowicz, and Mark Selden. *Chinese Village, Socialist State.* New Haven: Yale University Press, 1991.

Fu Chonglan. *Zhongguo yunhe chengshi fazhanshi* [A history of the development of cities along China's Grand Canal]. Chongqing: Sichuan Renmin Chubanshe, 1985.

Fu Feiwen and Quan Yuyuan. "Xiangcun shougongye diaocha" [Survey of rural handicraft industry]. *Jingji Zhoukan*, no. 65 (1934).

Fujita, Masahisa, Paul Krugman, and Anthony J. Venables. *The Spatial Economy: Cities, Regions and International Trade.* Cambridge, MA: MIT Press, 2000.

Fukutake Takashi. *Chūgoku nōson shakai no kōzō* [The structure of Chinese rural society]. Tokyo: Tokyo Daigaku Shuppankai, 1976.

Gaoyang County Communist Party Committee and Gaoyang County Archives, eds. *Hebei Sheng Gaoyang Xian zuzhi shi ziliao, 1930–1987* [Historical materials on party organization in Gaoyang County, Hebei Province, 1930–1987]. Shijiazhuang: Hebei Renmin Chubanshe, 1992.

Gaoyang County Government. "Gaoyang gongshang ye de chubu diaocha" [A preliminary survey of Gaoyang commerce and industry]. Manuscript, 1948. Held by the Gaoyang County Archives.

Gaoyang Party History Editorial Committee. *Gaoyangxian geming douzheng dashiji* [A chronological account of revolutionary struggles in Gaoyang]. Yazhou Chuban-she, 1992.

Gaoyang Party History Research Office. "Xin guomin yundong dui Gaoyang renmin de zanhai" [The cruel impact of the New Citizen Movement on the people of Gaoyang]. *Hebei Wenshi Ziliao Xuanyi* 15 (1985).

"Gaoyang Ranchang Changshi" [Factory history of the Gaoyang Dyeing Works]. Mimeograph, 1988.

"Gaoyangxian dierqu Yanfuxiang mianzhi shougongye jiben qingkuang diaocha bao-gao" [A report on the basic economic conditions of handicraft weaving in Yanfu-xiang, Gaoyang County].Manuscript, 1954. Held by the Gaoyang County Archives.

"Gaoyangxian disanqu Yanfuxiang mianzhi shougongye jiben qingkuang diaocha baogao" [A report on the basic economic conditions with regard to weaving coop-eratives in Yanfun Xiang of the third district of Gaoyang County]. Manuscript, 1954. Held by the Gaoyang County Archives.

Gaoyangxian Mianzhi Lianshe. "Gaoyangxian zuzhi qilaide mianzhi shougongye diaocha baogao" [A report on the recently organized weaving cooperatives in Gaoyang County]. Manuscript, 1954. Held by the Gaoyang County Archives.

Gaoyangxian Renmin Zhengfu Caizheng Jingji Bangongshi. "Gaoyang Xian 1954 nian shougongye diaocha gongzuo zongjie" [A summary of work on the Gaoyang County 1954 survey of handicraft industry]. Mimeograph, 1954. Held by the Gaoyang County Archives.

"Gaoyangxian zhi jingji gaikuang" [An outline of economic conditions in Gaoyang County]." *Zhong-Wai Jingji Zhoukan* (1926), 8–15.

Gerth, Karl. *China Made: Consumer Culture and the Creation of the Nation*. Cam-bridge: Harvard University Asia Center, 2003.

Gold, Thomas, Doug Guthrie, and David Wank. *Social Connections in China: Insti-tutions, Culture and the Changing Nature of Guanxi*. Cambridge: Cambridge Uni-versity Press, 2002.

Gongshang Banyuekan [The commerce and industry bi-monthly].

Gore, Lance L. P. "The Communist Legacy in Post-Mao Economic Growth." *The China Journal*, no. 41 (1999): 25–54.

Greenhalgh, Susan. "Families and Networks in Taiwan's Economic Development." In *Contending Approaches to the Political Economy of Taiwan*, edited by Edwin A. Winckler and Susan Greenhalgh. Armonk, NY: Sharpe, 1988.

Grove, Linda. "Creating a Northern Soviet." *Modern China* 1, no. 3 (1974): 243–70.

———. "International Trade and the Creation of Domestic Marketing Networks in North China, 1860–1930." In *Commercial Networks in Modern Asia*, edited by S. Sugiyama and Linda Grove. Richmond, Surrey: Curzon, 2001.

———. "Mechanization and Women's Work in Early Twentieth Century China." In *Yanagita Setsuko-sensei koki kinen Chūgoku no dentō shakai to kazoku* [A vol-ume in honor of Prof. Yanagita Setsuko's seventieth birthday—traditional Chinese society and the family], edited by Yanagita Setsuko-sensei Koki Kinen Ronshū Hen-shō Iinkai, ed., 95–120. Tokyo: Kyūko Shoin, 1993.

———. "Rural Manufacture in China's Cotton Industry, 1890–1990." In *The Fibre That Changed the World: The Cotton Industry in International Perspective,*

1600–1990s, edited by Douglas A. Farnie and David J. Jeremy, 431–59. Oxford: Oxford University Press, 2004.

———. "Rural Society in Revolution: The Gaoyang District, 1910–1947." Ph.D. thesis, University of California, Berkeley, 1975.

Guo Lanjing, ed. *Tianjin gudai chengshi fazhanshi* [A history of the development of pre-modern Tianjin]. Tianjin: Tianjin Guji Chubanshe, 1989.

Guo Yunjing. "Qingdai Tianjin shangye chengshi de xingcheng chutan" [A preliminary investigation of the formation of Tianjin as a commercial city during the Qing period]. *Tianjin Shehui Kexue*, no. 4 (1987): 77–82.

Hamashita Takashi. *Chūgoku kindai keizaishi kenkyū* [Economic history of modern China—Maritime Customs finance and open port market zones in late Ch'ing China]. Tokyo: Tōyō Bunka Kenkyūjō, 1989.

Hamilton, Gary, ed. *Business Networks and Economic Development in East and Southeast Asia*. Hong Kong: Centre of Asian Studies, University of Hong Kong, 1991.

Hamilton, Gary, and Nicole Woolsey Biggart. "Market, Culture and Authority: A Comparative Analysis of Management and Organization in the Far East." *American Journal of Sociology* 94 (1988): S52–S93.

Hamilton, Gary, and Kao Cheng-Shu. "The Institutional Foundations of Chinese Business: The Family Firm in Taiwan." *Comparative Social Research* 12 (1990): 135–51.

Harrison, Henrietta. *The Making of the Republican Citizen: Political Ceremonies and Symbols in China, 1911–1929*. Oxford: Oxford University Press, 2000.

Harvey, David. *The Condition of Postmodernity*. Oxford: Basil Blackwell, 1989.

Hebei Gongshang Yuebao [Hebei commerce and industry monthly review].

Hebei jingji nianjian 1995 [Hebei economic almanac, 1995]. Beijing: Zhongguo Tongji Chubanshe, 1995.

Hebei Provincial Government. *Hebei Sheng gong shang tongji* [Statistical review of Hebei commerce and industry]. Tianjin: Hebei Provincial Government, 1931.

Hebeisheng shangye zhi [Commercial gazetteer of Hebei Province]. Shijiazhuang: Hebei Renmin Chubanshe, 1988.

Hebei Sheng Yinhang Yuekan [The Hebei bank monthly].

Hebei shengli gongxueyuan xiaoyoulu [A list of graduates of the Hebei Gongxueyuan], 1947.

Hebei Yuekan [Hebei monthly].

Heng Zhiyi. *Qingdai Zhili zongdu yanjiu* [Research on the Governors-General of Zhili during the Qing dynasty]. Beijing: Zhongguo Wenlian Chubanshe, 1999.

Hershatter, Gail. "Flying Hammers, Walking Chisels: The Workers of Santiaoshi." *Modern China* 9 (October 1983): 387–419.

———. *The Workers of Tianjin, 1900–1949*. Stanford: Stanford University Press, 1987.

Hokushi Keizai Chōsasho, ed. *I-Ken dofugyō chōsa hōkokusho* [A report on the native cloth industry of Wei County]. Mantetsu Chōsabu, 1942.

Howe, Christopher. *The Origins of Japanese Trade Supremacy: Development and Technology in Asia from 1540 to the Pacific War*. London: Hurst, 1996.

Hu Guangming. *Huabei—Jianjing Shang Hui shi* [A history of the Chambers of Commerce in North China, Tianjin and Beijing]. Unpublished paper, 1991.

———. "Kaipuqian Tianjin chengshihua guocheng ji naimaoxing shangye shichang de xingcheng" [The process of urbanization in Tianjin before its opening as a treaty port and the formation of a commercial city based on trade]. *Tianjin Shehui Kexue*, no. 3 (1987): 85–91.

———. "Lun zaoqi Tianjin Shanghui de xingzhi yu zuoyong" [The form and functions of the early Chamber of Commerce in Tianjin]. *Jindaishi Yanjiu*, no. 4 (1986): 182–223.

Hu Rengui. *Youjiqu jingji wenti yanjiu* [A study of economic problems in the guerrilla areas]. Shanxi: Huanghe Chubanshe, 1939.

Huang, Philip C. *The Peasant Economy and Social Change in North China*. Stanford: Stanford University Press, 1985.

Imazu Kenji. "Kōgyōka ni hatashita kangyō seisaku no yakuwari: Nōshōmushō shōkōgyō gishi ni meggute" [The role of industrial promotion policies in industrialization: On the commercial and industrial technicians employed by the Ministry of Agriculture and Commerce]. In *Nihon no kōgyōka to gijutsu hatten* [Japanese industrialization and technological development], edited by Kiyokawa Yukihiko and Minami Ryoshin, 237–59. Tokyo: Tōyō Keizai Shimposha, 1987.

Ishida Hideji. *Chōkakō menpu bōeki* [The cotton trade in Zhangjiakou]. Mitsui, 1919.

Ishii Tadashi. "Toyota Saekichi to shoki gijutsu no hatten." *Hatsumei* 76 (January-June 1979).

Jequier, Nicolas, ed. *Appropriate Technology—Problems and Promises*. Paris: Development Centre of the Organisation for Economic Co-Operation and Development, 1976.

Ji Hua. "Guohuo Shoupinsuo shimo" [Complete history of the National Products Sales Promotion Center]. *Wenshi Ziliao Xuanyi* 31 (1962): 221–36.

Jia Jianhua. *Cuican ce qunxing* [Flourishing constellations]. Haikou: Hainan Chubanshe, 1994.

Ji-Cha Diaocha Tonji Zongkan [Ji-Cha survey and statistical journal].

Jiefang Ribao [Liberation daily; official newspaper of the Communist Party of China during the war years].

Jin Zheng. "Shixi ersanshi niandai Ding Xian nongmin gengdi zhi buzu" [The distribution of farming land in Ding County in the 1920s and 1930s]. *Hebei Daxue Xuebao* 2 (1991): 79–85.

Jinchaji Ribao; official newspaper of the Jinchaji base area.

Jing Rui. "Aiguo shangren Song Zejiu." *Tianjin Gongshang Shiliao Congkan* 5 (1986): 57–74.

Jizhong Daobao [Newspaper of the Central Hebei Resistance Movement], 1942–47.

Jizhong Yiri Xiezuo Yundong Weiyuanhui. *Jizhong yiri* [One day in central Hebei]. Tianjin: Baiyua Wenyi Chubanshe, 1959.

Kasahara Tokushi. "Boikotto undō to minzoku sangyō—Shanghai o chūshin ni" [Boycotts and Chinese-owned industries in Shanghai]. In *Kōza Chūgoku Kingendaishi* [Lectures on modern and contemporary Chinese history], vol. 4, 117–47. Tokyo: Tokyo Daigaku Shuppankai, 1978.

Kawakatsu Heita. "Ajia momen shijō no kūzō to tenkai" [The structure and development of the Asian market for cotton textiles]. *Shakai Keizai Shigaku* 51, no. 1 (1985): 91–125.

———. "The Emergence of a Market for Cotton Goods in East Asia in the Early Modern Period." In *Japanese Industrialization and the Asian Economy*, edited by A. J. H. Latham and Heita Kawakatsu, 9–34. London: Routledge, 1994.

Kikuchi Takaharu. "Keizai kyōkō to Shingai Kakumei e no keisha" [Financial panics and movements leading up to the 1911 revolution]." In *Chūgoku kindai no shakai kōzō*, edited by Kyōiku Daigaku Bungakubu Tōyōshi Kenkyūkai, 73–110. Tokyo: Kyōiku Shoseki, 1960.

Kim San, and Nym Wales. *The Song of Ariran*. San Francisco: Ramparts Press, 1972.

Kiyokawa Yukihiko. "Chūgoku sen'i kikai kogyō no hatten to zaikabō no igi" [Development of the Chinese textile machinery industry and the role of the Japanese mills in China], *Keizai Kenkyū* 34 (January 1983): 22–39.

———. "Gijutsu kakusa to dōnyu gijutsu no teichaku katei: Sen'yi sangyō no keiken o chūshin ni" [The technology gap and the process of indigenization of technology: Evidence from the experience of the textile industry]. In *Kindai Nihon no Keizai Hatten*, edited by Ogawa Kazushi and Minami Ryoshin. Tokyo: Tōyō Keizai Shinposha, 1975, 249?82.

———. "Nihon orimonogyō ni okeru rikishokukika no shinten o meggute" [Questions with relation to the adoption of the power loom in Japan's weaving industry]. *Keizai Kenkyū* [of the Keizaigaku kenkyūkai of Tokyo University] (April 1984): 150–70.

Kiyokawa Yukihiko, and Minami Ryoshin, eds. *Nihon no kogyōka to gijutsu hatten* [Japanese industrialization and technological development]. Tokyo: Tōyō Keizai Shinposha, 1987.

Kobayashi Hideo. *Daitōa kyōeiken no keisei to hakai* [Formation and destruction of the Greater East Asia Co-Prosperity Sphere]. Tokyo: Ochanomizu Shobō, 1975.

Kohama Masako. *Kindai Shanghai no kōkyōsei to kokka* [The public and the state in modern Shanghai]. Tokyo: Kenbun Shuppansha, 2000.

"Kōnichi seiryoku no shokōsaku to shin seiken no katsudō jōkyō chōsa hōkoku—kahokusho seitei oyobi Kōyō-ken ni okeru" [A report on early activities of anti-Japanese forces and the current state of affairs—a case study of Zhengding and Gaoyang Counties]. *Rikushi Mitsu Dai Nikki* 46 (1939).

Kubo Tōru. *Chūgoku keizai 100 nen no ayumi* [The development of the Chinese economy over the last century]. Tokyo: Sōken Shuppan, vol. 1, 1991, vol. 2, 1995.

———. "Nanking seifu no kanzei seisaku to sono rekishiteki igi" [The Nanjing government's tariff policy and its historical significance]. *Tōchi Seido Shigaku* 86, (January 1980): 38–55.

Kuhn, Philip. "The Development of Local Government." In *The Cambridge History of China*, vol. 13, part 2, edited by John K. Fairbank and Albert Feuerwerker, 329–60. Cambridge: Cambridge University Press, 1986.

Kusano Fumio. *Chūgoku sengo no dōtai* [Trends in postwar China]. Kyoto: Kyōiku Shuppansha, 1947.

Li Bingxi. "Zhili Gaoyang buye zhi enge jilue" [A short account of the history of the Gaoyang weaving industry]. *Quanguo Shanghui Lianhehui Huibao* 1–3.

Li Daben. *Gaoyang Xianzhi* [Gaoyang gazetteer]. Reprint. Taibei: Chengwen Chubanshe, (1931) 1967.

Li Feng. "Wushinianlai shangye ziben zai Hebei xiangcun mianzhi shougongye zhong zhi fazhan jincheng" [The process of development and the role of commercial capital in the Hebei rural weaving industry over the last fifty years]. *Zhongguo Nongcun* 1, no. 3 (December 1934): 61–76.

Li Jinzheng. "Shixi ersanshi niandai Dingxian nongmen gengdi zhi buzu" [A consideration of the land shortage in Dingxian in the 1920s and 1930s]. *Hebei Daxue Xuebao,* no. 2 (1991): 79–85.

Li Qingwei, ed. *Zhongguo shangye wenhua dazidian* [The great dictionary of Chinese commercial culture]. Beijing: Zhongguo Fazhan Chubanshe, 1994.

Li Rui. "Hebeisheng gexian nianlai zhi junshi zhiying" [Annual expenses of various Hebei counties on military affairs]. *Da Gong Bao* (September 20, 1933).

Li Xiaoti. *Qingmo de xiaceng shehui qimeng yundong, 1901–1911* [Enlightment movements directed at the local society in the late Qing: 1901–1911]. Taibei: Institute of Modern History, Academia Sinica, 1992.

Li Yuyi. *Qingmo minchu Zhongguo geda duhui nannu zhuangshi lunji, 1899–1923* [Essays on male and female fashion in various Chinese cities at the end of the Qing and the beginning of the Republic, 1899–1923]. Hong Kong: Chung Shan Book Co., 1972.

Liang Guochang. *Gaoyang sili zhiye zhongxue yilan* [A survey of the Gaoyang industrial middle school]. 1934.

Liang Xihui. "Gongshang fazhan yu renkou zhi guanxi" [The relationship between the development of commerce and industry and population]. *Da Gong Bao* (March 31, 1937).

Liang Zhao. "Gaoyang dizhi meihuo jingyan" [Gaoyang's experience in boycotting American goods]. *Jizhong Daobao*, February 15, 1947.

Lin Jubai. *Jindai Nantong tubuye* [The modern Nantong native weaving industry]. Nanjing Daxue Xuebao Bianjibu, 1984.

Lippit, Victor D. "The Development of Underdevelopment in China." *Modern China* 4, no. 3 (1978): 251–328.

Little, Ian M. D., Dipak Mazumdar, and John M. Page, Jr., eds. *Small Manufacturing Enterprises: A Comparative Study of India and Other Economies.* New York: Oxford University Press (for the World Bank), 1987.

Liu Fenghan and Li Zongtong. *Li Hongzao xiansheng nianpu* [A chronological biography of Li Hongzao]. 2 vols. Taibei: Zhongguo Xueshu Zhuzuo Jiangzhu Weiyuanhui, 1969.

Liu Foding, and Chen Zhengping. "Gaoyang zhibuye de lishi he xianzhuang" [History and contemporary status of Gaoyang weaving]. Tianjin: Nankai University, Institute of Economics, 1984.

Liu Foding, and Wang Yuru. "Gaoyang nongcun lianhuban qiye de fazhan" [The development of rural enterprises based on lianhu in Gaoyang]. *Nankai Jingji Yanjiusuo Qikan*, no. 4 (1988): 23–26, 70.

Liu, Tessie P. *The Weaver's Knot: The Contradictions of Class Struggle and Family Solidarity in Western France, 1750–1914.* Ithaca: Cornell University Press, 1994.

Liu Xiusheng. "Qingdai mianbu shichang de bianqian yu Jiangnan mianbu shengchan de shuailuo" [Changes in the cotton market during the Qing period and the decline of Jiangnan cotton production]. *Zhongguo Shehui Jingjishi Yanjiu* [Xiamen], no. 2 (1990): 54–61.

———. *Qingdai shangpin jingji yu shangye ziben* [Commodity economy and commercial capital during the Qing period]. Beijing: Zhongguo Shangye Chubanshe, 1993.

Lo, Dic. "Reappraising the Performance of China's State-Owned Industrial Enterprises, 1980–1996." *Cambridge Journal of Economics* 23 (1999): 693–718.

Luo Fu, and Li Tielin. "Gao-Li baodong [The Gaoyang-Lixian uprising]. *Beiguo Chunqiu* 1 (1960): 1–13.

Ma Min. *Guan shang zhi jian—shehui jubianzhong de jindai shenshang* [Between gentry and merchant—the modern gentry-merchant in the midst of dramatic social change]. Tianjin: Tianjin Renmin Chubanshe, 1995.

Ma Min, and Zhu Ying. *Chuantong yu jindai de erzhong bianzou—wan Qing Suzhou Shang Hui gean yanjiu* [Dual processes of tradition and modern—studies on the Suzhou Chamber of Commerce in the late Qing]. Chengdu: Bazhou Shu She, 1993.

MacKinnon, R. *Power and Politics in Late Imperial China—Yuan Shikai in Beijing and Tianjin, 1901–1908.* Berkeley: University of California Press, 1980.

Mantetsu Hokushi Jimukyoku Chōsabu, ed. *Kahokusho zeisei chōsa hōkoku* [A report on taxes in Hebei Province], 1938.

Mantetsu Tenshin Jimusho Chōsaka. *Shina in okeru san, sōda oyobi chisso kōgyō* [The alkaline, soda and nitrogen industries in China]. 1936.

Marshall, Alfred. *Principles of Economics.* Eighth ed. London: McMillan, 1920.

"Miansha mianbu pifashang de lishi qingkuang" [Circumstances of the yarn and cotton wholesale merchants]. Manuscript, 1980. Held by the Tianjin Zhengxie.

Minami Mantetsu Chōsabu. *Tenshin no ginkō* [Native banking in Tianjin]. 1942.

Minamisato Tomoki. "Chūgoku seifu koyō no Nihonjin" [Japanese employed by the Chinese government]. In *Kindai Ni-Chū kankei shiryō*, vol 2. Tokyo: Ryūkei Shosha, 1976.

Mitani Takashi, ed. *Chūgoku nōson henkaku to kazoku, sonraku, kokka—Kahoku nōson chōsa no kiroku* [Rural change in China: Family, village, and state—records of field research in North China]. Vol. 2. Tokyo: Kyūko Shoin, 2000.

Myers, Ramon. *The Chinese Peasant Economy.* Cambridge: Harvard University Press, 1970.

——— . "Cotton Textile Handicraft and the Development of the Cotton Textile Industry in Modern China." *Economic History Review* 18, no. 3 (1965): 614–32.

——— . "The World Depression and the Chinese Economy 1930–36." In *The Economies of Africa and Asia in the Inter-War Depression*, edited by Ian Brown, 253–78. London: Routledge, 1989.

Nagano Akira. *Dōhi, guntai, kosokai* [Bandits, armies, and the Red Spears]. Tokyo: Shinmondai Kenkyūjo, 1931.

Nakamura Takafusa. "Nihon no kahoku keizai kōsaku" [Japan's economic policies in North China]. In *Kindai Nihon to Higashi Ajia*, edited by Kindai Nihon kenkyūkai. Tokyo: Yamakawa Shupan, 1980.

Nankai University History Department, ed. *Tianjinshi Santiaoshi zaoqi gongye ziliao diaocha* [A survey on early industry in Tianjin's Santiaoshi]. Mimeograph, 1958.

Nan'yō Kangyōkai Nihon Shuppin Kyōkai, ed. *Nan'yō Hakurankai kakusho shuppin chōsasho.* Tokyo, 1912.

Naughton, Barry. *Growing out of the Plan—Chinese Economic Reform 1978–1993.* Cambridge: Cambridge University Press, 1995.

——— . "Implications of the State Monopoly over Industry and Its Relaxation." *Modern China* 18, no. 1 (1992): 14–41.

Negishi Tadashi. *Shōji ni kan suru kankō chōsa hōkokusho— "Hegu" no kenkyū* [A report on a survey of commercial customs—a study of Chinese-style business partnerships]. Tokyo: Tōa Kenkyūsho, 1943.

Nihon Yushutsu Men Orimono Dōgyō Kumiai Rengōkai. *Naigai shijō ni okeru honpō yushutsu men orimono no gensei* [Current status of Japanese cotton textiles in foreign and domestic markets]. 1929.

Nishikawa Hiroshi. *Nihon teikokushugi to mengyō* [Japanese imperialism and the cotton textile industry]. Kyoto: Minerva Shobō, 1987.

Nishikawa Kiichi. *Menkogyō to menshi menpu* [The cotton industry and yarn and cloth]. Shanghai: Nihondō Shobō, 1924.

Odaka, Konosuke, and Minoru Sawai. *Small Firms, Large Concerns: The Development of Small Business in Comparative Perspective*. Oxford: Oxford University Press, 1999.

Oi, Jean. "Fiscal Reform and the Economic Foundation of Local State Corporatism in China." *World Politics* 45 (1992).

———. "The Role of the Local State in China's Transitional Economy." *China Quarterly* 144 (1995).

———. *Rural China Takes Off: Institutional Foundations of Economic Reform*. Berkeley: University of California Press, 1999.

Oi, Jean C., and Andrew G. Walder. *Property Rights and Economic Reform in China*. Stanford: Stanford University Press, 1999.

Osaka Furitsu Shōhin Chinretsusho Soritsu Sanjunen Kinen Kyōsankai. *Kaiko Sanjunen* [Recollection of thirty years of the Osaka Commercial Exhibition Hall]. Osaka, 1920.

Ōshima Tadashi, and Kabayama Yukio. "Jikenka ni okeru Kōyō shokufugyō" [The Gaoyang weaving industry since the China Incident]. *Mantetsu Chōsa Geppō* (1942): 21–62.

Peng Zeyi. "Minguo shiqi Beijing de shougongye he gongshang tongyehui? [Beijing handicraft industry and trade associations during the Republican Period]. *Zhongguo Jingjishi Yanjiu*, no. 1 (1990): 77–86.

———, ed. *Zhongguo jindai shougongye shi ziliao* [A collection of materials on China's modern handicraft industries]. 4 vols. Beijing: Sanlian, 1962.

———, ed. *Zhongguo gongshang hanghui shiliao ji* [Collected materials on Chinese commercial and industrial guilds]. 2 vols. Beijing: Zhonghua Shuju, 1995.

Piore, Michael J., and Charles Sabel. *The Second Industrial Divide*. New York: Basic Books, 1984.

Pyke, Frank, Giacomo Becattini, and Werner Sengenberger. *Industrial Districts and Inter-Firm Co-Operation in Italy*. Geneva: International Institute for Labour Studies, 1990.

Pyke, Frank, and Werner Sengenberger, eds. *Industrial Districts and Local Economic Regeneration*. Geneva: International Institute for Labour Studies, 1992.

Qi Rushan. *Qi Rushan huiyilu* [Reminiscences of Qi Rushan]. Taibei: Zhongyang wenwu gongyingshe, 1956.

Qing Ye. "Xingji pimao ming tianxia" [Xingji leather trade is famous everywhere]. *Hebei Wenshi Jicui*. Jingji Juan: Hebei Renmin Chubanshe.

Quan Guobao. *Zhongguo mianye wenti* [Problems of the Chinese cotton industry]. Shanghai: Shangwu Yinshuguan, 1936.

Quanguo Shanghui Lianhehui Huibao [Journal of the National Federation of Chambers of Commerce].

Quanguo Zhengxie Wenshibian. *Zhongguo jindai guohuo yundong* [The national products movement in modern China]. Beijing: Zhongguo Wenshi Chubanshe, 1995.

Rawski, Thomas C. *Economic Growth in Prewar China*. Berkeley: University of California Press, 1989.

Rawski, Thomas G. "What's Happening to China's GDP Statistics?" Paper prepared for the *China Economic Review* (2001). (Available at http:www.pitt.edu/~trawski/papers2001/gdp912f.pdf.)

Remer, C. F. *Foreign Investment in China*. New York: MacMillan, 1933.

Reynolds, Douglas. *China, 1898–1912: The Xinzheng Revolution and Japan*. Cambridge: Harvard University Press, 1993.

———. "A Golden Decade Forgotten: Japan-China Relations, 1898–1907." *Transactions of the Asiatic Society of Japan* 2 (1987).

Rhoads, Edward. "Merchant Associations in Canton, 1895–1911." In *The Chinese City between Two Worlds*, edited by Mark Elvin and G. William Skinner. Stanford: Stanford University Press, 1974, 97–117.

Rinbara Fumiko. "Qingmo Tianjin gong-shangyezhe de juexing ji quhui guonei yangbu shichang de douzheng" [The consciousness of Tianjin merchants and industrialists in the late Qing and their struggles to recover the market for western-style cloth]. *Tianjin Wenshi Ziliao* 41 (1987): 1–34.

———. "So Sokukyu to Tenshin no kokka teishou undo" [Song Zejiu and the Tianjin native products movement]. In *Kyoto Daigaku Jinbun Kagaku Kenkyūjo Kyōdō Kenkyū Hōkoku, Go-Shi undō no Kenkyū*. Kyoto: Dōmyosha, 1983.

Riskin, Carl. "Surplus and Stagnation in Modern China." In *China's Modern Economy in Historical Perspective*, edited by Dwight H. Perkins, 49–84 (Stanford: Stanford University Press, 1975).

Robinson, Austin, ed. *Appropriate Technologies for Third World Development*. London: Macmillan, 1979.

Rowe, William. *Hankow*. Stanford: Stanford University Press, 1984.

———. "The Problem of 'Civil Society' in Late Imperial China," *Modern China* 19, no. 1 (1993): 139–57

———. "The Public Sphere in Modern China." *Modern China* 16, no. 3 (1990): 309–29.

Sabel, Charles, and Jonathan Zeitlin. "Historical Alternatives to Mass Production: Politics, Markets and Technology in Nineteenth-Century Industrialization." *Past and Present* 108 (August 1985): 133–76.

———. *World of Possibilities: Flexibility and Mass Production in Western Industrialization*. Cambridge: Cambridge University Press, 1997.

Salais, Robert, and Michael Storper. "The Four 'Worlds' of Contemporary Industry." *Cambridge Journal of Economics* 15 (1992): 169–93.

Sato, Shinichi. "Tei Kanei ni tsuite" [On Zheng Guanying]. *Hōgaku* (Tohoku University) 47, no. 4 (1983): 56–106.

Scranton, Philip. "Diversity in Diversity: Flexible Production and American Industrialization, 1880–1930." *Business History Review* 65 (Spring 1991): 27–90.

———. *Endless Novelty: Specialty Production and American Industrialization, 1865–1925*. Princeton: Princeton University Press, 1997.

——. *Proprietary Capitalism: The Textile Manufacture at Philadelphia, 1800–1885.* Philadelphia: Temple University Press, 1983.

Shangyebu Fangzhipinju, ed. *Xin Zhongguo de fangzhipin shangye* [Textile trade in new China]. Beijing: Zhongguo Shangye Chubanshe, 1989.

Shangyebu Shangye Jingji Yanjiusuo, ed. *Geming genjudi shangye huiyilu* [Recollections of commerce in the revolutionary base areas]. Beijing: Shangye Chubanshe, 1984.

Shen Bao, 1918.

Shen Fandeng. *Fangzhi gongye jingji guanli* [Management in the textile industry]. Beijing: Fangzhi Gongye Chubanshe, 1989.

Shina Kenkyūkai. "Kōyō no kairyō menpu" [Improved cotton cloth in Gaoyang]. *Shina Kenkyū Shiryō* 1917, 394–95.

Shirk, Susan. *The Political Logic of Economic Reform in China.* Berkeley: University of California Press, 1993.

Shue, Vivienne. *The Reach of the State: Sketches of the Chinese Body Politic.* Stanford: Stanford University Press, 1988.

Shōgyō Kaigisho Shuhō [Journal of the Japanese Chamber of Commerce]. Tianjin.

Shuili Shuidian Kexue Yanjiuyuan Shuilishi Yanjiushi, ed. *Qingdai Haihe Luanhe honglao dang'an shiliao* [Archival materials on natural disasters in the Hai and Luan River basins]. Beijing: Zhonghua Shuju, 1981.

Soda Saburo. "Shinmatsu ni okeru 'shōsen' ron no tenkai to shōmukyoku no setchi" [The development of theories on 'commercial war' in the late Qing and the founding of the Bureau of Commerce]. *Ajia Seikei Gakkai Ajia Kenkyū* 38, no. 1 (1991): 47–78.

Solinger, Dorothy. *Chinese Business under Socialism: The Politics of Domestic Commerce, 1949–1980.* Berkeley: University of California Press, 1984.

——. "Commercial Reform and State Control: Structural Changes in Chinese Trade." *Pacific Affairs* 58, no. 2 (1985).

——. *From Lathes to Looms—China's Industrial Policy in Comparative Perspective, 1979–1982.* Stanford: Stanford University Press, 1991.

Stark, David, and László Bruszt. *Postsocialist Pathways: Transforming Politics and Property in East Central Europe.* Cambridge: Cambridge University Press, 1998.

State Statistical Bureau. *Woguo gangtie, dianli, meikuang, jichi, fangzhi, zaozhi gongye de jinxi* [Recent developments in our national manufacturing industries, steel, power, mining, machine manufacturing, and textile industries]. Beijing: Tongji Chubanshe, 1958.

Storper, Michael, and Robert Salais. *Worlds of Production: The Action Framework of the Economy.* Cambridge: Harvard University Press, 1997.

Su Bai, ed. *Su Bingqi Xiansheng jinianji* [In memory of Su Bingqi]. Beijing: Kexue Chubanshe, 2000.

Su Bingzhang and Li Futian. *Jiangnan shiye canguan ji* [Records of an inspection tour of Jiangnan industry]. Gaoyang: Privately published, 1936.

Sugiyama Shina. *Japan's Industrialization in the World Economy, 1859–99.* London: Athlone Press, 1988.

Sun Xuemei. *Qingmo Minchu Zhongguoren de Riben guan—yi Zhilisheng wei zhongxin* [Chinese views of Japan during the late Qing and early Republican periods—with a focus on Zhili Province]. Tianjin: Tianjin Renmin Chubanshe, 2001.

Suzuki Tomoo. *Yōmu undō no kenkyō* [A study of the Yangwu movement]. Tokyo: Kyūko Shoin, 1992.

Szelenyi, Ivan. *Socialist Enterpreneurs—Embourgeoisement in Rural Hungary*. Madison: University of Wisconsin Press, 1988.

Takamura Naosuke. *Kindai Nihon mengyō to Chūgoku* [The modern Japanese cotton industry and China]. Tokyo: Tokyo Daigaku Shuppankai, 1982.

Tanimoto Masayuki. *Nihon ni okeru zairaiteki keizai hatten to orimonogyō—shijō keisei to kazoku keizai* [Indigenous development in Japan and the weaving industry—market formation and the household economy]. Nagoya: Nagoya Daigaku Shuppankai, 1998.

Teng Maochun. "Lun hua-sha-bu guanli zhengci" [On the control policies for cotton, yarn, and cloth]. *Gongye Yuekan* 5, no. 4 (1948).

"Tenshin chihō ni okeru shokufuki" [Looms in the Tianjin region]. *Tenshin Nihonjin Shōgyō Kaigisho Hannenhō* [The semi-annual report of the Japanese chamber of commerce in Tianjin]. 1916, no. 1–6: 61–66.

Thompson, E. P. *The Making of the English Working Class*. London: Penguin, 1968.

"Three Towns on the Peking-Hankow Railway." *Chinese Economic Journal* 1, no. 6 (1927): 544–63.

Tianjin Dang'an Guan, Tianjin Shehuikexueyuan Lishi Yanjiusuo, and Tianjinshi Gongshangye Lianhehui, eds. *Tianjin Shanghui dang'an huibian* [Selections from the archives of the Tianjin Chamber of Commerce]. 10 vols. Tianjin: Tianjin Renmin Chubanshe, 1989–1998.

Tianjin Gongshang Ye [Tianjin commerce and industry]. Tianjin Tebieshi Shehuiju, 1930.

Tianjin Historical Museum and the History Department of Nankai University, eds. *Wusi yundong zai Tianjin* [The May Fourth Movement in Tianjin]. Tianjin: Tianjin Renmin Chubanshe, 1979.

"Tianjin Li Li Gongchang diaocha" [A survey of the Li Li Factory in Tianjin]. In *Pingjian gongye diaocha* [Surveys of industry in Beijing and Tianjin], edited by Beijing Shili Gaoji Zhiye Xuexiao. 1937.

Tianjin Local History Association, ed. *Tenshinshi: Zaisei suru toshi no topoloji* [Tianjin: The topology of a multifaceted city]. Tokyo: Tōhō Shoten, 1999.

Tianjin Shehuikexueyuan Lishi Yanjiusuo, ed. "Zhili Gongyi Zongju zilian xuanbian" [Selected materials on the Zhili Industrial Institute]. *Tianjin Lishi Ziliao* 16 (1982): 1–78.

Tianjin Shehui Kexueyuan Lishi Yanjiusuo Tianjin Jianshi Bianxiezu. *Tianjin jianshi* [A short history of Tianjin]. Tianjin: Tianjin Renmin Chubanshe, 1987.

Tianjin Shi Fangzhi Gongyeju Bianshizu. "Jiu Zhongguo shiqi de Tianjin fangzhi gongye" [The Tianjin textile industry before liberation]. *Beiguo Chunqiu* (1960).

Tōa Dōbun Kai. "Gaoyang weaving industry." In *Shina shobetsu zenshi* [Comprehensive gazetteer of Chinese provinces], 825–30, 1920.

Tōyō Bōseki. *Tōyō Bōseki nanajunen shi* [A seventy-year history of Tōyō Bōseki]. Osaka: 1953.

Tsūshō Ihō [Japanese commercial consular reports].

Uchiyama Sei. *Bōeki jo mitaru Shina fūzoku no kenkyū* [Chinese customs as seen through a study of trade]. 1915.

Unger, Jonathan. "Bridges: Private Business, the Chinese Government and the Rise of New Associations." *China Quarterly* 147 (1996): 795–819.

Wakeman, Frederic. "The Civil Society and Public Sphere Debate: Western Reflections on Chinese Political Culture." *Modern China* 19, no. 3 (1993): 108–38.

Walder, Andrew G., and Jean C. Oi. "Property Rights in the Chinese Economy: Contours of the Process of Change." In *Property Rights and Economic Reform in China,* edited by Jean C. Oi and Andrew G. Walder, 1–24. Stanford: Stanford University Press, 1999.

Walker, Kathy Le Mons. *Chinese Modernity and the Peasant Path: Semicolonialism in the Northern Yangzi Delta.* Stanford: Stanford University Press, 1999.

Wang Huaiyuan. "Jiu Zhongguo shiqi Tianjin de duiwai maoyi" [Tianjin's foreign trade in the pre-revolutionary period]. *Beiguo Chunqiu* 1960, no. 1, 4, 7: 65–86, 29–48, 98–109.

Wang Ling. *Beijing yu zhouwei chengshi guanxi shi* [A history of the relations between Beijing and surrounding cities]. Beijing: Beijing Yanshan Chubanshe, 1988.

Wang Yaoyu. "Gengdi suoyouquan de fenpei he tianchang fenge zhuangtai: Yige shilie de yanjiu [A study of the division of ownership rights and division of fields]. In *Zhongguo jingji yanjiu,* edited by Fang Xianting, 378–84. Changsha: Shangwu Yinshuguan, 1938.

Wang Yuru. "Economic Development in China between the Two World Wars (1920–1936)." In *The Chinese Economy in the Early Twentieth Century: Recent Chinese Studies,* edited by Timothy Wright, 58–77. New York: St. Martin's Press, 1992.

Wang Zongpei. *Zhongguo zhi hehui* [Chinese credit associations]. Zhongguo Hezuoshe, 1941.

Wank, David. *Commodifying Communism.* Cambridge: Cambridge University Press, 1999.

Watanabe Kisaku. *Menshipu no kiso chishiki* [Basic knowledge of cotton yarn and cloth]. Tokyo: Konan Shoin, 1950.

Watson, Andrew, Christopher Findlay, and Du Yintang. "Who Won the 'Wool War'?: A Case Study of Rural Product Marketing in China." *China Quarterly* 118 (1989): 213–41.

Wong, Christine P. W. "Between Plan and Market: The Role of the Local Sector in Post-Mao China." *Journal of Comparative Economics* 11 (1987).

——— . "Central-Local Relations in an Era of Fiscal Decline: The Paradox of Fiscal Decentralization in Post-Mao China." *China Quarterly* 128 (1991).

——— . ed. *Financing Local Government in the People's Republic of China.* Hong Kong: Oxford University Press, 1997.

——— . "Interpreting Rural Industrial Growth in the Post-Mao Period," *Modern China* 14, no. 1 (1988), 3?30.

Wong, John, Rong Ma, and Mu Yang. *China's Rural Entrepreneurs: Ten Case Studies.* Singapore: Times Academic Press, 1995.

Wong Siu-lan. "The Chinese Family Firm: A Model." *The British Journal of Sociology* 36, no. 1 (1985): 58–72.

Woo Wing Thye. "The Real Reasons for China's Growth." *The China Journal,* no. 41 (1999): 115–37.

Wu Chengming. "Zhongguo minzu ziben de tedian [Special characteristics of Chinese national capital]. *Jingji Yanjiu*, no. 6 (1956): 111–37.

Wu Zhi. "Cong yiban gongchan zhidu de yanjin guancha Gaoyang de zhibu gongye" [Reflections on the Gaoyang weaving industry in comparison with the development of general industrial systems]. *Zhengzhi Jingji Xuebao* (October 1934).

——— . "Gaoyang zhi tubu gongye" [The native cloth industry of Gaoyang]. In *Zhongguo jingji yanjiu*, edited by Fang Xianting, 677–700. Changsha: Shangwu Yinshuguan, 1938.

——— . "Gongnong liguoxia Zhongguo xiangcun gongye de xin pingjia" [A new evaluation of Chinese rural industry as part of the effort to establish China on the basis of industry and commerce]. *Da Gong Bao* (1935).

——— . *Xiangcun zhibu gongye de yige yanjiu* [A study of the rural weaving industry]. Shanghai: Shangwu Yinshuguan, 1936.

Xiao Weizhao, Wang Minsheng, and Liu Qing, "Hehuo siying qiye cunzai de wenti ji yindao duici" [Latent problems in private cooperative firms and strategies for dealing with them]. *Gaige yu Lunli* 6 (1990): 34?35.

Xu Dixin. *Shanghai Shanghui shi, 1902–1929* [A history of the Shanghai Chamber of Commerce, 1902–1929]. Shanghai: Shanghai Shehuikexueyuan Chubanshe, 1991.

Xu Dixin and Wu Chengming, eds. *Zhongguo zibenzhuyi fazhanshi*, vol. 2, *Jiu minzhuzhuyi geming shiqi de Zhongguo zibenzhuyi* [Development of Chinese capitalism, vol. 2, Chinese capitalism during the age of the old democratic revolution]. Beijing: Renmin Chubanshe, 1990.

Xu Jingxing. "Tianjin jindai gongye de zaoqi gaikuang" [An outline of the early development of Tianjin modern industry]. *Tianjin Wenshi Ziliao Xuanyi* 1 (December 1978): 124–61.

Xu Junxing, ed. *Hebei chengshi fazhanshi* [The development of Hebei cities]. Shijiazhuang: Hebei Jiaoyu Chubanshe, 1991.

Xu Xinwu. *Jiangnan tubu shi* [A history of native cloth in Jiangnan]. Shanghai: Shanghai Shehui Kexue Chubanshe, 1992.

——— . "The Struggle of the Handicraft Cotton Industry against Machine Textiles in China." *Modern China* 14, no. 1 (1988): 31–49.

——— . "Zhongguo he Riben mianfangzhiye zibenzhuyi mengya de bijiao yanjiu" [A comparison of the "sprouts of capitalism" in the cotton industries of China and Japan]. *Lishi Yanjiu* no. 6 (1981): 69–80.

Yan, Yunxiang. "The Culture of Guanxi in a North China Village." *The China Journal* 35 (1996).

——— . *The Flow of Gifts: Reciprocity and Social Networks in a Chinese Village*. Stanford: Stanford University Press, 1996.

Yan Zhongping. "Dingxian shougong mianzhiye zhi shengchan zhidu" [The production system in handicraft weaving in Ding County]. *Shehui Kexue Zazhi* 7 (1937): 395–409.

Yang, Mayfair Mei-hui. *Gifts, Favors and Banquets—the Art of Social Relations in China*. Ithaca: Cornell University Press, 1994.

Yang Ximeng. *Zhongguo hehui zhi yanjiu* [A study of Chinese credit associations]. Shangwu Yinshuguan, 1934.

Yeh Shuzhen. "Tianjingang de maoyi dui qi fudi jingji de yinxiang" [The economic influence of Tianjin trade on its hinterland]. M.A. thesis, National Taiwan University, 1984.

Young, Susan. *Private Business and Economic Reform in China*. Armonk, NY: Sharpe, 1995.

Yu Heping. *Shanghui yu Zhongguo zaoqi xiandaihua* [The chambers of commerce and Chinese early modernization efforts]. Shanghai: Shanghai Renmin Chubanshe, 1993.

Yu Jianwei. "Zhongguo jingji fazhan zhongde zhongqi podung" [Middle-range cycles and Chinese economic development]. *Tianfu Xinlun*, no. 4 (1989): 23–33.

Yu, Tony Fu-Lai. *Entrepreneurship and Economic Development in Hong Kong*. London: Routledge, 1997.

Zeitlin, Jonathan. "Industrial Districts and Local Economic Regeneration: Overview and Comment." In *Industrial Districts and Local Economic Regeneration*, edited by Frank Pyke and Werner Sengenberger. Geneva: International Institute for Labour Studies, 1992.

Zelin, Madeleine. *The Magistrate's Tael: Rationalizing Fiscal Reform in Eighteenth-Century Ch'ing China*. Berkeley: University of California Press, 1984.

Zhang Hongxiang, and Wang Yongxiang, eds. *Liufa qingong jianxue yundong jianshi* [A short history of the Diligent Work and Study Movement in France]. Harbin: Heilongjiang Renmin Chubanshe, 1982.

Zhang Limin. "Tianjin zaoqi de fangshachang—Lisheng Shachang" [Tianjin's earliest spinning mill—Lisheng Spinning Mill]. *Zhongguo jindai fangzhishi yanjiu ziliao huibian* 8 (1990): 43–46.

Zhang Peigang. "Qingyuan de nongjia jingji" [Rural family economy in Qingyuan]. *Shehui Kexue Zazhi* 7–8, March, June, March (1936–1937): 1–65; 187–266; 53–120.

Zhang Shiwen. *Dingxian nongcun gongye diaocha* [Rural industries in Dingxian]. Dingxian: Zhonghua Pingmin Jiaoyu Juojinhui, 1936.

Zhang Si. "Shijiu shijimo Tianjin de yangsha yangbu maoyi" [Trade in foreign yarn and cloth in Tianjin in the late nineteenth century]. *Tianjin Shizhi*, no. 4 (1987): 30–34.

Zhang Xiaohe, Weiguo Lu, Keliang Sun, Christopher Findlay, and Andrew Watson. "The 'Wool War' and the 'Cotton Chaos': Fibre Marketing in China." *China Quarterly* 91.

Zhao, Minghua, and Theo Nichols. "Management Control of Labor in State-Owned Enterprises: Cases from the Textile Industry." *The China Journal* 36 (1996): 1–21.

Zheng Kecheng. "Anguoxian yaoshi diaocha" [A survey of the Anguo Drug Market]. *Shehui Kexue Zazhi* 3, no. 1 (1932): 94–124; no. 2: 186–233.

Zhilisheng Shangpin Chenliesuo. "Diyici diaocha shiye baogaoshu" [A report on the first survey of commerce and industry]. Tianjin: Zhili Provincial Commercial Exhibition Center, 1928.

Zhili Shiye Zazhi [Zhili provincial industrial gazetteer].

Zhonggong Gaoyang Xianwei Dangshi Yanjiushi, ed. *Gaoyang xian geming douzheng da shiji* [A chronological account of revolutionary struggles in Gaoyang County]. Xushui: Yazhou Chubanshe, 1992.

Zhonggong Tianjin Shiwei Dangshi Ziliao Zhengshu Weiyuanhui, et al. *Zhongguo zibenzhuyi gongshangye de shehuizhuyi gaizao; Tianjin* [The socialist transformation of Chinese capitalist commerce and industry: Tianjin]. Beijing: Zhonggong Dangshi Chubanshe, 1991.

Zhongguo Dier Dang'an Guan, ed. *Beiyang junfa tongzhi shiqi de bingbian* [Military uprisings at the time of Beiyang warlord rule]. Nanjing: Jiangsu Renmin Chubanshe, 1982.

Zhongguo Fangzhi Jingji Yanjiu Zhongxin. *Zhongguo fangzhi gongye nianjian* [Almanac of China's textile industry]. Beijing: Zhongguo Fangzhi Chubanshe, 1994.

Zhongguo Kexueyuan Jingji Yanjiusuo, et al. *Beijing Reifuxiang* [Reifuxiang Company of Beijing]. Beijing: Sanlian Shudian, 1959.

Zhongguo Renmin Daxue Gongye Jingjixi, ed. *Beijing gongye shiliao* [Historical materials on Beijing industry]. Beijing: Beijing Chubanshe, 1960.

Zhongguo Shehui Kexueyuan Nongye Jingji Yanjiusuo, ed. *Nongcun gugong jingying diaocha yanjiu* [Surveys on the use of hired labor in rural enterprises]. 1983.

Zhongguo Zibenzhuyi Gongshangye de Shehuizhuyi Gaizao Ziliao Congshu Bianjibu, *Zhongguo zibenzhuyi gongshangye de shehuizhuyi gaizao* [The socialist transformation of Chinese commerce and industry]. Beijing: Zhonggong Dangshi Chubanshe, 1991.

Zhongyang Gongzuozu Diaocha Cailiao. "Gaoyangxian jingji jiben qingkuang; Jiefanghou Gaoyangxian shougongye zhibuyezhong de siren ziben" [Basic economic conditions in Gaoyang: Private capital in the Gaoyang weaving industry after the war]. Manuscript, 1954. Held by the Gaoyang County Archives.

Zhongyang Nongyebu Jihuaci. *Liangnian laide Zhongguo nongcun jingji diaocha huibian* [Collection of survey materials on Chinese villages over the last two years]. Shanghai: Zhonghua Shuju, 1952.

Zhou Errun. *Zhili gongyizhi chubian* [Gazetteer of the Zhili Gongyiju, first series]. Tianjin: Zhili Gongyiju Printing Office, 1907.

Zhou Xibao. *Zhongguo gudai fuzhuangshi* [A history of costume in traditional China]. Beijing: Zhongguo Xiju Chubanshe, 1984.

Zhou Yan. "Zhou Xuexi yi gongkuan banshiye fajia de neimu" [An inside account of how Zhou Xuexi got rich by promoting public industrialization]. *Wenshi Ziliao* 53 (1965): 32–34.

Zhou Zhijun. "Beiyang shiyejia Zhou Xuexi" [Zhou Xuexi as a Beiyang industrialist]. Mimeograph held by the History Department of Nankai University, 1977.

Zhu Chunfu. "Beiyang junfa dui Tianjin jindai gongye de touzi" [Investment by Beiyang warlords in Tianjin modern industry]. *Tianjin Wenshi Ziliao Xuanyi* 4 (October 1979): 146–62.

———. "Zhou Xuexi yu Beiyang shiye" [Zhou Xuexi and Beiyang development projects]. *Tianjin Wenshi Ziliao Xuanyi* 1 (December 1978): 1–28.

Zhu Shangying. "Gaoyang buye diaocha ji" [Record of a survey of the Gaoyang weaving industry]. *Fangzhi Zhoukan*, June 15, 1935, 571–76.

Index

accounts: credit/debit in, 61; profit underreporting for, 52; repayment schedules of, 61–62; trimester settlement for, 61

agencies. *See* sales agencies

agriculture: cooperativization of, 191n38; developments for, 197, 220n6; farm size, decline in, 40n35; "five small industries" for, 191–92n41; income from, v. industry, 178–79, 191n36; investments in, for living standards, 197–98, 220n9; as involution, 24; land distribution in, 24, 40n35; living standards from, 197–98, 220n9; poverty within, 24, 197–98; reforms on labor supply in, 195; reports on productivity in, 197, 220nn6–7; weaving v., for income, 24

all-rayon: development of, 33–34; high profits of, 34; production of, for boom period, 33; subsidiary industries from, 34

America: cotton, for Chinese production costs, 189n16; dyestuffs from, boycott for, 189n17

"anti-Japanese worsted," native origin of, 37

apprenticeship: competitive, v. introduction, 59; entrepreneurial legacies and, 161; home, at business for, 54; lifestyle of, 75n15; managers, from, 51, 75n14; technical education v., 64; of weavers, 87–88

assets and liabilities, wholesalers, in Wu Zhi study, 60, 75n25

bank(s): credit from, 62, 207; failure of, for weaving growth cycles, 28; firm as, 76n31; for industrialization, 46, 74n7; native (*hang*), 50

bankruptcy (*chi huoguo*): investors and, 63, 75n29; in war, 149–51

boom period: all-rayon production for, 33; foreign competition v., 31

boycott: for American dyestuffs, 189n17; CCP on, 190n21; CCP, v. Nationalist Party on, 171; fabrics industry boost from, 37, 116; forced sale, for, 172, 190n22; state-owned v. private firms and, 171–72; yarn supply, v., 35; years, summary of, 173–74

business: advantages, in Gaoyang, v. Tianjin, 70; environment, 73; history, large firms in, 6; model, economic v.,